Rocamora
Man of Masks

Donald Michael Platt

Also by Donald Michael Platt:

A Gathering of Vultures

House of Rocamora

Bodo the Apostate

Close to the Sun

Rocamora

Man of Masks

Donald Michael Platt

www.penmorepress.com

Rocamora: Man of Masks
By
Donald Michael Platt

Copyright © 2008 and 2011 Donald Michael Platt

All rights reserved. No part of this book may be used or reproduced by any means without the written permission of the publisher except in the case of brief quotation embodied in critical articles and reviews.

ISBN-13: 978-1-942756-28-6(Paperback)
ISBN -13:978-1-942756-29-3 (e-book)

BISAC Subject Headings:
HIS045000 HISTORY / Europe / Spain &Portugal
FIÇ032000FICTION / War&Military
FIC031020FICTION / Thrillers / Historical

2nd Edition, 2011

Editing: Chris Paige
Front Cover Illustration by Pam Marin-Kingsley,
Front cover: portrait of Vicente de Rocamora and **Back Cover:** portrait of the Infanta Doña Maria by Pam Marin-Kingsley, www.pammarin-kingsley.cm

Back cover: We chose to use a depiction of an Auto de fé, painted ca. 1495 by Pedro Berruguete. This work is housed in the Prado Museum in Madrid, Spain and was originally from the sacristy of the Santo Tomás church in Avila, Spain and its proper title is *Saint Dominic Presiding over an Auto de fé*. While this is not a 17th century image from the time of Vicente de Rocamora, it is one of the best representations of this kind of religious trial and public condemnation of heretics.

Address all correspondence to:
Michael James
Penmore Press LLC
920 N Javelina Pl
Tucson AZ 85748
mjames@Penmorepress.com

"In Spain, the dead are more alive than the dead of any other country in the world."

—*Federico Garcia Lorca*

Spain & Portugal
Showing Major Cities in Vicente de Rocamora's Time

This map does not show Spain's provinces and former kingdoms because some of their boundaries have changed since the 17th century.

Author's Note

Seventeenth century Spain was obsessed with *limpieza de sangre*, purity of blood untainted by mixture with Jews, Moors, and recent converts. Spaniards who could prove they were *limpio*, untainted, were known as Old-Christians; with few exceptions, only they could serve the Crown, rise to high rank in the Military, and reach the uppermost levels in the Church.

Conversos were Jews who converted to the Roman Catholic faith during the fourteenth and fifteenth centuries, usually during and after massacres to avoid death or exile. Before the expulsion of Jews in 1492, *conversos* and old-Christians frequently intermarried, especially among the nobility. In the seventeenth century, any Spaniard or Portuguese descended from a *converso* was known as a New-Christian regardless of his or her devotion to Catholicism and even if only one ancestor had been a *converso* or New-Christian.

Most historians estimate that a miniscule number of Spaniards practiced Judaism in the seventeenth century; while at the same time, around twenty-five percent of the Portuguese practiced some form of hidden or crypto-Judaism. The words "Portuguese" and "Jew" were synonymous in seventeenth century Europe.

Although I wrote *Rocamora* in modern prose, whenever historical speeches and quotations were available and seventeenth century descriptions could be converted to dialogue, I used Spanish vocabulary and syntax to give the reader a more accurate flavor of the times.

Because the spelling of proper Spanish names and places varies from book to book and region to region, I made arbitrary decisions in that matter. As examples, I chose Olivares over Olivarez and Elx over Elche. I used the Spanish spelling of Portuguese names when those individuals lived in Spain, and I anglicized others to allow smooth dialogue. For example, I used Philip instead of Felipe when referring to the Kings of Spain and certain titles such as count-duke.

Habsburg Spain was an empire made up of the kingdoms of Aragón, Navarre, Castile, and Valencia, Iberian provinces, parts of Italy and France, and overseas colonies. *The Empire*, also Holy Roman Empire or HRE, refers to lands ruled by the Austrian branch of the Habsburg dynasty, including Austria, Hungary, Bohemia, Bavaria, the Rhenish Palatinate, other German principalities and the Austrian Netherlands now modern Belgium. Within the Habsburg family, first cousins and even uncles and nieces married over several consecutive generations during the sixteenth and seventeenth centuries. The Empire was originally ruled by German kings chosen by Popes, but long before the seventeenth century, those rulers had split with the papacy. Thus, historians who claim the Empire was "neither holy, nor Roman nor an empire" are correct.

Vicente de Rocamora was reputed to have been a gifted poet who wrote in Spanish and Latin. Except for his signature on a few registries in the Netherlands, his poems, sermons, and writings no longer exist. His poems appearing in *Rocamora* are created by the author.

Because the Church had a history of altering, forging, and destroying evidence viewed as embarrassing or contrary to its dogma, much written by and about Vicente de Rocamora in Spain may have suffered such a fate. The Crown even had the Count-Duke de Olivares painted over as if he never existed in one of Velázquez' paintings after he fell from power in 1643.

What is historical truth? Often it is difficult to discover because the victors' versions usually prevail, and if, as Napoleon has said, "History is a myth men have agreed upon," let mine be the definitive myth. So, as other authors have done with fiction set in earlier times, I altered and created when necessary the actions, dialogue, and presence of historical personages as well as certain events in *Rocamora* to further character development and plot. Which, the reader may ask? Most of the answers are in the Historical Note section at the end of this book.

A list of characters appears at the end so that the interested reader may know who is fictional and who is not. A monetary conversion table and partial cost of living also are included at the end for the reader's convenience.

Donald Michael Platt
November 2008

Yo soy un hombre . . . I am a man . . .
Limpio de sangre y jamas Pure of blood and never
De hebrea o mora manchada. Stained by Hebrew or Moor.

Lope de Vega,
Captain Alonso de Contreras, and other Spanish Old Christians

PART ONE

Blood and Honor

In the Kingdom of Valencia, 1617

I certify over my signature . . . that they are of pure descent, without any family taint, and they can intermarry with the most honored families in Israel; for there has been no admixture of impure blood in their maternal or paternal antecedents and their collateral relatives . . .

Rabbinical decision, ca. 1300 AD

Chapter 1
Shrove Tuesday

El jorobado, the hunchback, reached under his tattered cloak and gripped the hilt of his dagger. He had spent hours honing the blade until it could split the finest strand of hair.

A perfect day for vengeance.

So thought the hunchback while he sat high and grotesque as a gargoyle upon the broad shoulders of San Martín's statue on the Puente de Serranos, one of two bridges spanning the Turia, the great dark green river that snaked through Valencia towards the port of El Grau three miles away. Yet, he reminded himself, every day in Valencia was perfect for vendetta and revenge. No city in all of Spain had as many blood feuds and murders, and the killing increased during Shrove Tuesday, the debauchery preceding Ash Wednesday and forty days of Lenten contrition and denial.

Carne vale. Farewell to the flesh.

Farewell to blood enemies.

All about him, men and boys clung to the statues and pedestals of saints and kings lining both sides of the bridge. Below, thousands of boisterous Valencians pushed towards the span and overflowed the banks of the Turia as they returned from the meadows across the river where nobles and knights had competed in a joust.

The hunchback paid no attention to the soldiers who moved through the mob and opened a path along the bridge for drummers and trumpeters heralding a cavalcade of civic dignitaries and their ladies, who were carried in litters covered with velvet and damask. He searched beyond them for his quarry riding with the knight-combatants on caparisoned chargers escorted by liveried equerries carrying javelins and lances with silk flags and pennants bearing their lords' coats-of-arms.

Most of the señores and *caballeros* wore short capes, velvet doublets, elaborate white ruffs, and broad-brimmed felt hats with dyed plumes; others had dressed and armed themselves in the Moorish or Turkish fashion. Each man flaunted a shield of wood and leather painted in his own colors or those of his *encantadora*, the enchantress he honored. The sun reflected off their gilt, silks, and silver saddles, but it was hatred that blinded the hunchback when he espied one particular *caballero* mounted on a white Andalusian charger: Enríque de Anglesola Suárez y Talens, the coward who had murdered his beloved father and caused the death of his saintly mother three years ago.

Very well then. Today, he would pay back the haughty swine in his own coin.

As Anglesola and his four equerries rode past him, the hunchback climbed down from San Martín and followed the *caballero* through the arches of the Serrano Gate towers and into the city of Valencia. Thousands of peasants had poured into the city to participate in the pre-Lenten revelry and added their numbers to the crowds that obstructed his movement.

He pushed his way through the mass of humanity watching the processions and assorted festivities in the plazas, along wide boulevards, and narrow streets. He brushed past hawkers and peddlers selling their wares from festooned booths and carts. Intent on the hunt, he did not hear them or the minstrels singing bawdy songs as men accosted women and young girls and demanded favors. He ignored the jugglers, magicians, and strolling players amusing the multitude while cutpurses gorged on the unwary.

Never losing sight of Anglesola, the hunchback dodged rotten eggs and overripe fruit that pranksters threw at him. He sidestepped howling maimed dogs and screeching cats whose tails had been set afire. He avoided a bag filled with the fresh contents of a chamber pot, which splattered two rustics next to him. At a congested intersection, he tripped over a rope and pretended to be confused while onlookers laughed and called him *el jorobado* as they ridiculed his hump, scars, and hairy wens.

He scrambled to catch Anglesola, who had turned a corner ahead of his escort, and saw him lash out with his whip to clear a way through the unmoving mob transfixed by a procession of papier-mâché figures in the shapes of giants and dwarfs. Trapped in the narrow street, out of his equerries' sight, and surrounded by the crowd, Anglesola cursed when a blacksmith pulled the whip from his hand. His threats went ignored.

The hunchback muscled ahead, drew his dagger, and leaped onto the rear of the charger. In two practiced swift motions, he wrapped an arm around Anglesola's mouth and slit his throat above the white ruff.

"For my father and mother."

He stood on the rear of the charger, seized hold of the forged iron railing of a nearby balcony, and climbed past its occupants, whose attention was fixed on a colossal mechanical winged serpent on wheels. Atop a tiled roof, he watched the crush of celebrants below pressing against Anglesola's legs and horse as the *caballero* slumped forward in his saddle. No one in the crowded street had yet to notice crimson blood saturate Anglesola's ruff and the mane of his white Andalusian. Satisfied his enemy was dead, the hunchback scurried across more rooftops, dropped onto a street leading to the Turia, and shouldered his way through the throng along the embankment towards El Grau.

He loped along the reeking docks on a carpet of rotting carcass leavings, fish bones, and scales. Survival was the one law in El Grau, a waterfront community of squalid wooden shacks situated between docks and city, and that could be guaranteed only by quickness of wit and blade. More than a seaport, the waterfront community was a haven for the *pícaro* underclass of merchant smugglers, impoverished nobility, unemployed soldiers, degenerate priests, fugitive slaves, actors, prostitutes and pimps, violent criminals, professional gamblers, quacks and charlatans.

The setting sun briefly balanced atop the foothills to the west. Rising smoke from thousands of torches and cooking fires serpentined upwards above cypress and taller palm trees. Under the darkening sky, a ghost fleet of sailing ships and galleys lay at anchor. Normally, their crews would have been hauling cargo, working ropes and pulleys, repairing tawny red-lateen sails, scraping and tarring hulls, and greasing beached vessels below the water line. On this Shrove Tuesday, the sailors were drinking themselves senseless in taverns, brawling in brandy houses, carousing with whores, or falling victim to local felons. No such good fortune for the slaves and prisoners chained to their benches in the stinking galleys.

The hunchback turned away from the docks and entered a narrow alley between rows of multistory buildings where top floors almost touched to form an archway. He rapped a code on the back door of a structure situated between a bawdy house and a tavern. The door squeaked open. He entered a shuttered, candle-lit room and inhaled a familiar aroma of ointment and incense. Cabinets and tables were filled with bottles and jars. Masks and costumes hung from the ceiling. Assorted surgical knives and saws lay organized at the end of a bloodstained wooden table equipped with leg and hand irons.

A bald and bent man in a dark green velvet robe, toothless, with a wispy graying beard and scarred face, bolted shut the door behind the hunchback. Damaged vocal cords allowed him to speak only in a hoarse exhale over the shouts and cries penetrating the thin walls.

"Where have you been?" He saw blood on the hunchback's hand. "What have you done?"

"I have restored honor."

"Enríque de Anglesola?"

"Yes, Don Lope. He is dead."

"Are you certain?"

"I severed his larynx and jugular. The way you taught me."

"You may have acted precipitously, but retribution has come at last to Anglesola, extortionist and murderer."

"I wish I'd had the time to disembowel the pig, to make him die a slow death."

"Rejoice in what opportunities fate bestows upon you."

Don Lope held a candelabrum and led the way upstairs through a cluttered storage area to a small room. Beside the bed where he slept whenever he stayed in El Grau, the hunchback faced the mirror he used when he applied his disguises. He took off his cap and peeled away the wax and gum that had twisted and scarred his features. Hairy wens came off with them. He stripped more blackened wax from his strong white teeth, removed his rags, and undid the straps of his false hump. He stood straight and stretched, naked except for the gold chain and cross his mother had bequeathed him, and dropped the hump onto the floor.

Adios el jorobado.

Chapter 2
Mentor and Student

Vicente de Rocamora needed no mirror to show him that his family blood and good fortune had blessed him with superb health and handsome features. Almost sixteen, he had attained exceptional upper-body strength from climbing ropes hand-over-hand without using his feet. Although his quickness made him a gambler's favorite to win rope races from deck to mast-top against all comers, he had rejected all opportunities to join the *pícaro* gangs as a *grumete*, a burglar who used rope ladders to break into the upper levels of houses. He had developed his body and mind for one specific purpose, to avenge his parents.

"And no one recognized you? No one followed you?"

"No one." Vicente emptied his bladder in a chamber pot, opened a shutter, and tossed the contents out into the alley below. "The disguise worked perfectly." He put on his white linen shirt, black breeches, and leather boots. "Don Lope, I've tasted vengeance, yet why do I feel so unsatisfied?"

"Revenge can redeem one's honor and remove the stain of an affront, but it never brings back the dead whom we continue to love and mourn."

"Someone had to eliminate the arrogant pig."

"I would have done the deed myself, if I did not have this pitiful wreck of a body. And so, Vicente, you have killed your first man."

"A man? Anglesola was a filthy dog." Vicente spat on a rag and wiped the blood from his father's dagger. "I feel no guilt or remorse even though I've broken one of God's great commandments. The Lord will understand and forgive me, if He bothers to pay attention to what men do. If He actually exists. No matter, an eye for an eye is sanctioned by the Bible, and the right to personal vengeance is ageless unwritten law in Valencia as well."

"I loved your parents too, Vicente. Despite my condemnation as a Judaizer by the Inquisition and imprisonment in the galleys, Don Luís and Doña Gabriela believed in my innocence and treated me with respect. That is why, after Anglesola's crime against them, I undertook to protect you from our mutual enemies and to supervise your education."

Vicente embraced his mentor and second father. "And I shall be forever grateful for all I have learned at your unique University of El Grau."

He could not imagine any traditional college preparing him so well for the real world, not even the great universities of Zaragoza and Seville. In El Grau, his classrooms had included dock, street, and tavern where he learned French, Italian, Arabic, Turkish, German, English, Dutch, and every Spanish dialect from sailors, soldiers, and merchants. Brawlers gave him lessons in eye gouging, ear biting, and groin crushing. An exiled Catholic English knight instructed him in swordplay and taught him all the tricks of gambling so he would never starve or be cheated. A brandy-sotted *hidalgo* revealed cunning tricks with his dagger. A slant-eyed sailor from far-off Asia taught him how to throw a man many times heavier than himself and to shatter a thick piece of wood with the edge of his hand.

Here, in El Grau, he had mastered the vocabulary of the *pícaros* that differentiated those rogues, thieves, and murderers. *Capeadores* specialized in the theft of clothing. *Salteadores*, highwaymen, robbed their victims on streets and country roads for money and jewels. *Apóstoles*, like St. Peter, had keys to every home and public building. *Satyrs* rustled cattle. *Devotos* looted church alms boxes and stripped precious ornaments from statues of saints. *Matones* were professional killers. The *pícaro* jargon, which varied from city to city, also included clever metaphors, juxtaposition of alphabet, altering initial consonants of syllables, speaking fast or slurring, and "frenchifying" words by dropping the last syllable,

Vicente had the greatest respect as well as love for his mentor. The *pícaros* called Don Lope a *polidor*, one with many interests. He sold stolen goods, forged documents, and created lifelike masks from wax and resin as well as scars and deformities for bogus beggars. A master forger of false genealogies for those who wished to conceal their new-Christian origins or denounce enemies to the Inquisition, Don Lope also dealt in rare books and manuscripts, including those placed on the *Index of Forbidden Books*, and he had encouraged him to read the prohibited writings of Jews, Erasmus, Machiavelli, heretics, and infidels.

After they went downstairs to the library that also served as a workroom, Vicente saw lying on a table sheets of parchment baked to appear centuries older. "Why don't you create a document to prove that the Anglesolas and all our enemies are descended from Jews, and that they Judaize in secret?"

"One day, my boy, one day. They shall all pay for their crimes against me and mine, and yours."

Vicente was familiar with the history of his mentor and family's physician. At the turn of the century after failing to extort money from Diego Fernández y Vega, Anglesola had produced questionable documents and denounced him as a crypto-Jew. During his two years in prison and three years in the galleys, his wife and son passed away from fever, having been weakened from their own torture and imprisonment. A condemned Judaizer and banished from the Kingdom of Valencia, he became known as Don Lope after he sneaked back into El Grau with the help of Vicente's father and perfected the skills necessary to thrive within the criminal brotherhoods.

"You never told me which torture caused you to confess."

Don Lope touched one of the scars on his face, then his throat, which had been damaged by the Inquisition's brutal interrogators. "The tortures? Nothing unusual. The rack, fire, the water treatment, ropes, rods, and pulleys. One can almost get used to pain. Almost. But it was what they did to my beloved wife and son in my presence . . . may they rest in peace . . . which is why, in the end, I falsely confessed to practicing certain customs of the hated Jewish religion. Then, as you know, I repented before the Inquisitorial Tribunal and was reconciled at a public *auto-de-fé*."

"I wonder how much torture I could bear."

"There are worse agonies than those caused by physical torture, Vicente. The horrors they forced me to watch while they tortured my wife and son. Insults to pride, honor, and name. The public ridicule heaped upon me when they marched me through the streets of Valencia. Scourged in public. Forced to wear the *sambenito*, the yellow robe transversed by a black St. Andrew's cross and covered with flames pointing downward, and the similarly decorated *coraza* on my head. Most humiliating of all, they repeatedly inspected my penis to see if I had been circumcised or if my foreskin had been pierced symbolically."

Vicente's genitals tightened. "Circumcision is a barbaric practice."

Shouts and coarse laughter from the tavern next door were heard through the thin walls as Don Lope placed on a small table a skin of red wine and an earthen pot filled with a mix of garbanzo beans, shellfish, chorizo sausages, garlic, onions, and pimento. Because he had no teeth, he ate only the softest morsels.

Vicente squirted wine from the bag between heaping mouthfuls of stew and relived the moment when he slit Anglesola's throat and avenged his parents. He fought back tears at other memories. Again, he saw his father shot by blasts from the harquebuses of Anglesola and his henchmen. Again, he watched helplessly while his mother miscarried and died of hemorrhaging after hearing the news of her husband's assassination. His surviving half-brother, sickly and slow of wit twenty-year old Alonso, was now the Fifth Señor de Benetorrente and married to Doña Violante de Suárez, a cousin of his father's first wife and the Anglesolas who had masterminded their father's murder.

"Vicente, it is only a matter of time before the Anglesolas perpetrate some terrible act against you."

"I'll strike first at the swine."

"They are too many, too powerful. You cannot expect to survive every attempt on your life, even with my help."

"Then what am I supposed to do?"

"Leave Spain. Spain is finished."

"But we're the strongest power in the world. Our banners fly over every continent. Our armies and fleet triumph against all heretics and enemies."

"A last gasp of a once-great giant. We fight everywhere and win no permanent peace."

"I can't believe it. Ships loaded with gold and silver come from the lands and peoples ruled by our King Philip. We must be the wealthiest, most powerful empire since Rome."

"Spain is debt-ridden, and still we attempt the impossible task of trying to be *alguacíl* mayor, head sheriff, of the entire world for the Catholic faith."

Although Vicente believed Don Lope to be the wisest of all men, he refused to accept what he was hearing. He remembered an important lesson taught by his mentor: Before arguing demand further explanation. "Why do you say such terrible things about Spain?"

"All our problems can be traced to one cause, proof of *limpieza de sangre*, purity of blood. Everything bad in Spain is a result of our poisonous obsession with *limpieza*. In England and Holland, even the Ottoman Empire, men who achieve great deeds can become influential and powerful. In Spain, achievement and being count for nothing. Old-Christian pedigree takes precedence over ability and wealth, even if the superior new-Christian is a devout Catholic. Here, all men struggle every waking moment to prove the peculiar condition of not being."

"Not being, Don Lope?"

"Yes, Vicente. Not being industrious and hard working is proof one has no Moorish roots. Not being skeptical, not being a clever merchant, not being a skilled physician, and not being brilliant in finance is proof one has no Jewish origins. Not bathing, washing, and keeping personal hygiene are external proofs that one is an untainted old-Christian. The stench of filth is respected as the odor of sanctity. You can see it everywhere. Each Spaniard is consumed with fear that some unknown ancestor may have been tainted. Our mad compulsion to prove purity of blood is so all-consuming no one is excluded from suspicion and investigation, neither bishop and saint, nor monarch and *grandee*."

Vicente shared the Spanish obsession with lineage. His tanned naturally swarthy complexion suggested Moorish origins despite his unusual green eyes inherited from his mother, verdigris Don Lope called them. Yet he was as *sangre azul* as any old-Christian *hidalgo* of Castile, who used the visual test of blue veins against pale skin to proclaim purity of blood.

Yes, he was *limpio*. Clean. Of old-Christian stock, untainted by mixture with Jews, Moriscos, or recent converts. Each certificate of his parents' *limpiezas de sangre* included statements signed by reliable witnesses who had further confirmed their purity of blood and stated that none of their forebears had been punished by the Inquisition. Furthermore, the de Rocamoras had proven consanguinity to Kings of France, Counts of Toulouse, Lords of Septimania, and señores, *caballeros*, and barónes throughout Orihuela and Murcia.

"Even if what you say is true, Don Lope, because I am *limpio*, I can rise as far as my abilities will take me."

"Listen to me, my son. My body may be twisted and ravaged, but my mind, eyes, and ears are keen. I listen to sailors, soldiers, and merchants, men who have sailed the seas and seen the world. I believe the future is in the north, in England and Holland, where they have no Inquisition, no test of *limpieza*. There a man is rewarded for his accomplishments, not for being born into a great house or for having the sole condition of being *limpio*. If I were younger, physically fit, and did not have more scores to settle, I would leave this night."

"Are you suggesting I live as a Protestant heretic?"

"And since when are you so devout a Catholic?"

"Belief is not necessary. To be Spanish is to be Catholic. If one appears to be religious, that should be enough."

"Machiavelli's advice to rulers." Don Lope nodded at him, his scarred face made more diabolical by candlelight. "You have learned some of your lessons well, Vicente. If it were a matter of external appearances, there would be no need for the *limpieza* statutes. But even you, Vicente, will have to produce your own *limpieza de sangre* when you choose a career or marry. Can you, can anyone ever be certain no ancestor was tainted, or that an enemy will not produce a lie superior to your truth? Listen to me. You must make your future in one of the Protestant lands, not here in Spain. Decide now, this very night, before your enemies destroy you. Do not return to your home. Stay with me until you can sail."

"I prefer to send all the other Anglesolas to hell. Only then, will I leave to bring great honor to Spain and the name de Rocamora. When Alonso dies, I shall claim my señorio and spend the rest of my days here along the Costa del Azahar. What other paradise offers more than our lazy, hot sunny days when I can dive into the refreshing turquoise surf along the palm-lined brilliant white sandy beaches, inhale the blossom-scented air from the orange groves, and feast on delicious golden apples, melons, and fruit from the sea?"

"Vicente, you may yet become an eloquent poet, and I would prefer you to be a live poet. The Anglesolas are many and powerful."

"I am not yet ready to sail from Valencia, but I will follow your advice and stay away from the señorio. Except . . ."

Shouts and music came from the street. Vicente opened the front shutters and gaped at a young Gypsy girl dancing a *chaconne* in front of an appreciative audience outside the tavern. She wore a saffron yellow skirt, no blouse or shoes. Her bronze body and budding breasts glistened with perspiration. Jewel-like drops of moisture on her bushy armpits reflected light from the torches. As she snapped her fingers and turned in time to the guitars, her skirt swirled above her thighs.

Don Lope watched Vicente stare at the girl. "Do you remember when you began to show a natural interest in the younger, more aggressive *mujeres perdidas*, prostitutes, and lupine Gypsy girls?"

"Yes."

"And I warned you to beware of *mal frances*, the French sickness from the one and a knife in the back from the other?"

"I remember."

"Have you made love with a woman yet?"

"I don't know."

"A most peculiar answer"

"I've had dreams."

"A natural function of the body when fluids build up."

"No, my dreams were different. Last week, for three nights in a row, a succubus came to me."

"A succubus? You doubt the existence of God, yet you believe in the superstition a female demon can visit you in the middle of the night and drain the juices of your manhood?"

"What else could explain it?"

"Many a wish becomes a dream." Don Lope pulled at his wispy beard when he saw the boy was dissatisfied with his response. He closed the shutters to prevent further distraction. "Tell me everything that happened, Vicente."

"I was sleeping, and a presence in my room awakened me. At first, it was a black shadow. Then it changed into a huge bird and sat on my chest. A soft, warm bird, but with no feathers, and it had female breasts. I could not see her face. She touched me all over my body with her hands, then her mouth and tongue."

"Didn't you struggle?"

"I couldn't move." Vicente described how the succubus had sat on his erection, and then rolled him over so he was on top of her.

"A very strange dream, indeed. Three nights in a row, you said?"

"Yes, and then the dreams stopped."

"In the morning, did you find any evidence of the succubus?"

"Each day when I awakened, I detected a strange, lingering odor. It was a mix of woman-scent, and perfume, and something else. An unfamiliar essence, both sweetish and acrid."

"You must not return to your home."

Don Lope took Vicente into the back room, and as he withdrew a small terra-cotta jar from his cabinet of medicines, they heard yelling and repeated banging on the back door. Vicente drew his dagger. Don Lope peered through the shutters, and then motioned for him to put it away and unbolt the door.

A servant from the tavern burst in with a professional gambler whose thigh had been ripped open in a brawl. Vicente needed no instructions. He often used his physical strength to restrain Don Lope's patients whenever his mentor took on yet another more despised role as a surgeon to cauterize wounds, suture cuts, or saw off limbs. He wrestled and pinned the gambler to the table, locked his wrists and ankles in the irons, and cut open his breeches to expose a long and deep gash.

The man screamed and twisted his body as if he were a victim of the Inquisition. Don Lope opened the small terra-cotta jar and mixed some of its contents with water until it liquefied. He passed the potion under Vicente's nose before administering it to his struggling patient.

He inhaled a familiar bittersweet scent. "Don Lope, this is the same odor I told you about. I thought I was familiar with all your medicines. What is it?"

"A mold. It arrived at the end of last year from New Spain. Used by savage shamans during their shape-shifting rituals, I have been told. It will put him to sleep, and he will feel no pain while I sear and sew his wound. It also causes one to hallucinate, to have visions, to dream. To dream perhaps of a succubus?"

Chapter 3
Violante

I should have listened to Don Lope.

Ash Wednesday. And still to come was the Edict of Faith, which commanded all Christians to confess their sins and denounce family and friends for Judaizing and other heresies, to be followed by the awesome Anathema and possible investigation by the dreaded Inquisition. Then Holy Week would arrive with somber processions culminating in the sanguinary Good Friday parade of penitents and flagellants.

On the first evening of Lent, Vicente was to suffer his own Edict and flogging. Two burly lackeys forced him to his knees at a *prie-Dieu* beneath a realistic crucifix in the de Rocamora chapel. They spread his arms wide, secured his wrists to the railing with wet leather thongs, and ripped apart the back of his white linen shirt.

He had failed to heed Don Lope's advice and had returned home one last time to collect some precious mementos of his parents. The instant he crossed the threshold, his sister-in-law's servants had seized and locked him in a small room until now.

The entire household gathered in the chapel to witness his humiliation. All in black, Violante, Alonso's eighteen year old wife, stood at Vicente's right. He wondered how someone so beautiful of face could be so repellent. Her wolf's eyes, reflecting candlelight from sconces and candelabra burned like live coals. Her full red feral lips might drain a man of his blood. He believed she was evil incarnate. *La bruja*, the witch.

Behind Vicente were the *mayordomo*, valets, maids, and lackeys Violante had brought to Alonso as part of her dowry. He thought of them as an army of occupation while he listened to the phlegmy coughing of his sallow half-brother.

Rocamora

Alonso slouched in a chair deep in the shadows of the chapel. His dull blue eyes saw nothing. Unwashed lank blond hair fell to the shoulders of his ill-fitting purple velvet doublet. Alonso was in a hashish-induced stupor and would not be giving him a perfunctory, harmless flogging this night. Violante had invited her obese cousin, Dominican Inquisitor Bernardo de Anglesola, to carry out the beating, a man of monstrous appearance with a thick vertical scar from the top of his forehead past where his left eye used to be to his fleshy jowls.

Vicente stared at the gilded crucifix illuminated by tall tapers in silver candelabra on the family altar and focused on the agonized features of The Savior, whose wounds ran with blood of garnet and rubies. This was the moment to ask Him for the strength not to cry out, but he was unable to pray. He no longer believed God, His Son, the Virgin Mary, nor any of the saints paid attention to prayers or to what humans did. Why had God allowed his father to be assassinated and his mother to die so young and in pain? No prayer or relic had brought them back to life, nor had His wrath fallen upon the murderers.

While waiting for the first blow from the Dominican's whip, Vicente fought his fear by brooding over the origins of his father's feud with the Anglesolas. It had begun with his injudicious first marriage to Valeria de Anglesola, who died giving birth to feeble Alonso. He then infuriated his former in-laws after he married Gabriela de Cornel, who presented him with a healthy son.

A ruthless clan, the Anglesolas' armed bands extorted mulberry cuttings, leafage, and silkworms from defenseless landowners and smuggled their plunder to the silk makers of Toledo without paying duty. They had planned to steal Benetorrente and its valuable mulberry groves legally and eventually through slow-witted Alonso because the señorio had been entailed to Vicente's great-great-grandfather and could never be sold, transferred, or seized no matter how great the rapacity of others nor for unpaid debts. It could only be inherited.

Convinced that Alonso's father and brother would outlive him, the Anglesolas decided to assassinate Luís de Rocamora before the señorio would be forever lost to their clan. After his father's murder, Alonso allowed his uncles and cousins, their notaries and lawyers, to handle all business and accounts, giving the Anglesolas control of the Benetorrente mulberry groves, and he accepted Violante for his wife, willing cat's-paw of her avaricious family.

Vicente imagined the unpleasant surprise and frustration Violante must have experienced on her wedding night when she discovered her husband was incapable of making love to a woman. He believed that if she ever got herself with child to secure their hold on Benetorrente, the Anglesolas would murder him and his half-brother before he revealed why Alonso could not possibly be its father.

Bernardo tapped Vicente's back with the whip. "Boy, do you repent your many sins?"

"What sins?" He tensed every muscle for the first stinging snap of the whip.

"For the sin of insolence." Violante said, and the Dominican lashed him.

Vicente clenched his teeth and stifled a cry as a streak of fire scorched his back.

Before each subsequent burning cut of the whip, she enumerated more of his transgressions. "For disrespect. For lack of contrition. For vanity. For pride. For repeated absence from your school. For disobedience. I forbade you to leave this house during the week before Lent. For causing grief to your brother. For questioning scripture."

Vicente almost passed out from shock. Better if he had.

Bernardo pulled at his hair and forced him to look into his one pitiless blue eye. "Now, I will put the question to you, plain and simple. Account for your whereabouts at the time of my brother's murder."

"Whoever did it deserves to be made a *grandee*."

"You disrespectful pup." Bernardo hit Vicente in the mouth. "I'm tempted to deliver this insolent dog to the Inquisition. They will make him talk."

Vicente spat blood. "And I'll sing a pretty tune. I'll tell the inquisitors that I've seen you washing before meals, changing linen on Fridays, Judaizing . . ."

"Silence." Bernardo flashed a dagger and placed the tip against Vicente's upper lip. "Do not tempt me to remove your impertinent tongue. Answer my question."

"I'm not answerable to you."

"Then I will make you speak."

"No, Bernardo." Violante took the whip from the Dominican. "He has had enough for the time being. I still need him alive."

In the small room that had become his prison cell, Vicente lay on his stomach atop a coarse mat, head to one side, his mouth swollen, his bloody lacerated back and arms stinging. Had he been scarred for life as any common criminal? Marks on his body did not matter, but he had felt true fear when Don Bernardo held the dagger to his mouth. In one quick movement, the Dominican could have split open his cheek, cut off his nose, or sliced away an ear.

He had to escape to a new life. He envisioned himself sailing for King Philip to discover new lands, or battling against Turks, Barbary corsairs, and heretic Protestants. Or, he could join a wandering troupe of actors to live the free, adventurous life of a poor but proud young noble *pícaro*, appear on stage or write poetry and plays. He enjoyed the banter of those free spirits whenever they came to El Grau to purchase costumes and disguises. Don Lope had encouraged him to learn their techniques of acting to mask his thoughts and feelings. Such skills could be a better defense than any armor, with informers and spies of the Inquisition everywhere.

Vicente blamed himself for his predicament. Yes, he should have listened to Don Lope. Now he had allowed his enemies to decide his fate, possibly his murder.

He moved, bit his forearm to stifle a cry of pain, then heard someone unlock the door. From the corner of his eye, he saw a shadowy form and inhaled a familiar scent, woman-smell mixed with strong perfume. Had he fallen asleep and begun to dream again?

The door was bolted shut. He heard the rustling of a dress. The musty scent became stronger, asphyxiating. The intruder turned him onto his side, held his head, and placed the rim of a silver cup against his mouth.

"Drink, Vicente, drink," Violante said. "I have brought you cold strawberry water. It will refresh you."

He was thirsty and drained the cup without thought. The aftertaste was sweet, then bitter.

Have I taken poison?

Moonlight angled through the iron grilles of an open window, and he thought Violante had never looked more beautiful or threatening, a dark angel of death. She placed him on his stomach again and rubbed a soothing ointment into his lacerations. Her soft hands were warm. So was her almond scented breath on his neck.

He felt Violante move her hands along his back and pull his breeches. She stroked his bared buttocks, then between and under until she turned him over onto the soft velvet of her black cloak.

As in his other dreams, Vicente was paralyzed, but he could see the erect dark nipples of Violante's high breasts. So was he. She straddled his waist, and rolled over until he was on top. She pulled Vicente's face to hers, and clung to him throughout his first ejaculation to final secretion.

Why hasn't Don Lope rescued me?"

A prisoner in his own house, Vicente had been told his isolation would continue until he confessed, repented all his sins, and revealed where he had been and with whom when Enríque de Anglesola was murdered.

He saw his brother and Violante for the first time when they went as a family to the Cathedral of the Virgen de Los Desamparados for masses and sermons as part of the Edict of Faith, and on this day the Anathema. Armed lackeys separated him from them and other Anglesolas.

He recognized Don Lope's name written on a placard beside his *sambenito* and *coraza*. They were displayed beside those of other confessed Judaizers who had been condemned over the centuries, to identify and dishonor them and all their descendants. "He keeps his credentials at church" was a common expression of ridicule.

Forced to attend ritual and listen to clerical harangues for the first time since his parents' deaths, Vicente experienced a new appreciation for the pageantry and drama attendant to the Catholic Faith. The relentless chanting and cloying scent of incense was hypnotic. No *comedia* had a more spectacular set than Valencia's Cathedral, with its spacious transept, lengthy nave, and majestic high altar between pillars and in front of an elaborate baldacchino.

Shafts of sunlight angled through stained glass windows and reflected off marble columns as if of Divine origin. Those beams of light irradiated gilt and jewel covered statues of the Holy Family, saints, and a dark green agate bowl set with precious stones and pearls believed by all to be the Holy Grail, the chalice used by Jesus at the Last Supper, one of many in Spanish churches

Vicente also paid close attention to the effect the preachers had on their congregations when they threatened all sinners with eternal hellfire, torments, and damnation unless they denounced heretics and blasphemers and ended their evil ways. Men trembled; many embraced their enemies. Women wept; some fainted. Others denounced their kin. Prostitutes required by law to attend sermons during Lent promised to leave their sinful trades and enter convents or hospital service for a lifetime of penitence.

He wondered what it must feel like to sway an entire congregation with dramatic words and gestures. Were these preachers sincere or master actors manipulating a gullible audience?

Vicente smelled fear among the congregation when three priests appeared and raised their large crosses for all to see, the one in the center covered in black velvet between two aflame. They marched three abreast and led a procession of black hooded friars carrying torches along the center aisle towards the altar.

At the pulpit, the principal sermonizing friar further intimidated the credulous with the awesome words of the Anathema:

"We excommunicate and anathematize in the name of the Father and of the Son and of the Holy Ghost, in the form of law, all apostate heretics from our Holy Catholic Faith . . .

"May they be accursed as members of the devil and separated from the bosom and unity of our Holy Mother Church . . .

"May the same sentence of divine excommunication encompass them as it encompassed the people of Sodom and Gomorrah who all perished in flames . . .

"May all the maledictions and plagues of Egypt come to them. And may they be accursed in eating and drinking, in waking and sleeping, in coming and going . . .

"Accursed be they in living and dying, and may they ever be burdened by their sins . . .

"May their days be few and evil . . .

"May their possessions be enjoyed by others, their wives widows, their children orphans . . .

"Accursed be they to Satan and to Lucifer and to all the devils in hell, and may these be their lords and accompany them by night and by day."

After amen and more admonitions, the priests and friars resumed their procession and sang the *Miserere*. As the great bells tolled and monks extinguished torches in the fountain of holy water, the sermonizer uttered his final terrifying words: "As these flames die in the water, so shall the souls of sinners burn in the eternal fires of hell."

Yes, good theater, but neither God nor Satan . . . only man guarantees those punishments here on earth.

The Tuesday after Easter Sunday, Vicente stood on colorful Turkish carpets over blue and yellow tile in the grand reception salon and faced his captors. Alonso slouched in a high-back chair, pale and cadaverous in loose fitting brown doublet, breeches, and wrinkled hose. His prominent blue veins would have incited the envy of any Castilian *hidalgo*.

Violante squatted in the Moorish fashion on an embroidered velvet cushion beside her husband. She wore a chaste black velvet dress with a white ruff. A jeweled golden crucifix hung from her neck. Bernardo stood beside her.

Alonso spoke as if trying to remember words not of his creation. "Vicente, you have . . .have caused me much pain."

"My brother . . ."

"Be silent, you miserable whelp." Bernardo growled, pointing a finger at Vicente.

Violante motioned for her husband to continue. When he could not recall the words, she said, "Alonso has decided. Nothing more can be done here to improve your behavior. That is why I . . .why he is acceding to a surprising request that arrived by courier. Don Jerónimo de Rocamora, Señor de Rafal, has summoned you to Orihuela."

"The head of the senior branch of our family has summoned me? Why?"

"That is not for you to question. And, Bernardo has been appointed Executor of Justice for the Tribunal of Murcia."

Vicente was not surprised the sadistic friar had been selected to be the Inquisition's principal interrogator during torture. "What has that to do with me?"

Violante exchanged sly looks with her cousin. "Because Murcia is no more than a day's journey beyond Orihuela and Bernardo is expected there as soon as possible, he will accompany you, to make certain you arrive as summoned by Rafal. You leave at once. And understand this, Vicente. Benetorrente is no longer your home. By right of entailment and primogeniture, all lands, rents, and duties of the señorio belong to Don Alonso. You have been living here and eating here and clothed here because of my husband's generosity. But no longer. You will go, never to return under pain of death."

Vicente's eyes misted. They were exiling him from his own home, from familiar surroundings, from the graves of his parents. He turned to his half-brother. Alonso looked away.

"If you still believe you will outlive Alonso and return to become lord of this señorio, know that it shall never be." Violante placed a hand on her belly. "I am with child. I have announced to the world that we shall have an heir. You are forever excluded from any inheritance."

He gaped at Violante. Now he understood that she had been the succubus of his recurring dreams. No, they had not been dreams. The clever witch had drugged him to sire her child and kept him prisoner until her conception was confirmed. Don Lope had suspected as much. The Anglesolas had outmaneuvered him. He could not speak out. If he attempted to tell the authorities what Violante had done, either her cousins would assassinate him, or they would condemn him to the galleys as an adulterer.

One day, Violante, one day I shall return to take my revenge on you and all the Anglesolas. And I shall reclaim Benetorrente and my child. I swear it. On my honor.

Chapter 4
The Nandi Variation

"Excuse me, young *caballero*," the elderly wine merchant apologized when his mule bumped against Vicente near the outskirts of Valencia and a group of street urchins distracted Bernardo with their persistent begging.

Vicente nodded at Don Lope and concealed the dagger and bag of gold coins the disguised *polidor* had handed him during their brief encounter before heading in opposite directions. Thanks to his wily mentor, he now had the means to deal with Bernardo and escape, although he preferred to continue on to Orihuela and learn why he had been summoned. From earliest memory, he had dreamed of soldering for the Crown, achieving honor and glory, and gaining admission into one of the knightly military Orders like Rafal, his kinsman in Orihuela, who was a renowned soldier and Knight of Santiago.

Surely, he has summoned me to ride off to war with him.

On foot while Don Bernardo burdened a mule with his weight, Vicente kept a wary eye on the Dominican as they departed Valencia for the more than weeklong journey to Orihuela. Clans like the Anglesolas often hired clerics to arrange murders. Priests and friars were beyond the jurisdiction of His Majesty's courts and only their ecclesiastic superiors could try them.

Just let Bernardo make a move. Vicente welcomed any opportunity to take him on man-to-man. In the meantime, he ignored the friar's relentless religious lectures and homilies while they progressed along the coastal road on a thin strip of land rimmed with rice fields and pine woods that separated the sea from the Albufereta Lagoon.

Farther south, they passed through orange and lemon orchards. Both flower and orange grew on the same tree in springtime and gave forth waves of blossom-perfume in the balmy air at night. They traveled through palm and mulberry groves, market gardens of melons, and fields of sugar cane. The land also produced wine, olive oil, rice, wheat, and barley, with many droves of goat and sheep on the barrens; and the gulf teemed with tuna, scrod, and shellfish. That was why Valencia was known throughout Spain as *la regalada*, the offering, as if it were a gift from heaven,

Yet, much of the country lay desolate and untended. It had not recovered from the expulsion of its most industrious population, the Moriscos, in 1609, and two of the past three years had been arid.

When they entered a deserted village, Bernardo cursed and spat. "Everyone knows the accursed Moriscos only pretended to accept Christianity like those Jew-pigs, who converted out of convenience and in secret continued to practice their false religion. And just like the perfidious Jews, they were banished from Spain." He pointed towards the hills and mountains to the west. "Over there, about twenty-one miles away, is la Muela de Cortes, where the Moriscos who refused exile gathered for a last stand, then surrendered without a fight. They begged for mercy and safe passage to the embarkation ports, but we could not let their defiance go unpunished. We executed their leaders. Our soldiers had their way with the women and sold the children into slavery."

"You were there?"

Bernardo touched the scar on the left side of his face. "In my capacity as confessor to the soldiers."

Vicente imagined the Dominican would have had much to confess himself after the massacre. Was it there Bernardo had lost his eye? Talk of Moriscos also caused Vicente to remember a lost best friend of his childhood, Pablo Royaya, who had been expelled from Spain with his family in 1609. Where was he now? Had he been enslaved upon reaching North Africa?

Vicente felt his loins stir when the darkening violet sky reminded him of Pablo's beautiful older sister, enchanting Moraíma of the blue-violet eyes, who used to chase him with the threat of many kisses.

Ay, Moraíma. I would not run from you now.

They spent their nights at inns instead of monasteries. At first, Vicente would not close his eyes and give the friar an opportunity for murder or buggery. He need not have worried. Each night, the Dominican drank wine and brandy until he passed out. Nevertheless, Vicente had difficulty falling asleep. At the inns, voracious bedbugs and fleas assaulted him and by mid journey left him looking as if he had the pox, with no space left for another bite. The fifth night out of Valencia they sat in a corner of another filthy inn on the outskirts of Alicante. Bernardo guzzled from his second jug of strong wine, reached across the table, and gripped one of Vicente's hands. "I am the most miserable of men."

He saw he was in no immediate danger. The wine had made the friar sentimental, but his own words shocked him. Any priest hearing confession might have said as he, "Why are you so miserable, Don Bernardo?" At least he had not added, "my son."

"I once loved a *morilla*, a beautiful Morisca. Josefa was her name, but I was forced to give her up."

"Why did you give her up?" *Incredible. I* am *behaving like a stinking confessor.*

"My illustrious family would never allow me to marry a girl of tainted Moorish blood." The Dominican swilled from his jug. Rivulets of blood red wine soaked his chin as he slurred. "I was not allowed to marry anyone. I was a younger son, and they forced me into the clergy against my wishes. That November in 1609, when I rode with the army into la Muela de Cortes, I found my Josefa. She was married, twice a mother . . ."

"Did you help her to escape?"

"No, I became enraged because she had lain with another. No matter that he was her husband. Flames of desire consumed me. Hotter than the fires of hell. She was the most gorgeous creature I had ever seen and completely at my mercy. Only God knows why we do such terrible things. I took Josefa. And afterwards, I killed her. God forgive me."

While Vicente stared at him horrified, Bernardo pleaded, "Absolve me. Give me absolution for my sins. Forgive me."

The friar passed out. Vicente pulled his hand away and wiped it on his breeches. He would not have been surprised to see pustules of *mal frances* under the Dominican's filthy robe.

The following morning, Bernardo did not recall his confession. They continued on their way through Alicante, a port on the Costa Blanca, the White Coast so-called because of the blinding light reflecting off its sandy beaches, and headed inland along the high road to Elx, the next town of importance before Orihuela.

Passing the last blossom-scented orchards of oranges and groves of date palms, Vicente turned and glanced one last time across the terraced vineyards to the palm and carob tree-lined Gulf of Alicante. He always dreaded being more than five miles away from the sea.

Valencia, lost paradise of the Moors. My Fragrant Coast, lost paradise of Vicente de Rocamora?

Bernardo turned to Vicente after they entered a pine forest in the hills beyond Elx. "What was that sound? They say bandits lurk everywhere in these woods and hills."

"No one will dare harm us here. I am a de Rocamora. We approach domains where my kinsmen are . . ."

Someone seized Vicente. Another stuffed a cloth into his mouth and tore away his cross, dagger, and bag of coins. Others trussed him onto a long pole like a goat ready for slaughter and carried him deeper into the steep pine forest. *Has Bernardo arranged my murder after all?* Then he heard the Dominican squealing in pain behind him.

Vicente's captors dropped him to the ground in the middle of a large clearing as the sun set behind the pine trees and mountains. One of the men pulled the rag from his mouth. Another cut his bonds. Vicente bolted to his feet ready to defend himself. A horde of armed men surrounded him, their hostile expressions made more grotesque because of scars, missing ears, noses, and eyes. They were as vicious a collection of *matones* as any in El Grau. Some held torches, and behind them several dozen women and children of varying ages stared at him and Bernardo, who lay on the ground a few feet away, still bound and bleeding from cuts on his arms and legs.

Vicente had a good eye for regional faces. Although the band included renegade Moriscos and a few Gypsies, most were typically short and dark Valencians or Murcians. A head taller, a shirtless African had scars on his torso and arms from flogging, torture, and tribal mutilations.

The bandit leader stepped forward. He had the swarthy hawk features of an Arab, trimmed spade-beard, and silver filigree earrings. He carried himself with dignity in the tattered blue and white livery of some unknown señor. The Arab kicked Bernardo in the ribs and beckoned to a boy no older than Vicente.

"You say he is the one?"

"Yes, he is the pig who tortured my father and raped my mother. Ay, Yusef, I was forced to watch when he cut off her breasts and split open her belly."

"You are certain?"

"On my life, he is Bernardo de Anglesola, who rode with Augustín Mexia's soldiers when they massacred our people at la Muela de Cortes." He drew his knife, but the African prevented him from plunging it into the friar.

The black man pushed the boy aside and rested his foot on the friar's belly. "I also recognize him. I slaved in his father's fields." He touched several of his scars. "He gave me these."

Vicente called out at the shock of sudden recognition, "Pablo . . . Pablo Royaya."

The youth sauntered over to him. "Vicente, *mi amigo*. It is really you."

Pablo's demeanor became hostile again when Yusef, the African, and a noseless Murcian approached them. He pretended to threaten Vicente with his knife. "And what are you doing in the company of this Dominican pig?"

"He's my jailer. He's taking me from Valencia to my kinsman in Orihuela, Don Jerónimo de Rocamora, Señor de Rafal. If you value your lives, you'll release me, or retribution will . . ."

31

"Silence, you sack of oral diarrhea." The Arab, whom Pablo had addressed as Yusef, rested the tip of his scimitar against Vicente's chest. "Who is this babbling fool?"

"He is Vicente de Rocamora, best friend of my childhood, son of Don Luís. My father managed his father's mulberry groves and silkworm production. The Señor de Benetorrente was a good man. He protested against our expulsion and tried to protect us."

Yusef ran the flat of his blade across Vicente's chest. "A fine physique for field, quarry, or galley. He would bring us many gold pieces."

Noseless reached out to touch Vicente's cheeks. "A pretty face too. Mulay Zidan, the Sultan of Morocco himself, might fancy his . . ."

Vicente struck the *matone* with his fist and dropped him unconscious to the ground. Yusef laughed and said to the African, "Koitalel, perhaps we can persuade this young hothead to join us after we settle scores with the friar." He read a scroll taken from Bernardo's bag. "By the beard of the Prophet, this Dominican swine has been appointed chief interrogator and torturer in Murcia for the Inquisition. What shall we do with this Christian dog?"

Vicente stepped forward. "Let me fight him man-to-man with whips, knives, or bare hands, to the death."

"And deprive the rest of us of our entertainment?"

The band of robbers, thieves, and murderers called out for the usual common tortures, mutilations, and slow deaths. Flickering light from the torches further distorted their disfigured features. When the women became part of the circle, Vicente fixed his attention on a beauty whose straight blue-black hair fell to her waist. *From my thoughts to God's great gift.* She had to be none other than Pablo's sister, the enchanting Moraíma.

The nineteen-year old *morilla* stood beside her brother. Nothing of the hatred she felt marred her face. "This cowardly dog would have raped and murdered me, the same as he did our mother, and he would have killed Pablo too. Fortunately, I had a knife and cut out his eye, and we were able to escape. He deserves the foulest punishment imaginable."

Yusef arched an eyebrow and grinned in anticipation. "Which is?"

"He would condemn us to the rack, pulleys, fire, and water treatments of his Inquisition. Give him the equivalent of the last, the *aselli*, but with a variation, the Nandi tribal death Koitalel has spoken of."

All cheered when Yusef nodded at the African. Koitalel instructed the men to spread-eagle Bernardo on an incline, face up, head lower than feet. They tied his limbs to pegs driven deeply into the ground and secured his head with leather thongs between a pair of stakes.

Pablo cut open the Dominican's filthy robe and exposed his flabby body to ridicule. Individual men and women squeezed and pinched the friar's folds of fat, heavy breasts and nipples until they bled. Bernardo screamed loudest when they shoved pine needles under his fingernails and abused his genitals. A hag stretched his genitals, waved her dagger, and threatened to circumcise, then geld him.

Koitalel trimmed a small section of a branch and forced it into Bernardo's mouth as a wedge. On reflex, the friar attempted to clench his jaw. The pressure from the sharp ends of the wood caused blood to ooze into his throat and out from the corners of his mouth. The Dominican gagged and coughed, unable to move his head or close his mouth as he looked at the full moon and stars with his one good eye.

Yusef turned to Pablo. "I give you the honor of going first."

Pablo stood over the terrified friar and undid his breeches. The Gypsy girls whistled and made obscene comments when he exposed his penis and urinated into the Dominican's gaping mouth. "For you, Christian dog. ¡Agua muy rica! The water is very rich!"

Bernardo choked on urine and blood and gasped for breath. The bandit gang cheered again when Koitalel peed into the friar's throat.

The Nandi death disgusted Vicente. Torturing a helpless human went against his code of honor no matter how voracious his appetite for revenge. Moraíma also did not participate when her turn came.

"Yusef, I am satisfied to have selected this pig's death."

The Arab followed Koitalel, then all the bandits and their women, who squatted over the Dominican's face. They urinated in his mouth and peed into his nostrils until he drowned in blood and urine.

Vicente recalled the emptiness he had felt after killing Anglesola. "Tell me, are you satisfied with your revenge, Moraíma?"

"No, but evil must be punished."

While Koitalel, Pablo, and other members of the band took turns kicking Bernardo's corpse away from the campfires, Moraíma pressed against Vicente. "You do not run from me anymore?"

He stared into the deep pools of her blue-violet eyes, aroused in spite of the danger he still faced. "I am no longer eight years old."

"I know," she said grinding her hips.

Yusef, Koitalel, Pablo, and several *matones* approached them. Vicente stepped back from Moraíma. He looked for a rock, a branch, anything to defend himself. No one was going to piss in his mouth. He would die fighting like a man, like a de Rocamora.

Yusef handed Vicente his dagger, purse, and cross. "I also give you the friar's mule. It is tethered down the hill with all your belongings. You are free to go or stay."

Vicente could not take his eyes away from Moraíma. "My kinsman is expecting me."

Pablo embraced him "Stay the night, my old friend. We have so much to say to each other."

Moraíma took Vicente's arm. "Yes, stay the night. Stay the night with me."

Chapter 5
Second Sight

They sat around one of the campfires and ate chicken stolen from a local señorio. Pablo asked questions and Yusef interrogated Vicente, while Moraíma clung to him and threatened any girl bold enough to come too close. The men were impressed with his account of Anglesola's assassination, and the Arab demanded to know everything about Don Lope's enterprises. He then described how he had been captured from a sinking Barbary pirate ship and sentenced to labor as a slave on the Duke of Gandia's estates. Like Koitalel, he escaped and later organized his company of desperados, which included other runaway slaves, hardened criminals, Gypsies, and hunted Moriscos like Pablo and Moraíma. They thieved throughout the south of Valencia and parts of Murcia. "Feuding señores and *caballeros* hire us, even your kin, the de Rocamoras."

"And you, Moraíma, what are your specialties," Vicente asked

"I dance and sing at fairs, while Yusef's band plucks the pigeons who gawk at me."

"And I've become a skilled gambler," Pablo said.

"I'd like to see how good you really are at cards and dice. Don Lope and his friends taught me how to recognize cheats, deal seconds, and control the outcome of any throw at knucklebones."

Pablo raised his eyebrows. "Deal second cards? You'll have to teach me that one, Vicente."

Several men at another fire strummed guitars and the women shook tambourines. A quartet of girls in skirts and blouses of vivid primary colors began to dance. They snapped their fingers, turned and twisted their bodies. Skirts twirled above their thighs as their comrades clapped hands and moved their feet to the rhythm.

"Moraíma. Moraíma." Her name became a rhythmic chant.

Two of the girls pulled Moraíma to her feet, and Pablo began to play his guitar. She smiled at Vicente. "Tonight, I sing and dance only for you."

At the first chords from Pablo's guitar, Moraíma opened her arms to Vicente and sang a centuries-old Castilian ballad in the most soul-wrenching voice he had ever heard:

> *Yo me era mora Moraíma,*
> *morilla de un bel catar;*
> *christiano vino a mi puerta*
> *cuidada, por me engañar.*
> *Yo me . . .*

> I was the Moorish Girl, Moraíma
> a Morisca with a pretty face,
> a Christian came to my door
> To deceive me, oh, beware.

> *Yo me . . .*

Another girl continued the tragic song when Moraíma bent back her torso, raised her arms, and shook her shoulders. Unlike the Gypsy girls and all of the other developed women Vicente had ever seen, she had no hair under her arms.

Moraíma danced a three-quarter-measure chaconne and snapped her fingers in time to the music accompanied by Gypsy women clicking pieces of ivory and seashells. She devoured Vicente with her expressive blue-violet eyes and twirled her skirt higher.

Entranced by the turn of her head, the way she tossed her hair, the movement of arms and hands as if they were snakes, Vicente's pulse raced in time with the accelerating tempo until Moraíma pulled him to his feet. "Come with me, Vicente, come with me to paradise."

On an unseasonable warm spring night beneath a full moon and sky filled with stars, atop a bed of fragrant orange blossoms, Vicente experienced conscious lovemaking for the first time. Because he was rough and awkward as any male adolescent, Moraíma guided, instructed, and transported him to a new world of ecstatic delights. She performed tricks with her mouth and tongue he never imagined possible. Her sweet scent, cleanliness, and lack of body hair further aroused him. She had even waxed her eyebrows and replaced them with artificial lines to draw attention to her eyes.

Vicente compared Moraíma to the sea, mysterious, turbulent and infinite. He rode crests of passion with her, then became passive clay in her hands during moments between.

Once while he rested on his back and gazed at the moon, he heard her say, "My unfortunate Vicente."

"Why am I unfortunate?"

"I have spoiled you for other women."

"You have." He rolled over on top of her. "I want no other, only you Moraíma."

"You say that now, but tomorrow there will be another."

"Never. And would you take another lover?"

"When we are apart, I must do what I can to survive."

"I'll kill anyone who . . ."

"My hot-blooded Valencian lover." Moraíma pulled his face to hers for a passionate kiss.

"Why have you honored me so, Moraíma?"

"To pay my father's debt to your father."

"Oh," he said disappointed.

"And because you are a rare young man of perfect face and form. You have your father's manly features and your mother's unusual green eyes. You are truly blessed, Vicente. And perhaps cursed."

"God forbid. Why do you say such things?"

"I am a *morilla*, and you are sinning with me, Christian."

"I can never sin with you. We are not married to others, so what we're doing is not forbidden by any of the Ten Commandments."

"Yes, you are right. Allah will pardon me for whatever I do with men. I am different. He knows the reason for my behavior and that I must follow my road. God is compassionate and understanding."

Vicente also could rationalize his lust as well as any Spaniard and kissed her hand. "A Christian who loves such infidel beauty deserves to be pardoned by God, and I truly love you, Moraíma. You are like the most delicate rose planted in a secluded garden. So white is your face in the moonlight, more pure than crystal, that when I gaze at your perfection I see my own face reflected in its brightness. Your breasts are perfect globes, which Aphrodite herself must envy. May God bless and honor the mother who bore you."

Moraíma rewarded him with another kiss. "My sweet Vicente. You are a poet."

"You have made me a poet, Moraíma. You make the sun shine at night. You illuminate the depths of my dark soul. Tonight, I almost believe in God, for only a divine being could have created one such as you. I will forever sing praises of your great beauty."

"Yes, I believe you will. But on the morrow, we must travel our separate roads."

"Moraíma, you are breaking my heart."

"It is true. You will continue your journey and meet your fate in Orihuela, as Pablo and I must travel in an opposite direction."

"With Yusef's band?"

"A necessary association for our own safety and profit. One day I will act and sing in Madrid, before King Philip himself."

"Then I will go with you. I can create masks, wear disguises. I can act and win money for us at cards."

She rested her head on Vicente's chest. "A fanciful dream."

He buried his face in Moraíma's scented hair and caressed her smooth body. "Yes, I must honor my family's summons, but I will love no other. I will return to claim you."

"You are very young, my Vicente. I know you will doubt me when I say you will love many women."

"Never, I swear."

"I know men. Whenever you remember tonight, you'll feel fire in your loins and want every woman you see. María the servant. Dolores the lusty widow. Inéz the virginal daughter of some señor. And when you're close to those unwashed Christian bitches, you'll retch at their stench of week-old fish. You'll cringe at the sight and smell of their sweat-stinking bushy armpits. Their breath of rotting teeth will nauseate you. The lice in their filthy hair will distract you. That is why Christian men will sell their souls to receive love from a *morilla* like me."

"You already have mine."

She caressed his genitals. "And when you get close to those reeking Christians, you'll have difficulty raising your lance."

"Not with you, Moraíma. Never with you."

Sunlight sliced through the trees and awakened them. When Vicente moved to kiss Moraíma, she pushed him away. "The breath of dawn can be fouler than a priest's chamber pot."

She peeled an orange with his dagger, and after they sucked on the fruit to sweeten their mouths, they made love. Afterwards, he lay on his side and watched Moraíma put on her red blouse and purple skirt. Dappled morning light fell on her blue-black hair. Vicente believed he would never again see anyone more beautiful. "I have decided. I cannot go to Orihuela. I love you, Moraíma. I'll follow you anywhere."

With her hand, she weighed the bag of coins he had placed under his clothes. "There is not enough gold here to keep me."

"Do not torment me."

Moraíma tossed Vicente the bag. When she held his cross, she cried out and clutched her abdomen.

Vicente went to her. "What is it?"

She doubled over. "Your mother. I can feel her . . . see her dying in agony when she was with child. It is too much. Too much." She held the neck-chain and let the cross dangle in front of her eyes.

Vicente gaped at Moraíma as any rustic might. "Is that what you do at the fairs? Tell fortunes like a Gypsy?"

"I never do it for money. These accursed visions come without warning. Sometimes, when I touch an object or enter a room, I live what has taken place. Often, terrible happenings. Rape, murder, a fatal miscarriage. I also see what will be."

If anyone other than Moraíma had spoken those words, Vicente would have rejected them. "Will I marry you?"

"You shall have better fortune than that."

"How could I ever prefer another to you?"

"My young naive gallant." She ran the chain through her fingers as if telling a rosary. "We are not fated to wed each other. We must follow the separate paths kismet has chosen for us. May God protect you."

"You're pretending to tell my fortune to rid yourself of me."

"Hush." Moraíma closed her eyes. Moisture formed on her brow. "I see you with three loves. Yes. Three loves, one of them not yet born. And you will have many children."

"If I love you, why would there be others? Who are the others?"

"I see a golden fire, flaming brilliantly, but burning under thick ice. I also see a ruby and a pearl."

"What does it mean?"

"And you will wear many masks."

"Then I'll be an actor after all."

"An actor, yes. You will be a great actor, but on a different stage." Moraíma trembled. "Mother of God!"

"What is it?"

"You will face a powerful enemy . . ."

"Then I'll deal with him the way I took care of Anglesola."

"No, not a man, you will have many such enemies. As you defeat one, another will take his place. Many enemies, multiple manifestations of your great adversary."

"Who? Tell me who?"

"Spain, your enemy is Spain."

"Impossible. How can Spain be my enemy when it is my land?"

"Vicente, you must accept your fate and travel on to Orihuela."

"And what will happen to me there?"

"The great adventure of your life will begin."

"I believe it has already happened."

Drenched in perspiration, Moraíma opened her eyes and thrust the cross and chain into Vicente's hands. "No more, I wish to see no more."

"Moraíma . . ."

"No more."

After Vicente put on his clothes, they held hands and walked back in silence to the camp. In the pine clearing, Yusef, Pablo, and Koitalel were waiting for them with Bernardo's mule. The Dominican's silver crucifix hung from the African's neck.

Pablo embraced Vicente. "We must not let so many years pass before we meet again. May God watch over you."

"And a long life to you, my friend."

Yusef also embraced him. "You will always be welcome among us. I believe I can do good business with your friend in Valencia. Last night I sent my men to deposit the friar's corpse in the Segura River near the gates of Murcia, so you will not be blamed for his drowning and for poisoning the river."

Vicente thanked the Arab, but doubted if Violante and the Anglesolas would believe the deception. He hesitated before mounting. "Moraíma, you have shown me the blessed paradise promised in your Koran."

"Fortunate Christian, and you did not have to die in battle for Allah to experience it." She waited for him to sit astride his mule, then pulled his face to her so she could kiss him. "We shall meet again, Vicente, when we least expect it."

"I'll pray for our next meeting every day until we do."

"Go with your God, Vicente."

"Then I go alone."

Vicente looked back to wave one last time at Moraíma, but she had disappeared between the pines. Later in the day when he rested in an orange grove, its sweet scent took him back to those magical moments amidst their bed of fragrant blossoms. He also recalled Moraíma's dancing, her sweet affecting voice, and he sang his own improvised variations of popular Andalusian *coplas*:

> I am jealous of the air
> that touches my Moraíma's face;
> if the air was a man
> I would kill him.
>
> If I knew the stones
> my Moraíma walks on in the street
> I'd turn them upside down
> so that no one else may tread upon them.

Chapter 6
Rafal and Ballebrera

During the last hour of siesta, Vicente entered Orihuela, a provincial town of about five hundred families situated on a narrow strip of land between the Segura River and a rising wall of foothills. The late afternoon sun reflected off whitewashed houses and bathed the silent, empty wider avenues and squares in amber light. Cool shadows fell at angles from eaves, shuttered balconies, and towers of the Gothic Cathedral, the Monastery of Santo Domingo, the Romanesque-Gothic cloister of the Episcopal palace, other churches, convents, and hermitages. He calculated Orihuela held almost as many religious structures as private homes.

As church bells tolled the hour, he reached the Rafal *Palacio* and its façade of quarried stone, iron grill balconies, and heavy wood shutters. The de Rocamora coat-of-arms hung over the portico. Over waves of silver and blue atop a golden rock against a sky-blue field stood a tower of gold with a flowering mulberry branch above and flanked by golden fleur-de-lys, identifying the clan's French origins.

The mulberry: Genus *morus* in Latin, *mora* in the vulgate. Rocamora: Rock, both of the Moors and of the mulberry.

Vicente dismounted and rapped the massive oak front door until it was opened by a half-dressed portly *mayordomo*. He identified himself as the son of Don Luís de Rocamora, cousin to the Señor de Rafal, and handed over the written summons. "I am expected by Don Jerónimo himself."

The *mayordomo* stared at Vicente for signs of family resemblance and pretended to read the document until he recognized his master's seal. He called out for someone named Sanchito. A small boy in loose breeches scurried to the door and rubbed his eyes. The *mayordomo* slapped Sanchito's head, ordered him to take the mule to the stables, and let Vicente into the zaguan, a rust-tiled vestibule with whitewashed walls.

The *mayordomo* escorted him to an *estrado* where the de Rocamoras were drinking post siesta chocolate with water to wash down the thick and sweet beverage, which was the most popular refreshment in Spain and consumed day and night. Vicente presented his summons to Rafal and went through introductions and formal civilities. Years on the waterfront of El Grau had sharpened his natural aptitude for reading individuals. The women and youngest children would not be a factor in his future. A typical subservient provincial wife dressed in black, the Señora de Rafal held prayer book and rosary in her lap. So did her daughter, Isabella, a girl close to his age who blushed and looked away when their eyes met. Five-year old Gaspar stared at him until his interest waned. Two-year old Juan slept in the arms of an elderly servant.

Vicente felt instant animosity from Jacinto, Rafal's oldest son, about twelve years of age, he guessed. The thin, high-strung boy's remorseless blue eyes and feminine features reminded him of children who tortured small animals for amusement.

Don Jerónimo de Rocamora y Roda, Señor de Rafal and Benferri and Barón de la Puebla de Rocamora, sat in a plain high-back wooden chair as if astride his charger. At age forty-six, Rafal was lean and fit with a graying mustache, spade beard and close-cropped hair. Dressed all in black in the style of the previous century with a white ruff of modest size, his inscrutable expression was impossible for Vicente to read.

Slouching in a more comfortable chair, Don Ramón de Rocamora y Riquelme, Señor de Ballebrera, was shorter and darker with a stocky torso. He reeked of perfume, wore make-up, and was festooned in the current fashion of the Court, at which, Don Lope had told Vicente, homosexuality was accepted when not flaunted. The dark brown hair of Ballebrera's wig fell to his shoulders in curling locks, and he had waxed the ends of his upturned, exaggerated mustachio and beard. Tight-fitting dark blue velvet doublet with balloon sleeves was embroidered in gold and silver thread. Blue and gray breeches puffed out and tightened above his knees over silver silk stockings and square-toed gray leather shoes with oversized silver buckles. A fragile ruff and cuffs of fine white linen with lace edges completed the fabulous costume.

Rafal dismissed the women and children. At the doorway, Jacinto toyed with a dagger as if intending to throw it at Vicente.

Ballebrera appeared to be the friendlier of the two kinsmen, and Vicente intended to be on guard if they ever were alone until he knew the reason why. In El Grau, he had learned how to fend off men who preferred boys.

Rafal asked questions about Vicente's father and the Señorío de Benetorrente. At no time did facial expression and manner betray his thoughts. Vicente sensed a wall between them.

Has Jerónimo taken an instant dislike to me?

"Your brother is the eldest son," Ballebrera said to Vicente "Why has he not acted against the Anglesolas?"

"I regret to say that Alonso is feeble of mind, with little stamina and less will."

"Despicable coward," Rafal said.

"No, Don Jerónimo, it is not cowardice. What could we do? The Anglesola faction is the most powerful in the city of Valencia."

"The boy is right," Ballebrera said. "They are kinsmen of Lerma, His Majesty's favorite, and supported by all the might of Madrid."

Rafal sipped his chocolate and water. "Why then, did Alonso marry a daughter of your enemies?"

"I believe she bewitched him."

Ballebrera twisted an end of his mustachio. "She is beautiful then?"

"I'm not sure. At times Violante seems to be very beautiful. And she can be ugly. I believe she cast a spell over my brother."

"And over you as well?"

"No, Don Ramón." Vicente thought it best not to tell them of his experience with the succubus. "I hate that *bruja*. She controls Alonso with hashish."

"Violante has announced to the world that she is pregnant," Ballebrera said, "which eliminates you from inheriting Benetorrente. Yet, we have heard rumors that your brother is incapable of producing an heir."

When Vicente did not speak, Rafal leaned forward in his chair. "Tell us. Who is the father?"

Vicente responded with a half-truth. "Any man would do for the purposes of that evil brood. At least Enríque de Anglesola, my father's assassin, died on Shrove Tuesday."

The two men looked at each other. Ballebrera got out of his chair and circled Vicente. "Handsome face, superb physique. Exactly how old are you?"

"On the fifth day of this month I turned sixteen."

Ballebrera sighed. "To be just sixteen again. Have you had any schooling?"

Vicente recited his knowledge of dialects and languages. He omitted what Don Lope had taught him about medicine, forgery, and disguises, and boasted of his skill with knife, sword, and ciphers to impress Rafal who sustained his unreadable expression.

"Cousin, I would take Vicente to Madrid with me, place him as an equerry in a great house, and arrange a marriage with an heiress or wealthy widow . . ."

"Who may lose her fortune the day after the wedding," Rafal finished for Ballebrera.

"Or, better yet, establish him in the royal household, where he might become a favorite of Infante Philip, our future king."

"Favorites come and go according to the sudden whims of kings."

"I can teach him to play the game better than anyone."

"And he may come to enjoy the game more than working to achieve our ends. Vicente is much too handsome. If the Infante does not become jealous of his looks, he may become enamored of the boy, as they say James of England is with his favorite, Villiers. Is either what you want?"

"Of course not."

In spite of Don Lope's advice to wear a mask, Vicente could not hide his displeasure at being discussed as if he were invisible. He wanted no arranged marriage, nor did he aspire to attend a pampered prince. He saw his future as a soldier, riding to war against Spain's enemies.

"I may have something else in mind for the boy," Rafal said.

Vicente could no longer keep silent. "Don Jerónimo, I want to fight beside you against Spain's enemies. Is that why you summoned me?"

Ballebrera waved a white handkerchief in a gesture of surrender. "He is a typical de Rocamora soldier, and all yours."

The *mayordomo* entered the *estrado*. "My lord, your kinsmen have arrived."

Rafal stood and approached Vicente. "Will you promise to serve the cause of our family as I so command?"

Vicente placed his right fist on his heart and again saw himself charging into battle against Protestants and Turks alongside the renowned soldier. "Don Jerónimo, you have my word of honor, the word of a de Rocamora and a Spaniard. I will do whatever you so command."

Chapter 7
Family Aspirations

In Rafal's *estrado de cumplimiento*, a salon used for ceremonial receptions, Vicente met three more kinsmen for the first time: Rafal's elderly uncle, António de Rocamora, Dominican rector of Orihuela's renowned College of Confessors of Santo Domingo; Don Francisco de Rocamora, Señor de la Granja de Rocamora, also a distinguished soldier and veteran of the recent Italian campaign; and Tomás de Rocamora, Francisco's younger brother, who had been appointed Dominican lector at the University of Zaragoza.

Soldiers and Dominicans. Vicente knew which family career he preferred to the exclusion of the other.

Chairs had been placed in an extended circle for a light supper of breads, cheeses, and cold meats. Small tables between them held food and drink. Servants lit tall tapers on silver candelabra and sconces as dusk faded into evening. Odorless olive pits burned in metal braziers mounted on wooden stands and provided heat.

The candles illuminated Rafal's valuable family treasures. Paintings depicted the Nativity and Crucifixion of Jesus and the martyrdom of saints. Delicate chests of drawers were inlaid with mother-of-pearl and ivory. Carved sideboards and cabinets had been crammed with plates and dishes of silver. Boxes contained religious relics, some possibly genuine. Ballebrera, sitting on Vicente's right, identified booty from wars against the heretics that included more fine plates and goblets, small sculptures, and a Flemish tapestry of The Annunciation.

"Don Ramón, why has Don Jerónimo summoned the men of his family?"

"Because here in Spain, Don Nobody wishes to become Don Somebody, Don Somebody desires to become Don Somebody Important, and Jerónimo aspires to the titles of conde or marqués, and perhaps even the *grandeza*. And he may have a very important role for you to play in his endeavors."

"What role? To soldier with him?"

"We must wait for him to say." Ballebrera explained what had transpired earlier in the day before siesta. He, Rafal, and Francisco had signed documents reaffirming that in the event of no heirs all property and titles would devolve to the head of the most senior surviving branch.

Vicente understood why. He had passed through their adjacent señorios. If they were ever joined together, the lord of that vast estate would be the most powerful in the area.

He observed Rafal looking with distaste at Ballebrera and guessed what the reserved soldier must be thinking. Ramón's flamboyant appearance contrasted with the close-cropped hair, trimmed mustaches and spade beards, and sober black elegance of Jerónimo and Francisco, and an affront to the tonsure, white woolen robes, silver crucifixes and plain sandals of the Dominicans.

Vicente suspected that Ballebrera's affectations disguised a cunning mind as he studied the other men. Don Lope had taught him to identify specific signs of illness. The eyes of António, whom everyone affectionately addressed as Tío, revealed he was ill with intestinal worms, too weak to do more than offer counsel. He also suffered from gout, dozed off at short intervals, and appeared not long for this world. Vicente needed more time to evaluate Francisco, a taciturn robust man of ruddy complexion younger than Rafal by about a decade.

"Francisco also aspires to a title and membership in Rafal's military Order of Santiago," Ballebrera said as if reading Vicente's mind. "As for Tomás, although only twenty-one years of age, that narrow-minded humorless prig is older in spirit than any other man in the room. Dangerous too, because he is brilliant and already a skilled polemicist. Stay clear of him."

As with Jacinto, Vicente had marked the Dominican as a possible adversary.

António snorted himself awake and gripped the silver crucifix of his Order hanging from his neck. "Do you attend Church regularly, my boy?"

"Yes."

"Tell the truth, Vicente," Ballebrera said. "Any *caballero* who listens to sermons has either no girl or no money. The young men of Spain are more capable of killing in defense of our Church than entering its front door."

"Ignore our wicked kinsman," António said with good humor. "And, my son, did you confess your sins this past Easter?"

"As I do every year."

"Not all, I hope." Ballebrera leered and added, "No Spaniard with balls confesses every one of his sins. Confession is an act of humility, which is alien to our racial character."

"We are all humble before our Lord, Don Ramón, and pray for His Divine Mercy."

"Amen," the other men said as one.

"Time to change the subject, I see." Ballebrera, the only one present drinking wine, raised his glass. "This is what I enjoy most about my infrequent visits to Orihuela. Here in the Kingdom of Valencia and in Catalonia wines are stored in wooden casks and served in decent goblets. Throughout the rest of Spain, even at Court, the best wines are spoiled by the pitch and resin in those vulgar pigskin and goatskin bags. Absolutely criminal."

Tomás crossed himself. "Wine is brewed in the bowels of hell, where Satan himself prepares the seductive vintage to lead men astray."

Ballebrera shrugged off his cousin's homily. "What can I say to counter such constipated wisdom?"

At the end of supper, the men moved about the room, except for Antonio who dozed off again. Servants arranged their chairs in a tighter circle and placed a selection of desserts on a sideboard. Vicente admired the silver bowls and plates overflowing with the sweetest grapes, pomegranates, and oranges from Rafal's orchards, as well as almond cakes, fruit pies, egg yolks preserved in sugar, and a selection of iced orange juice, strawberry water, and chocolate.

After the servants left, Rafal opened and shut all doors to make sure no one was listening and caught Jacinto hiding outside on the balcony. He admonished his son and ordered him to bed.

"The boy lurks about," Ballebrera said to Vicente, "and he has an exceptionally vicious streak. Rotten to the core before he's become half-ripe."

"Jacinto has taken an instant dislike to me."

"Take no notice of the insect."

"And Tomás stares at me as if he suspects I'm guilty of some blasphemy or worse."

"It is his nature. He believes everyone has sinned, is sinning, or intends to sin." Ballebrera sneered at the Dominican, who appeared to be praying over each of Rafal's holy relics. "The fool believes those are real splinters from the True Cross. There must be enough such shavings in Spain to build an entire city of wood."

"And enough saintly bones to populate every house with a skeleton."

"At last. Someone with wit in Orihuela."

Rafal called for his guests to take their seats in the small circle. "I pray tonight's discussion will ensure that in the near future all de Rocamoras shall have titles and palaces worthy of our blood."

And a place in the armies of Spain for me as well.

Tomás pointed at Vicente. "Why is he still here?"

Rafal turned to the young Dominican. "He represents Benetorrente and is old enough to understand everything. Now then, as we know all too well, no de Rocamora has yet been raised to conde, marqués, or duque, and Tío was denied the Bishopric of Orihuela in spite of our outstanding military careers and distinguished lineage. Tonight we must decide on our strategy and tactics to achieve our goals. Ramón, what is the current situation at *la Corte?*"

Ballebrera quartered an orange in the Valencian manner and tasted a section. "First, you ought to know that our King will not have a long life."

Tomás crossed himself. "God forbid. Surely, you are not speaking of regicide?"

"No one would dare harm His Majesty, but he is sickly, scrofulous. His eldest son and heir to the throne, Infante Philip, is an impressionable boy of twelve and relies upon Gaspar de Guzmán, Count de Olivares, his tutor, who has ambitions to become the next king's *privado.*"

Francisco made a fist for emphasis. "Then we must ally ourselves with Olivares."

Ballebrera fussed with his artificial locks. "I have already laid the foundation for our success. In Madrid, I have a considerable reputation as a wit with certain wives of influential men, whom I advise in matters of appearance. Although, the Countess de Olivares is rather plain, she has considerable charm and is interested in gossip and the latest fashions. I have been of value to her in both instances, and, therefore, to Olivares. Remember, we are both Knights of Alcántara."

Vicente gaped at Ballebrera. *A Knight of Alcántara? It seems I have much more to learn about you.*

"Because Tomás is a Dominican we might be able to install him as a royal confessor for one of His Majesty's other children. As you may or may not know, His Majesty's confessor, Luís de Aliaga, and the Infante's confessor, António de Sotomayor, also are Dominicans."

Tomás gripped his cross. "I prefer to have a seat on *la Suprema*, the Supreme Council of the Inquisition, and continue our holy war against all heretics and infidels. As for Olivares, I would like to know where he stands regarding the *limpieza de sangre*. I have heard he is a new-Christian."

Rafal frowned at Ballebrera. "Is it true? Is he tainted?"

"Lope Conchillos, Secretary to Emperor Charles V and father of the First Count de Olivares' wife, was an Aragónese of *converso* ancestry. That same First Count de Olivares also was related by marriage to the *converso*, Juan Sánchez de Toledo, grandfather of Teresa of Avila, whom many believe will become Spain's next saint."

Rafal's face clouded. "As a new-Christian, he will collect enemies before he has earned them."

"In God's name, Olivares' Jewish blood has been diluted by subsequent Guzmánes' marriages to untainted old-Christians over several generations."

Tomás rose to his feet. "One drop is enough to pollute. Our great King, Philip II, said he would prefer not to reign at all than to reign over heretics."

Ballebrera glared back at him. "A taint is not heresy. So an extreme interpretation of the *limpieza* has deprived Spain of its best minds, driven great wealth into exile, stifled industry and creativity. Exiled new-Christians and *conversos* help the Dutch challenge our might. They are welcomed in other northern lands, and by the Turks as well. When war comes, we may not be able to defeat the next coalition of our enemies."

Vicente listened in awe to Ballebrera's argument. His wisdom was no less than Don Lope's.

Tomás raised his silver crucifix as if to call for a crusade. "Better to go down in honorable defeat as a cleansed, pure Spain than win victories with tainted blood."

Ballebrera shook his head in disbelief. "You're being illogical."

"The honor of our True Faith and that of Spain require no logic." Tomás stalked out of the *estrado*.

The Dominican's exit ended the meeting. Francisco and Tomás left for Granja de Rocamora, António returned to his cell at the monastery, and Rafal continued to confer with Ballebrera.

In the stable, Vicente lay on a pile of straw unable to sleep. His thoughts alternated between his night in paradise with Moraíma and his expectation that on the morrow Rafal would begin training him to soldier for the Crown.

Chapter 8
Test of Honor

"Although recent years have been exceptionally dry, the Segura and its irrigation canals built in previous centuries by Arabs still channel life-giving water to field and grove," Ballebrera said to Vicente as they rode out of Orihuela on horseback. "Throughout the Kingdom of Valencia, the prevailing belief is that rain or no rain, Orihuela will have wheat."

The Segura might appear wide and refreshing to the natives of Orihuela, but for Vicente it was no more than a weak trickle when compared to the limitless turquoise horizons of the open sea. He had begun the day

disappointed. After the required morning prayers, he had expected Rafal to reveal the plans for his future. Instead, Ramón arrived with a second spirited chestnut horse from his stables and invited him for a ride through his señorio.

Vicente was still recovering from his surprise at Ballebrera's changed appearance. The *caballero* wore no wig nor had he applied make-up, and he had covered his balding head with a simple brown felt cap. A tight white linen blouse constrained powerful arms and hirsute muscular torso. A plain black cape, gray breeches and hose were functional rather than decorative, as were gloves, boots, saddle, and spurs. Although his short legs seemed to belong to a different body, Ballebrera sat tall on his mount with the bearing of a soldier. He had dropped the Castilian lisp and affectations in favor of the more robust and flavored Valencian dialect.

An hour beyond Orihuela and the mulberry groves of Ballebrera's señorio, they passed through mostly untended vineyards and orchards and entered a deserted Morisco village, where, Ballebrera told him, several dozen families of his vassals had lived before their expulsion. After tethering their mounts at the ruins of a bathhouse by a limpid spring surrounded by date palms, Ballebrera removed his gloves, dropped to one knee, and scooped the water with his hands. "¡*Agua muy rica!*"

Vicente had heard Pablo speak those same words when he urinated into Bernardo's throat. There would be plenty of hell to pay when the Anglesolas learned that the inquisitor never reached Murcia. He could not worry about it now. Instead, he also drank the delicious water.

"I would not confess it to just anyone, Vicente, but I might sell my soul for a leisurely bath. As you know, the only water permitted externally by our Church is Holy Water." He forced a mirthless laugh. "And the only Spaniard who ever gets enough water has to be a drowning man."

"Do you bathe in Madrid?"

"Secretly when I can. As you might expect, the spies of the Inquisition lurk everywhere. In Madrid, even a superficial scrubbing is uncommon, although some will on occasion wipe their faces with the white of an egg. Instead, we must drench ourselves in perfume."

"Except for ascetics, shouldn't personal comfort triumph over religious scruple?"

"So, one would think. I suspect those who most flaunt their filth are more than likely trying to conceal the existence of a *converso* Jew-ancestor." He splashed water on his face and neck. "The Church's prohibitions are absolute torture on hot summer days and nights."

"Any day and night." Vicente took off his shirt, shook it free of pests, and washed himself with the spring water.

Ballebrera praised Vicente's musculature and sympathized when the boy told him how he had received the stripes on his back. He drank again. "Is this not proof that the Moriscos knew how to live?"

"You didn't see them as a threat?"

"In my opinion, they were essential to our economy. The losses in rents and unpaid debts are still incalculable. Valencia lost the most productive one third of its population, and Spain more than a million innocent souls."

Vicente remembered Tomás' support of the most extreme *limpieza* statutes. "And the Jews?"

"Why, surely everyone knows no Jews are left in Spain."

Vicente had become used to Ballebrera's ironic inflections. "I meant to say new-Christians."

"One might ask how new is new? The Count de Olivares is of relatively *old* new-Christian stock."

"Then Santiago, the patron saint of Castile, must be the oldest new-Christian of them all."

Ballebrera laughed and shook a finger at him. "Be careful where you expose your clever wit, Vicente. If you had spoken thus of Santiago last night, Tomás might have handed you over to the Holy Office for insulting Castile's most venerated saint, and me as well, if he knew what I had done here in my youth."

Ballebrera went on to recount his many assignations with the loveliest daughters of his Morisco vassals, and Vicente was surprised to hear that he had made love to so many girls. Perhaps he had misjudged his kinsman's predilections. He had more questions to ask, but Ballebrera had begun to croon a centuries-old popular Castilian song:

> *Tres Moriscas me enamoram en Jaen,*
> *Axa y Fatima y Marién . . .*
>
> *Three Moorish girls captivated me in Jaén:*
> *Axa, and Fatima, and Marién . . .*

The poignant ballad of the three *morillas* more beautiful than Toledo girls, who went to harvest olives already gathered, intensified Vicente's yearning for Moraíma and his curiosity regarding the loves of Ballebrera.

> *Dixayales quien sois señoritas,*
> *De mi alma robadoras,*

Christianas de ramas Moras en Jaén:
Axa, Fatima, Marién.

Say who you are girls,
Robbers of my soul,
Christian girls of Moorish roots in Jaén:
Axa, Fatima, Marién.

"What happened to your *morillas*, Don Ramón?"

"God only knows. Years before our expulsion, I had already left my señorio to seek fame and fortune."

In response to Vicente's probing, Ballebrera described how he had fought in Flanders against the Dutch heretics and earned a martial reputation equal to Rafal's and Don Francisco's, which qualified him for the military Order of Alcántara. Unlike his cousins, he had seen enough of war and settled in Madrid to enjoy the good life.

"Will Don Francisco also become a knight of one of the great Orders?"

"Yes, I believe he will. As you know, only a man of proven untainted bloodlines can be accepted into one of the military Orders. Once he is a knight of Alcántara, Santiago, or Calatrava, he becomes more desirable for marriage, his daughters too, which means he need not provide expensive dowries."

"Don Ramón, did you ever marry? Did you ever love one lady above all others?"

His eyes clouded with memory. "Yes, when I was your age, I loved my cousin, Yolanda, Jerónimo's fair sister, who died too young of fever. Then life offered too great a banquet for me to select from only one particular plate. In Madrid, I was corrupted by lovely women and pretty boys."

"Which do you prefer?"

"Give me fine drink, delicious food, a fair companion, and I am content."

"You're so intelligent and talented, why aren't you an advisor to the king?"

"You have a courtier's flair for flattery, Vicente. To answer your question, I know how to complain and find fault, but I could never offer King Philip remedies in finances, or advise how to conduct foreign policy."

"You couldn't do worse than his chief minister, the Duke of Lerma."

"But no better, I fear. To tell the truth, my skills are limited to literary matters and getting along in fashionable society. I may appear immodest, but I speak the truth. All the important people seek my company. No social event is considered a success unless I am present. They hang on my every word, especially playwrights and authors such as Lope de Vega and Quevedo. They listen to me too carefully, for when I see their plays or read their satires,

Rocamora

my spontaneous thrusts are metamorphosed into their brilliant dialogue and aphorisms without anyone giving me due credit."

"Then why don't you write?"

"When I think it, I say it. Once said, it bores me to repeat it." Ballebrera took bread, cheese, and a jar of wine from his saddlebag, and they sat amidst the ruins of the bathhouse sharing the repast. "I have been talking too much about my sinful life."

"If I've asked too many questions, I apologize."

"You have a soothing way about you, Vicente, like a confessor who encourages his parishioner to speak openly. You could be a very successful priest."

"God forbid. Never."

"I regret I must tell you that is exactly what Jerónimo requests of you. He will have you enter the clergy."

"Don Ramón, not even in jest."

"No jest, Vicente. Hear me out," Ballebrera said over his protests. "Last night, Jerónimo and I discussed your future. In spite of my objections, he would not alter his decision. Given his bluntness, I offered to break the news to you."

"No, I'll never be a stinking priest."

Ballebrera held Vicente's arm and prevented him from leaving. "Where do you intend to go?"

"Back to Valencia."

"And there for certain you will be murdered by your enemies, the Anglesolas."

"I'll sail as a cabin boy."

"No captain can be trusted. You would have more value to them as a commodity worth many gold escudos at the slave marts."

"Then I'll be a *pícaro*. Join a troupe of actors."

"And live amidst the most despised."

"Don Ramón, I can never be a priest. I'm the most unrepentant sinner in Spain."

"So every Spaniard believes of himself."

"I've broken most of the Ten Commandments."

"Surely you exaggerate."

"I'm not sure if God exists, or if He does, He does not intervene in the affairs of men. And I've taken His name in vain."

"None of that will disqualify you from the clergy."

"I've dealt with stolen goods." Vicente described the errands he ran for Don Lope.

"Petty sins."

"I've coveted my brother's title to the señorío."

"A common desire among younger sons. You'll soon value your freedom not to be tied down with burdensome family responsibilities and worries of debt, dowry, and drought."

"I've killed." Vicente described how he had slit Anglesola's throat.

"I thought as much. If justifiable revenge were a sin, every Valencian would be headed straight for hell. And the Bible allows an eye for an eye."

"I've fornicated." Vicente told Ballebrera of his passionate night with Moraíma.

"Fornication is the most favored sin of the clergy, and it is not forbidden by any of the Ten Commandments."

"Adultery is. I've sired my brother's child."

"*¡Madre de Dios!*" Ballebrera saluted him. "You have lived more during the past two months than most men in a lifetime."

"Please, let me speak to Don Jerónimo. I won't be a priest."

"Yesterday, you promised to do whatever he asked for the good of our family. Are you a man of your word? A man of honor?"

"Of course I am." Vicente cursed the quickness of his own tongue. He had spoken before thought when he made his pledge of honor to Rafal.

"I will not deceive you. While you study at the Dominican College of Confessors . . ."

"Friars? Does Don Jerónimo have so little respect for me?"

"Heed me, Vicente. Because of your youth and limited experience, you have been exposed to only a small part of the Spanish Church. The Dominicans are the most powerful men in Spain. Dominicans control the Inquisition. They *are* the Inquisition. And they *are* the royal confessors. For the next four years, you must be more Dominican than the Dominicans. Memorize their teachings and question nothing."

Vicente plunged his dagger into the soil. "You've described a prison."

"A temporary prison. We can arrange a freer life for you in Madrid. You say you have thought about becoming an actor. Vicente, you have been given a significant role to play, as the most pious and eloquent of men."

"A dismal role, a minor role. With two Dominicans in our family, why must I become the third?"

"Tío is elderly and ineffectual, and Tomás is too bigoted to work with Olivares and his faction. Jerónimo wants you in the Madrid clergy at *la Corte* to help him gain his title."

"And I promised to do whatever he asked."

"Yes, you did."

"Don Ramón, do you believe everything that the Church teaches?"

"If I answered you honestly, I would be placing my life in your hands."

"I believe you are a freethinker."

"Believe what you will, but listen to me, Vicente. The Church can satisfy any man who desires fame, wealth, and power. Fat benefices are available, and they rise in value faster than land and other investments. Your privileges will include immunity from taxation and civil law. You would be answerable only to ecclesiastic authorities."

"But what about women? I can't . . . I won't be celibate."

"Nor shall you be." Ballebrera twisted an upturned end of his mustachio. "Although celibacy is a noble concept, it is contrary to normal human behavior. And, it is most unnatural for us hot-blooded Spaniards. Even the Popes have sired children, which is why the Church recognizes and tolerates priestly sin within reason. Consider this, Vicente. No man is closer to a woman than her confessor. Not her husband, not her father. As such, you will have more opportunities than any *caballero*."

Vicente adjusted his cap to shield his eyes from the sun's rays angling through the palms. He whittled a dead branch to a fine point while he listened to Ballebrera describe the Church's prevailing vice, the seduction of female penitents by their confessors.

"Women in the Church are no different from men. Convents are filled with widowed women of quality and unwanted young daughters of the nobility put there against their wishes and inclinations because even the great families cannot afford ruinous dowries. Certain convents accept only women of noble birth where contemplation and penitence are strangers. Nuns there may have as many as four maids. Visitors of both sexes frequent their parlors and participate in fetes and amateur dramatics. In Madrid, my favorite convent entertainments are the poetico-theological jousts. For example, which is better in love, desire or fulfillment? What is your answer, Vicente?"

Vicente recalled his night of paradise with Moraíma. "I desire fulfillment."

"Excellent. You have a talent for playing with words and turning phrases. You will have much success in Madrid courting the nuns and dedicating yourself to a fair lady of noble birth."

"Courting nuns? How is it possible?"

"The same as one would court any señorita by demeanor and fond looks. It is amusing to watch sighing lovers congregate outside a convent. The gallant of the grilles, lay or clerical, makes every endeavor to see his love from a distance, behind the choir grille of a church, or through the bars of her cell. He dedicates verses to her, smuggles messages, and creates pretexts for a visit. They may meet in the convent parlor and plan how to consummate their passion."

Vicente did not believe Ballebrera's portrayal of lusty clerical life. "Don't the authorities disapprove?"

"Government decrees prohibiting intercourse between sexes of all religious orders have never been published. The Church takes the position conditions must not be imposed on clergy that oppress them more than other men."

"Surely the Inquisition intervenes?"

"Only in notorious cases, when homosexuals or heretical mystics are involved. The Holy Office considers a priest who fornicates relatively harmless. As a sinner, he can repent and do penance. If the same priest is celibate and preaches that fornication is not a sin, he is perceived as a danger to our True Faith and treated as a heretic."

"That's logic turned upside down."

"In any case, Vicente, as a Dominican you may have more women than you can imagine. You are handsome, fine of figure, with a rich baritone voice that can be trained to ooze sincerity. You may well become a fashionable confessor, desired by all the ladies, especially the widowed and the married who are neglected by their husbands and are the most vulnerable because they remember what they are missing."

"Aren't such women kept in seclusion or chaperoned all the time?"

"Yes, but always free to summon their confessors, which offers many opportunities for seduction."

"I'd rather have them without the tonsure. I know I could never preach sincerely."

"Sincerity? It's all a matter of style. Tone and cadence. Vivid similes and metaphors. I'm sure you've seen how even a mediocre preacher can spellbind an entire congregation. When you preach about hell, threaten them with all the horrors you have seen and imagined. No mythic Satan can match the torments devised by humans. Attach the words *abominable* to all sins and *eternal* to all punishments. When you refer to the Virgin, imagine that you are praising your Moraíma."

"I did at prayers this morning and said *amor* instead of amen."

"By all the Virgin's mercies, I would take you to Madrid this day."

"Then please, I beg you, help me. Let us both speak to Don Jerónimo. I have always pictured myself wearing armor and sword, not robe and tonsure."

Chapter 9
The Codicil

Rafal's austere study had a brazier, two armless high-backed wooden chairs, and a rectangular table at which the soldier sat in front of a centuries-old large wooden cross. Weapons and trophies of war belonging to their heroic ancestors covered the other walls.

Rafal pushed aside the pile of documents he had on his desk "Have you told the boy?"

"I have, but his greatest desire is to ride with you as a soldier. And, I want to champion his cause, convince you to change your mind."

"Ramón, we have enough soldiers. As I told you last night, Vicente must serve our cause here in Spain. Royal confessors and chaplains are often in office for life, with greater influence than any courtier. Consider this. What if Vicente becomes the conscience and advisor of our next king?"

"I must concede the point. That would be ideal."

"And there is another possibility. The boy told us he knows some English. If the Infanta marries the Prince of Wales, would it not be useful for her to have an English speaking, Spanish Catholic confessor, a de Rocamora?"

"An English marriage may never happen."

"I have decided. We shall place him in the Church. He gave me his word of honor that he would do whatever I commanded for the good of our family." Rafal beckoned Vicente to approach. "You will attend the College of Confessors here in Orihuela. Tío will ease your way into the Dominican Order. We will protect you from the Anglesolas who dare not ride into Orihuela. Ramón will use his connections to ensure that you shall receive an appointment to the royal clergy."

"Why? Why are you doing this to me?" Vicente repeated how he had broken many of the Ten Commandments and told of his desire to take revenge on Violante and the Anglesolas, and to claim his yet unborn child. He showed off his physique, agility, and dexterity as he demonstrated his skill with sword and knife from Rafal's collection.

Ballebrera applauded. "You must agree that so superb a physical specimen would be wasted among the Dominicans."

"My decision is final."

"Then answer his question. Tell the boy the underlying reason for your decision."

"You may never be permitted to rise to significant command, or be eligible to enter any of the great military Orders of Santiago, Alcántara, and Calatrava. You may never qualify for Royal service, or be allowed to attend a major university." Rafal selected one of the documents and stared at it for a few moments before he looked Vicente in the eye. "This is my family's *mayorazgo*, the document that entails the inheritance of my señorios, to which my blessed father, may he rest in peace, added a codicil. It excludes all descendants born of Doña Gabriela de Rocamora from any inheritance."

Vicente took the *mayorazgo*, which had a magnificent frontispiece engraving of San Francisco at prayer surrounded by a variety of animals.

"Read sections 147 to 151."

Vicente opened the document written in the legal style with Latin phrases and words of indirect meaning: "*Porque el licor mas puro, y de mas virtud, podrá resistir un vaso de otros menos legitimo, pero si le incluyessen dos, aunque pudo vencer el primero, queda a vencido del Segundo.* The most pure and virtuous liquid can be rendered illegitimate by mixture with an impure fluid, as the quality of fruit produced by the most noble plant degenerates when it is transplanted in alien soil."

"I do not understand, Don Jerónimo."

"To avoid exciting the interest of the Holy Office, my father ensured this codicil never directly mentioned the fact that your father's pure and noble de Rocamora blood when mixed with tainted . . ."

"No, my mother was *limpia*. I am *limpio*."

Ballebrera intervened. "What he means is that we cannot risk the slightest chance you *may* be tainted. It could lead to relentless investigations of all who carry the de Rocamora name. And if they were to reach back to . . ."

"You go too far."

"No, let me finish, cousin, so that he will understand our situation. Vicente, Jews had lived here for centuries and prospered before and after Pedro Ramón de Rocamora helped King Jaime the Conqueror liberate Orihuela from the Moors three-hundred-and-fifty years ago. Some were ennobled and later married Christians after the year 1391 when each and every one of them in Orihuela chose conversion to our True Faith rather than face death."

"But not one of Pedro Ramón's descendants ever married someone from a *converso* family, until Vicente's father."

"How can you be so sure?" Ballebrera countered.

Vicente no longer listened to them. His entire world, all his hopes, dreams, and expectations had come crashing down. Was the *limpieza* his parents had shown him a forgery? Had Don Lope created it? If his mother had lived, what would she have told him? Was there anything to tell? She had never spoken of her family or their origins. Had her ancestors chosen baptism rather than exile or death between the great massacres of 1391 and the Edict of Expulsion in 1492? All he knew about Gabriela de Cornel was that she had been an orphan, a ward of an unnamed uncle somewhere in the northernmost reaches of Catalonia or beyond in Roussillon. No matter, she had to have been *limpia*. He could not imagine his father marrying one who was not.

Yet, could it be that his baptismal name was a deliberate ironic deception? He had been baptized Vicente after the patron saint of Valencia, Vicente de Ferrer, the fiery Dominican preacher whose eloquence had sparked the great massacres and conversion of Valencian Jews in 1391. Ferrer had proselytized the survivors and brought nobles, *caballeros*, and even rabbis into the bosom of the Holy Mother Church, which had earned him his sainthood. His parents had selected the day of San Vicente's death for his own name day. Had it been an act of defiance? Mother of God. Had she also . . .?

Ballebrera saw his distress. "Vicente, I can assure you of one thing. No proof exists, aside from the innuendo in this codicil, that your mother may not have been *limpia*." He turned to Rafal. "Tell the boy. Is there any evidence that Doña Gabriela, or anyone in her family, ever Judaized?"

"No."

"Who else knows about the codicil?"

"Only you and I, now that both our fathers are no longer with us, may they rest in eternal peace. No one else, not Tío, Don Francisco, and Tomás, and it must forever remain a family secret because we will all be interviewed by the Holy Office before Francisco qualifies to become a Familiar and Knight of Santiago."

Ballebrera motioned towards the fireplace. "Burn it."

"Honor forbids."

"Then I ask you one more time, let Vicente rise to wherever his abilities take him."

"No. Can we be certain no other documents exist that might imply or even prove that Vicente's mother had new-Christian origins? The most we can do for the good of our family, and the boy, is to maintain silence. If anyone discovers this secret, the scandal could end our ascent to the *grandeza*, or lead to worse."

Ballebrera placed his fists on the table and leaned forward. "One more question, cousin. Why did you send for Vicente if you suspected he might be tainted? He would have been murdered by now and no longer a potential threat to be used by our enemies to disgrace us."

Rafal handed him the summons. "I did not send for him. His arrival yesterday took me by surprise. I do not know who wrote it. I do not know how and why it was done. As you can see, it is a perfect copy of my writing and my seal."

"You could have refused to see him."

"My first instinct was to do so, but I was curious and wanted to meet the younger son of Don Luís, whom I had always admired as a man of honor. Then I saw a way for him to help my cause despite the potential liability of tainted blood. Vicente, who forged this summons?"

He did not reply. His entire life had changed. Even if he were not tainted, the merest suspicion that he might have even one drop of new-Christian blood, would deny him everything Spain had to offer *limpio* old-Christians. Had Don Lope known? Is that why he had urged him to leave for Protestant lands? The physician must have sent the forged summons to save his life once Violante was secure with her pregnancy and the Anglesolas had no further use for him.

Save my life for what?

"Don Jerónimo, Don Ramón, if I cannot be a soldier or enter the royal administration, how can I become a royal confessor?"

"The Church has always been ambivalent about the rule of *limpieza* despite its pronouncements," Ballebrera said, "and it is relatively free of privileged descent. Anyone can become a member. Purity of blood has never been a requirement for becoming a priest or bishop. Vicente, unless the taint is obvious, the Church can be very accommodating. Most Holy Orders do not require their students to show genealogies. No one will question Tío if he sponsors a cousin. And, I have good reason to believe that once the Count de Olivares is securely in power, he will do all he can to remove the *limpieza* from Spanish life. Jerónimo, I have no doubts Vicente will acquire a new unassailable *limpieza de sangre* from the same source who created the summons, which will make him eligible to be a royal confessor and perhaps even an Inquisitor."

Vicente's despair gave way to defiance. Even if proof lay hidden somewhere that he was part-new-Christian, he would never whine, cringe, or feel shame. He was still as good a Spaniard as any. He could always take pride in his accomplishments and his de Rocamora name no matter what others might say. A passion to learn his true maternal ancestry overwhelmed him. At first opportunity, he would go to the northern reaches of Catalonia and Roussillon and discover more about his mother's people. If some were Jews, then they must have been of the aristocracy. His father would not have married less. And, even if he was a partial new-Christian, he could still be a Spaniard of full-blooded honor.

Honor. He had given Rafal his word of honor. Maintaining honor was more important than life to a Spaniard. Without it, better to be dead. Don Lope had taught him honor was as fragile as a mirror; the slightest breath of taint was enough to fog it. The *hidalgos* accepted it as a condition of birth. Men like Rafal and Ballebrera believed it was acquired through noble deeds and behavior. Regardless, no one was going to force him out of Spain. Rocamoras had ruled their señorios since the thirteenth-century, and earlier in Septimania-Languedoc. He was Spanish as much as any man. And he still might not become a priest. If Moraíma had correctly seen his future, he would be reunited with her, have other loves, many children, and a long life. Perhaps this detour was necessary after all for him to fulfill his destiny.

Ballebrera gestured towards the door. "Vicente, again I say the choice is yours. Ride back to Valencia and certain death or take the *pícaro* road. Discard honor, or go for the greatest prizes of all. Seize the opportunity to become a royal confessor, advisor, and the King's conscience, and yes, even Inquisitor General of all Spain."

Vicente stood tall and thrust out his chest. "I am a man of honor, and a de Rocamora. I have given my word. I will do whatever I can to fulfill my promise to you, Don Jerónimo. I will enter the Dominican Order, and there I shall remain until you have your title."

Rafal placed the *mayorazgo* and codicil in a strongbox and locked it. "Only the three of us will ever know of this matter."

Vicente turned his head. Had he heard footsteps retreating from the other side of the door?

Those who enter the holy orders are the bravest, healthiest, best-formed men of great wit and ability, and amongst them not a single cripple, and scarcely any who are small, ugly, and dull; while amongst the laity remain the ignorant dregs.

Archbishop Gaspar de Criales to Philip IV

PART TWO
Man of Masks
Madrid, 1621-1623

Friars are the shrewdest of men: they do not go to war, they do not pay taxes, they enjoy the best things; and people give them money . . . they beget children, and other people raise them . . .

Lope de Vega's letter to the Duke of Sessa

Chapter 10
Bufónes

And so, vengeance must be put off for another time.

Now a graduate of the College of Confessors in Orihuela and ordained a friar in the Dominican order, Vicente had to abort his plans to travel to Madrid via Valencia, take revenge against Violante and the Anglesolas and claim his daughter. She had been baptized Brianda the same day Alonso died or, most likely, was murdered. Don Lope had sent him a warning. An army of Anglesola assassins awaited him should he approach Valencia and Benetorrente. He also advised Vicente to travel to Madrid by a specific route and arranged for his men to rendezvous with him in La Mancha where they delivered two mules laden with valuable goods.

Will I ever be warm again?

An icy blast of wind sliced across the sere Castilian plain. It cut through Vicente's muddied black cloak and hood and white woolen Dominican robe as he rode his mule and led its burdened mate along the road to Madrid. He had not yet adapted to the harsher elements of Castile and he was unable to sleep unless exhausted. Another bone-chilling gust buffeted him. The cold was the reason why, despite an infestation of hair lice, he had not shaved his mustache, beard, and tonsure during the journey.

The wind shrieked as if a woman labored through a painful childbirth. *Too much like a woman.* Vicente threw back his hood and listened. Not the wind, the sounds were those of a female screaming over drunken laughter beyond some brush.

Vicente guided his mules off the road and dismounted. He hurried through thorny scrub, passed a covered cart and two mules, and crossed a dry ravine. On the other side, two armed men were about to assault a female child. He identified them as *golondreros*, parasites usually army deserters, who formed the most vicious of the bandit gangs infecting all of Spain.

A toothless assailant had spread apart his tiny victim's legs. His one-eyed comrade held the girl's wrists over her head with one hand and pulled her skirt over her face with the other.

Toothless dropped his breeches and exposed running *mal frances* sores. Before the rapist could penetrate the girl, Vicente lifted his robe, kicked the man from behind, and took the sword the *golondrero* had left on the ground.

"Stop this sin. In the name of God."

One-eye released the girl's hands and drew his wheel-lock pistol. "Leave us, Friar, and you won't be hurt. It's none of your concern."

"All God's children are my concern."

"Maybe he wants to take his turn with the little bitch," his syphilitic comrade said. "He's probably a *matone* in disguise. No Dominican I know has the balls to take on armed men."

One-eye cocked his pistol. "Friar, go now, or say your own final rites before you join your maker."

Vicente lunged with the sword and slashed the pistol away from the outlaw's hand along with thumb and forefinger.

"What kind of friar are you?" One-eye screamed.

"You should confess more often." Vicente pressed the tip of the blade against Toothless' throat, drew blood, and shouted at One-eye, "You. Take off your buckler and leave your sword, dagger, and pistol here. The money and her jewels too, or your friend will breathe his last. And you will be next."

After One-eye obeyed him, Vicente motioned with the sword. "Now go. And don't let me see your faces again, or I'll dispatch you to hell without last rites."

As they scurried away, Vicente bent over the unconscious female. He gaped in surprise at the tuft of thick black hair on her delta. No child, she was a perfectly proportioned midget, whose pretty face was bruised and swelling where she had been struck. He carried her across the ravine to the cart, where a battered and similarly proportioned male midget had been tied to a wheel. He placed her inside atop a blanket and attended to her small companion.

Vicente freed the midget, who swept his plumed felt hat from the ground, slapped away the dirt, and put it on. His soiled and torn dark brown velour doublet and silk breeches were of the finest quality. Vicente thought his graying mustachio, goatee, and attempt to preserve his dignity gave him an air of a miniature *grandee*.

"Friar, did you arrive in time before they . . ."

"She is intact and not seriously hurt."

He crossed himself and kneeled to kiss the hem of Vicente's robe as was the Spanish custom when encountering priests and friars. "Thank God. And you too, my holy deliverer. I am forever in your debt. How are you called, Friar?"

"Vicente de Rocamora y Cornel of Valencia and Orihuela." He went on to recite his paternal lineage and kinship with Rafal, Ballebrera, and Francisco.

"And I am Sáncho de Fonseca." With a Castilian lisp in a high-pitched monotone that sounded like a quacking duck, he cited his old-Christian

Castilian lineage and kinship to the late King's Chaplain, Juan de Fonseca. "Doña Inéz is my cousin and bride."

"A difficult honeymoon."

"And not yet consummated. We departed for Madrid after our wedding ceremonies in Alarcon. Our masters are impatient for our return."

Vicente surmised they were attached to someone powerful. Dwarf and midget companions were common in the households of *poderosos* throughout Spain. "Which great house do you serve?"

"The greatest of them all. I am one of the Royal *bufónes*, originally from Seville. I was brought to Madrid in 1615 by the Count de Olivares and given to King Philip III as a gift. I soon became one of the old King's favorite fools. Now I serve our new King, Philip IV, as *mayordomo* for all of His Majesty's jesters, midgets, dwarfs, and drooling idiots ... at least those of us who are small of physical stature. I take no responsibility for imbeciles of normal size who inhabit the Court and influence the royal councils."

Vicente concealed his excitement and smiled at the midget's wit. Surely, these grateful tiny creatures he had rescued would be able and willing to facilitate his entry into the Court Clergy.

"In the palace, I am addressed by the impressive title of Marqués de Hombrecillo, Runt-Marquis, and I expect my bride will receive a similar baptism from her new mistress."

"Queen Isabel?"

"No, she will serve Her Most Illustrious Highness, Infanta Doña María, His Majesty's younger sister, who is a very cold, difficult, and demanding child." Hombrecillo went to his bride and placed a pillow beneath her head. "Don Vicente, you have preserved my honor, which is more valuable than life itself."

He helped Hombrecillo lead the mules and cart back to the roadside where he had left his two beasts. "I have some medicines."

Hombrecillo watched Vicente administer salves to his wife's bruises and cuts. "You are a most unusual Dominican. You attack and defend better than any experienced soldier, and you have medicines. Perhaps you are a *pícaro matone* in monk's robes?"

"What you see is who I am, a Dominican friar."

"And what business have you in Madrid?"

"I aspire to serve as a royal preacher or confessor and help advance the cause of my noble family." He told them of his vow to Rafal.

"Then honor requires we do all we can to help you."

Exactly what I had hoped to hear.

After Inéz whispered in her husband's ear, he studied the young friar's features. "My bride believes you will cause a sensation at the palace because you are handsome, with those unusual penetrating green eyes. I agree. You also have youth and a rich voice. The women will wait in line to have you hear their confessions and, perhaps, tempt you."

Vicente donned his mask of pious humility and crossed himself. "The man who resists temptation is greater in the eyes of God than one who is never put to the test."

"Well said, Don Vicente. We would be honored if you accompanied us for the rest of the journey."

"The honor is mine."

Vicente rode beside his small friends who sat together in their cart under its brown and gray striped canvas top. Behind a vintner's wagon laden with barrels of wine, they had become part of a slow-moving caravan that included herds of cattle, droves of sheep, wagons filled with merchandise, and hundreds of men and women riding and trudging who hoped to make their fortune in Madrid, still a good week's journey away.

Hombrecillo offered Vicente a piece of bread. "You should know that Madrid produces nothing and exports nothing. It has no resources, no major river. Because all necessities must be transported over land, our caravan will soon expand to more than sixty miles in length. Others will also converge on the city from the wheat fields of Salamanca, the vineyards of Valladolid, and the tablelands and sierras where great flocks of sheep are raised."

"Impressive."

"Madrid depends completely upon imported goods and imposts are exorbitant, but customs officials will not search your belongings. Although the Crown is in desperate need of money, you clergy are exempt from taxes."

And they will not discover my medicines, books forbidden by the Index, and other contraband supplied by Don Lope in the bulging bags on my mules.

"Be on your guard in the capital and the Alcazar. As is said, *Hijos de Madrid, uno bueno entre mil.* Sons of Madrid, one good man in a thousand."

"And I've heard the lament, what shall I do in Madrid when I don't know how to lie?"

"I suspect you will do well enough, Don Vicente, for the Valencians' violent temperament is legend throughout Spain. It is well-known that no one draws knife or sword more quickly there. All Spaniards believe the climate makes your women too passionate, which drives their men to insane acts of jealousy, and that your Valencian soil throws up criminals in the same way it sprouts wheat or barley."

"It may be that all Spain envies us, but then again, no city is spared contempt. Is it not said throughout our kingdom that in Cariñena neither the donkeys nor the women are very good, and in Andujar, she who is not a whore is a witch?"

"You may be right." Hombrecillo recited more regional chestnuts: "Badajoz, which many justifiably call God's country, because cuckolds walk two by two. Valladolid, land of pungent wines, where the men arrive clothed and leave naked."

To pass the time, Vicente discussed the war with Hombrecillo. Much had happened during the four years while he had studied in Orihuela. In 1618, the Bohemian Protestants had rebelled against their Catholic Austrian Habsburg masters, and another revolt in the Swiss Val Telline provided a pretext for the Spanish Governor to establish garrisons in the strategic valley linking Milan and Austria. That same year, Frederick V of the Rhenish Palatinate and son-in-law of James I of England usurped the titles of King of Bohemia and Holy Roman Emperor at the request of Bohemian and German Protestants. Ridiculed as "the Winter King," Frederick was defeated in 1619 by the disciplined troops of Spanish General Ambrosio de Spinola. Spinola then seized control of most of the Palatinate between the Rhine River and France, Flanders, and the United Provinces, which opened a direct route from Spanish Italy to the Spanish Netherlands. With the German Protestants demoralized and the English neutralized, Spain had felt free to resume its war against the United Provinces when the twelve-year truce expired in April of 1621, and Rafal and Francisco were in the forefront of the battles.

"Do you know how and why our King died so suddenly, Don Sancho?"

"It was a most miserable death, ridiculous and unnecessary, a matter of *punctilio* carried to the extreme. It is true that King Philip was very ill with a skin ailment, but not fatally so. His courtiers had place a brazier beside his bed to keep him warm, and the smoke began to suffocate him. By rank and precedence, only the Duke of Uceda had the honor of removing it. Because he was absent, no one dared usurp his position. Thus, Philip III, ruler of an empire greater than Rome, choked to death because his gentlemen of the bedchamber would not violate court etiquette. And I am called a royal fool."

"Where were the King's sons?"

"Away hunting in the company of the Count de Olivares, who, according to his enemies, may have anticipated . . . I dare not say precipitated . . . an event that would advance his career."

The evening temperatures dropped lower, and frigid winds were relentless. Vicente heard his own teeth chattering faster than a Gypsy's castanets while Inéz prepared a spicy mutton stew over a fire and Hombrecillo described Court gossip and anecdotes about the ridicule he had to endure.

"Why do you not leave *la Corte* for a better life than that of a *bufón*?"

"Where would I go? Who would protect me from cruel sport? I would be a penniless *hidalgo*. The King is generous. Like you ecclesiastics, I pay no taxes. I am ridiculed, it is true, but when I play the fool, I give back twice what I get. Furthermore, am I not better off as an old-Christian of small size than to be a rich and powerful *grandee* who is tainted with the accursed blood of Jews? I have learned a valuable lesson that I will pass on to you. If one cannot be great, he must attach himself to greatness."

"I shall never forget your excellent piece of advice." A powerful gust almost blew out their fire, and Vicente built it again with more scrub.

"Now you can understand why we Castilians had to conquer the world. We were desperate to escape from so dismal a land."

"Couldn't you have at least selected a capital in a more hospitable climate?"

Hombrecillo postured by the fire as a miniature conquistador. "When has reality ever mattered to Spaniards? Because Castile is the center of the universe, our capital city must be in the middle of Spain regardless of climate, distance, or elements. As the saying goes, in Madrid, one must wait until the fortieth of May before removing his cloak, then two days more. But the worst thing about our capital is not the weather. Madrid has become the great refuge for Jews."

"How is it possible," Vicente said repeating Ballebrera's ironic comment, "when everyone knows that there are no Jews in Spain?"

"Bleed a Portuguese new-Christian *hombre de negócio*, and you'll vomit from the stench of his accursed blood."

Vicente listened without interrupting Hombrecillo's screed against the influx of Portuguese men of business coming to Madrid in increasing numbers. *Is my new friend a bigot, or is his excessive zeal superficial conformity in the presence of a Dominican?*

Late afternoon, Vicente saw in the distance one of the great postern gates leading into Madrid set in the middle of a vast central plateau high above sea level that reached to the Guadarrama Sierras in the west. Under their heavy cloaks, Hombrecillo wore his finest gold trimmed burgundy velvet doublet and breeches and Inéz her most elaborate dress of black and silver-trimmed velour.

The *bufón* said for his bride's benefit as well as Vicente's, "Impossible to imagine that less than a hundred years ago this was a village of five thousand. Now it has more than a hundred thousand souls and again as many in the surrounding communities."

"More than twice the population of Valencia." When the direction of the wind shifted towards them, Vicente wrinkled his nose at the stench emanating from Madrid. "Poor sewage."

Hombrecillo doused handkerchiefs in perfume for himself, Inéz, and Vicente to hold against their noses. "Yes, Madrid can be foul and nasty. Its streets and alleys are scented every day with excrement from the population, and from even more horses, donkeys, mules, and smaller animals. In winter, the rains turn it all into a nauseating sludge. In summer, the sun will dry it to a fine golden powder carried everywhere by the wind, even into wells and rivers." He beckoned Vicente closer and whispered so his wife would not hear, "What one shits in winter, one drinks in summer."

"Amazing that everyone isn't dead from plague."

"Our air is blessedly pure. In the heat of summer, it can dry a corpse in an instant with absolutely no putrescence. Even dead dogs and cats do not give off any bad smells during those months. Too hot in summer, too cold in winter, recurring fevers from bad air . . . Madrid is the ideal Castilian paradise."

The capital disappointed Vicente. He had expected to encounter grandeur everywhere. Instead, they moved along narrow cobblestone streets between austere buildings of stone, brick, and masonry topped by roofs blending into a burnt-red sea of tiles.

As their mules sloshed through the muck and fecal sludge, he almost retched at the intolerable stench coming from the crowded streets and squares. He soaked his handkerchief with more perfume and never took it from his face. Chilled and uncomfortable, he felt every individual flea and louse under his robe.

They stopped at a cross street while a long caravan of supplies passed in front of them, and Hombrecillo explained, "It is said that Madrid annually consumes fifty thousand sheep, twelve thousand oxen, sixty thousand goats, ten thousand calves, and thirteen thousand pigs; and because of fasting days, the city requires a limitless supply of fish: carp, cod, trout, sole, bream, and sardines. The municipal government struggles to ensure a good inventory of regular provisions to prevent rises in the prices of necessities. We all fear famine or someone cornering a market. Authorities keep a vigilant watch on the sale of wheat and baking of bread."

"*¡Agua va!*"

Vicente sympathized with several pedestrians who had no room to maneuver after they heard the warning that a chamber pot was about to be emptied from above. Hombrecillo told him that "Beware of water" was heard with discouraging regularity at all times of day along the crowded streets and alleys of Madrid. The angry victims could only curse at the guilty servant who disappeared behind closed shutters.

"It is the same in Valencia and Orihuela."

At the Plaza Mayor, he exchanged farewells with Hombrecillo and Doña Inéz whose destination was the Alcazar. The *bufón* again thanked him for saving their lives, his wife's virtue, and most important of all, his honor, and he promised they would meet again and soon.

"A final piece of advice, Don Vicente. Hurry to your kinsman. After dark, the streets of Madrid belong to the armed."

Vicente watched the tiny couple ride towards the palace and remembered Moraíma's prophecies. *What is my place to be in Madrid? What is my true destiny?*

Chapter 11
The Astórquia Palacio

This is more like the grandeur I expected.

Ballebrera resided beyond the center of town near the lush green park of the Prado in a tree-lined neighborhood of mansions, monasteries, and convents. High walls protected the square one story residence, larger than any Vicente had seen in Valencia. A young and handsome blond in dark blue livery trimmed in scarlet opened the great front door. After Vicente identified himself, the youthful *mayordomo* clapped his hands for lesser lackeys to take his bags and stable the mules and escorted him through salons and antechambers to a luxurious carpeted sitting room filled with valuable objects of art.

Dressed in wrinkled gray doublet and breeches, Ballebrera sat in a comfortable armchair beside a brazier. He placed his cup of hot chocolate on a side table and rose when he saw Vicente. "Here at last. I feared you might have run off."

"Honor prevented me," Vicente said with a sarcastic edge to his voice. He moved closer to the brazier to absorb its heat as a pretty servant girl appeared and served him hot chocolate.

"What news from Orihuela?"

"Tío died shortly before I left."

Ballebrera crossed himself. "He had a long life."

"And he was a good and kindly man. The Church could use more like him. Unfortunately, zealots like Tomás continue to thrive. I expect him to head an Inquisitorial Tribunal one day, or rise to Bishop. He is a strange, humorless man, who is renowned for his good works helping the poor and as a gifted polemicist."

"Beware of such men who cannot be influenced by money, women, or boys. They are the most dangerous of all." Ballebrera contorted his face as if inhaling the stench of Madrid's streets. "And Jerónimo's son, Jacinto?"

"A beautiful boy, fair of face and form, which masks the fact that he is a veritable demon. He tortures animals, beats the servants, and has raped numerous servant girls and peasant daughters. Boys too, if the rumors are true. I have often caught him smirking, as if he knows something about me. Jacinto is sixteen and has joined his father and Don Francisco in Flanders."

Vicente did not mention several incidents he attributed to Jacinto and the Anglesolas: A poisonous snake in his pallet; a knife thrown that missed him by a few hairs; and the occasional arrow that seemed to come from nowhere.

Ballebrera pinched his nostrils when Vicente came nearer. "We must give you a bath."

"Those are the best words I've heard in four years."

Ballebrera took him to the austere Astórquia family chapel and locked the door behind them. He twisted the railing of a prie-Dieu and turned it until a trap door opened on the floor in front of it. He led Vicente down a flight of steps into a vast underground stone chamber. At the far end a hearth was ablaze and heating a cauldron filled with water. A table near a large metal tub held soap, scissors, blades for shaving, and towels.

"For my daily bath. This palace once belonged to a rich and powerful noble who was burned at the *quemadero* for Judaizing. I can bathe another day. Get out of your clothes and into the tub. My servants will wash your robe and cloak after your bath as well. You will not need them until tomorrow."

"Still a stinking ecclesiastic. And will I have to acquire a lisp like you to progress in Madrid?"

"When necessary." Ballebrera tested the water and put out the fire. "The temperature is perfect." They poured the water into the tub and he watched Vicente get out of his robe. "Your looks have improved with maturity."

"And you haven't changed." A flattering lie. Ballebrera's face was puffier, more dissipated, with dark shadows under his eyes. "I didn't expect to find you in so impressive a *palacio*."

"It belongs to Doña Xímena, the widowed Duchess of Astórquia, who is quite elderly and fatigues easily. She is wintering at her estates in Vizcaya. You will meet her eventually. Xímena is content to let me handle all her affairs and gives me the run of her house."

"Will you marry her and become el Duque de Astórquia? That would free me from my promise to Rafal because you are childless and the title would be passed on to him."

"It is a possibility, but who can say? As we both know, life has many surprises in store for us."

Vicente climbed into the tub. "Drown and go to hell all you accursed fleas and lice."

"Did you first return to Valencia and take your revenge?"

"I was well advised my life would be forfeit. But be assured of this. One day I shall return to take my revenge on Violante and claim my daughter."

"Vicente, I regret to say that it may be later rather than sooner. Jerónimo aspires beyond a title to the *grandeza*, Castilian nobility with the highest degrees of rank. As you know, they are most privileged and likely to receive appointment as viceroy, governor, or ambassador. There are fewer than fifty *grandees*, all of them Castilian, and they are divided into three classes. A *grandee* First Class is allowed to put on his hat before addressing King Phillip. Those of the Second Class speak first and then put on their hats. *Grandees* of the Third Class remain bareheaded while addressing the King, until they return to their places."

"It seems much ado about nothing."

"Perhaps, but even before adultery, precedence and lineage dominate existence at Court. How those *grandees* and *títulos* . . . *duques*, *marquéses*, and *condes* . . . all quarrel over status. And, let me illustrate further the difficulty of the problem we face. As powerful as he is, the Count de Olivares himself is not yet a *grandee*."

Vicente had assumed that Olivares was of the *grandeza*. "Then unless you marry your duchess, I will never be able to fulfill my promise to Rafal. I shall forever be a stinking friar unless I choose to leave Spain or join my *pícaro* friends."

"True, you have a daunting task, but not impossible. Have patience."

"I've had plenty of that these past four years." Vicente wiped soap from his eyes. "What can you tell me about the *bufónes*."

"Why do you bring those repugnant little creatures into our conversation?" Ballebrera listened while Vicente described his rescue of Hombrecillo and Inéz. "How fortuitous. If your little friends speak on your behalf to an influential personage at the most propitious moment, you may be in the royal service sooner than we hoped. But know this. Although the royal fools make everyone laugh, they also repeat *murmuraciónes*, rumors, gossip, and lies to Olivares and His Majesty no one else dares to voice. In that way, they learn much of what the Court and subjects truly think regarding important matters."

"Then should I find a place at Court, I shall become their greatest friend. Until then, what specific plans have you in mind for me?"

"Tomorrow, I shall begin introducing you to the wives of influential men. Most will want you to be their confessor, and they may ask you to preach sermons in their family chapels. It shouldn't be too long before the Countess de Olivares hears of you."

After his bath, Vicente put on the dressing gown and slippers Ballebrera had brought him, and they traversed the lush garden patio and tiled pool to his room in another wing of the *palacio*. It had a narrow bed, small table and chair, and brazier. A massive oak crucifix hung on the wall above the bed. Servants had brought in his bags.

"My first real bed in more than four years. I believe I shall sleep a week."

""I will give you until midday tomorrow. We have much to do."

A pretty servant girl brought a pitcher filled with water, a basin, and a chamber pot, then lit the brazier. Ballebrera saw Vicente admiring her. "Did Cupid's arrows find you as I promised?"

"Exactly so, but acting upon my opportunities was more difficult. I was more prisoner than divinity student, and Jacinto spied on me relentlessly."

Ballebrera inclined his head towards the girl as she was leaving. "Do you want her?"

"Yes, of course I do, but I will have to deny my desires of the flesh for the moment."

"Why?"

"Here in Madrid, I must establish an unassailable reputation for piety. No one must ever accuse this friar of fornication."

"Wise, even heroic, but most of all amazing. How will you control your basic urges?"

"At night whenever I can." Vicente took out a small wig and covered his tonsure. "With this, a false beard, and proper garments, I can pretend to be

Don Somebody de Somebody." He produced other material for disguises. "Or a vicious *pícaro matone*."

Ballebrera watched him place medicines, rare books, and maps on the bed. He read the titles. "All on the Index of Forbidden Books, I presume."

"And all of them for the Count de Olivares."

"Yes, he is an obsessive bibliophile, and it is well known that the new Inquisitor General has given him dispensation to read Indexed material. These books for Olivares may gain you a more rapid entry to the palace than I can arrange. And what do you have in those packages?"

"Special essences, bases for perfumes smuggled out of France and Italy for Don Lope's business associates here in Madrid."

Ballebrera took Vicente outside into an arbor and walked with him towards a heavy gate. "Your private entrance. I will provide a key."

"So, I may come here as a friar, and leave through this gate as a human being?"

"It seems that four years studying to be a Dominican has not changed you."

"I will confess that I've come to respect the Church for its ideals of helping the poor, its interference with secular authorities to prevent injustice, and its attempts to make men better, more ethical, but it would be better served if the clergy accepted only those with a true calling. I have met decent friars like Tío, who served God and man selflessly until the day he died. Unfortunately, many others are venal, lecherous, intolerant, and uneducated."

"We live in an imperfect world, Vicente, and I see no alternative to our flawed Church. Lutheranism, Calvinism, and the Church of England are heresies created to accommodate the dynastic ambitions and greed of kings and princes. The religion of the Jews is all superstition and lies. Islam is an unbelievable mix of paganism, Arab fantasies, and misunderstood Christianity. One man's religion is another man's myth. We must make the best of ours."

Chapter 12
La Corte

"Wake up." Ballebrera shook Vicente and pulled off his covers. "You must dress immediately."

He yawned and stretched. "What is the hour?"

"Lauds, as you friars call it. Her Royal Highness, Infanta Doña María, has sent her carriage for you with a personal escort . . . your small friend, the Marqués de Hombrecillo."

"Why didn't you say so?" He leaped out of bed and used the chamber pot.

Ballebrera summoned a servant to shave Vicente's face and tonsure, and another to serve him hot chocolate. Although many clerics wore mustachios and beards as elegant as any *grandee*, he preferred to be clean-shaven so he could create varied disguises for himself and reduce nesting places for ubiquitous hair lice.

"So it begins, Ramón."

"And sooner than either of us expected."

After Vicente got into his wool robe and sandals and hung the silver chain and crucifix of the Dominican Order around his neck, he greeted Hombrecillo in the formal *estrado*. "Don Sáncho, I apologize for keeping you waiting. I did not expect to see you again so soon."

"The Infanta wants to thank you for rescuing Doña Inéz from a fate worse than death, and for saving me from eternal *vergüenza*."

"The eternal shame and dishonor would have been mine had I not interfered." Vicente attached his cloak and put on his cap. "Don Sáncho, will you advise me in the ways of the Alcazar?"

"Be respectful, and be yourself."

"Surely, there is more you can tell me."

"Then I must drown you in verbiage."

Passersby gawked as Hombrecillo and Vicente stepped into a gilded carriage with the Habsburg coat-of-arms displayed on each door. While they rode along the Calle Mayor towards the Alcazar, Vicente paid little attention to the morning activities going on throughout the populous city. He listened to his little friend, who told him all he knew about the Infanta and the clerical cliques within the palace. As before, the *bufón* characterized the Infanta as an ice-princess, strong-willed, imperious, and a paragon of unapproachable Spanish reserve. Of most importance for Vicente's purposes, María practiced her religion with all the intense devotion of a true Spaniard.

"The Infanta lives a life not to be envied, more restricted than any nun. Her world does not exist beyond the confines of the Alcazar. She is a prisoner of Court etiquette, protocol, and imperial expectations. Only three men in all of Europe are eligible to marry her. Charles Stuart, Prince of Wales, provided he converts to our True Faith; a Dauphin of France, yet to be born; and her cousin, Archduke Ferdinand of Hungary."

"Then she must be as guarded as the rarest of jewels."

"Yes, she is. Except for formal Court appearances and an occasional procession of short distance and duration, the Infanta is limited to her cloistered apartments and gardens. Day and night, awake and sleeping, she is watched over always by her ladies and chaperones. The only young men she speaks to informally are her siblings, all cut from the same mold. How could it be otherwise? Their parents were first cousins and their paternal grandparents, Philip II and Anne of Austria, uncle and niece."

Hombrecillo went on to describe the royal clergy. The six members of the Supreme Council of the Inquisition were the most influential. *La Suprema* met in its council chambers beneath the Alcazar, and Inquisitor General de Aliaga was an ally of Olivares, although not sympathetic to all his policies. King Philip's confessor, António de Sotomayor, headed a second powerful clerical force. A Dominican and dedicated Olivarista, he supervised all the palace confessors: One each for the Queen, the two Infantes, the Infanta, Olivares and his family; and numberless others for courtiers and servants, countless clerical secretaries, and ministerial aides. The principal chaplain, traditionally the Archbishop of Santiago, led a third group of clerics and was responsible for maintaining standards of Court religion and morals. He also managed the royal chapel with its lesser chaplains, organist, chapel-master, and chorister. Under his supervision, royal preachers took turns giving sermons to the King and Queen in the royal chapel. He also gave orders to the Grand Almoner, who distributed alms in accordance with Royal wishes and dressed the poor for the ceremonial washing of feet by the King on Maundy Thursday.

"The palace supports a veritable army of God."

"And most live there." Hombrecillo stared at him thoughtfully. "The ideal milieu for an ambitious friar."

The carriage cut across the great plaza in front of the Alcazar and stopped in a vaulted yard on the southern side. They got out and proceeded on foot through the main gate into one of the two great courtyards surrounded by porticos ornamented with busts of saints and Catholic kings. Hombrecillo told Vicente that the Alcazar had been built on the western side of Madrid at the edge of a plateau above the Manzanares River. Erected as a fortress in the fourteenth-century, it was converted to a residence for Philip II two hundred years later. Flanked by four dissimilar towers facing the city, the Alcazar was of rectangular shape, with walls of stone, brick, mud and majestic marble ornaments with balconies built around two large patios, the King's and the Queen's Courtyards.

Vicente saw royal guards stationed everywhere. The Spanish wore scarlet and orange-gold striped uniforms with silver breastplates and moines, visorless high-crested helmets. The German guards had become a tradition during the previous century when King Charles II also was Holy Roman Emperor Charles V. They dressed in gold-trimmed crimson satin uniforms with white hose and plumed caps, and each held a halberd, a battle-ax and pike mounted on poles taller than most men.

He observed mingling throughout the quadrants of the Alcazar solicitors, curates, captains-general and officers returned from the Indies and European battlefields, courtiers and officials of the royal households, counselors and secretaries of state offices, magistrates, and governors, all in uniforms and cloaks of office. *Titulo*s and their ladies strolled accompanied by liveried pages and equerries.

Hombrecillo pointed out the *mentidero*s where *madrileños* gathered to hear and pass on the latest *murmuraciónes*, gossip. Near them, shopkeepers did business from booths specializing in jewelry, perfumes, and other luxury goods. Hawkers pushed carts through the throng and called out their wares. Stalls exhibited work by court painters.

"*Mentideros* can be found everywhere in Madrid, Don Vicente. I find them to be both enjoyable and invaluable because *madrileños* of all classes can meet to hear current gossip, discuss the most recent literary works, assess the merits of various actors, and criticize the government. There newsmongers wait for courtiers to tell them tales from within the palace and distribute lampoons, verses, and satirical pamphlets. The *murmuración* might be the result of a battle, a decision in foreign or economic policy, and who is in or out of favor. It might be accurate, partially true, completely false, or a malicious lie. Frivolous topics are the most popular: The King's current mistress, the escapade of a *grandee* with an actress; and Olivares' latest pact with Satan."

The *bufón* mocked litigants and their notaries who awaited appointments with some austere council magistrate. "All are quite prepared to grovel for favors or rulings on cases, some of which have been dragging on for months, even years. If Death appointed only Spanish bureaucrats to come for us, we would be guaranteed eternal life."

He stopped and oriented Vicente. "To the right, through those porticos, the chambers and offices of the Councils of State, Castile, Finance, Aragón, Portugal, and the Indies all open onto the northern wing of the Queen's Courtyard. There are vaults beneath them for more council rooms and secretarial offices. Farther to the right, through that archway is the Eastern Annex, the Casa del Tesoro. It holds an armory, kitchens, bakery, lodgings for clergy and servants, studios for court painters, and the Treasury House for which it has been named."

Vicente had seen the massive, four-story addition from the outside when they arrived. Its southern facade was wider than the main palace. "Is that where you and Doña Inéz live?"

"We have the honor of sleeping at our masters' doors, sometimes at their feet, but never the greatest privilege of all."

"Which is?"

"To compete for the honor of emptying Their Majesties' and Highnesses' chamber pots, an honor to which only a true fool would aspire." Hombrecillo pointed at a monumental marble staircase between the two courtyards. "At the top, is the royal chapel. His Majesty's suite is to the west, Her Majesty's to the east, above their patios. Infante Don Carlos' apartments are up there next to King Philip's, and the Count de Olivares has a suite adjacent to His Majesty to facilitate his access. In theory, the only married man permitted to sleep in the palace is His Majesty, but exceptions have been made for Olivares and this *bufón* who has taken a bride. The Count's main suite of apartments is at the northeast rear of the palace and includes a private oratory, spacious book-lined study, and an office with an extensive collection of maps and charts. Olivares' wife and daughter have suites on the third floor."

The *bufón* motioned for Vicente to bend so he could whisper. "I now give you your first lesson in court intrigue. Queen Isabel and Olivares despise each other. The Count fears that every moment he is absent from his King's side, someone else might replace him as the royal favorite. He enjoys the privilege of sleeping in Philip's bedroom, which infuriates and humiliates Isabel. The King leaves her in the middle of each night to be available in his apartments for Olivares first thing in the morning, which has led to malicious gossip that he uses homosexuality, witchcraft, and other unnatural powers to control His Majesty."

"And who lives on the uppermost floors?"

"Above the King and Queen, the third and fourth floors serve as quarters for the four-hundred women of the Queen's household. Some are duennas. Only widows may qualify as chaperones. Others are ladies-in-waiting, or maids-of-honor called meninas because of their low-heeled shoes, and of course innumerable female servants who must also live in the palace."

"Where are the Infanta's apartments?"

"Over there off the King's Courtyard. And I must warn you. Although she turned fifteen this past eighteenth of August, the Infanta is the most regal of them all."

Partial Genealogy of The Spanish Habsburgs Showing Consanguinity

FERDINAND of Aragón (m) ISABELLA of Castile
d. 1516   d.1504

Juana la loca (m) Philip von Habsburg   Katherine of Aragón (m) Henry VIII
of Castile   Duke of Burgundy
d 1555   **Philip I of Spain**
d. 1506

CHARLES I of Spain (m) Isabella of Portugal
CHARLES V HRE
d. 1558

PHILIP II (m) **niece** and fourth wife, Anna of Austria
d. 1598

PHILIP III (m) **first cousin**, Margaret of Austria
d. 1621

Ana (Anne) m Louis XIII   Carlos   Fernando, cardinal-infante
b.1601   b. 1607   b. 1609

Louis XIV   María (m) **first cousin**, Ferdinand III, HRE
b. 1606

Isabel (m-1) PHILIP IV (m-2) **niece**, María Anna
(Elizabeth   b. 1605
de Borbón)   d. 1665

CHARLES II (last Spanish Habsburg)
d. 1700

Baltazar Carlos   Maria Teresa (m) **first cousin**, Louis XIV
d. 1646

Chapter 13
Doña María

Vicente and Hombrecillo entered a small candle-lit *estrado*. At the far end, on a small platform covered with brown velour under a canopy of beige and white damask, the Infanta sat in a plain straight back ebony chair. Still in mourning for her father, Philip III, she wore an unadorned black silk guardinfante, an exaggeration of the farthingale, with a modest white ruff and a plain golden cross hanging from her neck. The dress covered her feet, which rested on a black satin cushion. Tiny Inéz stood below the platform at her mistress' feet in an identical dress. Two meninas and a duenna, dressed all in black, attended her.

Rajosa, her aged Dominican confessor and a reactionary bigot according to Hombrecillo, stood next to the chaperone and measured Vicente with a sour expression as he approached. Behind them, a boy in scarlet robes and biretta stepped forward for a closer look. Vicente did not need to be told he was María's twelve-year old brother, Infante Fernándo, Cardinal and Archbishop of Toledo.

When they stopped at a respectful distance and genuflected, Vicente summoned all his skill to sustain an inscrutable expression. Despite Hombrecillo's descriptions, he had not expected to see so un-Spanish a beauty. The Infanta's braided hair shone as pure gold in the candlelight of the somber *estrado*. Her eyes were a clear pale blue, her flawless pink and white complexion unblemished by cosmetics. Her narrow hands and slim graceful fingers held prayer book, rosary, and a large fan of black satin and ivory. Her most attractive attribute, Vicente decided, was her full and luscious lower lip, which appeared to be in a permanent kissable pout.

Vicente heard whispers of approval and saw flirtatious glances from the meninas before his eyes met and held María's, which to him reflected external light and exuded inner fire as if they were perfect blue diamonds. All else, all others in the *estrado* disappeared when unfamiliar emotions overwhelmed him. What he felt was inexplicable, beyond mere flesh, more noble. The brown and white canopy and the tapestry of dark green and gold thread behind the Infanta suggested she was the Virgin Herself, ensconced in a baldacchino, the platform itself a celestial pedestal for a chaste golden goddess.

Maria spoke in a forced formal monotone: "Friar, we wish to hear from you how it happened that you rescued the Marqués and Marquesa de Hombrecillo."

If Vicente thought he could affect humility and minimize his heroics, he was mistaken. Fernándo wanted to know every detail and repeatedly interrupted him. The little Cardinal-Infante, in spirit more soldier than prelate, brought Vicente a sword from one of the guards outside and commanded him to demonstrate how he had slashed away the *golondrero's* wheel-lock pistol.

After Vicente recreated his rescue of the *bufónes*, Fernándo asked, "Did you study under a great swordsman?"

"Your Eminence, when I was your age, I received useful lessons from an exiled Catholic noble Englishman."

"Then you must show me everything he taught you."

María said, "We thought the days of warrior friars had passed."

Rajosa confronted Vicente. "Yes, is it not a sin for one of our Order to take up the sword and shed blood?"

He measured the friar before he spoke. The frail Dominican was in his seventies and suffered from sciatica. His thin lips suggested inflexibility and intolerance. "I spared their miserable lives. If defending the helpless is a sin, then I will leave it for wiser men to assign me penance. But surely, would it not have been a greater sin to do nothing?"

Vicente had the Infanta and everyone else in the *estrado* hanging on his every word. Instead of shouting, he spoke the purest Castilian in a passionate theatrical whisper. He applied everything Don Lope's actor friends had taught him. He paused and emphasized for dramatic effect and gestured as if he were on stage.

"Did not my actions prevent the breaking of God's commandments? Who can say those criminals would not have murdered Don Sáncho and Doña Inéz? At the very least, they would have violated her, infected her with the foulest of diseases, taken their property . . . and worst of all, stolen their honor. To have done nothing would have been the same as participating in the crime."

Rajosa raised his voice over the sighing, moaning, and weeping of the Infanta's *meninas*, "Fray Vicente, tell us why have you come to Madrid."

"To serve my Church and my King, if I am so permitted."

"At which house of our Order are you lodging?"

"I arrived in Madrid yesterday morning, and for the present, I am staying with my kinsman, Don Ramón de Rocamora, Señor de Ballebrera and Knight of Alcántara." Vicente began his campaign for Rafal's title. "We are cousins to the Illustrious Don Jerónimo de Rocamora, Señor de Rafal, commander of *tercios* in Flanders." Vicente recited his lineage as well as any haughty Castilian *hidalgo*, which initiated another torrent of questions from the little Cardinal-Infante about strategy and tactics in the Netherlands.

"And your education in the church?"

After Vicente described his studies at the College of Confessors of Santo Domingo in Orihuela, the Infanta said, "Then you hear confessions."

Vicente perceived that the Infanta wanted him to be her confessor and modulated his voice to a normal tone. "Yes, *Alteza*, Your Highness. Before I left Orihuela, I confessed the Bailiff General and his family."

The meninas sighed. Vicente believed they would have formed a line to confess here and now if María were to give her consent. He also saw her confessor scowling and counted him as his first enemy at *la Corte*.

Rajosa turned to the Infanta. "*Alteza*, it is past the time for your lesson in English."

"A barbaric, heretic language."

"If you are to marry the Prince of Wales . . ."

"He should learn Castilian Spanish. The noblest language of all."

Vicente spoke in English, "Highness, if I may assist you in your studies . . ."

The Infanta lost her composure. "You speak English?"

"I know many languages."

"Their grammar makes no sense to us."

"*Alteza*, we all know their heretical language is confused and causes erroneous thought. It is essentially a German tongue, forced into a Latin grammar, with many words stolen from the French. May I speak further?" She nodded permission, and he continued, "If they are not on the Index of Forbidden Writings, I suggest you learn English through the plays of their great playwright, William Shakespeare."

She glared at Rajosa. "Well? Are they on the Index?"

"*Alteza*, I know nothing of this Shakespeare."

"Then find out if we may learn English from his plays. But first, we must find a position for Don Vicente at Court." When her meninas murmured approval, she silenced them with an icy stare.

Vicente experienced a surge of pride. The Infanta had referred to him not as Friar but respectfully as Don. How he wanted to kiss her delicious mouth. When their eyes met again, he silently cursed God and all the treacherous fates for his intense attraction to this unattainable princess.

Rajosa would not give up. "We must proceed according to protocol, Your Highness. Fray Vicente, produce your certificates of *limpieza de sangre*."

"They are at the house of my kinsman."

María pointed her fan at Vicente. "Bring them with you tomorrow morning after lauds." She turned to her confessor. "You will then escort Don Vicente to His Majesty's Confessor, Don António de Sotomayor, who will accept him into the royal clergy."

Rajosa played one more card. "How old are you Fray Vicente?"

"I turned twenty this past April."

"Impossible. Too young, too close in age," Rajosa said over giggling from the meninas.

María said to the old Dominican as more threat than request, "After Don Vicente meets with Don António, you shall bring him here so we may know that our commands have been obeyed." She shut her fan indicating the audience had ended.

The moment they were outside the Infanta's *estrado*, Hombrecillo said, "We will have to protect your flank from Rajosa."

By now, Vicente had come to suspect that his little friend spied for the most powerful man in Spain. "So much has happened I've neglected to tell you . . . I have brought a very important package from Valencia for the Count de Olivares."

"*La Suprema* and Olivares? Tomorrow will be another interesting day for you, my amazing young friend."

And this afternoon as well.

Chapter 14
La Hermosura

"Again Vicente, I am delighted to say that you have run far ahead of my plans for you."

"I am not yet a palace friar, and there is still the matter of my interrogation tomorrow in the chambers of *la Suprema*."

Armed with rapiers and daggers, Vicente and Ballebrera rode in the Duchess of Astórquia's luxurious carriage to the theater el Paraíso. Both men wore black velour doublets, silk breeches and hose, and plumed broad-brimmed black felt hats. Vicente had applied a false mustachio, goatee, and bushy eyebrows to complete his disguise.

When they arrived, the theater doors had just opened, and angry patrons demanded free entrance because of their station and their claims to be friends of the playwright. Vicente watched ushers in buff doublets and *alguacíles*, officers of the law, struggling to maintain order because the theater had no reserved seats. He recognized a member of Yusef's band, and parted from Ballebrera. After a brief conversation, the man took Vicente to a side door and guided him upstairs to an office suite.

"What are you two bandit scum doing in so fine a place?" At the insult, they reached for their daggers. "Peace, Don Yusef and Don Pablo, or whatever you're calling yourselves these days."

Pablo gaped at him. "Can it be?"

Vicente bowed and lisped, "Don Jaime de Algorfa y whomever at your service, gentlemen."

Yusef and Pablo each hugged Vicente, who then took several small parcels from his doublet.

Pablo opened them and handed the vials to Yusef. "The essences we've been expecting."

Yusef expressed his undying gratitude to Vicente for telling him about Don Lope. They had gone to work for and then with the *polidor*. During the past four years, they had made so much money smuggling his perfumes and other desirable luxury goods into Madrid that they were able to finance el Paraíso.

"And so," Yusef concluded, "we have created a paradise worthy of the Koran with more virgins and feasting than even our Holy Book promises."

"And Moraíma?"

"My sister is well. You will see her soon."

"Where, when?"

Pablo took his arm. "Patience, Vicente. Come, let us show you our other more profitable enterprises before the play begins."

They took him into a sumptuous *estrado*. Accustomed to the dangerous and filthy waterfront *garitos* of El Grau where professional gamblers fleeced gullible victims with marked cards and shaved dice, Vicente was unprepared for the gaming room's plush interior. Elaborate golden sconces and glass chandeliers held enough candles to illuminate the mirrored great room as bright as daylight. The floor was of honey-colored marble tiles, and along the walls gilded couches and divans upholstered in striped green and gold velvet offered comfort for the clientele. Green and gold liveried servants circulated throughout the room with trays of complimentary flavored water, brandy, wine, and chocolate.

At glass-topped tables, fashionably attired patrons wagered gold escudos and silver reales de ocho. Some risked rings, necklaces, jeweled crucifixes, and crosses to recoup their losses. Others wrote pledges of property on pieces of paper.

Yusef gestured towards a table. "As you might expect, the most popular card game is lansquet, also known as pharaoh. In other rooms, we have tables for dice, knucklebones, and wheels of chance. Which game do you prefer?"

"The game of love." Vicente ogled several voluptuous courtesans in bare-shouldered dresses exposing delicious cleavage. Like predatory birds, they hovered over the wealthiest gamblers. "I'm about to explode."

"How long has it been?"

"Too long, due more to prudence than virtue. Unfortunately, the French sickness is rampant in Orihuela."

Pablo sighed. "Regrettably, it is the same here in Madrid. But, if one is careful . . ." He pointed to a pair of doors at the far end of the great room. "You will find the choicest selection in there, and you can take your slut to one of the private rooms after the play."

"And have you found love, Pablo?"

"I have a wife and son in Valencia, a sweet young girl I rescued before the brothels claimed her."

"And you, Yusef?"

"I am content to spread my Arabic seed to repopulate Spain with the blood of True Believers. Koitalel prefers to remain with Don Lope in Valencia."

Vicente observed a houseman dealing second-cards for the benefit of certain players. "Your dealer over there is cheating."

Yusef shrugged. "It is the easiest way for us to pay off certain officials and Familiars so that we may stay open. Others prefer women or our servant boys. You still have an eye for cards, Vicente. Perhaps some night you will deal for us."

Yusef returned to his office, and Pablo sat with Vicente in one of the balconies overlooking the theater. El Paraíso was set between rows of two-story houses with a stage and colorful curtain at one end. *Titulos* and other gentry occupied balconies on the second floors. Several rows of benches had been set up close to the stage, and the rest of the throng stood or mingled as vendors moved about offering food and drink. Women sat in ground level covered balconies along the walls and threw assorted debris at men making ribald comments.

Pablo directed Vicente's attention to the men seated on the benches. "Those posturing peacocks are known as musketeers, each one pretending to be a *caballero*, presumptuous critics all and easily bribed to spread positive *murmuraciónes* about the play."

"When does it begin?"

"This time of the year at two past noon. At four during the summer. Daily performances. We're always filled beyond capacity."

"What play is being performed this day?"

"*The Scorned Sweetheart.*"

"You really make money off such trash?"

"We prefer to believe our theater is filled because of la Hermosura."

"The Beauty?"

"She is the real attraction. She sings and dances between the acts. All the men adore her. All the women envy her."

And by your expression, my friend Pablo, she must be none other than Moraima.

Vicente observed drawn daggers and swords throughout the restless throng below and *alguaciles* preventing confrontations from escalating to duels and murders. He saw Ballebrera speaking with a slender blond *caballero* in a pastel blue silk doublet and fawn breeches. After a brief angry exchange, the young man minced away in a huff.

An actor emerged on stage from behind the curtain, and Vicente suffered through a bombastic prologue and trivial first act. He sat forward when attractive young women and girls in bright colored blouses and skirts took turns on the small stage singing lewd songs of desire, clicking their castanets, and moving sensually to guitars. A puppet show followed them, which received derisive shouts and whistles from those clamoring for la Hermosura.

La Hermosura. The Beauty had been aptly named. She wore a blouse and matching skirt of diaphanous voile the color of her blue-violet eyes and designed to expose her golden shoulders, shapely arms, and the cleavage of her majestic breasts. While Vicente listened to her sweet affecting voice, he relived yet again that special balmy night of orange blossom perfume and imagined what might have been had he taken the *pícaro* road instead of the other to Orihuela.

After la Hermosura completed her songs and dances, several men leaped onto the stage and surrounded her. Vicente dropped from the balcony and joined them. They praised her beauty and offered jewels and enormous sums of gold escudos for her favors. When one admirer, a slight wiry *caballero*, offered la Hermosura a king's treasury of diamonds, Vicente interrupted the auction and punned in the Valencian dialect, "Most Illustrious Hermosura, do you prefer *el diamante frío*, the cold of the diamond, to *el caldo de amante*, the heat of your lover?"

She stared into his green eyes. "Is it really you?"

He removed his hat and bowed, careful not to speak her *morilla* name. "Always at your service."

The *caballero* who had offered the diamonds to Moraíma flashed him a murderous look, and despite pleas from her disappointed suitors, she took Vicente to her private suite and bolted the door. The scented room was furnished with oversized damask pillows on Turkish rugs under a mirrored ceiling.

"I don't know if I approve of your mustache and beard."

"Then I'll remove them. My eyebrows too."

"What's this? One of the masks I foretold you'd wear?"

He took off his hat and removed the false hair covering his tonsure. "I am a Dominican."

"My unfortunate young poet, and have you been celibate for me all this time?"

"In my heart and soul."

"Liar."

"I swear. Every night and day, all these long years, my only sincere prayer was to hold you again."

Vicente took Moraíma in his arms and hungrily kissed her lips. He wallowed in her musty scent and caressed the smoothness of her skin.

"Ay, my Vicente, and how many escudos will I lose this day because of you?"

He suppressed his jealousy and repugnance at her trade. "Did you think of me a little?"

"I thought of you always and closed my eyes when there were others."

Better for me to believe your lies. "Then leave them open this day."

After he was through, Moraíma turned her back to him and cried. "What is it?" He reached to touch her, but she pushed his hand away.

"What has happened to you, Vicente? That night together in the orange grove, you were a strong but gentle lover then, a poet. The best I have known. But today you were a beast. I feel as if you've raped me. Ravished me. Used me. There was no love from you."

Vicente realized that he had indeed mounted his love like a filthy *golondrero*. He reached out again. "I promise, Moraíma. This time I'll be gentle."

"Not now. Act Two will end shortly. I have another performance, and afterwards, I must entertain my regular customers. Foolish Vicente. Do you realize you have wasted your opportunity to make love with the most expensive *puta* in all Spain?"

He winced at her use of that pejorative word. "I'll make it up to you."

"I know you will. By Allah's beard, a Dominican. When did you have your last woman?"

Everyone asks me that. "It's been more than a year."

Her expression softened, and she cupped his face with her hands. "Now I understand, my deprived Vicente. Return to me tonight, and I will let you make amends."

Vicente kissed her hands. If it became impossible for him to help Rafal receive his title, he would become a renegade friar and never again part from Moraíma.

Chapter 15
Among the Powerful

The following morning, Vicente sat on an uncomfortable stool facing a long table, at which sat six men in hooded black robes. Instead of taking him to the royal chapel for his interview with the King's confessor, Rajosa had brought him beneath the ground level of the Queen's Courtyard to the vault of *El Consejo de la Suprema y General Inquisición*, the Supreme Council of the Inquisition. The stone walls were bare except for an impressive realistic crucifix hanging between sconces. Administrative clerks sat at a smaller table with reed pens to record all that was said.

Vicente summoned all his acting skills to appear calm and humble before the most feared junta in all Spain. In an instant, he could be flung into a dungeon, tortured, and made to disappear without a trace.

Inquisitor General Luís de Aliaga was frail and did not appear to be long for this world. By way of contrast, Philip IV's confessor, Inquisitor António de Sotomayor, seemed much younger than his sixty-six years with an erect posture and pinkish fair skin.

A poor gambler, Rajosa played his best cards too soon. "Here is the friar of whom I spoke. You can see with your own eyes that he is too young to serve the Infanta or anyone else here in the palace. He needs seasoning. I recommend the Monastery of . . ."

"We will decide what shall be done with our young brother," Inquisitor Andrés de Pacheco interrupted, a lean clean-shaven ascetic with an intelligent face.

Vicente interpreted Pacheco's tone as one of annoyance. He suspected Rajosa's demand that *la Suprema* deal with the matter of his appointment as a Court cleric had interrupted more important matters.

Aliaga peered over his spectacles at Vicente. "May we see your certificates?"

Vicente gave the documents to the Inquisitor General, whose eyes were poor. After a cursory glance, the old man handed the scrolls to Sotomayor.

The King's Confessor read Vicente's *limpieza de sangre* and proof of his graduation from The College of Confessors of Santo Domingo and passed them to his colleagues on the Supreme Council. "Although everything appears to be in order, they will have to be verified."

The interrogation was non-threatening at first. The Inquisitors asked Vicente about his religious background, education, and why he had selected the Dominican Order.

He recited his lineage and praised the piety and gentle Christianity of the late Tío António as his ideal as well as the religious zeal of his repellent cousin, Tomás. He embellished the heroics of his kinsmen and mentioned their memberships in the Orders of Santiago and Alcántara.

After Rajosa urged the Inquisitors to probe his religious convictions and behavior, Vicente defended himself with skillful lies. No, he had never blasphemed nor spoken heresy. No, he had never been guilty of the seduction of penitents. No, he had never fornicated. Yes, he had done penance for lusting in his heart and would accept whatever penalty they gave him for defending Hombrecillo and Inéz. No, he had never read anything on the Index of Forbidden Books. Yes, he had kept all his vows.

"Easy for him to say," Rajosa said. "Fray Vicente is but twenty and from the small provincial town of Orihuela."

"I spent my first sixteen years in the magnificent city of Valencia," Vicente corrected him, "and Orihuela is a great cathedral city in its own right."

"Who can say he will not be tempted by the licentiousness at Court," Rajosa continued, "with hundreds of women living here, and men who behave like women? We have all heard their confessions, which reveal merely a small fraction of their many sins."

"We are well aware," Pacheco said, "that the laity never confess all their sins, not even the most pious, because they have trouble confessing matters of sexual conduct."

Vicente was not surprised. To squeeze a woman's hand could be interpreted as a mortal sin.

"And what are your views on the Doctrine of Immaculate Conception?" Sotomayor asked.

Even before he entered the Dominican Order, Vicente had learned from observation and discussions with Don Lope that worship of the Virgin was an essential part of the Spanish Catholic Faith, similar to a cult, with manifestations linked to local traditions, many of them pagan in origin. Although Immaculate Conception had been adopted as Church Doctrine less than a hundred years before, all Spaniards defended that relatively recent dogma. In

El Grau, Vicente had seen the most impious *pícaro* draw his sword in Her defense. The Dominicans were so devoted to the Doctrine they claimed that their love for Mary surpassed all other Orders, which they proved through their great public rosaries and processions any hour of the day or night.

"Regarding the Doctrine of Immaculate Conception, only a chaste and pure vessel could bear our Divine Jesús and carry Him to human form," he said to the satisfaction of all but Rajosa.

Aliaga cleared his throat as if to make his feeble voice stronger. "Should Teresa of Avila be canonized and made patron saint of all Spain, even above Santiago?"

The Inquisitor General had asked both a theological and political question. Santiago was the patron saint of Castile. His name had been the rallying cry of the *reconquista* and continued to be shouted to this day in battle by the Spanish military. If he preferred Teresa, who had a Jewish grandparent, over Santiago, he might be suspected of having tainted blood.

Presently, all Spanish religious Orders were pressing Rome to canonize their most outstanding candidates: Teresa, Isidore the Laborer, and Ignatius of Loyola, founder of the Jesuits. The people and the Crown supported them as grave affairs of State. The hunt for saints was a national pastime. Friar or nun, the holy person might be accredited with working miracles, being in two places at once, or reading thoughts. The funerals of these purported saints were as violent as war because the credulous fought over their clothes, hair, and even bits of skin and flesh. Any relic would do.

The great cathedral in Valencia displayed the Chalice used at The Last Supper. The Cathedral of Coria in Extremadura exhibited a jawbone of San Juan Batista, an eyetooth of San Cristobal, soil from the crib at Bethlehem and Mount of Olives, and the tablecloth from The Last Supper. In Burgos there were three crucifixes believed to be the work of Nicodemus. Laymen like Rafal owned precious gilded and jeweled reliquaries.

Vicente said, "It would be a great moment in the history of our Church if each of our deserving were to be canonized as saints. Do they not belong to all of Spain?"

Again, the members of *la Suprema* appeared pleased with his reply and impressed by his passionate eloquence, but not Rajosa. "You haven't said which you prefer, Santiago or Teresa."

He ignored the Infanta's confessor and faced the Inquisitor General. "Your Reverence, I submit to the wisdom of my elders and will heed their decisions. And if I may speak further the palace *bufónes* have no spiritual director of their own. Those unfortunates are also children of God. They need instruction and comfort from the bosom of our Holy Mother Church. If you find me worthy, I would be their confessor."

"A most charitable suggestion, Fray Vicente," Sotomayor commended.

"He is too young to confess anyone."

"Perhaps," Sotomayor said and added firmly to silence the old man, "but if the Infanta, who is the most pious of young women, sees virtue in this young man, he ought to be given an opportunity to serve. I see no reason why he cannot hear confessions during a period of probation and preach an occasional sermon too. And, if his certificate of *limpieza* is confirmed, he might even consider wearing the black robe."

"We have not heard his views on the Propositions," Rajosa persisted.

"Yes, I would test this young friar a bit further regarding the Propositions," Aliaga said.

Vicente understood that he was now on the most dangerous ground of all, control of thought and speech. Although the Spanish Inquisition had been founded to eradicate Judaizing and heresies, it held jurisdiction over all deviation from the True Faith and punished the slightest errors in theology, even when spoken in anger or inadvertently in jest. Religious fanaticism, greed, and malice gave everyone a motive to denounce. Family ties were no excuse. Men of the highest rank were arrested and tortured for even the slightest utterance connected to the most obscure point of theology.

He had witnessed Familiars of the Holy Office arrest a man at the Cathedral of Orihuela who had refused to believe God-in-Jesús was put to death between two robbers because the Supreme Being would never demean Himself to such a degree. The man had died under torture at the Tribunal in Murcia.

Tío had told him why he had never risen higher in the Church. He had made too many errors in his sermons that bordered on heresy and brought him to the attention of the Inquisition. Although never charged, those mistakes of dogma had been enough to prevent him from becoming Bishop of Orihuela.

The theologians of the Inquisition characterized the Propositions with specific vocabulary and meaning: Heretical, Erroneous, Savoring of Heresy, Ill-sounding, Rash, Scandalous or Offensive to pious ears, Schismatic or Seditious, Impious, Blasphemous, and Trivial.

After Vicente convinced the Inquisitors that he understood the Propositions, Rajosa said, "Let us hear a sample sermon from Fray Vicente and determine if he is guilty of . . . ."

"Guilty?" Sotomayor had wearied of Rajosa. "Has he been accused?"

"How can one know? I repeat . . . while we investigate if he truly is *ex puro sanguine*, of pure blood, let him be housed with our Order at the Monastery of . . ."

"So here is where you have kept him," a voice thundered from the entrance.

A huge stooping broad-shouldered man of olive complexion dressed in gold-trimmed black velvet entered the council chamber. Vicente did not need to be told the man was thirty-four-year old Gaspar de Guzmán, Count de Olivares and His Majesty's favorite. Hombrecillo must have burned his ear.

Olivares' head was large and square, with fierce dark eyes above an enormous nose, upturned twisted mustachio, and spade beard, which explained why the credulous believed rumors spread by his enemies that he had made a pact with the devil. He struck a haughty pose before *la Suprema* and bellowed, "Why are you wasting valuable time with this devout and courageous friar?"

Rajosa cringed and backed away from the intimidating Count, and Sotomayor said softly, "We were deciding where best to place him."

"And have you decided?"

"Not yet."

"Then I shall make up your minds for you. I'll take on this friar as one of my secretaries. I need him for important work." When Aliaga assented, Olivares beckoned to Vicente, "You. Come with me."

As they left, Vicente saw that Rajosa was drenched in sweat, and with good reason. The old man would have to report to the Infanta what had transpired in *la Suprema*, and she would be infuriated that his meddling had lost her young friar to Olivares.

Attracted as he was to María, Vicente preferred to work for Olivares, who held influence over King Philip as no other in Spain. He expected his proximity to the two most powerful men in the kingdom would better help him promote a title for Rafal.

Olivares stopped outside the chambers of the Council of State. "Hombrecillo says that you have brought me a package from Valencia."

"Don Lope has sent you Machiavelli's *Il Principe*, a Spanish translation of King Solomon's Song of Songs, a detailed map of Flanders, and another of Amsterdam."

"Where are they?"

"At the house of my kinsman, Don Ramón de Rocamora, Señor de Ballebrera, Knight of Alcántara . . ."

"Please, spare me the usual boring recital of lineage."

"One more thing, Excellency, I had an audience with the Infanta yesterday, and . . ."

"That capricious child." Olivares twisted an end of his great mustachio while he thought for a moment. "Still, she is a confidant of the Queen. Very well then, I will not complain if you are in occasional contact with the girl and Her Majesty, provided you report to me everything they say and all you observe. Ask for Fray Junipero at the palace annex. He will assign you your bed in the dormitory of priests. Come to my offices after siesta with my books and maps, and . . ." He dropped to his knees. "Your Majesty."

Philip IV and his younger brother, Infante Don Carlos, approached them with an escort of courtiers and Spanish Guards. The King was dressed in unadorned black silks while his entourage of noble courtiers glittered like peacocks and reminded Vicente of the youthful gangs that terrorized Valencia.

Sixteen-year old Philip was King of Castile, León, Aragón, the Two Sicilies, Portugal, Navarre, Granada, Valencia, Mallorca, Sardinia, the Canary Islands, the East and West Indies; he was Duke of Brabant and Milan, Count of Flanders and Barcelona, Señor de Vizcaya, and most of the New World. He had the fair hair, blue eyes, pale complexion, and heavy protuberant jaw characteristic of his inbred family. The identical features of his vapid brother, Carlos, were exaggerated into caricature. Having seen all four of the Royal siblings, Vicente thought the Infanta was fortunate to have the least extreme of the Habsburg jaws, and with her luscious lower lip, potential ugliness became a feature of beauty.

The procession swept past them into the council chambers, and the guards took positions inside and along the corridor. A bearded Spanish guardsman stopped to speak with Olivares, who nodded approval, then approached Vicente.

"Her Majesty commands your presence."

In a sumptuous *estrado* on a platform of woven silver under a gold and red damask canopy, eighteen-year old Queen Isabel sat upon a carved ebony throne-chair with burgundy velvet upholstering and foot cushion of the same plush material. Golden harps decorated her black velour dress, and her ruff was of the finest lace. Vicente struggled to contain his delight that Isabel was not alone under the canopy. María sat rigid and inscrutable beside her on a similar throne-chair.

Hombrecillo had told him much about the Queen of Spain. She had been born Elizabeth de Borbón, daughter of Henry IV of France and María de Medici, and was seventeen months older than her husband. She had taken the revered Spanish name Isabel on her wedding day, and with the Infanta, was renowned as one of the great beauties of European royalty. In Vicente's estimation, Isabel equaled her reputation. She was dark of hair, buxom, with an intelligent aquiline face, flashing eyes, and a charming smile.

The Queen's household was enormous compared to the small coterie Vicente had seen the day before in the Infanta's apartments. Her entourage included a *mayordomo*, hordes of duennas, ladies-in-waiting, maids-of-honor, a troop of *menins*, young pages from the noblest families, and several clerics. A short woman with a slight humped-back and of masculine appearance stood closest to Isabel. Day and night, Her Majesty was attended by the Countess de Olivares and her ladies-in-waiting so that no hint of infidelity might be spoken about her.

Isabel gave Vicente permission to approach the dais. He took an instant liking to the vivacious Queen, who appeared eager for an informal chat outside the boundaries of *punctilio*. The Infanta fanned herself when he came closer, and Vicente worried its rapid flutter indicated displeasure until he heard Isabel whisper in French to her, "As you described, he is indeed very handsome."

The Infanta did not comment, and the Queen signaled her entourage with her own fan. After bows and curtsies, all left the suite, except for the Countess de Olivares and two ancient *hidalgo* chaperones.

Isabel gestured for the Countess and the two old men to withdraw to the far end of the room. Satisfied they were out of hearing, she said in a charming French accent, "Don Vicente, why have you chosen to work for the Count de Olivares? Do you not prefer to serve her Most Illustrious Highness?"

"Yes, Your Majesty, but Fray Rajosa suggested to *la Suprema* that I was too young to be a palace cleric and I should go to a monastery."

The Infanta was horrified. "A monastery?"

Vicente faced María and thought her to be more beautiful than he remembered from the day before. "*Alteza*, your confessor brought me to their council chamber to subvert your wishes. Fray António de Sotomayor will confirm what I say." He went on to describe Olivares' appearance before *la Suprema* and his command that he would be one of his secretaries.

Isabel covered her face with her fan. She leaned closer to María. She spoke sotto voce in French but loud enough for Vicente to hear, "Rajosa is too old, too concerned about retaining his position with you. I see nothing wrong with having a young confessor. I should like one for myself, this one if he is not to be yours."

"I have lost him to Satan." María pouted and addressed Vicente, "Do you prefer working for the Count de Olivares to serving me?"

"*Alteza*, you will always have first call on my loyalty wherever and whenever you command," Vicente whispered with intense passion, delighted she had used the personal instead of the imperial collective pronoun. He had begun to draw out the e in *Alteza* to make his pronunciation of her title sound more like an endearment.

The Infanta blushed, again briefly covered her face while she pretended to cough. "There is a way we can make the best of the situation."

"Yes, *Alteza*?"

"We want information." She paused, glanced towards the Countess de Olivares, and lowered her voice. "The Count de Olivares would sell me to the heretics for the least gain in foreign policy. When he was on his deathbed, my beloved father . . ." Maria crossed herself, ". . . may God grant him eternal peace . . . he made my brother promise that I would become an empress. It cannot be here in Spain. Therefore, I must know Olivares' plans. If he attempts to force upon me a marriage with an English heretic, I shall enter a convent."

And I would be your exclusive gallant of the grilles.

Vicente masked his emotions. "We will need to arrange how and when I may report to you, Your Majesty, and you, *Alteza*."

Isabel giggled and huddled closer to María. "I so love a good intrigue, and better yet, an opportunity to defeat Olivares. Not even our greatest playwright, Lope de Vega, could devise a more complex plot."

While Queen and Infanta whispered behind their fans. Vicente recalled Ballebrera's promise that he would advance farther and fastest if he became part of the royal clergy. No one, not even his kinsman could have expected it to have happened so soon after his arrival in Madrid. He was a young man of twenty, a minor Dominican friar. Yet, by his third day in the capital, he had spoken with the Queen, the Infanta, and the Cardinal-Infante; and he had stood less than a body length away from the King and Infante Carlos. He had survived an interrogation by *la Suprema* and impressed Sotomayor, King Philip's Confessor. Within the past hour, he had entered the service of the most powerful individual in the Spanish Empire, the Count de Olivares. At the same time, the Infanta wanted him to replace Rajosa as her confessor.

Vicente remembered his youthful dreams of becoming soldier, sailor, conquistador, actor, or *pícaro*. None could offer as much adventure as the life he was about to lead.

Chapter 16
Two in Love

"No, Vicente, I can't." Moraíma left the divan and wrapped herself in a white silk robe with gold trim and pattern of crescents.

Her behavior confused him. Tonight he had been ready to be a patient attentive lover and worship at the altar of her beauty as he had done whenever he could get away from palace duties this past month. He had recited original poetry with metaphors praising his *morilla* as more desirable than Helen of Troy, more enchanting than Circe, and more beautiful than Aphrodite.

"Have I done something wrong?"

"I have not been honest with you."

"You love another?"

"I don't know if I love the boy or what he represents."

"Boy? How old is he? Who is he?"

"A stallion of sixteen."

"A sniveling child?"

"You were barely sixteen when we made love in the orange grove."

"I have never forgotten the most glorious night of my life."

"All that is in our past. King Philip has visited me."

"His Majesty? Well, why not? How could the King not have fallen under the spell of your beauty?"

Moraíma described the night Olivares brought the young monarch to see her perform. Philip had been attracted to her at first sight, and they had their first liaison. "I am expecting him later tonight."

Vicente rose from the divan. "Then it is over for us, Moraíma."

"No, we will always love each other, but from this day only as friends. Please understand, Vicente, Philip is not just any man. If he wasn't King, he'd still be the most sought after young man in all Spain. He is more than fair and handsome. Nature has endowed him with an astonishing appetite and endurance."

Moraíma's description of Philip's sexual prowess did not surprise Vicente, but he would not tell her all he knew about the King's intense affair with a noblewoman and his visits to attractive novices at the convents while still performing his conjugal duties with Isabel. His Majesty was not the only randy Habsburg. Vicente had heard *murmuraciónes* that Philip's older sister, Anne, Queen of France, also had many lovers. He had witnessed Infante Carlos indulging in every court vice. Although still a boy, Cardinal-Infante Fernándo adored the company of beautiful girls and women almost as much as his weapons and war maps. Even if the Habsburgs might be a family of satyrs and nymphs, he saw his golden Infanta as a chaste exception enthroned as the Virgin Herself in a baldacchino.

How am I to court her? Do I dare court her?

Moraíma held a silver candelabrum, illuminated Vicente's face, and reached for his golden cross. She held it in her hand and closed her eyes. "I thought as much. You have met *her*. I was your first passion. The second of your great loves is both pearl and ruby, and she has replaced me in your heart of hearts."

"You can see her?"

"Yes. She is fair."

"Then you know who she is."

"No, not who." She opened her eyes, placed the candelabra on a side table, and let go of his cross. "Tell me about her."

"She is the worst possible choice."

"Is she the wife or daughter of some powerful *grandee*?"

"That would create no great problem."

"Then she is a nun."

"No, but she lives in a prison more confining than any convent."

"Love must carry you along until it runs its course. All say our Queen is beautiful. Is she the one?"

"She is not Queen Isabel."

"Then who?"

"The Infanta."

After Vicente praised María's beauty and character, Moraíma said, "Now I understand everything. Tonight, you too have been somewhere else, as if on a shelf and merely observing."

"Perhaps I was."

"I'm wearying of this life, Vicente. I don't know how much longer I can continue. My beauty is fading."

"Never."

"It happens to us all. Those wealthy *grandees, títulos,* and bishops who purchase my time and favors today will seek fresher flowers tomorrow. And how much longer can I avoid the inevitable *mal frances*?"

"I know medicines. I can help."

Her eyes filled with tears. "No, Vicente, you cannot help me. Nor Allah. I must find my own peace."

"I should have run off with you four years ago."

She flashed her most captivating smile. "What might have happened will always give me pleasant thoughts."

Chapter 17
First Confession

Vicente shivered and pulled the black hood of his cloak over his head when he stepped out of Olivares' office into the north corridor. As an icy December wind howled throughout the upper floors of the stone-chilled Alcazar, torches dimmed and smoked above the bearded Spanish Guards and German Halberdiers stationed at regular intervals.

During his free moments, Vicente had familiarized himself with every nook and cranny of the palace. On this floor, the King's and Queen's apartments overlooked their patios and gardens. From Olivares' apartments, a passage went along the north gallery to the King's suite.

Philip's quarters and the suite of Infante Carlos were on the western and southern side and had to be approached through a series of galleries, antechambers, and rooms of State, connected by narrow corridors and staircases. Some were spacious and well lit; others were small and dark. Magnificent tapestries and paintings by Europe's greatest artists covered the walls.

Vicente walked towards the royal chapel located between Their Majesties' suites and stopped when he saw movement behind a large century-old Flemish tapestry depicting Ulysses and Circe. It was one of many covered entrances to secret passageways.

"You are a most difficult man to find, Don Vicente." Hombrecillo stepped out from behind the tapestry. A wide-brimmed black hat with dark blue plumes shaded his eyes, and he had drawn his heavy black cape across his face as if he were a character in one of Lope de Vega's cloak-and-dagger plays.

"The Count de Olivares has given me much work to do."

"Yes, Satan never sleeps."

Before Hombrecillo could continue, a horde of *bufónes* burst out from behind doors and other tapestries. They made faces at the guards, kicked at chamber pots, and aped courtiers and clerics passing along the corridor.

Vicente had encountered these liveried dwarfs and midgets everywhere throughout the Alcazar. Among them were idiots and cretins, some misshapen with humps, clubfeet, or from grotesque hydrocephaly.

He had long ago observed that to be deformed was not unusual in Spain. Outbreaks of epidemics ran their courses unchecked despite efforts of physicians, witches' spells, and prayers of priests. Pox and infections of the teeth left many a once attractive face sunken or swollen with abscesses. Disease, inadequate diet, and poor birthing procedures left much of the population stunted, afflicted with goiter, crippling limb-twisting gout, swollen necks and limbs, lameness, and humped backs

Vicente felt sympathy for the palace *bufónes* who were collectively known as *Sabandijas del Conde*, Count-Lizards. Like Hombrecillo, they had been given pompous or ridiculous names: Duke of Bavaria, Don Juan of Austria, Little Tattletale, Simpleton, El Niño de Vacellas, Pumpkin Head, Candle Wick de Valladolid, Red Beard, and Geography. They lived in the palace as equals with the royal family, their principal duties to amuse them and relate gossip. Their malicious rumors were embellished and repeated by *meninas, duennas,* and courtiers, which stirred feuds and quarrels between the nobles who ridiculed and bullied them.

Sponsored by Sotomayor and Olivares, Vicente had become the *bufónes'* principal confessor. Because he ignored their deformities and treated them with respect, many had become his allies. He blessed the jesters until Hombrecillo shooed the last of them away.

His midget friend motioned for Vicente to bend so he could whisper. "The Infanta commands your presence immediately."

"Where is she?"

"In her apartments. Wait, Vicente." Hombrecillo pulled at his arm. "I will show you a secret passageway so that you will not excite envy and become the subject of malicious gossip."

"I have seen the original plans of the Alcazar in Olivares' office, and I memorized the location of concealed passageways and stairs leading to known and hidden rooms. One night during an exploration of my own and before I learned King Philip's schedule, I hid in the shadows when His Majesty hurried to Isabel's chambers. He carried a small lantern to see, and a small glass vase should he need to pee."

"A nice couplet to end your description, but select well the time you explore. His Majesty also uses those secret passages to go to the royal chapel unobserved and for surprise visits to his counselors."

Vicente entered the Infanta's *estrado* through a sliding wall panel. At the foot of her dais, she sat next to a burning brazier in one of two wooden armchairs and wore her customary black dress of mourning. Also in the room were her loyal and discreet principal *menina*, Margarita de Tavara, and Inéz, whom he had confessed earlier in the day. After her chaperones retired to the far side of the *estrudo*, she gestured for him to sit beside her. They had not spoken to each other since the day of his audience with her and the Queen.

"Don Vicente, I am told that Olivares works you relentlessly."

No imperial tone this day, her natural voice was velvety and sweet. "There is always much to be done for Spain, *Alteza*."

She opened her fan and fluttered it impatiently. "Has it been decided? Am I to be married to the heretic or not?"

"*Alteza*, His Majesty and the Count de Olivares doubt that the Pope will grant a dispensation for your marriage to the Prince of Wales."

"But if Prince Charles converts to our True Faith?"

"It may make a marriage more likely, but then both sides would have to agree to terms I believe neither can possibly accept."

"Then despite my father's last request and His Majesty's qualms, marriage plans with the English are moving ahead."

"Cautiously and most delicately, *Alteza*. Anything can set them back."

"I mistrust Olivares and dislike his hostility to women. In my presence, he had the effrontery to say that friars were to be kept for praying and women for childbearing." María rapped her fan on the arm of the chair. Her *menina* and Inéz brought them a small table and tray with cups of chocolate and water, then withdrew again to the far side of the room. "If I must go to England, I will need steadfast allies within my entourage, as energetic, intelligent, and dedicated to the True Faith as Tomás de Torquemada."

"If only such a man existed."

"I believe he may. Don Vicente, throughout the palace all admire your piety. I am well aware you have resisted temptations that have destroyed other men."

"I honor my vows."

"I know, and that pleases me." The Infanta placed her hand on his arm. "I wish to confess."

Vicente required all his self-control not to respond to the excitement of her touch. "But isn't Fray Rajosa . . ."

"He is ill with the grippe, as is half the palace." María moved her hand lower to touch the top of his. "You tremble. Are you cold?" Before Vicente could speak, she said to her *menina*, "Bring the other brazier closer to Don Vicente, and then withdraw. Now then, about my confession."

"I am certain that with a soul so perfectly formed and beautiful, so noble and pure as yours, *Alteza*, you have no sin to confess."

"You flatter me like any courtier."

"If I were a courtier, I would praise only your external virtues."

"And what are they?" She asked before thinking, then blushed.

Vicente was aware that his voice, proximity, and maleness had affected this inexperienced princess who, except for her brothers, had never been alone with any young man. He wanted to please her vanity and recite poetical praises of every aspect of her physical being. Instead, he said, "To speak of them, I would be guilty of lèse majesté. No, *Alteza*, I see your true virtues, your purity and piety."

"Then hear my confession, Don Vicente, for I am the greatest sinner in all of Spain."

"As you command, *Alteza*."

"I confess to Almighty God, to The Blessed Mary, to Our Merciful Savior . . ."

Vicente listened to her litany, less of sin and more the normal behavior of a fifteen-year old girl: Loss of temper with servants, disrespect to brothers and elders, and lack of interest in studies. He gave her the most minor of instructional penances, as she had expected.

"I further accuse myself of paying little attention to Rajosa's sermon last Sunday."

Neither had anyone else.

"I also confess I prayed to The Blessed Mary that he would become ill."

"*Alteza.*" Vicente pretended shock to avoid laughing.

"I assure you, Don Vicente, I wished him nothing serious, just enough discomfort so that you could replace him as my confessor."

"If you prayed to Blessed Mary, then it must indeed be Her will that Fray Rajosa became ill."

She thought about what he said. "You must be right. But most seriously, I accuse myself of the sin of envy."

"And who could the Infanta of Spain envy?"

"My brother, the King. I have never told anyone this. I wish I had been born the eldest son so I could be King of Spain." María's pale blue eyes misted as she gazed at an undefined horizon, and she squeezed Vicente's hand. "Oh, how I could accomplish great things for our Faith with you at my side as confessor and Inquisitor General."

He dared not turn his palm to hers. "A great queen can do the same. Isabella . . ."

"She was Queen of Castile in her own right."

"And one day, you shall be the wife of an emperor or a great monarch."

"To be merely a brood mare, a pawn in Olivares' great game of diplomacy, not a great queen. But, I promise you this, Don Vicente. Whomsoever I marry, to whatever strange lands I may have to travel, you shall come with me as my confessor."

"If I am so permitted, *Alteza.*" *Come live with me and be my love. An English thought for an English adventure.*

"If I so wish, then so it shall be." The Infanta removed her hand from his. "Don Vicente, you must penance me for my sin of envy."

He thought for a moment. "For the sin of envy, you will serve the less fortunate and make bandages of lint for hospitals during the next month."

"A proper penance, and I accept it." The Infanta covered her face with the fan and lowered her voice. "Don Vicente, I wish you were my confessor now. It is so easy for me to speak with you. There is no one else."

"*Alteza*, I am always your humble servant."

"I will send for you again. Soon."

"I await your summons."

She was not yet ready to dismiss him. "To whom do you confess, Don Vicente?"

"Fray Junipero, the *mayordomo* of the clergy dormitories."

"What sins can you possibly have to confess?"

More sin than anyone else in all Spain. None your tiny ears may hear.

"*Alteza*, I also lose my temper too quickly when I encounter so much sinning throughout the palace."

Despite a conventional piety and occasional guilty bursts of prudish behavior from the King, adultery was the norm at *la Corte*. Bastards were raised with legitimate children. The haughty wives of titled philanderers regarded their husbands' lovers and mistresses to be so inferior it was beneath their dignity to take offense.

Almost daily, during one confession or another, Vicente had received overt propositions from wives of *grandees* and *títulos*, *duennas* and *meninas* of the Queen. He suspected that Isabel had sent several of the latter to test him.

Although tempted, Vicente had avoided these transient potentially dangerous liaisons. Well schooled by Don Lope, whenever Moraíma was busy with her most generous clients, he chose only the cleanest girls at el Paraíso. *Mal frances* was epidemic at the Alcazar. A classic example was the Marqués de Hinajosa, whose face was so ravaged by the disease he needed a special cork device placed in his mouth for his speech to be understood. Rumors abounded that Olivares and Philip were similarly afflicted.

Because Vicente had resisted all temptations and was in so short a time reputed to be a charismatic preacher, he had earned a reputation for piety as well as eloquence throughout the Alcazar and in Madrid among the titled women he met through Ballebrera. His virtuous conduct at Court was not solely the result of willpower or fear of betrayal. No court lady had yet aroused the earthy passion he still felt for Moraíma; none could overcome his idealized pure love for the golden Infanta. In Orihuela during his most extreme fantasies, he had never thought he would be enamored of an unapproachable princess. He had composed poems to María, which he dared not write down.

"And, *Alteza*, there are the sacrilegious writings I must read to help fight the lies of heretics. We must know what they preach so that we may effectively combat them. Therefore, one of my duties is to examine materials placed on the Index."

"Have you been given dispensation?"

"The Count de Olivares has."

"The devil himself. Tell me, what books and writings are on the Index?"

"The lies of Jews and Protestants, blasphemers like Machiavelli, heretics like Erasmus."

"But you have broken no vows?"

"This evening, I confess to you that I have indeed broken my first vow."

Vicente regretted his theatrical pause when he saw the Infanta's face redden, an indication she imagined him sinning with some lady of the court and was about to lose her temper. He continued in a passionate whisper, "I have broken my vow of poverty, for I am the richest man in the world when I am in the presence of so immaculate a soul."

María seemed about to swoon, recovered, and waved her fan at him. "You are dismissed, Don Vicente."

"*Alteza*." He bowed and left through the secret passage.

Chapter 18
The Card Sharp

In the spring of 1622, a significant event lifted Vicente's spirits because he believed it brought Rafal a step closer to his coveted title. At the Monastery of San Jerónimo in a room crowded with the highest nobility of Spain, His Majesty spoke the words, "Count de Olivares be covered." Made a *grandee* first class and Duke of San Luçar, he would be addressed henceforth by the imposing title of Count-Duke.

That same day Moraíma sent for Vicente, and he entered her apartment in disguise as Algorfa. "What is this urgent matter you want to discuss? Is all well between you and His Majesty?"

"Last night I become his mistress."

But for how long? "My congratulations, and have you so informed your many admirers?"

"I have, and because I did not mention my Philip's name, they have assumed I chose you, as the Señor de Algorfa, to be my exclusive lover. I want to warn you that you have a dangerous rival, one who does not like to lose. The man you outbid for my affections, Rodrigo de Lograno has sworn to kill you."

"The diamond merchant? So that is why he has been glaring at me in the casino."

"Vicente, Lograno is no diamond merchant. He is reputed to be the most feared swordsman in Madrid."

"As every Don Nobody claims to be. Do not worry on my account. Vicente de Rocamora might, but this mythical Señor de Algorfa can never be provoked into accepting a challenge. He has no honor to defend."

When Vicente returned to the gambling salon, Yusef took his arm and led him to Ballebrera's table. "Your kinsman is losing at lansquet."

"How much?"

"At least a thousand escudos."

"He can't afford it."

Ballebrera's adversary wore a wig of flowing dark brown curls, a satin doublet of pastel blue festooned with ribbons and pearls. His companion seated beside him in beige and pink gloated and toyed with stacks of gold coins beside promissory notes. He was the same blond young man Vicente had seen mincing away from Ballebrera at el Paraíso.

"My friend, can you do something before we have unwanted theater?"

"Have your special decks of cards brought to the table."

"Consider it done."

Vicente watched Ballebrera sign another note worth a hundred escudos and push it to the center of the gilded glass table. "Don Ramón, haven't you had enough?"

"I can live with the financial loss, but not the eternal smirking of that witless twit, Miguel de Mendoza."

"Let me play for you."

"What?"

"I'll win back your losses and more."

"How can you be so sure?"

"Much of my education took place in the gambling dens of El Grau."

Ballebrera lost again. "Do as you wish. Dame Fortune has abandoned me this night."

"You are through, Señor?"

"I am."

The older man snapped his fingers, and the blond took Ballebrera's note from the table. Because the aristocrat would not condescend to touch his winnings, Vicente surmised he was an important *grandee*. He sat beside Ballebrera and said to him in a Castilian lisp, "I will play against you, my lord."

"Indeed? Then be advised, that I have plucked clean all the other chickens at my table."

"Now you shall face a more formidable cock." Vicente clapped his hands. "Fresh cards."

One of Yusef's men brought a silver tray containing a dozen sealed decks. The *grandee* selected blue cards for himself and threw a red pack at Vicente, who recognized the subtle markings on the backs.

Lansquet was a simple game. A player selected three cards from his own pack, placed them face down on the table, and bet on each in sequence. His opponent shuffled the second deck, turned over cards one at a time, and said as he made two alternating stacks: "My win, your win. My win, your win." The stack on which the selected card ended determined who won the bet. To sustain his winning streak, the *grandee* preferred to select the individual cards rather than deal from the second deck.

Vicente shuffled, dealt, and won the first wager of ten escudos. The *grandee* doubled his bet, lost a second time, and doubled again. When necessary, Vicente dealt himself seconds and thirds with the marked decks, and after eight plays he recouped Ballebrera's losses and a profit of several hundred escudos.

"Enough." The *grandee* stood and scowled at Vicente through heavy makeup. Unlike Ramón, he wore padding for false calf muscles. "I will inspect these cards."

With a flourish, Vicente swept the cards from the table and rose with his hand upon the hilt of his sword. "Do you presume to accuse me of cheating?"

The *grandee* ignored Vicente, "Miguelito, pick up those cards."

"How easily he assumes the position for his master," Ballebrera said.

The *grandee* glared at him and Mendoza reddened with anger. Yusef diverted them with apologies while Pablo replaced the marked decks with clean cards. In the confusion, they guided the two men to another table.

Ballebrera tore his promissory notes and secured the gold pieces in his doublet. "I am forever in your debt, Vicente."

"How did this farce begin?"

"The Count de Sagunto ordered me to stay away from Miguel de Mendoza. I had great difficulty convincing him that because the boy is a vacuity I no longer wanted his company. Instead of a duel with swords, we battled over cards."

They ambled towards the exit where Pablo and an armed escort waited for them. Vicente watched the *grandee* fondle young Mendoza. "Who is Sagunto?"

"An irrelevant presumptuous poetaster."

"I suspect your animosity has deeper roots than rivalry over Mendoza."

"You are perceptive, Vicente. It is a serious matter of honor going back several years. Because I repeatedly bested him in wit and repartee at the salons of great ladies, he let it be known to one and all that he would not attend any entertainment to which I had been invited."

"I'm surprised he didn't challenge you to a duel with weapons instead of cards."

"He considers it beneath his station to duel with a mere señor even though I am a Knight of Alcántara. Tonight he expected to ruin me at lansquet."

"He almost did."

"And once again I thank you for saving my honor and precious escudos." Ballebrera glanced one more time at Mendoza and sighed. "Such perfect classic features. So shallow a mind."

Vicente wished Ballebrera would be more cautious. His kinsman's appetite for fair ganymedes could very well cost him more than losses at the gaming tables.

"And how is the fair Hermosura?" Vicente repeated Moraíma's warning. "She is correct in her assessment. Avoid Rodrigo de Logroño y Arce at all costs. He is a Familiar of the Inquisition, a Knight of Santiago, and a *poderoso* who won a fortune in gold and diamonds during his soldiering in New Spain and Africa. Dominican inquisitors, are counted among his kin. One of them aspires to become Inquisitor General."

"So he is indeed a man of parts and well-connected."

"There is more. Logroño is considered *the* master of *la Destreza*, the Spanish Circle. He has never lost a duel and has written a text on its geometry so arcane only he understands it."

"As Algorfa, I cannot be insulted."

"He may provoke you beyond endurance. He is no Sagunto."

They heard a commotion, and Moraíma's servant ran into the casino screaming. Vicente hurried to her apartment where she was naked and struggling with Logroño. He seized the man by the shoulder, spun him around, and threw him against a wall. He drew his dagger, but Logroño recovered in time to hold him at bay with his rapier. Yusef and Pablo arrived with several housemen and intervened. Ballebrera also entered the crowded room and drew his sword.

Moraíma put on her robe. "Kill the swine. He was trying to rape me."

Vicente waved them back. "Let me dispose of him."

Logroño lowered his rapier. "Algorfa, you have placed your filthy hands upon my person. Because I am the offended party, I have choice of weapon, time, and place. It shall be swords tomorrow at daybreak in the Pardo Woods. There is a meadow near the ruins of Santa Monica."

"I know it, and there I shall settle matters with you."

Ballebrera shook his head. "Vicente, what have you done?"

19.
Circles of Death

That night in the Astórquia cellar, Ballebrera faced Vicente, each with drawn swords. "You say you know how to use a rapier, but with which style?"

"My father taught me some French and Italian basics before the Anglesolas murdered him, and an exiled Catholic English knight taught me the fine points of English dueling."

"You mean tavern and street brawling."

"A well placed chair, a thrown candelabrum, a knee in the groin, all that and more can be just as effective as a thrust to ensure survival."

"And the last time you drew a sword?"

"Yesterday during my weekly exercise with the Cardinal-Infante."

"Then you are fit."

"But I will concede that I have not used a sword to engage an enemy since the day I rescued Hombrecillo and Inéz."

"I assume you know something of *la Destreza*."

"Only what I've heard, although Don Lope did expose me to geometry."

"May God and San Euclid help you."

"I had a more realistic hope that you might."

"Which is why we are here. Let us begin your lesson although without years of practice, it may be inadequate. First, know that as a Familiar of the Inquisition, who has witnessed tortures, and as a veteran soldier, Logroño knows where to strike at your vital organs and cause severe injury or death."

"As I have also learned, thanks to Don Lope."

"Now do as I do. Assume *la diestra*. Offer me a semi-profile, which gives me the least amount of target to attack. Next, place your heels slightly apart and extend your rapier at arm's length with your tip pointed at the guard of my blade or at my eyes. That tip is the edge of your circle. I am doing the same. At my nod, we will circle each other clockwise. Now. When our circles overlap, that is when you attack, defend, or step back. No sidesteps, and as we circle, you can apply assorted feints and other body positions, occasionally stepping towards me. Traverse, attack, retreat. Good, you avoided my thrust. Tomorrow, remember to stay at the edge of Logroño's circle while discovering his weaknesses and exploiting them."

"What are his weaknesses?"

"Technically, he has none. Your only hope may be to enrage him. Let his emotions overwhelm his good sense, and he will try to do the same to you. Excellent, you are applying subtle twists of your wrist, elbow and shoulder to gain control of my blade."

"Which changes the angle of your attack."

"If you feel my blade through your own sword, you should be able to anticipate my next attack. Yes, well done. Let us stop for a moment so I can tell you more about Logroño . . . and regain my wind. He will try to break your concentration and attempt to instill fear."

"Then I shall appear as the ultimate master of insouciance to throw him off, or I may act clumsily, uncoordinated. He will not be certain if I am aggressive, cautious, talented, incompetent, or a dangerous unpredictable amateur. Nor will he know at first which school or academy of swordsmanship I favor."

"Have you one?"

"The Academy of El Grau. I intend to use every unfair trick I know. I refuse to sacrifice my life on a point of honor for a mythical Algorfa."

Ballebrera gestured for them to resume their circles and feinted towards Vicente's face. "Good reaction. Logroño typically begins his duels with the Spanish Kiss, a sudden thrust to split an opponent's nose or lip. At worst it can be lethal, at best painful and disabling accompanied by a heavy flow of blood."

"He means to kill me slowly if I read the man accurately."

"Even if Logroño attempts the Spanish Kiss and fails, it can make you less likely to risk a counter move. You may concentrate too much upon defending your face, thus risking a thrust to your vitals. Like so. Good, your reflexes are excellent, your stamina too, but you have so little experience, especially against a master."

"I am beginning to feel at home with *la diestra*."

"One last important point. I have heard that he has rows of blunts on both cutting edges of his rapier two palm widths from the tip of his sword, thus giving the effect of a serrated blade. A fatal thrust from an unblunted sword may yet allow one's adversary to make a successful equally fatal counter thrust before death takes him. A serrated blade can cause instant shock, which incapacitates the opponent."

"Then, Ramón, we have much work ahead of us this night."

Because Logroño was a Familiar, Vicente would not allow Ballebrera to second him and risk denunciation. Instead, he selected one of Yusef's most reliable lieutenants, a hardened *matone*. In blouse, breeches, and boots, he stood opposite Lograño and his coterie of a half dozen *caballeros* at a glade deep in the Pardo Woods at misty dawn. Two others had emerged from a carriage during the preliminary rituals, a physician from the Inquisition, and a Black Hood who took great care to memorize his face.

Vicente had selected from Ballebrera's collection a rapier with a filigreed Italian guard, which they had blunted along both edges, and he adapted the mien of one terrified to be facing a master swordsman. He noted that Lograño had an ideal duelist's build: Lean and sinewy, with arms and legs longer than typical for someone of his limited height suggesting a spider. The man's innate arrogance might be his only weakness.

Lograño's expression shifted from contempt to amusement when the duel began. He taunted Vicente with a series of feints at his face and vitals and laughed at his clumsy reactions.

Vicente backed away from Lograño's first serious Spanish Kiss and surprised him when he adapted to *la diestra* while avoiding a second thrust to his face.

"Stoat, as does la Hermosura, I too reject your repugnant kisses."

"And I shall arrange it, Algorfa, so that your lips can never mention her name again."

They circled each other, and Lograño called out with each failed thrust, "Coward, afraid to attack, not even counter-thrusting. Shall I first slice your nose, split your lips, and scar your face? Perhaps first, I shall remove both ears, and then your eyes and tongue as well. Which will you defend first? Which do you value most? No matter, in the end your whore will vomit at the sight of you."

"She already does whenever she is in the presence your porcine stench, Lograño."

"And after I alter your face, I shall geld you."

"Vain boasting from one who already squats to piss."

No reaction. Vicente did not let his own frustration show. Ballebrera had been correct. Lograño had no technical or mental weaknesses.

"Algorfa, I shall make you wish you had studied geometry when I traverse your circle and do as I wish."

How do I end this madness? Vicente knew that the slightest cut to his face or other usually exposed parts of his body would ensure that the Dominican Inquisitor would learn his identity. He recalled every wile and guile he had been taught in El Grau, but there were no tables, chairs, crockery, and candelabra to use in the glade. He had one trick he had never applied except when practicing alone as a boy. He had shown it to Ballebrera, who called it ungallant and indecent and then urged him to select the best moment to use it. A dishonorable move to be sure, but after this duel, dead or alive, the Señor de Algorfa would disappear for good.

With deliberate lack of grace, Vicente offered Logrraño an opening. *Now. And please forgive me, San Euclid.* Instead of backing away, he sidestepped Logrraño's next attack counter-clockwise and stumbled forward ungeometrically. At the same instant, he twisted his body, switched his rapier to his left hand and thrust perpendicular to Logrraño's exposed sword arm. He penetrated flesh above the guard and sliced upwards with his own serrated blade. Logrraño dropped his rapier and fell to the ground seriously wounded. The physician and his second hurried to him.

The Inquisitor pointed at Vicente. "Seize him."

Logrraño's men drew their swords. Vicente and the *matone* leaped onto their mounts as Yusef and his masked band rode into the glade shouting, firing pistols, and waving swords. They dispersed Logrraño's men and the Black Hood, stole their horses, and overturned the carriage. Deep in the woods, Vicente parted from the bandits and stepped into the Astórquia carriage where Ballebrera awaited him.

"Thank God you survived."

"And without a scratch."

"Is Logrraño dead?"

"Only if they let him bleed to death. He did not expect me to be ambidextrous. If he survives, he may never again use his sword arm. I believe I damaged the nerves."

"You will become a legend now."

"Alas, I must say farewell to Señor de Algorfa, Spain's greatest swordsman." He recalled the Black Hood who had memorized his face. "Now I have other more fearsome enemies."

Chapter 20
Inferno

Vicente wiped persistent sweat from his brow. He had heard Hombrecillo's confession in the royal chapel at the canonical hour of sext and suffered in woolen robes during his first summer in Madrid. The Alcazar's rooms and corridors were stifling. Outside, temperatures were high, and hot winds scorched the skin. Worse, he bathed all too infrequently at the Astórquia *Palacio*. Deliberately so. A Dominican must never appear to be washed and scented.

"In summer, the strongest man can die of this wind which cannot snuff out a candle-flame," Hombrecillo complained.

Vicente recalled an old Morisco proverb he chose not to voice: *When Allah created hell, He did not find it bad enough. So, He created Castile.*

They paused by a window overlooking the banks and dry bed of the Manzanares. The river provided fairgrounds during religious festivals, rustic walks, and picnic sites for the *madrileños*. When water did flow, women washed their laundry at the river, although, as was commonly said, their gossiping tongues worked harder than their hands.

"Quevedo is correct to call our Manzanares the Apprentice River," Hombrecillo said. "Truly its name is longer than its course."

Vicente repeated one of Ballebrera's favorite puns. "I've heard it said that the Manzanares is the river people call rio, I laugh, because it laughs when people try to swim in it and there is no water."

"Our poor river. Still, others say perfect joy is to live by the banks of the Manzanares, and the second degree of happiness is to be in paradise, provided one can see Madrid through a window in heaven."

Inéz came upon them. "Vicente, the Infanta commands your presence immediately."

He took leave of his friends and found María seated on a stone bench under the shade of great elms and poplars in her walled garden attended by an elderly *duenna*, her principal *menina*, and an ancient *marqués*. In the Madrid furnace of August heat, her color had not changed, nor was there any hint of perspiration on her face even though she wore a high-neck pale yellow and orange satin-trimmed velour guardinfante.

Olivares had said of the Infanta, "No amount of fire or heat could melt that monolithic block of ice."

She motioned with her yellow and orange fan for him to sit beside her. Insects buzzed around them. The scent of flowers was heady. Sweat oozed from every pore under his woolen robe and down his face.

How ungallant, how repugnant I must seem to her.

The Infanta, who had celebrated her sixteenth birthday, gestured for Inéz and her chaperones to withdraw out of hearing. "You suffer from the heat, Don Vicente?"

"It is my first summer in Madrid, *Alteza*. Surely the Lord is testing me so that my spirit may triumph over discomforts of the flesh."

"We have been thoughtless." She rapped her fan on the bench, and her *menina* brought them iced almond water.

Vicente thanked the Infanta for the luxury. Ice and snow were important enough to be a city monopoly and used more for cooling drinks and sherbets than keeping foodstuffs fresh. In winter, snow was taken from the sierras about seventy-five miles from the capital and deposited in special pits to preserve it until summer.

"Are these months milder in Valencia?"

"No, *Alteza*, our summers are as hot, perhaps worse because of the high humidity." He dared not tell her they were more bearable because as a boy he swam in the Gulf of Valencia at will and had yet to wear the woolen robes of a stinking friar. "But there is a delicious fragrance in the air, and at night, the perfumed scent of flowers wafts in the gentle breeze."

"Tell me more about Valencia."

The Infanta closed her eyes while Vicente spoke of tall palm groves, scented terraced gardens, orchards of succulent fruit, fields of rice and plump melons, the clear turquoise sea, and vivid sails of great ships emerging from the horizon.

He saw a tear form in the corner of her eye. "*Alteza*, is something wrong?"

"You always move me with your words, Don Vicente, when you preach, and now when you paint your word pictures. If you did not have the calling, I believe you would have been a successful poet."

Vicente clenched his jaw to prevent himself from reciting one of his unwritten poems that revealed all he felt for her. In any case, she would not have heard him. María winced at a stab of pain and dismissed him.

Upon leaving the garden, Vicente reflected upon what was known as the Curse of Eve. Some were affected more than others. One might have to lie in bed for days, while another could work in the fields. A few became shrewish, fiendish in temper, and made life miserable for all.

The Infanta might be experiencing her first cycle of the Moon. He had confessed young girls in Orihuela and here in Madrid on such occasions. Throughout Spain, common practice was for the maidens to seek absolution from their confessors when their first bleeding surprised them. They wanted to know what sins they had committed to warrant God's punishment. Most confessors recited Eve's original sin. A few took the opportunity to seduce those naive, inexperienced girls. Vicente explained matters as best he could in Don Lope's empirical terms: Each month, the mature female body cleansed itself of impurities to prepare itself for conception.

He suspected the Infanta's cycle had not yet stabilized. All the Royal siblings were late maturers. Anne's wedding to Louis XIII had to be delayed, and Philip, although wed at age ten did not cohabit with Isabel until he was fifteen. At that same age, Carlos had just begun to revel in Court vices, and fourteen-year old Fernándo was still a boy who wanted to play soldier.

This might indeed be the year my sixteen-year old princess blooms into womanhood.

Chapter 21
"Our Torquemada"

Vicente finished penancing Sotomayor in the royal chapel after the old man had confessed the sin of envy, and they walked together toOlivares' suite of offices. At age sixty-seven, Philip's confessor had aspired to replace the recently deceased Luís de Aliaga as Inquisitor General. Instead, the King had approved Olivares' selection of Andrés de Pacheco who agreed with the Count-Duke's policy of hounding homosexuals, *alumbrados*, and sorcerers ahead of new-Christians.

Vicente believed that Sotomayor also would have been a good choice. The fair-minded Dominican had opposed the expulsion of sincere Christian Moriscos, and he agreed with Olivares' goal never to use the *limpieza* to persecute or limit opportunities for devout new-Christians.

Because Olivares was in a good mood and his clerical ally Sotomayor was present, Vicente took the opportunity to advance himself in María's entourage. "Excellency, the Infanta wants me to be her confessor and spiritual director."

Olivares turned to Sotomayor. "Do you know of this?"

"Yes, her Highness has more than once made her wishes known to me."

"What about Rajosa?"

"He is feeble," Vicente said, "often ill and unable to conduct mass or hear confessions."

Olivares frowned and twisted the end of his mustachio while he considered what Vicente had said. "Very well, confess the Infanta when Rajosa is indisposed, or when she requests you. But understand this. First and foremost you serve me . . . and, of course, His Majesty."

"Always, Excellency."

Shortly before Christmas, marriage negotiations between Spain and England intensified, and the Infanta became more dependent upon Vicente to confess and advise her. Instead of singing songs of the Nativity with him and her ladies this day, she set her formidable jaw.

"Don Vicente, put away your guitar. There are serious matters we must discuss with you."

"As you command, *Alteza*."

"We know that Spain's previous English marriages have been dismal failures. Ferdinand and Isabella the Catholic's younger daughter, Catherine of Aragón, married Henry VIII. Their divorce led to the founding of that abomination, the heretical Church of England. My grandfather, Philip II, married Mary Tudor, daughter of Catherine and Henry VIII, and might have made England permanently Catholic if she had given birth to an heir before she died. Now, His Majesty's advisors would deliver us into the hands of a heretic."

"*Alteza*, I believe it will never happen."

"Anything is possible when Satan intrigues. We might agree to the marriage if Prince Charles converts to Catholicism. Should we marry, we shall not go to England with an entourage of gossipy ladies and feeble elderly clerics. If God destines us to be Princess of Wales and then Queen of England, so be it, but we shall never be a victim like Catherine of Aragón or a failure like Mary Tudor. We shall be no less than our ideal queen, Isabella the Catholic, who conquered Granada, expelled all Jews from Spain, and used the Inquisition to ferret out heretics and blasphemers. We would rule England with an iron hand and wage our own *reconquista* against the Protestants. If we must go to England, let us accomplish what our armada failed to do, and you shall accompany us. You shall be our Torquemada."

"I shall be whatever you wish, *Alteza*."

He kneeled to pray behind the Infanta but thought only about the probable outcome of the marriage negotiations. England wanted the Palatinate, which Spain would never surrender; the Spanish would demand at the very least tolerance for Catholics in England, which the militant Protestant Parliament would not accept. Unless one side yielded to the other, the marriage would never take place.

God help the English if it did and María had her way.

Chapter 22
Ruff Trade

"It's good to be back in Madrid." Ballebrera sat beside Vicente in twin armchairs by a brazier in the sitting room of the Astórquia *Palacio*. He had returned from escorting the Duchess of Astórquia to her estates in Vizcaya, during which time her only surviving relation, a nephew, had passed away. Blankets covered their laps, and strong brandy warmed their innards. Tonight they were free to talk without interruption because Xímena had fallen asleep exhausted.

"Vicente, have you brought the matter of Jerónimo's title to Olivares' attention?"

"On more than a few occasions, but I have had no response. A pity we are not related. Although the Count-Duke runs the government *mano limpio*, he continues to apply the well-established tradition of nepotism to solidify his position. Kin and in-laws fill many of the choicest posts of the realm."

"Perhaps we ought to have a forgery created which would prove consanguinity with the Guzmánes."

"That would be something. Although Olivares is self-sacrificing for his King and country, he collects honors the way greedy men accumulate wealth. That is why he wears on his doublet the golden key of the Sumiller de Corps, Groom of the Stole, which identifies him as the highest ranking member of the royal household, and around his ankles the golden spurs proclaiming him Master of the Horse."

"As if the title Count-Duke is not enough."

"It is not enough because he regularly complains that his grandfather was denied the Dukedom of Medina-Sidonia. Now, Ramón, listen to me. Olivares intends to make life easier for his Portuguese financiers of suspect ancestry. As part of his plan, he has influenced *la Suprema* to direct the main investigations of the Inquisition away from new-Christians and concentrate on sorcerers, illuminati, and most especially homosexual behavior. As you know, one pebble of a denunciation to the Inquisition can ripple out until there is a tidal wave of arrests."

"Have no fears on my account. I am a cautious man."

"Caution may not be enough. Your vapid young friend Mendoza . . ."

"I told you. I spent only one evening with that twit, and he bored me silly."

"You would be well advised to avoid all such epicenes."

"Vicente, you know I am addicted to beauty, female or male, child or adult." Ballebrera sighed. "So perfect a profile. Mendoza might have posed for any statue of a Greek or Roman god. If only he had their personality and depth."

Vicente said no more on the subject. He expected his warning to go unheeded.

Ballebrera raised his glass of brandy. "Anyway, I have a more important matter to consider. Because Xímena is without an heir, I intend to court her after a respectable period of mourning."

Vicente gaped at him. "Why, she is at least seventy."

"Eighty-one, to be precise. Should she die without naming an heir, His Majesty will sell the Astórquia title and lands to a favorite. If we marry, by legal right I would become Duke of Astórquia and a *grandee* first class."

Vicente touched glasses with Ballebrera. "Then to your success, for that will free me from my oath to Rafal, who would inherit your title or one of his sons."

"I perfer to make you my heir if it is at all possible."

"Ahead of Rafal and Don Francisco?"

"I dislike the thought of Jerónimo's eldest depraved lump of excrement Jacinto prospering from my hard work after he dies. Now, tell me the latest gossip from the palace. And what are Jerónimo's prospects for a title of his own?"

"Olivares and the King are too busy reforming Spain to honor my requests on his behalf. I regret to tell you that glory without escudos is hollow glory indeed. My best efforts seem to have no effect on the matter. Jerónimo must come to Madrid and petition for himself."

"I agree, but my cousin has always been a poor courtier." Ballebrera touched his elaborate ruff. "Is it true Olivares has abolished the *leguichilla*?"

"Yes, and King Philip has already ordered collars made for himself and Infante Carlos."

"But why?"

Although he was often uncomfortable in his unwashed wool robe, Vicente thought himself fortunate as a friar that he never had to wear the ridiculous wide and stiff Spanish collar of fine linen adorned with lace known as the *leguichilla*. Some like Ballebrera's fanned far out over the shoulders. The ruff makers created its round shape by using several layers of linen pleated like a fan. In order to keep the *leguichilla* rigid, they inserted a metal frame between each pleat to support, stretch, and stiffen the material, which was then starched. Vicente had heard Olivares complain that the exaggerated ruff caused young men of intelligence and strength to be forever occupied ironing and fluting them.

"Surely, Ramon, you will agree it is the most extravagant article of male dress ever conceived. A single ruff of white linen can cost more than two hundred reales, and another six reales every time it is dressed. By the end of the year, its cost has been doubled by upkeep."

"If a man can afford it . . ."

"No matter."

"No ruff? Is Spain to become a nation of dour Calvinists? What then are we to wear?"

"Something called the *golilla*. A Madrid tailor has created a spread collar of cardboard covered with white or gray silk on the inner surface, and on the outside with dark cloth to match the doublet. By means of heated iron rollers and shellac, the cardboard collar can be molded into a curve, then bent outwards at the height of the chin to expose a surface of light colored silk. No washing or starching is necessary. It can last one year without further expenses. From now on, all men of Spain, Spanish Italy, the Spanish Netherlands, and the Indies will wear the *golilla*."

"What is the world coming to?"

"There is more. King Philip and Olivares have issued their edicts and injunctions against clothes embroidered with gold and silver thread as well as the use of silk in men's apparel. His Majesty has set an example by eliminating vivid colors from his own wardrobe. As in the days of Philip II, one cannot appear at Court unless he is dressed in black. Men of quality are permitted to wear a felt hat with a large brim and multi-colored plumes. Add a huge somber cape, and this new style is a perfect costume for amorous adventures, or camouflage for penury."

Ballebrera grimaced. "All in black."

"Do you really prefer those feminine pale shades favored by the French. Leaf-color, sea-green, lawn-green, laughing-monkey, kiss-me-my-love, wasted-time, and mortal-sin?"

"I do. Life should be theater not funereal. And what terrors lie in store for our women?"

"Stronger cages of iron and bone and more petticoats. Whatever protects their virtue most."

"Fashion as an important Matter of State." Ballebrera sighed and poured more brandy. "Now then, have you any delicious *murmuraciónes* for me?"

"Moraíma is exclusively Philip's mistress."

"If she gains influence over His Majesty, she may help you win a title for Jerónimo."

Vicente did not reply. He worried for Moraíma. Philip was incapable of being loyal to any woman, and he believed the stories about the King's former lovers having their newborn infants taken away and both disappearing forever behind the walls of convents. To lose her child and be forced into a nunnery would be no less than a death sentence for the vivacious *morilla*.

Chapter 23
Serious Questions

Only bad news.

Vicente read a sealed message from Don Lope, cursed loudly, and held a candle flame to its edge. The *polidor* had yet to discover any information about his mother's family in Valencia, Catalonia, and Roussillon. He also made it clear that the time was not yet propitious in Valencia for him to return and claim his daughter. Nor was it here in Madrid where he had become a prisoner of two demanding personalities. Olivares and the imperious Infanta summoned him regularly, each wanting to know the activities and thoughts of the other. Until he could get away from Madrid, vengeance would be delayed, and the matter of his mother's ancestry would remain a mystery to be exploited by his enemies and rivals.

How best to maneuver a title for Rafal and be done with it all?

He had yet to get the ear of His Majesty. Perhaps he could accomplish it through Moraíma if Philip became besotted with her. Otherwise, Olivares was his main hope. Vicente had drafted a cogent argument reasoning why Rafal deserved a title. The Count-Duke had replied he would consider the matter in due course.

Vicente returned to his duties encrypting messages for Olivares' spies. Other clerks were organizing reports coming in from all over the peninsula in response to the reforms and pragmatics of the *Junta Grande*. The nobles and King's ministers resented the Count-Duke's decrees reducing the size of their entourages at Court. Some had formed an opposition party supported by the Queen; others had withdrawn from Court to sulk at their provincial estates

He could not fault Olivares for trying to achieve so much. The Count-Duke sought tax reform. An end to price-fixing and debasing of the coinage. An inquiry into all ministerial fortunes acquired since 1603. And most difficult of all, to end the sale of offices and to control the enormous venal and powerful bureaucracy of all Spain from Madrid.

Along with forbidden excesses of dress, Olivares placed strict prohibitions on luxury imports and tried to control every aspect of Spanish life. The Count-Duke even regulated the use of chamber pots. They could no longer be thrown at will from windows or balconies; they were to be emptied only through the street door after ten at night in winter and eleven in summer. Violators faced severe punishments: Four years exile for the householder, six years exile and whippings for servants. He also enacted two measures to increase the population. For families too poor to marry off their daughters, he limited the size of dowries, and he decreed that all brothels were to be closed. Vicente had already alerted Yusef.

Olivares rushed into the office with documents stuck in his plumed hat and more bulging from the pockets of his doublet. He scanned the discouraging reports. In a rage, he sent his clerks scurrying in all directions except Vicente. "Has another package arrived for me from Valencia?"

Vicente produced a volume he had hidden under the piles of papers. "Yes, Excellency, a unique illustrated edition of Bocaccio's *Decameron*."

Olivares opened it to a page at random, read a story, and burst out laughing. "Featherless nightingale indeed." He closed the book and turned to his wall map of Europe. "Friar, you see the Infanta almost daily now. Tell me what she says about marrying the Prince of Wales."

"She fears damnation if she must share her bed with a heretic."

"Does anything really frighten that little dragon?"

"She is pious . . ."

"Yes, yes, I know. But if Rome gives dispensation for the marriage?"

"If it is to be, she is resigned to her martyrdom."

"Well, it may not take place after all. The Prince of Wales and his father's favorite, George Villiers, are visiting the French court for an alliance or, perhaps, to arrange a marriage with thirteen year old Henrietta María, Queen Isabel's younger sister." He scanned another batch of reports. "Friar, tell me your personal views regarding the *limpieza de sangre*."

Vicente had prepared himself to answer that inevitable question after wealthy Portuguese new-Christians offered to finance the cash-strapped Crown in return for concessions. Olivares devised several moderate proposals, two of which King Philip approved: No longer would anonymous denunciations be acceptable, and cases that had been closed could not be reopened for unscrupulous purposes. For personal reasons, Olivares supported a petition from the City Council of Valladolid that would have prevented investigations into family origins from going beyond one's grandparents. In this last matter, His Majesty sided with reactionary Castilians and vetoed the reform.

"Excellency, Spain needs the services of its best men. I have always believed that one should be judged by his abilities, not by blood. Because of the *limpieza*, the Crown is losing the potential services of its most valuable subjects. On the other hand, if anyone is proven to be a Judaizer..."

"Then, you will do all I ask of you if it leads to the abolition of the *limpieza* statutes?"

"Enthusiastically."

Olivares studied Vicente's features. "Perhaps too enthusiastically? Perhaps despite your certificate of *limpieza*, you may be tainted?"

Vicente gripped his silver crucifix. "Although I am *limpio*, I am no different from any other Spaniard who fears denunciation without proof, who fears interrogation, even torture, by the Inquisition as if the charges were true. More than anything else, the test of *limpieza* has harmed Spain. It encourages perjury, bribery, and slander for base motives. It denies talented men the privilege of serving the Crown, Church, and the military."

Vicente did not add how it also led to selective hypocrisy. His Majesty had raised Olivares who was known to have Jewish antecedents, to the highest position in the land. Both King Philip and the Infanta wanted the one-quarter new-Christian Teresa of Avila to be canonized and made Patron Saint of all Spain above Santiago.

"Go on, Friar. I find what you have to say most interesting."

"The law prohibiting honors to new-Christians is unjust and impious. It is against divine law, natural law, and the law of nations. Without crime, without sin or offense against God, they are condemned without being heard, and without the *possibility* of being heard... even when they excel all others in virtue, sanctity, and scholarship. In no other government or state in all the world do such laws exist."

"Excellent, I could not have expressed it better. Write down all you have said. It will make a most convincing argument when I bring this matter before the royal council." Olivares' eyes narrowed. "Now, tell me your views on the Inquisition."

The Count-Duke was leading him to dangerous ground. "Fray António de Sotomayor has suggested that I consider entering the Holy Office after I have had more experience."

Olivares twisted his mustachio. "Perhaps you should."

"Ah, midnight and you are still working." The Count de Gondomar, Ambassador to England, entered and greeted the Count-Duke with an outrageous smirk.

Olivares could not resist teasing the Anglophile. "You look as if you have brought me the King of England."

"If not the King, at least I have the Prince of Wales."

Chapter 24
A Royal Comedia Begins

Vicente had to wait until after lauds before he could tell María that Prince Charles and George Villiers had arrived in Madrid. "According to Gondomar, they traveled from France wearing false beards, calling themselves Tom Smith and John Smith, and escorted by one knight and a few attendants. The rest of their vast entourage is following."

She listened in icy silence until he finished. "Does Her Majesty know?"

"I cannot say, *Alteza*."

"The Queen must be told. Doña Inéz, go at once to inform Her Majesty. Don Vicente, if Prince Charles has risked a journey to Spain, it means he *is* willing to convert in order to marry me. For what other reason would he have come?"

"The Count-Duke believes there is no other reason."

"But what if a dispensation from Rome allows me to marry the English Prince even if he does not accept our True Faith?" María shuddered. "I shall never bear the children of a heretic. Never. Don Vicente, how do we prevent this marriage if he does not convert?"

He had given the matter much thought and began the opening act. "You can establish a mood, create a chilly atmosphere, *Alteza*. His Majesty respects your strength. And, I believe he would never force an unwanted marriage upon you."

"And Satan?"

"The Count-Duke dislikes dealing with strong women. He will not disagree with you openly, but behind your back . . . who can say? In the meantime, Her Majesty will be your staunchest ally."

"What is our first move?"

"Send for Fray Rajosa."

"Of what use can he be?"

"*Alteza*, Fray Rajosa will truly fear for your soul. If you perform convincingly, he will be an admirable witness to your distress. And, he is an incorrigible *murmurador*."

"I appreciate the way you think. Go to him."

Vicente left to tell Rajosa that the Prince of Wales had arrived to court the Infanta. As he expected, her confessor was appalled at the presence of heretics in Madrid and horrified they might set foot in the Alcazar.

When Vicente returned to her apartments with Rajosa, María was in her oratory praying at her prie-Dieu. "Holy fathers, help me. What shall I do?"

Vicente loomed over her, a hooded specter, his tone doom-shrouded. "Remember what life with a Protestant will be like, sharing your bed with a heretic..."

The Infanta let out a cry and implored the Blessed Virgin to intercede for her. Tears came to Rajosa's eyes, and he kneeled to pray with her.

Vicente intensified the imagery of his preaching. "The children you bear, they will be exposed to the Protestant heresy. They will be forever tainted by the blood of heretics. They will face the unspeakable agonies of eternal fire, the worst torments of hell."

He embellished those punishments from his memory of Dante's *Inferno* and from what he had heard about tortures in the Inquisition's dungeons. He punctuated his final sentence of eternal agony and doom with a blow from the edge of his hand that splintered a nearby table.

Rajosa cried out and gaped at Vicente.

María flushed and almost fainted. She gripped her prie-Dieu, recovered, and prayed aloud: "Thank you, Blessed Mary, for giving Don Vicente the strength of a Samson to carry out Your Divine Will on our behalf."

The Count-Duke discussed the Prince's surprise visit with the Council of State, his personal advisors, and a few trusted secretaries in his office before meeting with Prince Charles and Villiers.

Afterwards, Vicente reported in secret to both the Infanta and the Queen. He described all he had witnessed and heard, and he embellished the meeting between Olivares and the Prince of Wales for Isabel because he knew that she would never forgive the *privado's* open contempt for her, his dominance of Philip, and orchestration of her husband's sexual adventures. He soon had both Queen and Infanta laughing with his description of how the Count-Duke, upon meeting Charles, fell to his knees, kissed the Prince's hands, and hugged the young man's thighs.

"How His Majesty's arrogant favorite grovels before royalty," Isabel gloated.

Vicente next repeated what he had heard from spies placed within the divided English household. "King James' ambassador, the Earl of Bristol, is appalled by the Prince's unexpected arrival and outraged because Villiers announced that he would take charge of the marriage negotiations."

"Is that a good thing?"

"Your Majesty, Villiers is said to be a hothead and likely to shatter the delicate framework of the negotiations." Vicente turned to María. "*Alteza*, tomorrow you and Prince Charles are to see each other for the first time."

"So we have been told. What have you learned about him? What of his character? What of his appearance?"

"I have yet to see his Royal Highness, but this is what I know about the Prince of Wales. He turned twenty-two on the eleventh of November last. He is said to be short for an Englishman, clean shaven without mustachio and beard. Everyone agrees he is very handsome."

"We shall be the judge of that," the Infanta said. "Continue, Don Vicente."

"The Prince of Wales is difficult to understand because he stutters and speaks English with a Scottish accent. That particular disability gives him a natural lisp, which might allow him to speak Castilian Spanish more easily. Our spies also report that he is shy, somewhat delicate of constitution, with a great interest in paintings."

"Then he will get on well with His Majesty. Olivares is educating my husband in the arts and in everything else except kingship."

Vicente next described Charles' amateur passion for the theater. "It is said he loves Shakespeare more than the Bible."

María cried out in horror, "More than the Word of God? The typical blasphemy of a heretic."

"Perhaps, *Alteza*, but it gives us an understanding of his thinking. I would not be surprised if he attempted to court you personally and climb the wall to your balcony some evening, as in Shakespeare's play, *Romeo and Juliet*."

"Romeo and Juliet?" Isabel repeated

Vicente enthralled them with the story of Montagu and Capulet, and when he came to the famous balcony scene, he recited verbatim in a passionate whisper all he had come to feel for the Infanta.

María's fan fluttered more rapidly than a hummingbird's wings. "And how does the play end?"

"A tragic double suicide, which reconciles the two families."

The Infanta crossed herself. "Suicide is a mortal sin."

"It is a cautionary tale, *Alteza*."

"Even if what you say is true, I believe it should belong on the Index. Promise me, Don Vicente, that you will not permit such writing to corrupt you."

"Never, *Alteza*."

But perhaps it may awaken you.

"Tell us more, if you can, about this prince we are supposed to marry."

"Of course, *Alteza*. He is said to be conscientious, slow of mind, stubborn, and intolerant of others' frailties. To his credit, he is still chaste. All sources agree on one point. He is dependent upon his father's favorite, George Villiers."

Isabel giggled and whispered to María, who blushed before she could raise her fan, then faced Vicente again. "Is what they say true about King James' favorite?"

He would not repeat rumors about the Englishman's reputed endowment, nor the current gossip that he had seduced María's sister, Queen Anne of France. "I can tell you what I do know. Friend and foe describe Villiers as a handsome physical specimen. By reputation, he is perhaps the best dancer, leaper, and horseman in all Europe."

Isabel frowned into her fan. "Surely the man has flaws."

"I have seen reports describing him as one used to having his way, given to intemperate speech, with an eye for the ladies. If it is true that Villiers is impatient and hot-tempered, then he is the ideal amateur diplomat to ruin the marriage negotiations in our land of slow measure and *punctilio*."

"We care not about Villiers." The Infanta turned to the Queen. "Our only concern is how best to deal with Prince Charles."

Vicente set another component of his plan into motion "You can bury the English in our Court ritual and ensure that you are unapproachable."

María pointed her fan at Vicente. "Exactly who favors the marriage?"

"Gondomar, Prince Charles, and King James, the latter only if he can recover the Rhenish Palatinate for his son-in-law."

"And Olivares?"

"He prefers to draw out the negotiations. I would not presume to know his end game."

Isabel laughed again, her expression mischievous. "Then we are to become actors in a grand *comedia*. How exciting."

Vicente knew how much Isabel enjoyed watching plays. Every Sunday and Thursday evening during winter, and on holidays, professional actors performed comedies in her private theater. During the season of 1622-23, the Queen had spent almost fourteen thousand reales for forty-three plays.

What title might a playwright create for this royal comedy about to unfold?

The following day, Vicente relied on *murmuraciónes* to learn what was happening. Olivares had planned an accidental meeting between the Infanta and Prince Charles in the Prado. For reasons of diplomacy, it took place in full view of the Papal Nuncio and ambassadors from France and the Empire. Prince Charles waited in Bristol's *invisible* coach while the royal family on their way to church passed by him in their open carriages of state. María sat in the boot of the Queen's carriage behind the Cardinal-Infante. So that Charles could identify her, a blue ribbon had been tied to her wrist.

The Prince of Wales fell in love at first sight. He left his coach, approached the Infanta, and presumed to speak to her. María's face flushed in anger at his monumental breach of Spanish protocol, then turned livid as she regained her self-control. Bristol, who had followed Prince Charles as his interpreter, intervened and led the confused young man back to the coach.

As the royal family continued on to church, Olivares drew his cloak over his face and got inside the Prince's coach. Later in the day he related to his inner circle their conversation. Vicente would never tell María that the inexperienced young suitor had misinterpreted her indignant reaction as a maidenly blush and a natural sign of affection for him, nor would he repeat what Olivares said to the Prince: "If the Pope refuses to give dispensation for a wife, I'll give you the Infanta as a wench."

Vicente appreciated the setting for the Royal *comedia*. Each day, drumbeats and heralds proclaimed the welcome news that Olivares had suspended his reforms and sumptuary laws for the duration of the Prince's visit. Streets were to be repaved and houses painted. Nobles and *poderoso*s could again flaunt their wealth and richest garments, except for the replacement of the ruff by the *golilla*. To the delight of the courtiers and their ladies, ostentatious extravagance returned to the Alcazar. King Philip summoned *grandees* and *títulos* from all parts of Spain to entertain Charles with banquets, tourneys, processions, bullfights, and masked balls.

Heavy rains throughout the week cleansed the streets of filth accumulated during the winter. Most amazing and to the delight of the populace, the Manzanares filled with water. And as Vicente had anticipated, the Prince of Wales sank into the Spanish quicksand of court ritual, etiquette, and relentless diversions.

During the celebrations, the clergy debated and argued how best to deal with a royal heretic in their midst. Vicente suggested to Sotomayor and *la Suprema* that they first should convert Charles, Villiers, and their entourage to the True Faith.

Every style of flamboyant poetry and improvised songs celebrated Charles' arrival and passed from mouth-to-mouth. Throughout the city, men and women sang lines written by Lope de Vega for the occasion and said to be translated by Charles himself into English:

Carlos Estuardo soy,	Charles Stuart am I
Que, siendo amor mi guia,	Love guides me afar
Al cielo de España voy,	Into the Spanish sky I go,
Por ver mi estrella María.	To seek María, my star.

Vicente wrote his own poem of love, titled *Alteza*, and circulated it anonymously throughout the *mentideros* where it was well received:

> Bind thy silken favor 'round my wrist,
> Whilst I gird for knightly contest in the lists
> To joust and conquer Language;
> Thus, with metaphoric courage
> I fulfill sweet Ardor's duty
> And proclaim the perfection of thy Beauty.

Vicente and the Infanta watched through a window the Prince of Wales' arrival at the Alcazar. Musicians led the procession playing drums, fifes, and horns followed by civil functionaries in orange satin spangled with silver. The festive crowd cheered the colorful Spanish and German guards. Behind them riding two-by-two came the Infantes Carlos and Fernándo and assorted nobles and courtiers with their heralds and pages, each adorned in dazzling satin and velours of vivid colors trimmed with gold or silver. The sound of their spurs rang throughout as they put on a show with the most beautiful horses of Andalusia. Philip and Charles rode their mounts under a canopy of white and gold damask supported on silver pikes by six officers of the Guards. Also on horseback, Olivares and Villiers followed the royals with an escort of the leading *grandees* of Spain and English officers; and after them came the Knights of Santiago, Calatrava, and Alcántara, who displayed the crosses of their Orders on their *hábitos*.

"His Highness is a fine looking young man, *Alteza*," Vicente said hoping to learn her true impressions of Charles.

"But he is still a heretic. Knowledge of that abomination is always foremost in our mind, and tomorrow we must be seen at a disgusting spectacle. We confess, Don Vicente, unlike Queen Isabel who is an *aficionada*, we detest bullfights. It is a waste for men to risk death without a great objective, such as a *reconquista*."

Vicente noted that the Infanta used the royal plural because too many courtiers and ladies were within hearing. "They do it to achieve honor, which, for all Spaniards is the greatest objective of all."

"You have proven our point. Shallow honor is no honor at all."

"You are wise beyond your years, *Alteza*."

"You think so?" She turned from the window and proceeded to her apartments with Vicente at her side and her entourage behind. "There are times when we do not know what to do. Shall we be flattered or offended by that poem Lope de Vega wrote for the Prince of Wales?"

"I believe it was written with sincerity."

"Poets are clever with words, but do they have sincerity of heart?"

"Poets yes, but never the poetasters, *Alteza*. That is why the greatest endure over the ages."

Has she read my poem? Is this where our conversation is leading?

The Infanta said no more until after they sat facing each other in her *estrado* drinking flavored water. "Don Vicente, we are offended that so many poets have presumed to use our name in their poems and circulated them throughout the city."

"The populace adores you, and all *madrileños* love a good romantic tale."

"But to be wooed in public?"

"For reasons of state, *Alteza*, as you well know."

Her good humor returned. She beckoned her *menina*. "Give the poems to Don Vicente. He will read them aloud so we may judge their quality and sincerity. If any has crossed the line of propriety, we shall consign the offenders to the deepest dungeon in Spain."

She is playing with me.

"And should there be a winner, *Alteza*, what shall be his reward, a laurel crown?"

"It should suffice that we spare him. That he receives no punishment shall be reward enough. Now then, our eloquent preacher and confessor, let us hear what they have written."

By the time Vicente had read aloud and discarded the first four poems, María and her entourage were laughing at the bombastic efforts. "They love their words more than they love me," she said from behind her fan. "I have a better punishment than the dungeon. They should be made to marry their poems in front of the entire population of Madrid. Read on, Don Vicente."

The next was his, and after he finished, the Infanta did not laugh or exhibit anger as he had feared. During a long silence, he worried, *Did I read with too much feeling? Does she know? Has she already heard or read my poem and suspects I am its author?*

"What did you think of this poem, Don Vicente?"

"By far the best of them all, in my humble opinion. Is it the dungeon or the sacrament of marriage to his verse for the poet?"

"Ah, yes, the poet. We wonder who he is and if we can find out."

"Alas, it is anonymous, *Alteza*."

"Perhaps," she said coyly from behind her fan with all the practice of a *tapada* beauty, a woman who covered her face with a veil except for a flirtatious eye. "I have my suspicions though . . . that I would not have to look very far to find my eloquent admirer if I so choose."

She knows and approves.

Chapter 25
Reluctant Farewell

Although Vicente had little free time between attending the Infanta and carrying out his extensive duties for Olivares, he managed to get away one afternoon and meet with his friends at el Paraíso, which had survived Olivares' reforms and was doing more business than before because of the extra influx into the city of nobles and people with money.

Pablo gave him the latest news from Valencia. "Although Violante is leading an immoral life, she is a good mother and very protective of your daughter, Brianda. I regret to report that Don Lope has become more frail, but his mind is still active."

"Then I must find a way to go to Valencia."

"No, Vicente, he says the time is still not yet right for you to return and take your revenge."

Will it ever be? "Did Don Lope find out anything more about my mother's family?"

"No, and if the cleverest man in Spain cannot discover her origins, then neither shall your enemies."

"I have to know for my own peace of mind and survival. As I rise at Court, I accumulate rivals." Vicente lowered his voice. "Now about Moraíma . . . you say she is unwell?"

"We worry about her. My sister no longer performs and hasn't left her rooms in days. Please, go to her. Perhaps she will tell you what is afflicting her."

Vicente hurried to Moraíma's suite. Still beautiful, she was heavier, unnaturally pale, with dark shadows under her eyes and lines at the edges of her mouth.

They sat facing each other on chairs as confessor and penitent instead of lounging on cushions or her divan. Moraíma placed one hand in his and touched her stomach with the other. "I am four months pregnant."

Vicente knew that Moraíma was too clever to have a child by accident. "Does the King know?"

"I have not told him. I must know something first, Vicente. How does Philip behave in these matters. Does he adopt his bastards? Does he raise them at Court?"

He decided to tell her the blunt truth. "If the King is convinced the child is his, he will send you to a convent."

"Until my baby is delivered?"

"Forever, and after it is born, you will never see your child again."

She clutched her throat. "Allah protect me. What shall I do?"

"Leave Madrid this night. Go to Don Lope."

"No. I must tell Philip I am carrying his child."

"You are playing a dangerous game, Moraíma. You do not know the King."

"I do so know my Philip. I have lain beside him, heard his yearnings, his desires, his most private thoughts."

"And has he told you of the Queen's maid-of-honor, the wives of certain *títulos*, or the novice nun at the convent of San Plácido?"

She pulled her hand away from his. "You are cruel, Vicente."

"I speak the truth, for your own good."

"Yes, I know you do, but I believe that Philip will acknowledge my daughter as his and raise her at court where you could watch over her. Yes, I have seen. It will be a girl, and Philip will arrange a noble marriage for her."

Vicente let Moraíma dream aloud. Childless Isabel would never permit any of her husband's bastards to live at Court. It would be a permanent affront, and Philip would support his Queen in the matter. His Majesty could be pious and prudish when it suited him.

"Moraíma, listen to me. You must leave Madrid and give birth elsewhere. And always remember this . . . although your child may be half-Royal, it will forever be a despised *morilla*."

"As I am," and in tears she sang, "*Yo me era . . .*"

Vicente returned to the office and told his friends what he had learned. They agreed that Pablo should take Moraíma away from Madrid this night.

Yusef sighed. "I see the moving finger of fate writing an end to our enterprises here in Madrid. It is time to liquidate."

"After you close, what are your plans?"

"A return to Valencia for the usual smuggling and a very good business debasing copper and silver coins with alloy."

Pablo placed a hand on Vicente's shoulder. "Come with us."

He hugged the best friend of his boyhood. How many more opportunities would he be given to join Moraíma and Pablo in the adventurous life of a *pícaro*? He believed he saw all the roads Fate had laid out for him. Had he selected the most difficult course with no promise of certain success or happiness? *If it were not for the Infanta . . .*

Vicente embraced each man. "Go with God, Pablo, Yusef."

"And you, Vicente," Moraíma said entering the office. "I will do as you say and go to Valencia to have my child."

"May God grant we meet again, Moraíma."

"We shall, yet another time. Here. In Madrid. With my daughter. Then I shall present her to King Philip, her father."

Chapter 26
Block of Ice

At four in the afternoon, Prince Charles had his first opportunity to speak to his Star on Easter Sunday when he presented formal greetings to the royal family and thank them for their hospitality. Attended by their *meninas* and *duennas*, Isabel and the Infanta sat next to each other on a decorated platform three steps above the carpeted marble floor between two oversized carved ebony throne chairs upholstered in scarlet velvet. The Queen used a minimum of make-up and rouge, the Infanta none at all. Both wore dangling earrings and many jeweled rings and bracelets. María's chaste brown silk brocade dress covered her shoulders, neck, and arms to the wrist. Her white ruff was of modest size.

Philip sat in the throne-chair at the Infanta's left. As on the day of his formal entry into the capital, Charles had been placed to the right of the Queen. Bristol knelt at their feet to interpret, and Villiers' face froze into a permanent scowl when he was told that *punctilio* required him to stand before the royals.

The *grandees* jostled and argued over placement in the *estrado*. Because the occasion was so significant, the knightly Orders had been invited to attend. As a mere señor, Ballebrera initially stood at the farthest recess of the salon, but Vicente managed to bring him to his place behind Sotomayor and Rajosa.

The room filled with laughter when Hombrecillo entered at the head of a procession of palace fools. Dressed as miniature courtiers, they mocked, satirized, and ridiculed the assemblage.

Ballebrera whispered to Vicente, "That handsome devil, Villiers, have you ever seen so many pearls and gemstones on a man's doublet?"

"And diamond buttons. Olivares would have a fit if such extravagance became the new fashion at Court. But observe how all the ladies are taken with Villiers' looks."

Ballebrera sighed. "He must have been a beautiful boy."

Regarding Villiers, Vicente had helped create for Olivares a dossier that catalogued the man's faults. The handsome Englishman was too headstrong and direct for the ceremonious Spaniards and had been unable to control his sexual appetites. He ridiculed everything Spanish. His informality towards his Prince horrified the entire Court, especially when Charles and Villiers called each other by their nicknames, Baby and Steenie. Villiers stayed covered when his Prince bared his head. He sat when Charles stood. He even appeared without breeches in his Prince's presence. He also repeatedly expressed his hatred of the Count-Duke. The feeling was mutual.

An exception to protocol had been made in favor of the *galantes de palacio* who courted their ladies at the Queen's dinners, waited outside palace windows or under balconies for a glimpse of them, and followed their coaches with lighted candles. Even those who were not *grandees* had received permission to wear their hats while they gazed with adoration at their *encantadoras* and conversed in their private sign languages.

"King Philip is indeed merciful," Ballebrera said. "Because our ridiculous *galanteadores* have lost their heads, the King has allowed them to keep their hats."

All the Court ladies wore pink and vermilion facial paint over ceruse, a layer of white lead foundation cream they had also rubbed on the exposed parts of their shoulders. Rajosa was scandalized by their exposure of cleavage and bare shoulders. "Women who dress in such a manner would be more decent if they went about stark naked. They apply an entire box of paints to their faces, shoulders, and necks, even their ears. They spend all their time in the boudoir instead of praying to save their vain souls."

"A pity the Count-Duke was forced to suspend all sumptuary laws," Sotomayor agreed.

"Perhaps the ladies paint themselves so thickly to camouflage rather than beautify," Ballebrera said *sotto voce*.

Vicente was fascinated how clothing and make-up were the main preoccupation of women both at Court and on the streets. They painted their lips with a thin layer of wax to make them gleam. For the care of their hands, they used almond paste and ointments made from bacon fat. They also applied an abundance of rosewater, ambergris, and expensive imported essences. *Everything except bathing,* he lamented.

These highborn ladies were imprisoned by fashion unlike Moraíma and the Gypsy girls. Vicente believed their costumes had been created by *maracónes* who hated women, and the guardinfante was the most absurd garment ever created. An exaggeration of the farthingale, it had a framework of hoops made from whalebone, iron, and osier twigs padded to mold the petticoats and gown into a bell-shape accentuated by an even more tight-fitting jacket worn over a whalebone corset, which crushed the breasts and restricted the waist as if to cut the body in two.

To complete that distortion of the female body, sleeves ballooned at the shoulders, opened at the wrists to expose vivid linings, and ended in tight cuffs decorated with precious embroidery. The full-length gowns themselves were made of heavy satins, watered silk, or brocade, and hid the feet because it was immodest to expose them. Underneath, a barricade of corset and underskirts guaranteed their chastity, as many as twelve petticoats in winter, seven or eight in summer. The women also wore over their leather shoes clogs with wooden soles and cork heels, which gave them more height.

Vicente amused himself by observing his fellow friars and priests as they watched the women. Their expressions ran the gamut from sincere moral disapproval to open lust at the décolletage. Over the past decades, the fashion trend had been to expose Shallow honor is no honor at all more shoulder, back, and cleavage. Where would fashion lead to next?

The ceremony began. From his seat, Charles wished Isabel a Happy Easter and expressed formal gratitude for favors he had received since his arrival at Court. Because he could not address the Infanta across the Queen and King, he fixed his eyes on María with the expression of a lovesick swain. Not once did the Infanta acknowledge his existence.

After a half hour of formalities, the Prince of Wales left his chair. He bowed before the Infanta, and she rose, her eyes a glacial blue. Intimidated by María, Charles stuttered through his formal expressions of courtesies. "I . . . I w-w-wish to speak of the great friendship that exists between His Catholic Majesty Philip IV of Spain and my father, to reaffirm that friendship and pray that this friendship will continue to grow from the hour of this special occasion." He paused and then surprised all when he praised the Infanta's beauty and poured out his love for her. Bristol gulped for air like a fish out of water unable to speak while Charles recited poetically unaware that the diplomat had stopped translating.

Ballebrera tapped Vicente's arm. "What is he saying?"

"That he loves her, that he . . . My God, I cannot believe what I am hearing. He is quoting Shakespeare, *Romeo and Juliet*."

Vicente had spoken the same words to María, which Charles was now stammering, and he had the satisfaction of knowing that she had been more receptive to his subtler wooing. He translated for Ballebrera, "It is my lady, Oh, it is my love; Oh, that she knew she were."

Vicente relished Charles' unwise breach of etiquette. Better than anyone else, he knew that María had dreaded any wooing. Now the Prince would never be able to overcome her biases. More than despising Charles as a heretic, she would forever regard him as a buffoon.

While the Prince of Wales prolonged his gaffe, Philip fidgeted, and Isabel made her displeasure obvious. Courtiers and ladies whispered until the Infanta interrupted Charles in mid-sentence and coldly recited the formal words she had prepared for the occasion. "*Que quedava buena a servicio de Vuestra Alteza.* How good it has been to have received Your Highness."

Her tone implied dismissal, and Charles self-consciously returned to his place beside the Queen. After mutual formal compliments, the royals rose from their chairs, but before they could take leave from each other, a disturbance occurred below the dais. The buttons of diamonds, rosettes of precious gems, and pearl embroideries on Villiers' doublet fell to the floor and scattered among the Court ladies. Forgetting station and *punctilio*, they screamed and chased after the jewels. The debonair Englishman bowed and announced that they were theirs to keep, which aroused the ire of their husbands and gallants.

"A clever ploy," Ballebrera said. "And now all the women will cluster around him at every function."

The Infanta retired to her suite, and Charles went with Philip and his entourage to a window where they watched fencing exercises by masters-of-arms and *títulos*, followed by more courtesies and entertainments.

When Vicente entered her apartments, the Infanta was screaming and throwing cups, saucers, and vases at her *meninas*, *duenna*, and little Inéz. His appearance calmed her instantly. "Sit beside us. Don Vicente, you saw and heard everything?"

"Yes, *Alteza*."

"We have never been so humiliated. To be stared at so boldly. Are we an animal to be inspected before purchase, and by a heretic boor at that? What terrible things was he saying to us after his translator went silent? Because of his lisp, stammer, and Scottish accent, we could not understand a single word."

"He meant well. He recited from Shakespeare's *Romeo and Juliet*."

"What are we to do?"

"Bear the *comedia* as best you can. The marriage will never take place."

"But if it must?"

"You have said it yourself, *Alteza*. As a last resort, you can take the veil."

The Infanta crossed herself. "Yes, we shall. Should dispensation be given for the marriage before he converts, we will go to the Convent of the Barefoot Carmelites. There I shall reside with my *duennas* and *meninas* and invite the best people to my parlor for chocolate, fruits, and entertainments. You would be first to be summoned."

And I shall forever be your gallant of the grilles.

Chapter 27
Romeo, but no Juliet

Olivares pulled Vicente out of his chair and led him by the arm along the corridor towards Philip's suite. "His Majesty commands your presence."

"Excellency?"

"You are a subtle rogue, Friar. Do not deny it was your suggestion that Rajosa be part of the Prince's suite."

"As I said, Excellency, if he is to accompany her Highness to England . . ."

"Never. I will see to it that the old fool is rusticated to the most remote monastery in Extremadura. Just when our priests and friars believed their arguments were prevailing, Prince Charles proclaimed that he had almost converted Rajosa to his Protestant faith."

Concealing his glee, Vicente crossed himself. "God forbid. How appalling."

"When the Infanta heard of it, she went to His Majesty. She asked for Rajosa to be brought before *la Suprema*, or at the very least exiled. And she demanded that you replace him as her sole confessor and spiritual director. The Queen and Sotomayor supported her. And my wife. All at *la Corte* respect your eloquence and piety." He paused and searched Vicente's face. "Especially the women."

Vicente affected humility. "And the *bufónes*."

"Perhaps they are the wisest courtiers of all." Olivares gripped Vicente's shoulder. "Are you still my man?"

"Always, Excellency."

"Then continue to report everything you hear, and if the Infanta confesses something . . ."

Vicente feigned shock. "But the confessional is sacred."

"You understand my meaning."

They entered the great *estrado* where Philip was holding a diplomatic audience. King, Queen, and Infanta sat on throne-chairs covered with purple velvet on a gold-threaded dais under a gold and scarlet silk canopy. Philip was dressed in black, Isabel wore a burgundy satin guardinfante covered with jewels, and María shone brighter than the sun for Vicente in a pearl encrusted silk brocade dress the color of pink rose. Infantes Carlos and Fernándo stood at either side.

Courtiers, ambassadors, ladies-in-waiting, Spanish and German Guards, and clerics, among them Sotomayor and Inquisitor General Pacheco, filled the room. *Bufónes* aped and ridiculed the haughty *grandees* with impunity while spreading malicious gossip.

Hombrecillo whispered to Vicente, "Today, the Infanta. Tomorrow, all of Spain?"

Vicente glimpsed a smile of delight on the Queen's face and one of triumph from the Infanta. He had yet to decide if Philip was devoid of normal human emotions or the most self-controlled of actors. In public, the King moved like an animated statue; his sallow face and dull light blue eyes never expressed the slightest annoyance or delight, not even when his *bufónes* reduced the Court to helpless laughter. He had never seen Philip display affection for his brothers, although María seemed to be his favorite sibling. How could she not be?

The King said in a monotone, "Don Vicente de Rocamora, it is our pleasure to appoint you confessor and spiritual director for our beloved sister, Her Most Illustrious Highness Infanta Doña María."

"Your Majesty, the honor is most overwhelming."

"Don Vicente."

"*Alteza?*"

She beckoned him to come closer. "Your religious devotion and piety are well known throughout the palace." She nodded, and her *menina* handed him a golden cross encrusted with precious gems. "We all know that you despise material objects, yet we wish for you to have this gift to commemorate this special occasion."

Vicente raised the cross of diamonds, rubies, sapphires, and emeralds as if to bless her. "The greatest treasure of all is to serve one as saintly and pure as you, *Alteza*."

Fernándo, the little Cardinal-Infante, could not contain his delight. "And now my sister will have both cross and sword at her side if she must go to England."

On a sunny and cool afternoon early in May, Vicente met the Infanta within the private gardens of the Casa de Campo. He thought the Infanta had never looked lovelier dressed all in pale blue velour trimmed with gold satin. She held in her arms a fresh bouquet of roses as deeply pink as her lips. Her plaited hair, decorated with blue silk ribbons, reflected reddish gold in the bright sunlight.

She invited him to sit with her on a stone bench under the shade of great elms. Bees and other insects hummed about them in the scented air. It was spring, the time of songbirds, luxuriant plants, and a rainbow of flowers from the palest yellow to the deepest purple. Vicente's stirrings of desire would have shocked María had she been able to read his mind.

Her *duenna* slept in a chair at the far end of the garden. Her chaperone, an elderly *grandee*, also had dozed off on a wooden bench against a high, vine-covered wall.

"Is it true that a dispensation has arrived?"

"Yes, but I have good news, *Alteza*. After the Cardinals studied the Papal dispensation, they added more demands for religious guarantees. You and your household must be free to practice our Catholic faith. You and your priests would control the education of all children born of the marriage to the age of seven. Your children as heirs would be entitled to the throne, and prohibitions against the Catholic religion in England would be ended. Of course, these guarantees will require the prior agreement of King James, his Privy Council, and the English Parliament. Their House of Commons will most certainly refuse to accept them as did Prince Charles and Villiers this morning."

"They did?" She said delighted. "Tell me more."

"They objected to the additional clauses during a meeting with Olivares, and Villiers threatened to take matters into his own hands."

"What do you think he meant by that?"

"Who can say? As everyone knows, he is quite capable of anything."

"I am wearying of these interminable marriage negotiations." The Infanta placed her roses on the bench between them and opened her blue and gold fan. "I wish to confess." She sat shyly beside him in silence until she took a deep breath. "I confess to Almighty God, the Blessed Virgin, and our Holy Savior that I have sinned in my dreams."

"Dreams may be harmless, *Alteza*,"

"They are repeated nightly." María glanced at her chaperones, reassured herself that they still slept, and said barely above a whisper, "I believe I have been visited by an incubus."

Vicente recalled his own dreams of a succubus. But they had been drug induced and based on the reality of that witch, Violante. "Can you describe the incubus?"

She crossed herself. "God forgive me, but he was a most clever incubus. He wished to take me into his trust, for he looked exactly like you."

How I envy that most fortunate of demons. "And what happens in your dreams?"

"I have always awakened before . . ." Her complexion reddened. ". . . until last night."

Vicente told himself to tread carefully. María would be inexperienced about the ways of men and the functions of her own body until her wedding night. "*Alteza*, you believe you have sinned with an incubus who took on my form?"

"Yes."

"And after you awakened, was there any sign that you had been visited by an incubus?"

"My body . . . I . . ." She rose from the bench. So did Vicente. "Remain here. I must find the correct words before I confess all."

Vicente watched the Infanta walk to the bolted door of the garden. There had been no incubus. *He* had appeared in her dreams. They had made love. She had wet herself. If only he could dream the same, or better yet, share sweet reality with his beautiful María. Yes, the time had come to risk all. He would take her in his arms and confess his love.

Before Vicente took his first step towards the Infanta, a young man dropped from the high wall in front of her wearing plumed hat, silver doublet, and silver breeches. María cried out at the unexpected intrusion and retreated to her confused *duenna*.

Vicente watched from behind an elm as the aged *marqués* awakened to face none other than Prince Charles himself. The old marqués fell to his knees before the Prince of Wales and begged him, "Please, Your Highness, you must leave. I risk losing my head by letting Your Highness get so close to Her Most Illustrious Highness."

The Prince of Wales froze. He had not expected his love, his Juliet, to flee from his presence. Aware of his grand faux pas, he stood rooted to the spot undecided what to do next.

When the *hidalgo* opened the door to the garden, Charles gestured for him to close it again. After a sweeping bow to the aged marqués, he postured and declaimed as if performing one of Shakespeare's plays, "My g-g-good sir, I shall d-d-depart as I arrived." He searched in vain for María one last time and again climbed over the wall.

She hurried to Vicente. "Did you see?"

"Yes, *Alteza*, I saw and heard."

She fanned herself. "This is more insufferable than when he presumed to approach my carriage, more idiotic than the words he dared speak on Easter Sunday. What devil possessed him?"

Vicente had no doubts the devil was George Villiers. Charles still fancied himself in love with the Infanta, but the unfortunate wooer had never spoken to her in private. Villiers must have suggested to Charles that he break through the barriers of Spanish etiquette and Court ritual and play Don Juan. Ever a romantic, the Prince would have cast himself instead as Romeo, which would explain why he had followed his Juliet to the Casa de Campo.

Vicente believed that Charles should have selected another play by Shakespeare as his inspiration, but even then, could any Petruchio tame the imperial Infanta? He regretted the spell of their idyllic, intimate spring afternoon in the garden had broken. María's confession that she had been visited by an incubus would have to be continued another time.

Perhaps he ought to have thanked the Prince for possibly saving his life. If he had gone to María and declared his love for her, would she have summoned the palace guards?

Vicente took her bouquet of roses and brought the petals to his nose. By their own name, they would never smell as sweet as his golden Infanta.

Chapter 28
Seventeenth Birthday

The inferno of a typical Madrid summer caused the elderly to expire and the blood of younger men to boil. Fray Rajosa, Vicente's first adversary at Court, died in his sleep. High temperatures exacerbated the already overt hostility between the haughty *hidalgos* and the proud Englishmen of Charles' suite. Spanish pride was easy to offend; the arrogant British never stopped taking umbrage at any perceived slight.

Vicente would never repeat to María the latest rumor concerning Villiers and Olivares. In an attempt to humiliate his nemesis, the Englishman had propositioned the Count-Duke's loyal, ill-favored wife. When she informed her husband of the crude attempt at seduction, he told her to arrange a rendezvous. At night when Villiers sneaked into her bedroom for a coarse sexual encounter, he was unaware that the Count-Duke had substituted a diseased courtesan in his wife's bed to infect the randy Englishman with *mal frances*.

The summer heat also afflicted Vicente, who carried a basket of gifts wrapped in the finest cloths into the palace gardens where the Infanta awaited him. Even *that block of ice* had a fine mist of perspiration on her flushed forehead and cheeks.

"You are suffering, Don Vicente." She offered him a seat on their favorite bench under the shade of an elm and commanded her *menina* to serve him iced almond water.

"*Alteza*, I believe our Lord is showing me what lies in store for all sinners. I shall pray and give thanks to your grandfather, Philip II, for bringing these great elms from England. As the poet says, each leaf sings with the voice of the nightingale."

"Do you also write poetry?"

"I have tried."

"But surely not secular."

The Infanta's *menina* served him iced almond water. "No, only to the greater glory of God, our Merciful Savior, and the Blessed Virgin."

Two lies. One truth. He had indeed written of a virginal beauty named María. To his regret, she had never again discussed or confessed her dreams of the incubus.

"And what have you in that basket, Don Vicente?"

"For your birthday, *Alteza*."

"So many?"

"To make amends for all the others I have missed. But first, I wish to make you a present of good news. A thunderstorm took place in the Count-Duke's office less than an hour ago. Villiers demanded that Spain restore the Rhenish Palatinate to King James' son-in-law."

"My brother will never agree to that."

"And his Majesty did not. Olivares in the clearest language told the English that Spain will never surrender the Palatinate to the Protestants. Then Prince Charles said, and I quote directly: Look to it, sir, if you hold yourself to that, there is an end of all. For without this you may not rely upon either marriage or friendship."

María crossed herself. "Thank you Blessed Virgin. Then it is over."

"Yes, *Alteza*, the Prince of Wales has decided to leave Spain at the end of the month, with or without you."

She pointed her fan at the basket. "And now, what have you brought us?"

Inéz and María's excited *menina* and *duenna* gathered around her when she opened the first gift, an ivory and gold reliquary containing what was supposed to be a splinter from the table of the Last Supper. Vicente suspected Don Lope had selected the shaving from one of the ships rotting in the harbor of El Grau.

Another package contained a vial of viridian Venetian glass. The Infanta removed the top, inhaled the fragrance, and let her ladies sniff the rare perfume. "I have never breathed anything as sweet. However did you find it?"

"I have friends."

Squeals of delight followed the unwrapping of the larger packages. Don Lope had sent four dolls clothed in the latest fashions from France, and word for Vicente alone. Moraíma had given birth to a girl, fair as the Habsburgs, whom she had unwisely named Philippa.

"Don Vicente, were you not a friar, you would be a most successful *galanteador*."

Should I accept her comment as an open invitation to court her? Perhaps she is thinking ahead to the possibility of entering a convent after Charles leaves Spain.

The Infanta looked at him thoughtfully and motioned for her ladies to retire to the far side of the garden with her presents. "I know nothing about your life before you entered your Order."

"Not an interesting life."

"Have you ever loved?"

He wanted to confess all he felt for her. Instead, he shaded the truth. "Before my vows, I sinned in my thoughts and did penance."

The Infanta's eyes narrowed. "Was she beautiful?"

"Desirable."

"What is the difference?"

"Goodness and virtue can emanate like the warming rays of the sun from within one's soul. That is true beauty. It also is true, however, that there are women with perfection of face and form, with the symmetry one sees in statues of Greece and Rome. Cold as marble too because they have no soul. Yet, such women can arouse sinful thoughts and passions in men who are weak of will."

"Am I beautiful?"

Always use the personal with me. "Your soul . . ."

She tapped his arm with her fan. "I wish to know. Am I beautiful?"

"All who have seen you say you are the most beautiful princess in all Europe."

"Because there are so very few of us, it is no compliment, Don Vicente."

"If it were left to Prince Charles, he would change his country's religion to possess you."

"Would I have no other *galanteador*?"

Vicente held his breath. *Is she indeed asking me to court her?* "I am certain of this. If you were not Infanta of Spain, whose marriage possibilities are limited to two great princes, you would be desired as Aphrodite by all men free to court you."

"Be careful, Friar, that you do not encourage our tendency towards the sin of vanity." She turned to Inéz and her *menina* who were giggling. "What is it?"

"*Alteza*, we meant no harm," the *menina* said, "but we are all in agreement. If Don Vicente would grow a mustachio and beard he most certainly could pass as the twin brother of the new painter, Velázquez."

He allowed himself the sin of overweening pride when the Infanta said before thinking, "Don Vicente is more handsome by far."

Eleven days after María's seventeenth birthday, on the twenty-ninth of August, 1623, in Queen Isabel's great *estrado*, Vicente stood in the midst of nobles and clergy for the farewell ceremonies and exchange of lavish gifts.

Villiers took Olivares aside but said for all to hear, "I am obliged with profound gratitude to the King, Queen, and Infanta. As for you, Count-Duke, I offer you the least profession of friendship. From this moment, you must expect from me every possible opposition and enmity."

Olivares smiled at his remark. "I am most sincerely obliged that you do me the honor of thinking of me, and I accept whatever you offer."

Vicente appreciated why the Count-Duke was in good humor. He had succeeded in neutralizing the English for two years while waging war against the Dutch. He also had the pleasure of knowing that his riposte caused the Englishman he hated so very much to leave the ceremonies and Madrid in a snit, presumably infected with *mal frances*.

The following day, King Philip appeared in public dressed all in black as a gesture of mourning for Charles' departure when he escorted him to the gates of Madrid. At night in her apartment, the Infanta expressed her anger over appearances to Vicente.

"The Prince of Wales has left without me, yet he is pretending to the world he still wishes to marry."

"An intolerable insult, *Alteza*."

"And His Majesty's advisors . . . those dolts refused to let me present Prince Charles with a parting gift."

"They reasoned it would disqualify you from any future engagement."

"As if I would ever allow myself to be wooed twice."

But there was a distinct possibility she would, Vicente believed. A considerably more acceptable candidate for marriage to the Infanta was her Catholic first cousin, Ferdinand of Austria, son of Emperor Ferdinand II.

She invited Vicente to kneel beside her at the prie-Dieu in her oratory and offered thanks to Almighty God, the Merciful Savior, and the Blessed Virgin for answering her prayers that she would never be forced into marriage with a heretic. Vicente absorbed the essence of her delicious nearness and glanced at her saintly profile outlined in the darkness by candlelight. At this moment, life could not have been sweeter even if he were a boy again on the beaches of Valencia. He had made a place for himself at Court. He worked for Olivares at the center of power with opportunities to accomplish great things. Sotomayor looked upon him as a protégé. Most important of all, he was María's spiritual director, confessor, tutor, and confidant. If a Habsburg marriage never took place, then his cherished Infanta would enter a convent, and he could become her gallant of the grilles.

Three dark clouds still lay in the distant horizon, however. He had yet to satisfy himself that his mother was not descended from converted Jews. He had made no significant headway in helping Rafal receive a title. And, he had yet to take revenge on Violante and claim his daughter.

After María dismissed Vicente, he encountered Sotomayor in the corridor outside her apartments. As they walked together across the two torch lighted courtyards, the normally avuncular royal confessor's expression was uncharacteristically dark and forbidding.

Sotomayor stopped suddenly and shook a finger close to Vicente's face. "*Cave, cave frater, quia tu credis stare in alto, sed caveas de descenu et quomodo descendes.* Beware, beware, Friar, you may have risen high, yet beware that you may fall, and where you will descend."

For the first time since his arrival in Madrid, Vicente became concerned for his safety. "Fray António, have I sinned, done something wrong?"

"I have some advice for you to impart to Her Royal Highness. If it is true she believes she can take the veil and thereafter lead a freer life, she is completely mistaken. An Infanta of Spain would of necessity be sent to the most remote and austere convent, confined to her apartments, and let out only for prayer and meals under the strictest of supervision. No man, no one will be permitted to see her alone. Ever."

Although shaken by Sotomayor's vehemence, Vicente managed to appear nonchalant. "I will so advise Her Highness, Fray António."

Sotomayor's expression did not soften when he said good night and left for the royal chapel. His admonitions, with the power of *la Suprema* behind them, were not lost on Vicente. They were as clear and urgent as Don Lope's warnings for him to flee Valencia six years earlier, and considerably more threatening.

Like Odysseus, Vicente believed he had enough wit and guile to steer his love safely through the Scylla of an Austrian marriage and the Charybdis of a grim convent prison. But, to which harbor? Perhaps the romantic end he sought might be the journey itself, not any specific destination.

The pain was so great I screamed aloud; because I simultaneously felt such infinite bliss, I wished the pain to last eternally. It was the sweetest caressing of the soul by God.

Saint Teresa of Avila, from her autobiography

PART THREE
Royal Confessor
Madrid, 1624-1629

If one loses his self in God, he ceases to have responsibility, and even the possibility of sinning disappears.

Saint Teresa's exhortation against the alumbrados

Chapter 29
Rites of Spring

Vicente's hand shook when he inserted his taper in the Infanta's candelabrum. Ethereal in the dim light, María's hair fell as golden rivers down her shoulders and back. Her gauzy white linen robe clung to the contours of her luscious high breasts, revealed hints of her blonde delta, and exposed her small bare feet. When she smiled, her pale blue eyes misted with emotion. As she opened her arms, her robe parted.

Vicente embraced the Infanta intoxicated with her fresh clean scent of cinnamon. He kissed the soft moist cushion of her full lower lip and tasted the sweetness of her mouth. He stroked her hair and caressed her body.

He removed her robe and got out of his, which became their bed on the tiled floor. He drew María beside him. His swart muscular limbs entwined with the ivory smoothness of hers. They swore to love each other throughout eternity.

And then—

Vicente awakened on his pallet in the clerical dormitory. He bit his lip to prevent himself from crying out María's name and rousing the palace friars and preachers. He clutched at the straw in bitter disappointment and let his night dream run its course. So vivid, so real, he could still feel María's body against his. Her fragrance lingered.

The Infanta was almost eighteen, a restless virgin, vulnerable and inexperienced, deprived of love, with no possibility of escape from her cloistered life. Although her single-minded ambition was to be a Catholic Empress, she had expressed her resolve never to go through another humiliating courtship, which had yet to begin and might drag on for years.

Whenever they met at night in the secret passageway on the other side of her bedroom, Vicente summoned all his willpower to fight temptation and ignite the first embers of her passionate nature. His desire to make love with the Infanta had become near intolerable. Not since early January had he been able to satisfy his baser carnal needs at el Paraíso. He had been a prisoner in the palace because of María's and Olivares' demands. In the meantime, he had resisted countless opportunities to sin with assorted court ladies who came to him for confession, which solidified his reputation for piety.

Coughing, grumbling, and the usual pungent flatulence from his fellow friars and preachers awakening for matins prevented Vicente from reliving his dream.

Vicente's deep voice resonated throughout the Infanta's chapel as he concluded his sermon during lauds. "*Quid vobis videtur de illis perfidis Iudaeis, qui hodie Christum Dominum nostrum crucifuixerunt?*" What shall we say of the perfidious Jews who today crucified our Lord Jesus Christ?"

He waited for the traditional response from his small congregation. Each was to name a family of tainted lineage condemned for Judaizing. Kneeling at her prie-Dieu, the Infanta called out the name of a disgraced family. Standing in the shadows behind María, her *menina, duenna,* and Inéz damned several of the noblest houses of Spain.

Vicente pretended to listen to their interminable tirade. Ever since Rafal had shown him the codicil, he had come to dread Holy Week, specifically this day, Good Friday, when eloquent preachers described how the Jews first rejected the Son of God and then cruelly put Him to death. Good Friday and Easter Sunday when hatred for those presumed children of the devil reached a sanguinary boiling point.

How would the Infanta react if her confessor were denounced as a tainted new-Christian? María did distinguish between practicing Jews and devout partial new-Christians who accepted Jesus as Son of God and Savior. She was unwavering in her choice for patron saint of all Spain, the one-quarter-new-Christian Teresa of Avila. Even King Philip, who usually sided with the Castilian reactionaries, preferred Teresa over Santiago and could be tolerant enough to raise the partial-new-Christian Olivares to the most powerful position in Spain.

After the last damnation of a disgraced family, they heard drums coming from the city and the lugubrious wail of horns heralding the procession of *penitentes and pasos,* flat carts carrying images and people portraying the Passion.

María rose from her prie-Dieu. "Don Vicente, are you going to watch the procession of the *penitentes*?"

"I prefer prayer and meditation to ostentatious piety. San Juan de la Cruz wrote that it is an abomination to adorn holy images with profane luxury and fashions. They cease being objects of true devotion and instead become merely idols for vainglorious display."

Vicente had seen the sanguinary scene repeated each year. Spectators from all classes mingled along the entire length of Madrid's main streets.

Balconies and rooftops filled to capacity for the greatest of all Holy Week processions. The wealth that went into the elaborate *pasos* would have been better spent on the needy.

And blood everywhere. Jeweled blood, stained glass blood, and painted blood. On the *pasos*, blood dripping from His forehead under the crown of thorns. Blood oozing from His bony ribs where He had been pierced. Blood pouring from gaping nail holes on His hands and feet. Even carvings of the Virgin had tears of blood running down her cheeks. And all that followed by the real blood of the *penitentes*. To the measured beating of drums, they scourged themselves with ribboned leather whips, some with balls of wax at the ends containing shards of pottery and glass or slivers of bone and metal. Blood oozed from their lacerations and soaked their tattered robes. Some stumbled and fell to the ground, tore open their knees and elbows, and trailed blood from their bare feet cut by pebbles and sharp debris on the street. After the self-flagellants, men in imitation of Christ carried heavy wooden crosses that chafed their skin so raw they bled through their robes. Behind the cross-bearers trudged the *disciplinantes de amor* who whipped their bodies not out of religious devotion but to impress their loves.

"Don Vicente, have you ever prescribed flagellation during Holy Week as penance?"

"No, *Alteza*, the true purpose of penance is to instruct and improve and should never be meted out as punishment."

Vicente could hear *madrileños* cheering the *penitentes* and *disciplinantes*. Their blood-lust would continue the following day, Holy Saturday, when figures of Judas would be erected to be vilified and burned by the mobs. He had seen identical processions and Judas burnings in Valencia and Orihuela.

María commanded Vicente to stay in the oratory to hear her confession. They sat on plain chairs facing each other.

"I confess to Almighty God, to my Savior, Jesus Christ, to the Blessed Virgin that I may have sinned again in my dreams," she began

Has the Infanta shared my night dream?

Vicente wore his mask of clerical rectitude. "The incubus you spoke of before?"

"No, he was a man."

"Perhaps, *Alteza*, you experienced a moment of second-sight and dreamed of your future husband."

"No. I saw part of his face. He was very handsome, and . . ." She stopped in mid-sentence and hid her face behind her fan. "I have said too much. Leave me."

Vicente allowed his brain to rule his heart and withdrew. *Will I regret for the rest of my life what I have failed to do?*

"Vicente, beware."

Not Sotomayor this time. Hombrecillo had intercepted him in the Queen's Courtyard of the Alcazar. The *bufón* was all in black except for a fashionable *golilla* of gray silk around his small neck. His beard now completely white, at age thirty-five Hombrecillo was frail and resembled a grandfather. His high-pitched voice piped and wheezed like that of any old man.

"Vicente, you have aroused envy."

"I thank you for the warning, Sáncho, but can you be more specific?"

"You have risen high within the palace clergy."

"Thanks to you, my friend." Again, Hombrecillo had spoken Sotomayor's words.

"Risen high and quickly for one so young. You are confessor and spiritual director to the Infanta. The Queen and the Cardinal-Infante hold you in the highest regard. The Count-Duke relies upon you. You are Sotomayor's protégé. Who of the clergy would not envy you? Who of the *grandeza* would not sell his soul to be in your place as the man closest to the most desirable princess in all Europe?" Hombrecillo paused for emphasis before continuing, "And who would not conspire to ensure your fall? To see you blind, the envious man would pull out one of his own eyes."

Vicente was surprised, not by the warning, but by Hombrecillo's vehemence. After the Prince of Wales departed from Madrid, the Court had returned to its normal routine of vice, spying, and gossip. He had been under intense scrutiny by assorted preachers and confessors, specifically those who resisted Olivares' reform policies.

"Sáncho, are you saying there is a conspiracy against me?"

"Not yet organized, but the potential is there. Amazing, even to me, that you have behaved like a saint so far. No woman, maiden, or pretty boy has been able to report or even fabricate the slightest sin."

"Then what is it you are telling me?"

The *bufón* glanced around to make sure they were not overheard. "Inéz, my beloved wife, tells me the Infanta is very fond of you. I repeat, *very* fond." He motioned for Vicente to bend lower. "I cannot believe you have been unaware of it. Whenever you enter the room, her eyes . . . how shall I best say it? Her eyes, their expression, however subtle, betray an immoderate affection for you."

Vicente wanted to proclaim his joy aloud to the world. *In my heart and dreams, Infanta Doña María is simply María, and it is María who returns my love.*

Hombrecillo placed his hand on Vicente's arm. "Never forget that the Count-Duke looks upon the Infanta as his most valuable diplomatic card, to be played if and when necessary to seal an alliance with the Austrians."

The sun died in Vicente's soul. Had Olivares suspected his strong feelings for María and sent Hombrecillo with a warning? He believed the Count-Duke would cast him into the deepest dungeon of the Inquisition at the least suspicion of impropriety.

"Vicente, you above all others know that is normal for inexperienced maidens to become infatuated with their young and handsome confessors. I believe your reputation for virtue and chastity drives all women mad with lust for the unattainable. It would also be understandable, although inexcusable, for a young confessor and a princess to become enamored of each other."

Vicente silently vowed to tighten his mask whenever others were in the Infanta's presence. "What do you suggest?"

"It might be wise for you to begin using the confessional booth."

"She would ask why. The suggestion must come from Her Highness."

"Well, perhaps she will soon be married to Archduke Ferdinand."

"Perhaps." *But not for several years given the slow pace of Habsburg diplomacy.*

Chapter 30
Alumbrados

"Vicente, there is a matter I must discuss with you where we cannot be heard." Ballebrera wore all black except for a sky-blue *golilla* that matched the plume in his broad-brimmed felt hat and suede gloves with the de Rocamora crest embroidered in gold and silver thread. His waxed upturned mustachio and beard were more flamboyant than the Count-Duke's.

"And I have much to say as well."

Vicente walked with Ballebrera towards other strollers towards a deserted stretch along the dry banks of the Manzanares. The crisp fresh October air invigorated him. He almost forgot he was wearing a coarse, unwashed robe.

Ballebrera tossed a *quarto* copper alloy coin to a beggar. "And so I hallow the poor who are among us in the image of Christ."

Vicente saw two Dominicans nearby and intoned another common homily for them to hear, "To treat a poor man without courtesy is to affront the King of Kings, for the man who asks is a man sent from Heaven to ask you in the name of God to do a good deed."

"I have missed your company."

"And I have yearned for a good bath."

"Then what has kept you cloistered in the palace all this time?"

"A demanding master. And how is the courtship of your Duchess progressing?"

"Slower than our bureaucracy. Xímena fears the moment we marry she will lose control of her wealth and independence. I confess she is right to think so."

"But you will marry before she dies."

"Even if I have to obtain a forged marriage document."

"You know I can arrange that."

"I may ask you to. There is a problem concerning the Duchess."

"Is she ill?"

"In danger. And so am I, indirectly." Ballebrera glanced about to make sure no one could hear although they were a good distance away from anyone else on the dry riverbank. "The Duchess has fallen under the spell of an *alumbrado* she met this past summer in Vizcaya through her neighbor, the Marquésa de Zamárraga."

Vicente tensed. *La Suprema* condemned the *alumbrados*, also known as illuminati, as the greatest threat to the Catholic faith because the rot developed from within. *Alumbrado* heresies fell within the jurisdiction of the Inquisition. The Holy Office had a long reach, and all de Rocamoras could be endangered through Ballebrera and his association with the Duchess.

"Who is this *alumbrado*?"

"He goes as Padre Bartolomé Begoña, although I doubt it is his real name, or if he is even an ordained priest. He is definitely not of Spanish origin, to judge by his accent."

"I have not heard of him. Is he staying with the Duchess?"

"I thank God, no. Begoña has insinuated himself in the Zamárraga household. His followers believe that his spittle heals infections and his herbal potions increase potency. In Vizcaya, he convinced the Duchess that his brews and salves reverse the aging process. The man is a brilliant hypnotist who spellbinds his congregation."

"Which I also have done."

"And you could be the greatest *alumbrado* of them all. Let me tell you what I have heard about certain rituals practiced by Begoña and the inner circle of his most devout believers. They include ritual mutilation and circumcision of young girls they choose to be Mother of God. First, the chosen is repeatedly impregnated during an orgy. Then her left breast and clitoris are cut off, divided, and eaten by the congregation. If the girl gives birth to a daughter, the child is to be brought up as her successor. If a boy, he will be called Baby Jesús. On the sixth day after its birth, the male infant's heart is pierced with a spear and his blood drunk by all present, after which the body is ground into a powder and mixed into bread baked for the cult's communion."

"If what you say is true, these abominations must be stopped immediately. Has the Duchess participated?"

"Not yet. Because she is too frail, Begoña has given her a dispensation, for a large sum of course."

"When is the next mass?"

"Tomorrow night at the ruins of Santa Monica. The Duchess and I were invited to attend. It is not a sacrificial mass for the inner circle but a general orgy for the congregation and for those who wish to become followers. I have the password. Will you go in my place?"

Vicente looked northwards across the river to the Pardo Woods. "Yes, I want to see this Padre Begoña for myself. I will prepare a strong draught of powders to ensure that the Duchess and her servants will sleep tomorrow long after siesta."

"In my old age, Vicente, I find myself preferring the protective bosom of our Holy Mother Church to these faddish cults, even though I am still a skeptic."

Vicente tethered the horse Ballebrera had loaned him to a poplar in the dense woods near the ruins of Santa Monica. He wore an all black ensemble, mask, and a perfect copy of his kinsman's enormous upwards-turned mustachio to complete his disguise.

A fire had gutted the Romanesque convent at the turn of the century. Over the years, the credulous had come to believe that demons haunted the ruins, and many otherwise intelligent men shunned the area. It was an ideal setting for an *alumbrado* to delude his flock.

When the ruins came into view through the trees, Vicente understood why it filled so many with fear. Under a full moon and lit by candles from within, the front facade of the roofless windowless structure took on a Satanic visage.

He walked past several dozen carriages. Their owners had covered their crests with black cloth for anonymity. Armed men in satin red robes and matching conical hoods with narrow eye-slits patrolled the perimeter. He spoke the password Ballebrera had given him to other red robes guarding the entrance.

Inside, the congregation stood in the main chapel because the pews had long since disappeared. There was no need for candles except for purposes of ritual because moonlight illuminated the interior.

Vicente followed Ballebrera's instructions and joined the men and women in the center. Dressed in everyday clothes and wearing masks, they would be the Probationers. Those in red robes and hoods positioned along the walls and guarding windows and exits were known as Acolytes. Apostles were garbed in white robes.

This would be Vicente's first *alumbrado* mass. Although still a freethinker, he had come to accept the Church's existence as necessary mucilage to hold society together in ways governments could not. Roman Catholic ritual and pageantry kept the faithful in contact with orthodox doctrine, with priests as their sole guides to lead them along the path of faith and away from evil. The alternative, in his opinion, was an anarchy of individual mysticisms, most indistinguishable from lunacy or the bacchanalian practices of pagan cults. Such heresies appealed to mankind's natural desires to sin and afterwards to be redeemed; to descend to the depths of perverse lust and then rise to the heights of divine spirituality.

Begoña would not be the first lecherous priest or nun to manipulate the credulous. Among the forbidden books Vicente had read was the first significant *alumbrado* text, *Mirôr Des Simples Ames*, written by Marguerite de Porete, a nun martyred in 1310. She had taken the words of San Bernardo literally, that the freed spirit becomes one with God. Sor Marguerite believed the soul could be saved through faith only, without good works. Mental prayer alone was sufficient to achieve salvation. Priests as spiritual guides, confession, and indulgences were unnecessary, all later incorporated into the various Protestant sects.

Sor Marguerite also voiced the most religiously subversive message of all: Love is God and God is Love. By Love, she had meant carnal not spiritual love, with copulation as an act of the Holy Spirit.

She was not alone. The Beguines of Silesia, influenced by delusions resulting from extensive fasting, believed that once they achieved perfection through abstinence and flagellation they could gratify their carnal appetites. Their *spiritual* masses had included naked dances and ritual orgies presided over by a couple called Jesus and Mary.

Similar perversions practiced by certain women who took the veil were more abandoned than mere sinning with their gallants of the grilles. Some Brides of Christ professed the extreme Free Spirit belief that sexual union was union with God, and each night they embraced in love the Savior Himself, who was in reality a randy cleric.

Other *alumbrados* asserted that the body received merit only if it exposed itself to temptation and resisted, and that the soul would be liberated from the body solely in moments of complete physical abandonment. Consequently, as Saint Teresa had warned, unrestrained mysticism could descend to the depths of human depravity.

The congregation murmured when Begoña stepped behind a pulpit on a reconstructed dais at the far end of the chapel. Vicente moved closer to the front for a better view of the *alumbrado*, who wore a stained gray robe of coarse wool tied at the waist by a worn rope. Illuminated by the full moon and many candles, Begoña's flowing black hair and beard imitated paintings of the Savior. He was a malignant Christ, however. Thick eyebrows merged as a solid line above intense cobalt blue eyes and the bridge of a thick, prominent nose.

A crescent of disciples stood behind Begoña. A man in a red robe and conical hood was flanked on each side by three hooded men in white satin and three unmasked attractive girls in white robes with flame-colored sashes.

The *alumbrado* first welcomed his congregation and swore them to an oath of secrecy. Begoña's voice was deep, passionate, and trained as well as any actor's, and as Ballebrera had said, definitely not Spanish. Vicente remembered the languages he had heard on the docks of El Grau. Begoña's accent sounded Slavic. Perhaps the *alumbrado* had come from Poland or farther east from the mysterious land of the Russias.

Another unmasked girl, also in white, stepped onto the dais and handed Begoña a naked, newborn baby. He lifted the crying infant over his head and said for all to hear, "Four days ago, our Baby Jesús was born. On Saturday night, we take communion with him."

The congregation stirred. Vicente shivered. His sweat turned ice cold, as if an apocalyptic phantom had embraced him, when he recalled what Ballebrera had told him about the significance of *Baby Jesús*.

After the girl took back the infant and left, Begoña promised a new and better world. Master and servant, maid and mistress would be as equals and as one soul to be unified with God. Vicente was not surprised when the clever *alumbrado* sermonized verbatim from Sor Marguerite's *Mirôr*:

> "I am God, says Love, because Love is God and God is Love, and this Soul is God by love's condition, and I am God by divine nature . . .
>
> "God has sanctified His name in her and the divine Trinity dwells in her . . .

"She drinks the beverage no one else drinks, but the Trinity. And the soul, annihilated in God, is drunk with it, surpassingly drunk, more drunk than anybody ever was who drank or ever will drink . . .

"She is the fire of love herself, and she finds God in everything . . .

"And she is excused of everything because God is her will . . .

"She has taken leave of the virtues which are only anxiety and toil . . .

"She has crossed the sea in order to suck the marrow of the lofty cedar . . ."

"We are immersed in a sea of sin, but we need not drown. The more we sin, the greater we suffer, and the greater are our chances of salvation."

Begoña stepped to one side of the pulpit, removed his robe, and flaunted his priapic tumescence. "Carnal sin is the first step towards repentance. You cannot be granted redemption without confessing your sins. Sin is necessary. Sin with me and confess your sins. Then I shall redeem you. I have come to save you. Because God is within me, there is no sin, only union."

Begoña left the dais followed by the man in the red robe, the six girls, and the six hooded men. They formed a circle, faced inward, and turned from right to left. The rest of the congregation made a wider circle around them and sat on the floor. They clapped in time to the measured beating of drum, tambourine, and cymbal carried by red robed acolytes. As one, they chanted, "God is Love, Love is God".

The beat increased to a frenzied pace. One by one, the dancers entered a state of religious ecstasy. Acolytes and Probationers joined the expanding circle to participate. So did Vicente.

An unmasked girl in white staggered into the center of the circle, convulsed, and cried out, "Oh! The Spirit! The Spirit! He has entered me!"

Begoña seized the girl, ripped her robe, and fell with her onto the floor. Another Apostle screamed that the Spirit had entered her. The man in red was unaware that his hood had come off as he lifted the second girl's robe, then his, and penetrated her before they dropped beside Begoña and his partner. Vicente recognized him as an enemy of Olivares.

As Begoña's disciples began to couple, Probationers and Acolytes also shouted that the Spirit had entered them. Religious fervor became an indiscriminate orgy. Under an infernal full moon, writhing, moaning bodies of naked and semi-naked participants carpeted the chapel floor.

Vicente saw more than a few recognizable faces whose masks had fallen away. To conform as a member of Begoña's flock, he selected one of the Probationers he recognized as a lady-in-waiting to Queen Isabel and who had attempted to seduce him more than a few times. Tonight he would have his revenge. He was careful not to enter her for fear of catching one of Cupid's diseases. Fortunately, she was too possessed by the Spirit to know the difference.

Chapter 31
Foetor Judaicus

Vicente met with Olivares, Sotomayor, and Jerónimo Villanueva, the *Protonotario*, Secretary of State, of Aragón, and described the sermon and practices of Begoña as if he had heard it from an informant during confession. When he identified the man in the red robe who was the *alumbrado*'s host and apostle, the Count-Duke was delighted. The Marqués de Zamárraga, *Grandee* First Class and Knight of Santiago, was one of the most reactionary obstructionists in the *Camara de Castillo* who resisted his reforms and attempts to make Teresa patron saint of Spain.

"I will have that dolt arrested and handed over to the Inquisition. My opposition will be further weakened after he mentions certain names guilty or not during interrogation and torture. When and where is the vile event to take place?"

"This Saturday at midnight a mass and initiation ceremony for Begoña's new disciples at the ruins of Santa Monica."

Villanueva, a dark and handsome man with intense brown eyes, confronted Vicente. "I can understand why you have reported this *alumbrado* to the Count-Duke and His Reverence, but why have you asked for me to be present?"

"Forgive me, Excellency, but one of the ladies in attendance at Begoña's masses has been identified as Raquel de García y Villanueva."

"My niece." The *Protonotario* slammed his fist on Olivares' desk. "*Idiota*. I shall throw her into a convent this very night."

"If I may make a suggestion, Excellency, to imprison your niece now may alert Begoña that something is wrong. Say nothing to her, and when she leaves for the next blasphemous mass, we can intercept her carriage and guide her to your house."

"Very well, and then I will deal with the little simpleton. I'll not forget what you have done for me, Friar."

Olivares sent for the chief law enforcer of the Alcazar, Juan de Quiñones de Benevente, whose narrow nose was ideally suited for his predilections. When the *alcalde* entered, he sniffed at Villanueva as if seeking a specific odor.

This was not the first time Vicente had observed the *alcalde*'s peculiar behavior. He had begun to pay careful attention to the respected bibliophile, antiquarian, and dilettante who enjoyed hosting evenings for the literati of Madrid. Quiñones also was a self-righteous bigot with authority to pursue criminals and in general spy, denounce, arrest, and pass sentence on heretics. He often collaborated with the Inquisition, which depended on the secular authorities for much of its police work and for the actual sentencing and execution of those whom it had condemned. On several occasions, the *alcalde* apprehended individuals denounced as Judaizers and handed them to the Holy Office.

After Vicente repeated all he knew about Begoña, Quiñones said, "This is a matter for the Holy Office."

"Of course," Olivares agreed, "but as you know, we need to proceed first with secular authority. Select as many armed men and Familiars as you need to make the arrests."

"Did your informant tell you the size of Begoña's congregation?" Quiñones raised his eyebrows at the number. "Then I require several wagons to transport the heretics to prison."

"And you shall have them," the Count-Duke promised.

"Wear masks. Everyone is masked, I am told."

Quiñones squinted at Vicente. "How is it you know so much about these *alumbrados*? Who told you about them?"

"I cannot violate the sanctity of the confessional. Be assured that I have prescribed severe penance."

The *alcalde* stared at him unconvinced.

Vicente stood before the Infanta and her expanded entourage in her *estrado*. As marriage negotiations with the Austrians intensified, her value had increased, and so had the number of ladies and chaperones watching her. She wanted Vicente to confirm if it was true that he had denounced Begoña and the *alumbrados*.

He was aware that a tidal wave of *murmuraciónes* concerning the arrest of the *alumbrados* had swept over the Alcazar. Some rumors were so horrifying and bizarre that many refused to believe them.

Vicente had seen it all first hand after he joined Quiñones' troop of soldiers and Familiars and participated in the arrest of Begoña and his congregation. He spared the Infanta the most obscene and repugnant details. Nor did he mention Isabel's wayward lady-in-waiting. He had not trusted Quiñones to protect the Queen's interests and had alerted Olivares in private. The Count-Duke sought an audience with Isabel, and within minutes, her unfortunate lady was removed to a convent.

After he finished his narrative, the Infanta said, "Don Vicente, we are proud of you for protecting our Church from such abominable heresies. We must be patient, however, and wait for the day when we are Empress and you become our Inquisitor General. Then all heretics and blasphemers will cower in fear and tremble at the mere mention of our names."

Vicente crossed himself. "May it come to pass as you wish, *Alteza*."

"In the meantime, we would honor you for your great service to Crown and Church."

María pointed her fan at Inéz, and the tiny woman handed Vicente an ebony box inlaid with mother-of-pearl. He opened it and removed a needlepoint rendering in gold and silver thread of Mary Magdalene washing the feet of Jesús.

Vicente dropped to his knees. "*Alteza*."

"We made it for you, and so we honor you, Friar, for your piety and good works."

That evening Vicente confessed Xímena in her private chapel and absolved the terrified old Duchess of all sins connected with Begoña. He gave her minor penances of assorted Hail Marys and Our Fathers and urged her to marry Ballebrera for her own salvation and protection.

Afterwards, Vicente sat with Ramón in the *estrado*. "Xímena insists on penancing herself for a full year before she will marry you."

"May God grant she lives that long. And how soon will it be before Begoña and his followers face a public *auto*?"

"Inquisitor General de Pacheco is an Olivarista, so our Count-Duke will pull the strings at the time of his choosing."

"Will the Duchess and I be questioned?"

"Only if you are named, which is unlikely now. The Count and Countess de Zamárraga took a quick acting poison during the arrest. The Count-Duke suspects that Quiñones may have arranged it on behalf of Castilian reactionaries who continue to obstruct his reforms. The *alcalde* supports their views on maintaining and even narrowing the *limpieza*."

"Speaking of which and whom, let us hope both our tongues and mental acuity are at their sharpest tonight."

To celebrate the arrest of the most repugnant and dangerous cult of *alumbrados* in memory, Quiñones had invited Vicente and Ballebrera to his home, the latter for his wit. The other guests included the cream of Madrid's literati: Spain's greatest playwright, Félix Lope de Vega y Carpio; and the kingdom's master satirist, Francisco de Quevedo y Villegas, both men Knights of Santiago. Also present were the effete Duke of Sessa, Lope's patron, who paid him to write his love letters; Juan Pérez de Montalván, the playwright's friend and disciple; and Dominican Inquisitor Diego de Arce y Reynoso, whose handsome features resembled the stone carved saints watching over the churches of Spain.

Vicente had seen Arce on several previous occasions, the first time when he fatally wounded the Inquisitor's kinsman, Logroño, in a duel. After poor medical attention had led to infections and cost the *poderoso* his life, Arce had made it known that he would never rest until he uncovered the identity of the false Señor de Algorfa.

Not only Arce, he also had to be wary of his host, Lope de Vega, and Quevedo. The playwright often joined Quiñones in pursuit of heretics and had led a procession of his fellow Familiars to an *auto-de-fé*. His bigotry and hatred of Jews and new-Christians appeared in the themes, characters, and dialogue of his plays. *El Niño Innocente de la Guardia* was based on a notorious trial for the ritual murder of a child and used to justify the expulsion of Jews in 1492. *El Brasil Restitudo* dramatized how Jews had allied with the Dutch to betray Spain in Pernambuco.

Vicente had observed a contradictory characteristic concerning Lope, which he found to be common among certain men who expressed their hatred of Jewish blood. The playwright had many personal and literary friendships with new-Christians.

The shaggy graying hair, untrimmed mustache, and narrow vertical goatee falling from lower lip to the edge of spectacled Francisco de Quevedo's chin contrasted with the neat spade beards and flaring mustachios of the other guests. Although the satirist supported Olivares' sumptuary laws and puritanical reforms, he shared Lope's hatred of new-Christians and opposed any diminution of the *limpieza* statutes.

Vicente suspected the roots of their bigotry lay in envy of the wealthy Portuguese *hombres de negócio*, men of business. Payment for their writing was irregular and often meager, and plagiarists copied their work with impunity. Many writers entered the clergy to survive on its prebends and benefices. Even the great Luís de Góngora y Argote had served as Chaplain to Philip III. Others like Lope and Quevedo had to rely on powerful patrons, and Arce, who was a full Professor of Law at the University of Salamanca, Spain's most prestigious university, earned a paltry three hundred ducates per year.

In the *estrado*, Vicente sat between Montalván and Quiñones and opposite Ballebrera, Arce, and Sessa. He could well imagine his cousin's craving for wine or brandy while they drank chocolate or almond flavored water and nibbled fruits and cheeses.

Lope pointed an admonishing finger at his host. "I should be angry with you, Don Juan, for not inviting me along with the Familiars when you arrested the *alumbrados*."

"I did, but your servant said you were attending a meeting of your Order. We had to act immediately. It would have been a great sin to delay. Innocent lives would have been lost."

Arce squinted at Quiñones. "Then the rumors of human sacrifice are true?"

"And cannibalism."

Ballebrera brought tears of laughter to everyone's eyes, except Arce's, with a spontaneous verse certain to be repeated throughout the *mentideros*. "I have titled it End Result:

> The worst is not to be tasted,
> Devoured, and digested
> It is the victim's new nature,
> Once evacuated, to become ordure.

After the men jested and punned about cannibalism, Quiñones confirmed for all that they had interrupted horrors greater than anyone could have imagined. "Begoña's less fanatic acolytes and probationers confessed all the same night they were arrested to avoid torture and death sentences. They shall receive instead minor punishments and penances. During interrogations, they revealed that their cult had spread throughout the north of Spain and parts of the south. They also described their most repugnant practices, which thanks to the mercy of God, we have ended. The night of the arrest, we stripped Begoña naked. Although he was uncircumcised, the interrogators inspected his foreskin to see if it had been pricked ceremonially. Alas, there was no physical evidence of the slightest hole or incision, which was disappointing."

The Duke of Sessa spat out a grape seed. "How many followers does Begoña have?"

"Too many. Begoña had a genius for organization. He divided his followers into arks, as he calls them, with a Christ, a Mother of God, angels, apostles, prophets and prophetesses who proselyte and guide their adherents through those obscene rituals."

"They may be everywhere," Arce cautioned. "That is why I leave tomorrow for the Tribunal of Murcia with authority from *la Suprema* to root them out. Every last one of them." He looked at Vicente as if to read something in his eyes. "I shall also visit the Señorío de Algorfa on a personal matter."

"I apologize for my failure to discover that false señor's true identity," Quiñones said.

Vicente held Arce's gaze. *He suspects but cannot yet prove it.*

The conversation shifted to other topics. A restless man with many interests, Quiñones had helped eradicate a plague of locusts. He was an expert on Roman coins and wrote poetry and treatises on subjects as diverse as miracles, medicine, and famous battles.

Lope accused all his rivals, living and dead, of having tainted blood, the obvious proof being in their writing. Then Quevedo provoked laughter when he repeated his published allusion to the converso origins of the playwright's greatest antagonist:

"I'll send you my verses well larded, so that you will not be able to savor them, my dear Góngora."

Arce turned to Vicente. "I am told you have permission to read heretics and infidels."

Vicente feigned humility. "All the better to fight them. Still, it is an unpleasant duty that weighs heavily."

"You have my sympathy," Lope said. "Jew-lies and blasphemies always arouse my ire."

Quiñones wiped dirt from his spectacles. "Have you observed that there are too many Jews at court who claim to be Christians?"

Arce sliced a wedge of cheese with his knife as if cutting out the heart of a Jew. "You mean Olivares' pet swine, the Portuguese *hombres de negócio*?"

Quevedo adjusted his spectacles. "You might as well speak of the Count-Duke and his advisors as the synagogue, and throw in certain members of the *grandeza* as well."

"I can smell a Jew-taint without error, even if the ancestry is more than seven generations," Quiñones asserted and pinched his long, narrow nose for emphasis. "Have you noticed how an odor clings to partial new-Christians as well?"

Vicente suppressed a smile when he recalled the *alcalde*'s sniffing at Villanueva, whose enemies relentlessly spread rumors that the *Protonotario* was tainted.

"One drop of Jewish blood is enough to destroy the world," Arce intoned.

"And by blood, Jews suffer, as women do with menstruation, in punishment for the death of our Savior. I have Ruperto speak for me in my comedy *San Nicolás de Tolentino*: No Jew can do anything good. How hateful is this line of men."

"Exactly my sentiments," Montalván agreed.

"And mine," Ballebrera said conforming to their bigotry with an arched eyebrow for Vicente.

Quiñones continued with his theme. "My research in the matter has proven to my complete satisfaction an interesting fact. Every month many Jews bleed from their rumps as an eternal sign of dishonor and condemnation."

"And we all know that the Jews attempt to remove their blood-curse by drinking the blood of Christian children, which I illustrate in my play about Niño de la Guardia," Lope said.

"And a great play it is," Montalván declared.

"I was moved to tears," Sessa said.

Vicente despaired that so well educated an *alcalde*, erudite playwright, and brilliant satirist could hold such bigoted beliefs that they transferred Begoña's sanguinary rituals to the Jews. Yet, if Quiñones and other men had seen hard evidence of vile mutilations and cannibalism as practiced by the *alumbrados*, why should not they and the uneducated masses believe that Jews drank the blood of innocent Christian children and mixed it with bread on their holy days?

He tested the limits of their credulity and prejudice. "I read somewhere that each descendant of those who killed Our Savior is born covered with blood and with the right hand stuck to their head. Has anyone here seen evidence of that Divine Punishment?"

Arce glared at him. "If it is Divine Punishment, then it must be so."

Quiñones gestured towards his library. "Although the Lord works in wondrous ways, his punishments are not always mysterious. When I speak of Jews being cursed with bleeding posteriors, I am referring to hemorrhoids of course, which result from several factors. Jews eat food with no salt. They are a lethargic people and joyless, filled with fear and fatigue, which increases the listlessness of their blood. That is their Divine Punishment."

"Of course some believe the Jews menstruate only on Good Friday," Arce said. "That may be or not be true. But throughout the year, we can identify other external signs of Jewish guilt, especially their unique odor, which is not always related to the food they consume."

Lope touched his nose. "That is why Jews drink Christian blood. It is their mistaken belief that it removes their foul odor."

"Which only conversion to our True Faith can cure," Montalván added.

"Not even then." Arce brought his fist down on the table. "*Foetor Judaicus*, the stench of Jew, is the permanent Mark of Cain for that miserable race."

Vicente nodded at the Inquisitor, who did not understand his irony. "I agree with you, Fray Diego. If a child is missing, the Jews have stolen him. If he has been killed, the Jews are his murderers."

"Absolutely true, as they murdered Our Savior," Ballebrera said in support of Vicente, "which is why each of the Twelve Tribes of Israel has received its own unique curse."

Now everyone contributed to the lore of accursed Jews.

"Each year thirty men descended from Judah die as a result of betrayal."

"I have seen all green vegetation around those from Reuben wither in three days."

"Each noon to night the men of Gad develop fifteen thorns on their body that drip blood."

"Children of Asher are born with right hands shorter than the left by a palm."

"Naftali children are born with four teeth, like the pigs they are."

"At each new moon, those of Menasseh feel pain throughout their bodies and bleed all day."

"Every twenty-fifth day of March wounds appear on the hands and feet of Simeon."

"Levites cannot spit on the ground, and when they spew their vile saliva in the air, the spittle flies back into their faces."

Montalván, whose enemies had accused him of tainted blood, raised his voice: "But some theologians argue that many of these curses are false because not all tribes were present in Jerusalem, and, therefore, could not have participated in the crucifixion of our Savior. I believe that sincere New-Christian Catholics are not descended from the accursed. Otherwise, why bother to convert anyone?"

The Inquisitor dismissed his comment with a wave of his hand. "Absolute idiocy. If they had been in Jerusalem, those Jews also would have slain our Lord as they do each moment of their foul existence."

Vicente was aware that the Inquisitor watched him with the same manifestation of hatred as Jacinto. *Arce is my enemy. Does he fear me as a rival and despite my disguise that day recognize me as the swordsman who wounded Lograño? Regardless, he will prefer to believe I am tainted and attempt to destroy me.*

Chapter 32
An Unwanted Honor

Sotomayor invited Vicente to accompany him and Quiñones to the dungeons of the Toledo Tribunal as a reward for discovering Begoña and his blasphemous cult. The *alumbrado* and his followers were to be tortured until they confessed all to the inquisitors' satisfaction. Because Quiñones had arrested the prisoners, the garrulous *alcalde* was required to witness the interrogations and torture sessions, listen to their confessions, and verify all he heard.

Vicente had not wanted to be honored in this way, and his bleak mood did not improve when he rode his mule behind Sotomayor and Quiñones over an old bridge and past walls built by the Moors centuries ago. Seventy miles south of Madrid, the ancient city of Toledo had been built on a bare rocky precipice high above the stark Castilian plain and the Tagus River that surrounded it on three sides. Even on this sunny summer day, Toledo projected an image of austere inflexibility. Its narrow precipitous streets appeared to Vicente more like Stygian canyons between tall grim houses of stone, most with windowless walls, and appearing as one with the brown and gray rocky formations. Unlike other Spanish cities that shimmered with pleasing hues of sienna and dull old gold, Toledo loomed somber umber and funereal gray.

Perhaps no city or town could have cheered Vicente because of his destination. He knew what to expect. The accused would have been told nothing about the charges and flung into filthy cells. They could be held incommunicado from several weeks to many years as part of a softening process or because they had been simply forgotten. At trial, they were not allowed to confront their accusers. Anyone who tried to communicate with the prisoners committed a grave offense. Attempts to escape were regarded as proof of guilt. The Tribunal swore all accusers, witnesses, and officials to silence. Ultimately, the Inquisitors urged the prisoner to confess guilt, profess repentance, and entreat pardon. Denial and confessions given too quickly or perceived as insincere earned more torture sessions.

With Sotomayor's endorsement and presence as his credentials, Vicente gained access to the Toledo Tribunal's dungeons. Although an occasional cell held some wretched accused Judaizer, Olivares' government had generally succeeded in protecting the Portuguese new-Christians from unjust denunciations. Most were homosexuals, bigamists, sorcerers, and heretics. Rats scurried about the windowless cells where the prisoners lay in their own excrement on vermin-infested straw.

The chamber of tortures lay below the prison cells, and Vicente viewed it as Dante's lowest level of descent into Hell. All gray stone, it resembled a cavernous vaulted armory where soldiers trained. At one end, an enormous fireplace flamed and held boiling cauldrons for heating the instruments of torture. To terrorize the prisoners into confessing, the guards took them past a row of tables where they forced them to look at hooks, knives, clamps, and other devices no longer used such as thumbscrews and headbands that could be tightened. An open iron maiden stood at the end beside cages filled with hungry rats.

Depending upon the seriousness of the charges, three to five Inquisitors sat at a long table on a dais, with a clerk below at a smaller table. They commanded each prisoner brought before them to confess crimes and name accomplices. A refusal, denial, or unsatisfactory answer sent the victim back to the torturers' fiendish devices for more intense questioning. Several of the accused might be tortured at the same time.

Vicente needed all his willpower to maintain his composure, but he could not ignore the screaming and pleas for mercy. The Inquisition spared no one because of age, gender, or illness. Physicians moderated the torments, not out of charity, but to ensure that the prisoners would not die before confessing.

Am I as guilty as the torturers because I am doing nothing to save the accused? But then, what can I do beyond a futile gesture?

Hair and beard matted, his body covered with filth, vermin, and sores, Begoña came before the Tribunal. After he refused to speak, the torturers, who tied the *alumbrado's* wrists behind his back, inserted a wedge between the ropes, and fastened weights to the chains around his feet. They hoisted Begoña high off the floor by the *strappado*, pulley cords attached to his bound wrists.

An interrogator repeated a series of questions concerning the blasphemous rituals and demanded names of the participants and members of all his arks. Begoña ignored him, and the torturers jerked the pulleys. The other prisoners had screamed in pain when their arms were pulled back and up. Not Begoña. With each refusal to answer, the torturers added more weights to the next hoist and drop, which dislocated his joints.

Vicente struggled to visualize his beloved Fragrant Coast in this Hell and failed. He asked himself how anyone who called himself human could willingly inflict pain and injury on another, listen unmoved to the screams and pleas for mercy, or tolerate the stench of burnt flesh and released bowels and bladder. He answered his own question. A sincere zealot might if he believed torture, confession, and repentance could save souls. Sotomayor and another Inquisitor shed tears, frustrated that the accused might be eternally damned, but other inquisitors and most torturers found this vault of horrors to be heaven on earth. One interrogator stood over a naked terrified young woman tied along a bench. Torturers rubbed her soles with an oily combustible material and held lighted candles to her feet. Her screams and writhing excited the Inquisitor. And Quiñones was everywhere in the dungeon observing, listening, and writing.

After Begoña passed out, an Inquisitorial physician advised the tribunal that the *alumbrado* had taken enough for the moment and ended his torture session for the day and dragged him to his cell, That night, Sotomayor and the *alcalde* slept peacefully in the Inquisition dormitory. Vicente awakened often during vivid nightmares, in which he relived the hell of relentless tortures.

I cannot rescue those already in the hands of the Inquisition, but I will do everything possible to prevent unjust denunciations and arrests, and when possible, help them escape from Spain.

After matins, Vicente confessed Sotomayor, who believed that his painful toothache was God's punishment for his continuing sin of envying the Inquisitor General. He recommended oil of cloves as a balm, and the King's Confessor arranged for him to preach during the *alumbrado*'s next interrogation. Inspired by the manmade horrors he had seen in the vault, Vicente impressed the five Inquisitors on the dais with his powerful imagery of eternal torment while he harangued Begoña, who required support from two black hooded Dominicans in order to stand.

He concluded his sermon, and Inquisitor General Pacheco said, "Surely there are others we have not yet caught. Name them." When Begoña continued to stare at him with unblinking hypnotic cobalt blue eyes, Pacheco looked away. "Apply the *aselli*."

The torturers stripped Begoña naked and stretched him on a table of sharply edged rungs with his spine placed along an iron bar. They bound his arms and legs to the sides and placed his head on a section of the table lower than his body and secured it by an iron band.

At a command from Pacheco, Vicente raised his great silver crucifix over the *alumbrado*'s head and exhorted Begoña one more time to speak and reconcile with the Church. "Confess. Save your soul from eternal pain greater than any you have suffered and will suffer here on earth." He waited, then turned and faced the Tribunal. "He will not speak, Your Reverence."

Pacheco gestured for the torture to proceed. They forced open Begoña's mouth and shoved a strip of linen into his gullet, which reminded Vicente of Bernardo de Anglesola's fate years earlier.

A torturer selected a jar filled with water and poured its entire contents into Begoña's mouth. The liquid slowly oozed through the linen strip, filled the *alumbrado's* throat and nostrils, and almost suffocated him.

With each *jarra*, the cords around Begoña's arms and legs tightened, and veins popped to the bursting point. Vicente continued to exhort the *alumbrado* to confess, understanding that by now, Begoña would feel nothing in any limb or joint. After the torturer poured the fourth jar, he pulled the cloth from Begoña's throat. Water and blood gushed forth as the helpless prisoner gargled and gasped for breath. Vicente waited until the *alumbrado* breathed regularly before he commanded him yet again to confess. Begoña sustained his silence after two more *jarras* and during the fire treatment as well.

The following day, Vicente took his turn, addressed Begoña as Brother in Christ, and pleaded with him to confess. The *alumbrado* maintained his maddening silence, and as the torturers bound his right foot to the rack, an expression come over him as if he were at peace with himself. While Vicente repeated the same questions, the torturers stretched and tied each arm and foot to the rack and compressed the fleshy parts of arms and thighs with fine cords. After Begoña failed to respond to any question, they inflicted a simultaneous tension of the cords on each of his limbs and parts. He never cried out.

Vicente stood with Quiñones and watched the torturers drag the *alumbrado* back to his cell. The *alcalde* wrote a line in his notebook and said, "I have begun to write a treatise on the effect of pain on humans. I wish the Holy Office would accede to my request for an unlimited supply of condemned prisoners to use for my experiments. Anyway, this Begoña is an extraordinary man. Without uttering a single moan or cry of pain, he endured all without confessing. I believe he hypnotizes himself to withstand pain."

An art to be envied by all Spaniards who live under threat of arrest and torture by the Inquisition. "If what you say is correct, Don Juan, no amount of torture will ever break him."

"Not those currently permitted." Quiñones touched a thumbscrew on the table of forbidden devices. "However, I am acquainted with certain methods that have worked well and efficiently over the centuries, now prohibited by the Holy Office, but which ought to be reinstated. Don Vicente, surely you agree with me."

"You know I do."

"I will show you some very interesting and persuasive devices the next time you honor my home with a visit. With them, I know I could have made that *alumbrado* talk."

Chapter 33
Dreams and Reality

Vicente waited for María in the gardens of the Casa de Campo and enjoyed the late afternoon mellow sunlight and fresh air scented by May flowers. Legions of butterflies splashed tree trunks and walls with their vivid colors. Hummingbirds competed with swarms of bees for pollen. Swallows and larks sang their spring songs and inspired him to voice his own.

He picked up a lute left on a bench by one of the Infanta's ladies, sat under a great elm, and strummed until the words of Solomon's *Song of Songs* and those of Moorish poets merged with his own. He composed a melodic love song based on memories of his night dream, which he played and sang in a minor key:

> Come again, my beloved,
> Come visit my dreams.
> No gold more bright, no flower sweeter;
> Fairer than the moon, more brilliant than the sun.
>
> Your voice sings like the bird.
> Your movement more graceful than the swan.
> Your name spoken is as perfume poured forth.
> I breathe your rich fragrance.
>
> Come to me, my beloved,
> And let me drown in the sea of your beauty.
> Your face is as clear as a crystal goblet,
> Your hair, shining as a field of flaxen wheat,
> Your forehead a fair moon.
> Your bewitching eyes destroy my will,

The whites, pure like bowls of alabaster,
Your pupils as aquamarines.
Your nose as defined as the edge of a Toledo sword
Your cheeks, as sweet apples
Your mouth, a rosebud,
Your lips, as threads of scarlet,
So lovely when parted in speech,
With teeth as rows of fine pearls.
Your smile, as soft lightning, devastates me.

When you come to me
In my dreams, my beloved,
Your neck is a polished ivory tower,
Your breasts are full wineskins,
Your nipples pink cherries,
Your stomach as a rounded goblet,
Your navel brimming with spiced wine,
Your legs as marble pillars,
Your feet as tiny leaves of lotus on the lake.

When we embrace, my beloved,
Your arms and legs entwine me in gossamer,
Your skillful fingers dissolve my will,
Your skin as smooth as fine velour,
Your buttocks yield as Turkish pillows.
Your delta a silken tapestry of gold threads.

When we kiss, my beloved,
The taste of your mouth is pure virgin honey,
Smoothly gliding over my lips and teeth
And the perfume of your essence
Is sweeter than the fragrant coast of Valencia.
How much better your love is than wine

Come again my beloved,
Come visit my dreams . . .

Vicente sensed he was no longer alone. He turned to face the Infanta, an angelic vision in pale blue and gold velour. Only the identically dressed Inéz accompanied her. They had outpaced her *meninas* and *duenna*.

As Vicente genuflected, he felt his face burning. "*Alteza* . . . "

She cut him off with an imperious wave of her fan. Her face flushed with color. "Don Vicente, what were you singing?"

He tried to read her expression. How long had she been listening? "*Alteza*, I was remembering some songs of my childhood."

She motioned for Inéz to withdraw out of hearing. "And your loves?"

"I have never loved." *Until you.*

"But you called for your beloved to come to you again in your dreams."

"It's only a song, *Alteza*. Moorish in origins, I must confess, possibly as old as Solomon."

"A rather profane song, from our pious confessor." The Infanta permitted herself a slight, wry smile. "Tell me, Friar, who is she who visits you in your dreams? A vile succubus?" Her tone became more threatening. "A lady of the Court?"

Vicente let his silence speak eloquent sonnets of his great love for her. He held his breath when María seemed as if she were about to express her own true feelings. Instead, she looked away and covered her face with the fan.

"Perhaps you should be penanced, Don Vicente." The Infanta paused when the rest of her entourage entered the garden and glanced at the lute. "As we know, Don Vicente is quite competent with stringed instruments. One evening we shall summon him to entertain us with his liturgical songs."

Vicente appreciated her subtle humor. "It will be my pleasure, *Alteza*."

She bade him sit with her on their favorite bench under the shade of elms. "What news do you bring us today?"

"The Assembly of Castile has voted to enshrine Teresa as sole patron saint of Spain, and Olivares has sent a copy of her autobiography to Rome accompanied by a passionate plea to the Pope for his support in the matter."

She crossed herself and thanked God for hearing her prayers. "Have you nothing else to tell us?"

"No, *Alteza*."

She frowned. "Then you have not heard?"

"Heard what?"

"That cunning Satan. Olivares should have told you. Next month, on the first day of June, we shall be betrothed to our cousin Ferdinand, King of Hungary, and, henceforth, to be addressed as Queen of Hungary."

Vicente felt sick at heart even though he had expected her eventual betrothal. "My congratulations, Your Majesty."

"What congratulations? Now we must endure another humiliating courtship."

"Surely, King Ferdinand is not coming here?"

"No, and even if he should, we shall never consent to another public wooing. We can be certain of one thing. Our two great empires will be negotiating our dowry like merchants haggling over the market price of common goods."

"Of course you will not attend these insulting negotiations."

"They may take years. Our financial position is so weak our Austrian cousins will delay the marriage until sufficient dowry has been accumulated."

"And when the road from Italy to Vienna is safe for you to travel, *Alt* . . . Your Majesty." Vicente forced a smile. "Until then, your life will go on as before."

"No, there are to be changes that will affect us for the worst," she said in French when her duenna moved closer. "You know that the palace is to be renovated."

Vicente had seen the plans of the Royal Architect, Gómez de Mora, who had built the Plaza Mayor. De Mora had begun to improve and embellish the façade of the Alcazar and to create cool and pleasant summer quarters for the royals in the vaulted stone chambers below the palace.

"But the changes will not reach the hidden passageways and rooms," Vicente said also in French.

The Infanta glowered at her *duenna*, who backed away in panic, and said in Spanish, "As Queen of Hungary, we shall have our own household, our own *mayordomo*. We shall be surrounded by dozens of servants and ladies at all times, and the Countess of Lemos has been selected as our principal Lady of the Bedchamber. Imagine. She has even been granted the privilege of having rooms in the palace. Soon everyone in Madrid will have apartments here."

Vicente knew that she was referring to Olivares' only child, his sixteen-year old daughter also named María, who had been given rooms in the palace after marrying her cousin, Ramiro Nuñez de Guzmán, Marqués de Heliche and Duke of Medina de las Torres.

The Infanta raised her voice so that all in hearing would not mistake her will. "Of course, you shall continue as our confessor and spiritual director, Don Vicente, and, when the time comes, accompany us to the Imperial Court."

Chapter 34
Eloquent Preacher

María's betrothal to the King of Hungary was to be celebrated on the first Sunday in July with a great *auto-de-fé* of the *alumbrados* convicted in the Begoña affair. The populace had been promised a full menu that also included several dozen condemned Judaizers, heretics, bigamists, impostors, magicians, witches, sorcerers, and those guilty of making pacts with demons.

Excepting the *alumbrados*, all prisoners had been languishing in cells to be saved for a great show. Although the typical case averaged three to four years, with many taking up to fourteen years between arrest and sentencing, the Count-Duke had pushed Inquisitor General de Pacheco to speed the process for Begoña and his followers. He was eager for the ultimate destruction of his now dead enemy, de Zamárraga, whose decomposed corpse was to be exposed for ridicule and burned as a warning to others attempting to block his reforms.

Olivares also wanted to give the public a great *auto-de-fé* without disturbing his new-Christian financiers, who would be seated among the privileged spectators. The accused Judaizers were poor, mostly illiterate Portuguese.

Begoña had been condemned to the *quemadero* with four of his most fanatic disciples who had not reconciled and three inconsequential Portuguese Judaizers. Five men and women, who had been accused of Judaizing and fled Spain, were to be burned in effigy with the exhumed corpses of the de Zamárragas and two dead Judaizers.

The notaries had written almost a thousand folio pages of testimony for each of the accused and appended them to inventories of their household effects and property, depositions, and full genealogical minutia. Inquisitors and the *Consulta de Fé*, which included a representative of the bishop in each accused's diocese, had decided the sentences.

Public *autos-de-fé* were deemed necessary for several reasons: To stress the serious nature of certain crimes, to spread the glories and terrors of the Catholic Church, and to provide the credulous populace with spectacle. They were announced several weeks in advance with great fanfare and ceremony. Black hoods carried the standards of the Inquisition throughout the streets of Madrid. Notices were posted for the literate, and proclamations read to the public. The Holy Office guaranteed spiritual benefits for all who attended the spectacle, which always brought in hordes of rural louts from the countryside.

Carpenters sawed, hammered, and erected platforms and scaffolding in the Plaza Mayor. Balconies offering the best views and shade from the brutal July sun had been reserved for the royal family and the *grandeza*, who required the owners of the apartments to provide ample food, iced drinks, and comfortable seating for their illustrious guests.

Late Saturday afternoon, Lope de Vega, as a Familiar of the Holy Office, was given the honor of leading the procession of the Cruz Verde, the Green Cross of the Holy Office, from the Colegio de Doña María de Arago to the plaza. He carried the awesome standard of the Inquisition displaying its arms on one side, *Misericordia et Justicia*, and those of the King of Spain on the other.

Familiars and ecclesiastics followed Lope and carried more banners through the streets of Madrid. The somber procession passed the Alcazar and proceeded to the Plaza Mayor, where the Green Cross was placed at a specially constructed altar with an honor guard stationed around it. That same night, those condemned to burn heard their sentences at the Palace of the Inquisition and listened to exhortations for them to repent.

Before dawn on Sunday, a large crowd gathered at the square to celebrate masses at the altar of the Green Cross. Temporary platforms had been covered with colorful damasks and balconies shaded by bright canopies with silk hangings over the grilles bearing the vivid Royal and noble arms of their occupants.

At dawn, while the Dominicans sang another mass, troops of German and Spanish guards arrived to preserve order, and a company of royal archers took their stations to protect King Philip. Morning bells rang throughout Madrid, and the great square filled. Members of the Councils of Castile, Aragón, Italy, Portugal, Flanders, and the Indies took their seats on the balconies reserved for them.

After lauds, the royal family, Olivares, and other *grandees* left the Alcazar in coaches with their wives and attendants. That same hour, the accused were taken from the prisons of the Inquisition and paraded along the streets of Madrid to a dirge of drums and mournful wailing of horns. As the prisoners trudged towards the Plaza Mayor, the populace harassed and ridiculed them.

Each of the accused wore an identically decorated coraza, a tall peaked paper hat, and a yellow sambenito colored according to offense and punishment. Those abjuring their heresies *de vehementi* held lighted tapers in their hands and wore a sack transversed by a black St. Andrew's cross. Other prisoners convicted of formal heresy wore sambenitos with one diagonal stripe. They shuffled into the square between their guards and were led to one of two great platforms in the center where they stood between the pulpits and an altar draped in black velvet cloth.

If the prisoner had escaped the *quemadero* by confessing and reconciling, flames pointing downwards were painted on the garment. The men and women who had been condemned to burning carried a green cross in their hands and wore on their *sambenitos* representations of devils thrusting heretics into hell.

The royals were seated in their balconies. Vicente sat with the ecclesiastic and civic authorities on one of the two great raised platforms. Dignitaries and officials of the Holy Office and the city of Madrid entered the plaza. Inquisitor General Andrés de Pacheco went to the Royal Balcony where he administered an oath to the King. Philip swore to defend the faith and give all possible support to the Holy Office. Below them, a notary of the Inquisition raised a cross, and everyone present in the square repeated the same oath.

Drenched in sweat under his woolen robe, Vicente fought physical discomfort by concentrating on the tedious ceremony. The early morning heat and bright sunlight gave every indication that the day was going to be a pitiless scorcher. The prisoners, the clergy, guards, and spectators would have no relief, no siesta, and no break for meals until after the ceremonies ended. Only the royals and other dignitaries who had the good fortune to watch from the balconies would be able to take refreshments and relieve themselves in private. Some preferred to stand where slop-men plied their trade. Before the *auto* ended, bladders and bowels would burst, a number of clerics would faint, many of the laity too, and several of the elderly would die of sunstroke.

Sotomayor gave the first harangue against the condemned. Other preachers known for their eloquence followed the royal confessor and castigated the prisoners. Then Vicente's turn came. His piety and moving sermons were renowned throughout the Alcazar, and as a reward for denouncing Begoña's cult, he had been given the honor of preaching at this *auto-de-fé*.

Vicente stepped to the black pulpit. Under the bright, blazing late morning sun, he scanned the royal balconies and saw the Queen of Hungary fanning herself in anticipation of his sermon. What must María be thinking? Although they had never discussed the horrors of the Inquisition, he knew her uncompromising views on heresy. Had she not expressed her wish that he would one day be her Torquemada? He wanted to believe she pitied these unfortunates, the same as he, but dared not show her emotions.

Vicente squinted at the shamed prisoners. Don Lope must have suffered identical humiliation. He stifled those thoughts and began his sermon. His deep voice filled the square as he heaped opprobrium on the Judaizers and exhorted them to convert to the True Faith. Next, using his most theatrical gestures, he assailed Begoña and his disciples:

"These *alumbrados*, lost in the empty blind simplicity of their own essence, they feel no zeal, no inclination towards God. Not internally, not externally. To the contrary, they believe themselves to be God."

While Vicente preached, he felt a unique power. He had never held the attention of so large a congregation. He was one man among thousands, including the royal family, the *grandeza*, ministers of the Great Councils, and *la Suprema*. He was the one man who had every pair of eyes watching and each pair of ears listening to his performance. If he commanded them to leave, to massacre the prisoners, or to fall to their knees, he believed all would obey.

"These *alumbrados* lack true faith, hope, and charity. In their empty and naked state, they claim to have neither knowledge nor love. They claim to be excused from every virtue. They live without conscience, no matter how depraved their evil. They neglect the sacraments, virtues, and observances of the Holy Church. They esteem themselves above all things fit for imperfect men. For them, the highest degree of sanctity lies in following without restraint their own base natural instincts. They remain inwardly idle, with their spirit prone to evil. Outwardly, they indulge each impulse, thus satisfying the desires of the body, pleasing their flesh. And their abominations are many . . . "

Vicente recited specific examples of Begoña's abominations, which most of the horrified spectators in the square heard for the first time. Women screamed and fainted. Men shouted curses at the *alumbrados* and wept. Begoña saw nothing and heard nothing.

Vicente next described the terrors Satan and Hell had in store for the unrepentant, his usual variation on the tortures of the Inquisition and worse, those Quiñones would have applied. After he ended his sermon in a passionate crescendo of imagery, he looked towards María. In the shade of her balcony, the Queen of Hungary fanned herself with one hand and wiped tears from her eyes with the other.

After more preachers followed Vicente to the pulpit, the judges were sworn in one-by-one. Those prisoners who had reconciled with the Church took turns at the pulpit to hear the details of their indictments enumerated for the populace. They were asked by the Inquisitor General, "Dost thou believe that God is One in essence and Three in Person?"

"Yes, I believe," was their required response to each question.

Next, the prisoners faced a crucifix and swore adherence to the Roman Catholic faith in every detail. They expressed their hatred of all heresies, emphasizing those to which they had confessed, and accepted all punishments imposed by way of penance. Then they heard their sentences pronounced for the first time with specific warnings.

The men and women who were not to be scourged were stripped to the waists and forced to carry insignias of their offenses attached to sticks. A crier preceded them around the square and proclaimed the details of their crimes and punishments. Before the guards gagged a proud *hidalgo* bigamist, he screamed at the officials that he preferred death to such unbearable shame.

The Inquisitors warned the bigamists, sorcerers, and impostors who offered light abjuration that they would be held impenitent if they failed to comply with their sentences. They threatened the rest that failure to do penance would cause them to be treated as relapsed heretics and as such face certain death at the stake.

The crowd in the square was not interested in the light penances, which included fasting on Fridays for a specified length of time or reciting a number of Our Fathers and Hail Marys. The mob looked forward to public scourging and other humiliating punishments given to their social betters, even if in effigy or as exhumed corpses like the de Zamárragas.

Throughout the *auto-de-fé,* Vicente had been most interested in the fate of the new-Christians. Even if a male Judaizer confessed his crime and vehemently reconciled, he would still be sent to the galleys for a period of three years to life. A reconciled woman faced perpetual imprisonment and servitude in Houses of Mercy or Penance. When freed, some of the men might be exiled to the colonies. All were banned from specific cities, their houses and places of heretical worship razed to the ground.

Children of Judaizers and their descendants were to be denied public dignity and entry into Holy Orders as long as they lived. Professions closed to them were those of physician, apothecary, tutor of the young, scrivener, advocate, and farmer of revenue. They were forbidden to wear cloth of gold or silver, ride on horseback, although a mule or donkey was acceptable.

After the final sentence was passed, the Inquisitor General intoned *Immunde Spiritus.* Then the royal choir chanted the Psalm *Miserere mei Dominus,* followed by prayers urging all to turn away from heretical errors and depraved apostasies, which included Jewish superstition, Muslim sect, and all Protestant heresies.

The *auto-de-fé* ended twelve hours after it began. The crowd spilled out of the Plaza Mayor and onto the street to harass and ridicule one more time the penanced prisoners while they trudged back to their cells. Vicente took part in the procession of Dominicans led by monks carrying the Cruz Verde and their Order's Cruz Blanca to the Monastery of San Tomás. Because the Holy Office was limited to saving souls and combating heresies, they handed the condemned to the secular authorities for execution at the *quemadero* on the morrow.

The following morning Vicente marched in yet another procession of Dominican preachers and confessors ahead of the condemned who rode donkeys and were flanked by soldiers on horseback. Covered in corazas and sambenitos, the decomposed bodies, skeletons, and grotesque effigies of the dead and those who had fled also had been tied to mules. *Madrileños* pelted the prisoners with offal, contents of chamber pots, and refuse on the way to the *Quemadero de la Puerta de Fuencarral* outside the city gates.

Thousands had come to witness the burning of heretics, and as with bullfights, jousts, and *autos*, many paid high prices for windows and balconies with a good view. Arce stood among the Inquisitors, Lope de Vega in the forefront of the Familiars, and Quiñones at the head of the *alcaldes*. The crowd shouted curses and threats as the condemned rode out of the city toward the Puerta de Fuencarral. When Begoña dismounted, he almost touched a spectator with his sambenito. The man screamed and backed away in terror, afraid of contamination by a mere brush from the costume. Soldiers brought order and dragged the *alumbrado* towards his pyre.

Executioners tied the living to stakes between skeletons, effigies, and the rotting bodies of the Zamárragas and other corpses. Guards laughed at them and made jests. Vicente and other friars raised their crucifixes and once again exhorted the condemned to confess. A last moment profession of repentance could earn a merciful garrote before the pyres were lit.

Begoña regarded all with contempt until Arce began preaching to him. He spat at the Inquisitor and screamed at him in a language no one understood.

The lighting of the first brand was a pious honor usually bestowed upon royalty or a distinguished visitor. Vicente worried when the Queen of Hungary's carriage arrived at the *quemadero* and behind it another Royal Coach of State with an escort of German guards. He did not want to believe that María could or would watch living humans burn to death. He held his breath until the door of the Queen of Hungary's carriage opened. Not María, the Austrian ambassador stepped out of her carriage as Olivares and Infante Don Carlos emerged from the other coach.

Quiñones raised a finger to gauge the direction of the wind. "Today, the smoke will blow away from much of the city. That will please the women who always complain the ashes from the *quemadero* soil their Monday wash."

The Austrian ambassador, who had negotiated María's betrothal, took a brand from one of the executioners and applied the torch to dry wood at the foot of a Judaizer. As more pyres were lit, Vicente sang psalms with the other friars and preachers. He tried and failed to shut out the screams and moans of agony, the sickening sweet stench of cooked human flesh, and the infernal sight of vibrant bodies charred to cinders.

The crowd cheered.

That evening, the Queen of Hungary summoned Vicente to her new enlarged apartments. She was surrounded by her entire household of *meninas, duennas*, aged *hidalgos, mayordomo*, other royal confessors, *bufónes*, and watchful principal lady of the bedchamber, the Countess of Lemos, whose beady eyes missed nothing. The Austrian ambassador who had lit the first brand at the *quemadero*, Infante Don Carlos, the Cardinal-Infante, and Olivares also attended Her Majesty. Philip and Isabel were the only notables absent.

María looked every bit a queen on her gilded throne chair cushioned with a burgundy satin fabric highlighted by tendrils of gold thread. She stared straight ahead at no one in particular, yet she saw everything. Her hair and complexion shone gold and ivory against her velvet brown dress trimmed in silver and decorated with pearls. Inéz stood at her feet in identical miniature costume.

"Don Vicente de Rocamora, we have summoned you to let you know how pleased we were with your sermon yesterday."

"The Lord spoke through me, Your Majesty." He almost had said *Alteza*.

She turned her head towards the Austrian Ambassador to make it clear that what she had to say was intended for him to understand. "Don Vicente, we wish for all to know that we honor you for your piety, eloquence, and for your tireless service as our confessor and spiritual director. When the time comes for us to journey to our future husband, King Ferdinand of Hungary, we shall be pleased to have you come with us and continue as our confessor and spiritual director."

"As you command, Your Majesty." Vicente's joy dissipated and his heart became shrouded in darkness when he saw Olivares and the Austrian exchange looks of mutual understanding, as if they had agreed to deny the Queen of Hungary her wishes.

María tapped her fan on the arm of her chair, and her *mayordomo* presented Vicente with a flat box of polished wood an arms width in length and less than half as wide. He opened it to expose a magnificent miniature Flemish triptych of the seven sacraments painted in vivid tempura.

"Take this altarpiece as a gesture of our esteem."

"Your Majesty honors me far beyond my merits."

"Your humility is equal to your piety." She then gave Vicente permission to withdraw.

Afterwards in Olivares' office where the Count-Duke and the Cardinal-Infante admired María's gift, Fernándo said, "I think, Friar, you would have preferred a sword."

"First, as you well know, I would have chosen a title for my kinsman, Don Jerónimo."

"Then a word of advice," Olivares said. "His son travels in poor company."

Chapter 35
Tallest Man in Spain

Vicente stretched out next to Hombrecillo under the shade of poplars in the Prado during siesta, unable to sleep. It was too hot to do much more than breathe and dwell upon the radical changes in his relationship with the Queen of Hungary. He no longer had unlimited private access to María, except when she confessed, and even that was in jeopardy. The Austrian ambassador had insisted that they begin using the confessional booth, which she had so far refused to do.

Hombrecillo shared an orange with Vicente. "Did you observe how solemn the Queen of Hungary was yesterday during the celebrations of her birthday?"

"How could I not fail to see it? The Crown is too poor to give her a dowry adequate for an immediate marriage. No date has been set for her departure. She sees each detail of the negotiations as further humiliation."

"Alas, the Queen of Hungary has become the most experienced royal virgin in all of Europe." Hombrecillo paused and changed the subject. "Will you leave the Dominicans after Don Ramón becomes Duke of Astórquia?"

"Why should I do that?"

"As you have explained to me, his heir would be the Señor de Rafal. Surely, you would be freed from your pledge of honor."

"And still trapped in the clergy by my vows."

"Then keep an eye on the Capuchin Provincial of Castile, Diego de Quiroga."

Vicente had seen Quiroga in cozy company with the Austrian ambassador. "Is there something I have not been told?"

"Quiroga is fluent in German. He is quite at home at the Imperial Court and an Olivarista. I would not be surprised if he were to be appointed the Queen of Hungary's confessor when the time comes for her to leave Spain."

"She would never accept it."

"To be Empress, she would."

Vicente could not dispute that. His only hope was for María's marriage never to take place. "Is there anything else?"

"What you already know. The Queen of Hungary seems to be happy only in your presence."

Before thinking, Vicente uttered one of his most forbidden thoughts. "Do you think she might be allowed to marry a *grandee* if no king or emperor were available?"

"Never. Unimaginable."

"Will Inéz go to Austria with her?"

"No, the Queen of Hungary is a benevolent young woman who would never separate us. I would die if I should ever be parted from my beloved wife."

"She has a good soul."

"Speaking of souls and other clerical matters, can you tell me the reason for the great debate going on between your Dominicans and the Jesuits?"

"Aside from power and influence?"

"You mean it really is a theological dispute? As if the Santiago-Teresa dispute is not enough to divide our Church. Of course, you can explain the essence of the debate in one clear sentence." Hombrecillo yawned. "And put me to sleep in this miserable heat."

"We disagree over the best way to combat Protestant heresies, and we argue about the distinctions between essence and being, grace and predestination. Dominicans attach greater importance to Divine Grace than to human will and go along with the safest opinion in any moral question. Jesuits will follow any opinion accepted by two or more theological doctors of distinction, which has earned them the reputation of supporting a lax moral code. Over the years, the Jesuits have become too obsessed with solutions to cases which seldom, if ever, come up in real life."

"For example?"

"They worry about such questions as: Is it a greater sin to fornicate with an ugly rather than a beautiful woman? Is a man still obliged to fast if it renders him incapable of fulfilling his conjugal obligations? Is it a sin for a person who has killed his father while in a state of drunkenness to rejoice, not because his father is dead, but because he would inherit a legacy?"

"Then the Holy Orders may yet replace us midgets and dwarfs as the Royal *bufónes*." Hombrecillo pulled on the brim of his hat to shade his eyes. "I am content that my head is too small to support such weighty matters of theological masturbation. I rely upon you, my confessor, to explain them to me."

"I am no theologian."

"Then what are you? Who are you?"

"I am Vicente de Rocamora, Dominican Friar, Her Majesty's confessor and spiritual director."

"Are you deliberately misunderstanding my meaning? I know who I am and my place in the scheme of things. I had dreams and illusions once. Soldier, respected conquistador, honored by the King for service to the Crown. I soon learned never to dwell on what could have been or should have been, had I been born of normal size. In the end, I have accepted who I am . . . a *bufón* . . . no more, no less, a caustic bitter wit, who resents yet makes the most of his small size."

"You are the tallest man I know."

Hombrecillo looked away as tears filled his eyes. "Spoken like a good friend, Vicente. At least that much I do know about you. But again, who are you?"

Vicente pondered on Hombrecillo's difficult question. Did any man have an essence, or was he simply the sum total of his lifetime of actions? In Spain, as Don Lope had often complained, seeming to be was more important than being.

Who was any man at Court? Olivares was no more and no less than what he did. Ballebrera deliberately created his reputation as a wit. The *grandees*, *títulos*, *hidalgos* and *caballeros* were elaborate effigies on the outside and empty within, posturing like bad actors on the stage of life.

Vicente had contrived his own reputation as a pious and eloquent friar. *But who are you?* Hombrecillo had asked. He thought of his promise to Rafal, his loyalty to Moraíma and Don Lope, his restraint with María, and avenging his father's death by taking Anglesola's life. Violante's turn would come.

Calderón de la Barca had written: "To live is but to dream, and in living, man dreams what he is until he awakens." Vicente preferred his dream of love with María to grim reality.

"You asked who I am, Sáncho. I have dreams I dare not reveal, but I do know this. I am a man of honor and keep my word."

Hombrecillo tipped his hat to Vicente. "In the end, honor may be all there is."

Chapter 36
Fully Ripened & Wholly Rotten

Ballebrera was waiting for Vicente when he entered through the back gate of the Astórquia *Palacio*. "I thank God that I was able to hide your disguises and cabinet of medicines in time." Disgust distorted his features. "I have a visitor. He arrived unannounced this morning. Jacinto."

"And evil mischief is his inseparable companion."

Vicente paid his usual respects to Xímena, who was delighted to be the center of so much attention. He masked his hostile reaction to her guest, a slight, pretty young man fashionably dressed in dark brown velvet trimmed in gold.

Twenty-one-year old Jacinto de Rocamora slouched in an armchair. "The eminent Friar. We are honored to be in the presence of the Queen of Hungary's eloquent confessor."

Vicente sat on the couch beside the Duchess. "Is all well with your father?"

"Yes, but with no thanks to you. He wins battles and glory and still no title."

"The Count-Duke is reviewing his petition."

"Olivares surrounds himself with those of tainted blood, like himself. We all know once one of their ilk worms his way in, he makes room for others until the entire nest is infested."

"Be careful, *cousin*." Vicente emphasized the last word, which caused Jacinto to wince. "Such accusations can end a career before it begins and cause petitions to be lost permanently."

"Not if they are proven to be true." Jacinto pointed a delicate finger at Vicente. "I expected my father to have his title by now."

Ballebrera intervened. "You know that Vicente is the Queen of Hungary's confessor not a minister of state, nor does he have the ear of His Majesty."

"Well, no matter, when the Count-Duke falls, I intend to be on the winning side."

"How can one such as you know that he will fall?" Ballebrera asked.

Xímena interrupted them with loud snort. She had fallen asleep, and Jacinto sneered at the old woman. "How nice for you, Friar, that Ramón is to wed the Duchess. My father will probably release you from your promise the day he becomes Duke of Astórquia and our senior line is made his heir."

Vicente and Ballebrera looked at each other horrified. Jacinto must have been listening outside the door when Rafal had shown them the codicil and discussed the possibility of Vicente's new-Christian taint through his mother's family. The boy most certainly would have told Tomás what he had heard.

Vicente believed however much Jacinto desired to do so, he would never denounce him as a partial-new-Christian and bring suspicion and disgrace upon all de Rocamoras. Tomás would maintain a discreet silence as well because of his ambition to achieve high office in the Church.

"Olivares is hesitant in the matter of your father's title because he is displeased that you have chosen to associate with his enemies and is disgusted with specific aspects of your behavior." Vicente went on to cite examples of Jacinto's cruelty and bestiality that had been brought to the Count-Duke's attention.

"How dare a tainted Olivares tell a *limpio* de Rocamora how to live or what to do."

"Perhaps you are still unaware that the Count-Duke is the most powerful man in all Spain. He alone will decide whether or not your father receives his title."

"Which you should have seen to in any case."

Ballebrera shook a fist at Jacinto. "How many times must I tell you? Vicente has worked relentlessly on your father's behalf. And Olivares has at last agreed to consider his petition."

"Well, it really doesn't matter what he decides."

"What? You would destroy your father's chance to obtain a title?"

Jacinto sipped his wine. "After you wed the Duchess, we will have no need of Olivares. You shall be made Duke of Astórquia and a *grandee* first class. My father will become your heir, and as his eldest son, I will follow him as the Eighth Duke. And since you are both quite well along in years, I expect to be a relatively young *grandee*."

Ballebrera leaned forward like a bull ready to charge. "To prevent you from inheriting the title, I would select another heir."

"One of your pretty catamites?"

Ballebrera drew his dagger. Vicente sprang from the couch and stepped in front of him. "Ramón, he isn't worth it."

Ballebrera hesitated, shoved his blade back into its scabbard, and paced the floor. "Jacinto, you have presumed too much. On the day of my marriage,

I shall do what Julius Caesar did for Octavian. I will legally adopt Vicente and make him my heir."

His eyes expressing murderous intent, Jacinto forced a smile. "Ramón, it is unlike you to make so poor a jest. "

"No jest. And I shall write your father in detail why."

Even if Ballebrera had not lost his temper and revealed his plans, Vicente believed he could never inherit the title. Rafal and Jacinto would scheme and litigate until all were dead and the wealth of Astórquia fell into the hands of notaries and lawyers. In the meantime, both he and Ballebrera would be well advised to watch their backs.

After Jacinto left, Ballebrera stood at the edge of the patio pool and contemplated his reflection. "Ay, Vicente, next month I will be fifty years old, with nothing to show for my life."

"You once told me you lived a life of deliberate choice."

"True, but there are times when I wish I had created a family and produced heirs to carry on my direct line and to honor my name."

"You accomplished deeds great enough in Flanders to be made Knight of Alcántara."

"And nothing else since. I have gambled away the years the way I've squandered escudos at the tables. But at cards, I lost only money. I have pissed away my youth, and consequently, all my chances for happiness."

"You truly regret not marrying?"

"Only that I could not marry the great love of my life, Yolanda, my beautiful cousin. There has been no other true love. I am envious when I think of all the wide and long roads open to one as young as you, and the short, narrow alley left to a man my age. Tell me, Vicente, after Jerónimo receives his title will you continue in the clergy?"

Vicente could speak freely because no one was close enough to hear them. "Here in Spain I have no choice in that matter. Once a friar always a friar. Yet, because I serve Olivares, I see myself as less a cleric and more a member of the royal administration."

"And the Queen of Hungary?"

"More than confessor, I am her confidant and friend."

"You love her."

It was not a question. "God help me, Ramón . . . yes, I love her."

"I thought as much. I fear for you. You are careful to hide your feelings?"

"Yes."

"And does she?"

"The Queen of Hungary is a model of circumspect behavior."

"What will you do when she marries her cousin Archduke Ferdinand and moves away to the Imperial Court?"

"María said she would insist I accompany her and continue as her confessor."

"In your heart of hearts, Vicente, what is it you want?"

"I have my secrets, but I will tell you this. I have come to learn that we are all prisoners of events beyond our control and decisions made by the powerful. Our sole expression of free will is how we choose to act. Do we face those winds of change head on, or let them carry us to new adventures?"

"Kismet or God's will, it is all the same."

The following afternoon Ballebrera sought Vicente in the royal chapel. "I have never been so honored."

"What is it?"

"This morning, His Majesty went hunting with the Count-Duke and all the Knights of Alcántara. During our midday meal at the Monastery of San Jerónimo, The King's Chamberlain announced that the royal family and the *grandeza* would attend my wedding to the Duchess of Astórquia. Do you know what that means? After the ceremony, King Philip will call me cousin and make me a *grandee* First Class."

Vicente embraced him. "Can you wait the month?"

"It will seem forever." He took Vicente's arm. "Come with me. I want you there when I tell Xímena that she is to be honored by the Planet King himself."

The moment they arrived at the Astórquia *Palacio*, Vicente sensed trouble. Servants were nowhere in sight. He hurried with Ballebrera through the vestibule and antechambers to the patio where Xímena's lackeys, maids, and cooks were crying and moaning. When they saw Ballebrera, all surrounded him and spoke at once.

Behind them, Jacinto sat facing the fountain on a stone bench supported by cupids and insouciantly sipped his chocolate. The Duchess of Astórquia laid face down and motionless in the shallow patio pool.

"Xímena!" Ballebrera waded into the pool and lifted her out of the water.

"It is too late to save her," Jacinto said between sips. "I found the Duchess like this when I arrived. She must have tripped, fallen, and drowned."

Vicente calculated that either Xímena had walked into the ankle-high tile barrier and fell into the water, or Jacinto had murdered her. He did not doubt it was the latter.

Ballebrera placed the duchess on the patio tiles, crossed himself, and tried to read Jacinto's facial expression. "Xímena never walked unescorted."

"Today must have been an exception. You know how careless old women can be. It seems to have happened just before I arrived." Jacinto forced a sigh of regret. "If only I had come earlier."

Ballebrera reached for his dagger. "Assassin. You have ruined me."

Jacinto raised his hands. "I am unarmed. Surely, you will not murder your own kin."

Shaking with repressed anger, Ballebrera cursed Jacinto and stormed into the house.

After Vicente gave the Duchess last rites and told the servants to carry her inside, he seized Jacinto's doublet and pulled him to his feet. "You fool. Now your father may never earn his title."

"If that is the price we must pay, then it is worth it. How dare Ramón presume to make you his heir. The *grandeza* was meant only for old-Christians. Besides, after my faction destroys *Olivares*, I will gain a title on my own. And I promise you this. Once the Count-Duke is out of the way, you and I will have our day of reckoning. But be assured, I would never denounce you to the Holy Office. Unfortunately we carry the same family name, and the Inquisition might investigate me as well. I will choose other means to settle with you."

Vicente tightened his grip. "What cause have I given you to hate me so?"

"You exist. That is sufficient."

"Then let me earn your hatred by my chosen actions." In one swift move, Vicente reached under his sleeve, pulled out a dagger, and slashed Jacinto's cheek from mouth to ear.

Chapter 37
Irreplaceable Losses

Now Queen of Hungary, María suffered through meals as formal as those of King Philip's. Whenever possible, she invited Vicente to say grace and dine with her. Despite their lack of personal contact during the repast, he viewed the ritual at her royal table as great theater. The chief steward knelt and waited for his mistress to come to the table. After Vicente said grace, Doña María sat first, then the others by rank if she had company other than her chaperone and favorite *menina*. The *mayordomo* of the Queen of Hungary's household stood by her side and held a staff to indicate his status. Then carver, butlers, and cellar men served according to strict protocol. Each time she wished to drink, a cellar man fetched a goblet from a nearby dresser, uncovered it, and presented it to the physician attending the royal meal. He then covered the glass, and accompanied by two macebearers and a footman, knelt and presented it to her. After she drank, the cup was carried back to the dresser, while the cellar man brought a napkin to wipe her lips. Identical presentations followed each dish until the end of the meal, when Vicente gave thanks to God.

One rare evening after supper, the Countess of Lemos was absent due to a severe illness, and Vicente and Maria sat facing each other in her drawing room. She had dismissed her entourage except for an elderly *duenna* who had fallen asleep in a corner of the *estrado*, as elderly *duennas* were wont to do.

Although the windless August heat baked the palace walls and stifled the interiors, the Queen of Hungary was all in black. As if God had visited on the mighty a season of death, fetid gloom shrouded the entire palace. Philip and Isabel were beginning their third month of mourning for their daughter who had died shortly after birth, again leaving them without an heir. Within days of Xímena's funeral, Olivares' only legitimate child and beloved daughter died at age seventeen. Earlier in the year, the great literary giant, Góngora, had passed on, and only the day before, Hombrecillo's kinsman, Philip III's royal chaplain and patron of Velázquez, Juan de Fonseca, had been buried.

The Holy Office also had not been spared. Inquisitor General Andrés de Pacheco passed on and was replaced by seventy seven year old Cardinal António de Zapata who was so dedicated to the Church he renounced his title of Conde de Barajas. Yet again Sotomayor had been passed over. Vicente was more disappointed than the royal confessor. Zapata's protégé, the bigoted and ambitious Diego de Arce y Reynoso, now had unlimited access to supreme power within the Holy Office.

María spoke in a near whisper so as not to disturb her chaperone. "This morning the Austrian ambassador requested a private audience. He wished to tell me personally that I am now Queen of both Hungary and Bohemia."

"My congratulations, Your Majesty. You are acquiring an empire without leaving the Alcazar."

"Hollow titles. I can be called Empress of the World for all it matters and still I am unmarried and childless." Realizing what she had said, María blushed and briefly covered her face with her fan. "Don Vicente, is God punishing my brother for his sins?"

He understood that the Queen of Hungary had referred to Philip's affair with sixteen-year old María Calderón, the most popular singer and dancer in Madrid. "The question you posed is difficult to answer, Your Majesty. The little Infanta lived for only a few days, and Queen Isabel still grieves over the death of her child. Have mother and daughter sinned?"

"You never give a direct answer."

"All is revealed through faith. Life is the great test of our faith."

He did not voice his own question: Why would an all-powerful God, if He existed, need to use the death and suffering of innocents to punish the guilty or to teach mere mortals a salutary lesson? Why bother with mankind at all?

"Don Vicente, you are right as always. Forgive us. We have been in foul humor with so much death and sickness around us."

He agreed that the Alcazar had become more hospital than palace. The fever had put most of the court in bed, including the King.

"Don Vicente, how is it that you have not succumbed to the fever. Is it because of your virtue?"

From anyone else, he would have considered her question to be sarcasm. He crossed himself and said, "I thank God for blessing me with a healthy constitution and good fortune. And you, Your Majesty, even though you have behaved like a saint, tirelessly ministering to the ill in their beds, you also have been spared while your brothers have been laid low."

"We have not been spared more insults, with their endless haggling over our dowry as if we were a basket of fruit at a farmer's stall."

Vicente suppressed a smile when he recalled a common phrase: *Las mujeres y melónes, por casta se han de probar*, women and melons must be tested by their caste. He suspected one major cause of María's ill temper was that in two weeks she would be twenty-one, unwed, and still a virgin.

"How we hate the sound of our voice when we complain. You are a good man, Don Vicente. You are like a healing balm for our anguished soul. We will confess now what we believe may be sinful thoughts."

"Yes?" he said in the hope of hearing more about her dreams of an incubus.

"We rejoice in the one good outcome of all this sickness in the palace. It has given us an opportunity to meet alone."

Because the Countess of Lemos and most of her household were ill, Vicente might have rejoiced with the Queen of Hungary if little Inéz also had not gone to bed with fever. "And we have missed our conversations."

"We often think about you. How odd my confessor is the one individual who knows more about us than anyone else."

"Your Majesty, I know what I see and what you tell me. They are merely an infinitesimal part of you. The depths of your true self can be known only to God."

"But we have been confessed by other friars and priests. We have listened to the sermons of other preachers. This is different. We are more serene, happiest when you are here. We wish we could conjure you at will."

You have in your dreams. If only you would do so in reality as well.

Wearing his *hábito* of Alcántara and armed with sword and pistols, Ballebrera met Vicente in the Queen's Courtyard. Other knights of the Order clustered in groups in both royal patios. Olivares had summoned all his supporters to the palace with orders to spy and prevent any coup attempt. Rumors of a palace revolt had been running unchecked throughout Madrid while Philip lay ill in bed consumed with fever. Many believed and some hoped that his young life was ending. Olivares also was ill, or so he thought in his hypochondria. The Count-Duke's incapacity emboldened his enemies. The disgruntled Castilian ruling class closed ranks against him. Burdened by heavy taxes and increased food prices, the masses were on the verge of a general uprising. Some feared Aragón, Valencia, and Catalonia might declare independence from Madrid at any moment because they had not forgiven the Crown's extortions of the previous year. Powerful *grandees* and their followers clustered around their favorite candidates to replace Philip should he die. Most gambled that Isabel, who was pregnant again, would give birth to a healthy child. A few sought out retarded diffident Infante Carlos, next in line for the throne, or attached their important selves to the Cardinal-Infante.

María followed Vicente's advice not to participate in the intrigues against Olivares. She projected an icy aloofness. If her brothers died of fever and His Majesty's child did not survive, as the only living descendant of Philip III she would become Queen of Spain. Vicente dared hope for such an outcome. It might prevent the Austrian marriage from taking place. If María did become Queen of Spain, he saw himself as her only intimate, perhaps even her *privado*, and eventually her lover if she were to emulate her sister, Anne of France.

Ballebrera took Vicente aside. "Is it true His Majesty is dying?"

"Although our King is seriously ill, he will live, provided the doctors do not kill him."

"Then the rumors are false."

"Completely, but far worse than the palace gossip, enemies of Olivares' reforms are circulating lampoons against him throughout Madrid. Jacinto is prominent among those who are spreading slanderous *murmuraciónes* that Philip is dying as the result of *mal frances* or a wound he received from a jealous rival lover."

Hombrecillo, clad only in linen shirt and breeches, ran towards them. "Help me, help me, Don Vicente. My beloved Inéz is dying."

He left Ballebrera and carried the frail *bufón*, who directed him to a small room in the Queen of Hungary's apartments instead of the palace infirmary. María was applying cold rags to Inéz' fevered brow and ordering the Countess of Lemos and other harassed ladies-in-waiting to bring more ice and broth. She had nursed her little *bufóna* throughout the night.

Vicente looked askance at the attending white-bearded physician, an old-Christian of limited mind and narrow outlook, who fussed with filthy instruments and jars of leeches. He blessed María for her act of charity and kindness and held in check his emotions when he stood over Inéz. Hombrecillo's wife lay unconscious in bed, pale and skeletal, her black hair spread out medusa-like on a white satin pillow.

The physician coughed up phlegm, spat it into his hands, and wiped them on his bloodstained gown. Then he prepared to bleed her.

Vicente decided to speak to Olivares. If the Count-Duke could bring new-Christians to the palace to finance his shaky economic situation, then why not summon better qualified physicians who might be tainted?

"Can you assist us, Don Vicente? You saved her life once before."

"Don Sancho, she must be made to drink her broth."

"My wife will not waken."

"Your Majesty," the physician said, "I must bleed her again."

"Why? Has she any blood left?"

"Bloodletting induces vomiting. Constant application of purges and enemas are the approved methods for evacuating evil humors and cleaning out stomach and bowels."

"We have observed that such medical treatment often does more harm than good. More patients are killed by their doctors than cured."

Vicente admired María"s empiricism even if she did not know the meaning of that word. He had been present when this same doctor of medicine had recommended that an apoplectic *grandee* swallow a glass of urine from a healthy person mixed with salt to induce vomiting. He had seen Olivares' physicians apply earthworms to afflicted parts of the Count-Duke's gouty foot. Some blew dried and powdered human excrement into the eyes of patients as a remedy for cataract. Others prescribed medicines made from crushed human skulls mixed with other fantastic ingredients.

Hombrecillo confronted the physician. "No more. Let God decide if my wife will live."

The Queen of Hungary agreed and stifled the physician's protests with a wave of her fan. "Leave us."

"Your Majesty," Vicente said, "I will stay here with you and Don Sáncho and pray."

María silenced the Countess of Lemos' protest with a look that should have turned the woman to stone. Her eyes softened for Vicente. "You are a good man." She crossed herself and looked at her dying companion. "God be with you, my dear servant."

Vicente touched Inéz' forehead, raised her eyelids, and felt her pulse. "If only she would awaken and we could get her to eat something. I know of some helpful herbs."

María studied him anew. "It seems as if you have studied with physicians."

"I have observed, and I have read books on medicines."

"Will my wife live? I cannot survive without her."

Vicente placed his hand on Hombrecillo's shoulder. "My friend, we will hope for the best and pray for God's mercy." He did not expect the tiny woman to survive the night.

He kneeled with the Queen of Hungary and Hombrecillo at Inéz' bedside. To any observer, he appeared to be praying. Instead, he thought about the shortness of life and the failure of medicine to prolong it. The palace physicians were not completely to blame for their inability to cure. Regardless of their beliefs and skills, they were forced, under penalty of denunciation to the Inquisition for heresy, to apply Galen's theories despite recent discoveries by Vesalius who had proven him wrong.

One could make both theological and medical arguments to support Vesalius' opposition to phlebotomy. God was opposed to bloodletting; and empirical evidence proved that such purges removed life-giving blood and not evil humors. Nevertheless, in a land obsessed with blood, bleeding was the most common medical treatment. Physicians were all too eager to open veins as a cure for disease or to reduce inflammation, while at the same time they disagreed over where to bleed the patient.

Conventional practice in Spain was to bleed the patient's heel first, regardless of the ailment. Some physicians favored bleeding closer to the afflicted part. Others preferred to open a vein on the opposite side of the body at a distance from the ailing part, a treatment borrowed from Arabian medicine and methods advocated by Avicenna. Vicente had seen evidence to the contrary. Bleeding weakened the patient.

If given a choice of careers this night, he would have chosen to have the knowledge and skill to save Inéz's precious little life over royal service, the church, or the army. For a moment, he allowed himself to dream of working as a common physician with María as his wife and helpmate at his side.

At the bells of matins, Vicente awakened and found Inéz dead. Hombrecillo's lifeless body lay beside her. The Queen of Hungary and her chaperones continued to sleep. He hid in his robe the vial from which the *bufón* had drunk a poison. Better to let all know Sáncho had died of a broken heart so he would be buried with his wife in consecrated soil.

Vicente grieved over his loss of two good friends, irreplaceable comrades who had been his protective eyes and ears inside the Alcazar. He no longer had intermediaries he could trust to carry messages to and from María, nor spies to alert him against the intrigues of enemies.

Philip recovered from his fever during the second week in September, 1627. When the Count-Duke got out of bed the same day, dissident *grandees* and their supporters fled Madrid to escape his wrath.

During the following months, Vicente saw little of María because Olivares sent him on missions to the southern and western parts of Spain to confiscate books and manuscripts for his collection and to spy on the assorted kingdoms and provinces. He traveled everywhere but to his beloved fragrant coast of Valencia where he had scores to settle with Violante. Also, too many years had passed since he had seen his mentor, Don Lope and his *pícaro* friends. Eleven years would soon be his daughter's age.

Chapter 38
The Smile

Vicente returned to Madrid from yet another spy mission and quest for rare books in Andalusia, Badajoz at the frontier with Portugal, and the Asturias to the North. He went first to the Astórquia *Palacio*. Although Ballebrera had been deprived of a dukedom and the *grandeza*, Olivares had arranged for him to stay on as *mayordomo* while the Crown reviewed his petition to become Duke, which he would have been had he married the old woman. Because Spain needed money to finance the war, Olivares tried to auction Xímena's estates and title to the highest bidder. When no *poderoso* could afford the enormous price asked, her lands in Vizcaya were divided and sold to loyal Olivaristas, the title temporarily retired, and ownership of the *palacio* placed in limbo until a buyer could be found.

Ballebrera served Vicente hot chocolate while he bathed and repeated the latest *murmuraciónes*. Philip's mistress, Maria Calderón, known by the populace as la Calderóna, had given birth to a son baptized Juan after its paternal great-grandfather's bastard half-brother, victor of the great naval battle against the Turks at Lepanto in 1577. As with all women who had given birth to the King's illegitimate children, with the exception of Moraíma, la Calderóna was banished to a convent for life. Of more importance, Isabel was pregnant again.

Other *murmuraciónes* concerned the Englishman, Buckingham. Because of unfulfilled promises regarding French Princess Henrietta María's dowry and his flawed judgment, he had pressured Charles I to declare war against France. After the French annihilated two-thirds of the English fleet sent to aid the Calvinist Huguenots at La Rochelle, Charles opened peace negotiations with Spain. Many believed that Buckingham's brain had been addled by the *mal frances* he contracted from the diseased courtesan in the Countess-Duchess de Olivares' bed. How else to explain his insane act of going to war against France? As an added dividend, Richelieu had been forced to seek friendship with Spain because of the Huguenot revolt and unexpected war with England.

Ballebrera saved his most significant news for last. "You would not have heard, of course, that last week His Majesty made Francisco First Count de la Granja de Rocamora and Knight of Santiago."

Vicente found his voice after a few moments. "Why was he honored first and not Rafal?"

"His Majesty was quite moved by Francisco's gift of a magnificent tapestry of the Resurrection."

"Granted that Rafal does not know how to flatter . . ."

"There are other reasons. Francisco guaranteed a levy of fifty men for the Italian campaign, and Olivares weighed his brother Tomás, who has been appointed Regent at the Convent-College *de Nuestra Señora del Socorro* in Orihuela, against Jacinto, a known anti-Olivarista who attempted to denounce one of his most valued Portuguese bankers as a Judaizer. The Count-Duke also has received reports from Orihuela and Murcia detailing his cruelty and depravity."

"Were you present when Francisco received his title?"

"I was, and I must confess that Francisco's gift impressed everyone, most especially His Majesty's favorite painter, Velázquez, who has accepted an appointment as usher to the King's chamber. He aspires to titles and membership in the Order of Santiago even though he is, according to law, merely *oficio vil o mecánico*, engaging in manual trade, which has been codified in civil law by Olivares' sales tax levied on paintings executed and sold by living artists, as if they are ordinary articles of consumption. Also there to praise our cousin's gift was the Fleming, Peter Paul Rubens. The artist-diplomat had come from the court of Philip's aunt, Archduchess Isabella, in the Spanish Netherlands, to paint the royal family and to help negotiate a formal peace treaty between Spain and England. His Majesty enjoys extensive conversations with Rubens. One would wonder about the topic. Is it the diplomacy of art or the art of diplomacy?"

Vicente was in no mood to banter. "Rafal must come to Court so we can help him scheme for his title."

"We both know that he will not leave his men until victory or peace is achieved. He is no courtier."

"At least Francisco's title has freed me from my promise to Rafal. The irony is that if I choose to live in Spain, I must remain a friar."

When Vicente delivered his booty of rare manuscripts and codices to Olivares' office, a clerk told him that the Count-Duke had gone to Velázquez' studio.

"Is he sitting for another portrait?"

"No, the Queen of Hungary's painting has not been completed to his satisfaction. Although Velázquez prefers to work slowly, the Count-Duke has ordered him to finish with all speed."

Under the pretense of reporting to Olivares, Vicente hurried to the artist's studio so María might see for herself that he had returned. A grand assemblage filled the room: The King and Queen, Olivares, the Austrian Ambassador, Peter Paul Rubens, and the usual entourage of courtiers, clerics, and *bufónes*.

While Velázquez painted on a small canvas, Vicente took in each detail of his beloved María. She sat stone-faced and imperious on the edge of a throne-chair as if about to spring to her feet. Styled in a high crown of tight ringlets and covering her small ears, her flaxen hair was swept up in front to expose a perfect widow's peak above her high forehead. She wore a *guardinfante* of emerald green and cinnamon brown satin and moiré. A finely worked lace ruff covered her neck and grazed her chin. A gold necklace and crucifix of emeralds and rubies hung to her lap.

When Velázquez hesitated and shook his head, Philip, who had begun to grow a pale blond mustachio and beard, asked, "What is the problem? It is a perfect likeness."

"Your Majesty, I have not yet achieved the right expression."

"We see nothing wrong with the portrait."

"If I may speak freely, Her Majesty's expression is too severe, her posture too tense."

Philip's eyes went back and forth from his sister to the small canvas. He urged María to relax her face more. Several *bufónes* tried to make her smile, which caused her demeanor to become no less icy as on those occasions when Prince Charles had made an ass of himself. No amount of heat from the braziers could have melted her.

Vicente moved into María's line of vision. The instant she saw him, her complexion colored, her eyes softened, her body relaxed, and her lips moved slightly.

"Perfect, Your Majesty," Velázquez said, and he painted the left corner of her mouth with all the subtlety of a great master to suggest an enigmatic yet piquant smile.

Vicente genuflected before the royals and saw Olivares and the Austrian ambassador nod to each other as if they had reached a mutual understanding.

The Count-Duke beckoned him, "Were you successful, Friar?"

He fought an impulse to stare at María. "Yes, Excellency. I found all the codices and more. I left them in your library."

"Good. Report to me this afternoon."

"As you wish, Excellency."

On his way out Vicente glanced at the Queen of Hungary. María's expression had again become impenetrable, but her reaction to his presence, her slight suggestion of a smile, would forever be on that small canvas and etched permanently in his memory.

Chapter 39
Confessions

Vicente waited until María returned to her apartments and sought an audience. Chaperoned by the vigilant Countess of Lemos and two *duennas*, she met with him in her small chapel.

"Don Vicente, we have missed you . . . your wise counsel. We must now concern our Self with Austrian affairs." She reached out as if to take his hand, looked towards the Countess of Lemos, and instead waved away an imaginary flying insect. "Did you know that the Imperial Ambassador has had the temerity to suggest we dismiss you?"

"I am not surprised, Your Majesty. Emperor Ferdinand's confessor is a Jesuit, which is why Dominicans are unwelcome at the Imperial Court."

"There is more. The Ambassador does not like it that we are so close in age, even though everyone praises your piety and rectitude."

"Has His Majesty spoken on the matter?"

"Both Their Majesties are silent. We do not understand why. Our wish is for you to continue as our confessor and spiritual director although powerful forces are against us. Should they prevail, God forbid, I . . . we . . ." María could not speak the words he knew were in her heart. She crossed herself and regained control of her emotions. "At the moment we are treated as a mere pawn on Olivares' chessboard."

"If played skillfully, a pawn may yet become a powerful queen, Your Majesty, and when Emperor Ferdinand II dies, you will become Empress."

"As our father wished." She set her prominent jaw. "After we marry and settle in Vienna, we shall send for you."

If Olivares will let me go.

"Has a date been set for your departure, Your Majesty?"

"No. The war in Italy has made travel too dangerous, and they are still haggling over the details of our dowry." María pouted. "And now we are expected to sit for more portraits by the Flemish painter, Rubens, and our own Velázquez

Over the past five years, Velázquez had executed several magnificent paintings of the Count-Duke and the royal family, but not one of María until her brother demanded she pose for both artists. Olivares intended to send a special envoy to the Emperor in Vienna and present Spain's congratulations on her impending marriage to his son, His Esteemed Majesty the King of Hungary. The envoy would carry with him in advance of her arrival small portraits of Their Majesties and the Queen of Hungary.

Vicente attempted to cheer her. "Velázquez and Rubens are the finest artists in Europe."

"We have always tried to avoid the vain frivolity of posing for portraits. It is a waste of much valuable time better spent in spiritual contemplation or doing good works."

I have taught you lessons in Christian charity better than I had intended.

María leaned forward and whispered in English, "We must speak alone."

"Where?"

"In the secret passageway outside our bedroom. It has not yet been touched."

"How can you get away?"

María groped for the correct words in English, then covered her face with her fan when she spoke in French, "Sleeping draughts, can you arrange to bring me some?"

"Ensure that no one is in your bedroom during vespers. You will find them under your pillow. But when shall we meet?"

"It must be tonight." She signaled with her fingers the hour Philip was certain to be in bed with Isabel.

Vicente left María and returned to the Astórquia *Palacio* to inform Ballebrera about his plans. "Ramón, I am convinced that Olivares will send me on another journey to last until after the Queen of Hungary has left Madrid."

Ballebrera watched Vicente select specific small bags and bottles from his inventory of medicines, mix them into a potion, and pour it into an empty vial. "I have a spoken message for you that was delivered by some *pícaro* rogue. Don Lope is dying. Violante also is very ill. You are urged to return immediately and claim your daughter."

"Then no matter where Olivares sends me, I shall go to Valencia. The time to settle scores has come."

"Be careful."

"My enemies are the ones who should take care."

"There is another matter. I too shall be packing my belongings. This *palacio* has been purchased by one of Olivares' men of business"

Vicente was not surprised. Because of Spain's deteriorating financial situation, increasing numbers of *hombres de negócio* appeared daily within the Alcazar. Attracted by profitable dealings with the Crown, they had come to Madrid with their families under the protection of Olivares who had arranged for them an Edict of Grace from the Inquisition, a temporary indulgence that included permits to emigrate.

"Where will you go, Ramón? Back to your señorio?"

"I have found temporary lodgings. I cannot leave the joys Madrid offers."

During vespers, Vicente returned to the Alcazar, hastened through secret passageways, and delivered his sleeping potion to the Queen of Hungary's bedroom. Then he reported to the Count-Duke, who sat perpendicular to his desk scowling and in physical discomfort while a physician applied earthworms to his gouty foot resting on a pile of pillows. His forest green velvet robe trimmed in orange silk, white linen Turkish turban, and unwaxed drooping mustachio gave him the appearance of a fierce Ottoman Janissary.

"Excellency, I wish leave to go to Valencia."

Olivares searched his face. "You may go, and I expect you to pick clean Don Lope's inventory of rare books and codices. I also have a list of monasteries and convents in Aragón and Catalonia for you to visit along the way. Perhaps I missed some of their valuable manuscripts during the Royal Progress in the summer of 'twenty-six."

"I am pleased to carry out your wishes."

"You are an intelligent man, Friar. I will not require your valuable services here until after the Queen of Hungary departs for Austria with her entourage."

Vicente arrived first for the rendezvous. While he waited for María, he remembered his vivid dream of years past. Would she come to him in a sheer robe and be his for the taking, or would it be a cold imperial meeting? Should he seize the initiative or be passive? He expected María to behave with her usual self-discipline even if in her heart of hearts she loved him. Realistically, the Queen of Hungary's one path in life had been determined since her birth. She would be an Empress. All else was subordinate to that inevitability. He could only dream of what might be. Yet, to dream was to live.

If only I may live my dream.

A poem came to mind, which he would later commit to paper:

> Enchantress María mine,
> I am sick with love for thee,
> Forever thy captive lover,
> Love's victim sacrificed upon the altar of desire,
> To the heaven of thy fair grace.
>
> Enchantress María mine,
> Siren of my servile heart,
> Let me hear thine own love's expression,
> And with thy spoken word
> Lead my tormented soul to paradise.
>
> Enchantress María mine,
> Like the Casa de Campo,
> A garden enclosed is thy modest chastity,

A guarded flowering bower of beauty,
Death awaits he who would profane it.

Enchantress María mine,
Never to profane, always to worship thee,
Come open thy petals for me,
And like the hummingbird in spring,
I would drink thine own sweet nectar within.

María opened the secret panel to her bedroom suite wide enough for candlelight from within to illuminate the passageway. As she stepped towards him, Vicente kneeled and looked at her with adoration. She wore a black velvet hooded robe over her sleeping gown. Her bare feet were indeed as small as lotus pads. For the first time, except in his fantasies and dreams, he saw her in garments other than a guardinfante.

Agape and Eros. Sacred and Profane. Vicente simultaneously felt pure, idealized love for María and stirrings of tumescence when she pulled him to his feet and held his hands.

"Don Vicente, for how long will the sleeping potion last?"

"Through the night, Your Majesty."

She took a deep breath and sighed. "It has been decided. In two days, on the twenty-fifth of April, we shall be married by proxy to Archduke Ferdinand, King of Hungary and Bohemia."

Even though he had prepared himself for that inevitable fait accompli, Vicente felt a weighty stone settling in his stomach. "My congratulations, Your Majesty. And when do you leave Madrid?"

"His Majesty, our brother, intends for us to begin my long journey to Vienna at the beginning of September, while he waits here for Queen Isabel to give birth to their long-awaited heir, may God grant it survive this time. Then in October or November, depending upon when the child is born, he will leave to meet us in Barcelona before we embark for Naples."

María's face was a small distance from his. She had scented herself with one of the essences he had brought for her birthday.

Dare I kiss her delicious mouth?

"After you left the studio . . . despite our strongest protests . . . both His Majesty and Satan decided once and for all that we will not be permitted to take you with me to Vienna. Nor will we be allowed to send for you later. As we feared, they have selected Capuchin Provincial Quiroga to be my confessor. They say their decision was necessary because he is familiar with the intrigues of the Imperial Court and can better protect our interests there."

"Quiroga is a good man."

"Don Vicente, we must confess . . . we are to blame for losing you as our confessor and spiritual director."

"You, Your Majesty?"

"Yes, although we did not fully realize what we had done until Queen Isabel made us aware of it." María continued to hold his hands. "She told us that every man in the world would have envied you as the object of our spontaneous expression of delight when you appeared at the studio."

If they could have read my heart as well.

"Don Vicente, we truly regret that we were not clever enough to conceal our delight at your return."

"Please, do not blame yourself. His Majesty and the Count-Duke believe they are doing what is best for Spain. Their decision was as inevitable as your marriage."

She released his hands and stepped back into the darkness. "We will admit to a . . . an affection for you . . . an affection we have felt for no one else. It is different from that which we have for our brothers. We pray it is less than what we must feel for our future husband."

"Your Majesty, know that it is reciprocated."

"Yes . . . yes, we know. That is why we shall not see each other again, except under the most formal of circumstances."

Be bolder, Vicente told himself. "Your Majesty, you have often said I know you better than anyone."

"That is true."

"Yet, I do not know you well enough to have the confidence to say . . ."

All I have to lose is my life.

"You would be a poor diplomat. Your eyes speak clear volumes. They always have."

One kiss.

"I wish . . ."

"Say no more." María stepped forward into the light and touched his lips with her finger. "Hold out your hand."

Surprised, he obeyed her command. She took out a silken ribbon as blue as her eyes and tied it around his wrist.

"You knew."

"The first time we read the poem we heard your voice, and you confirmed our suspicions when you recited it aloud."

"There are others I dared not commit to paper."

"Perhaps one day you shall, and we will read them with the greatest of pleasure." María again reached into the pocket of her robe and brought out a gold box encrusted with diamonds. "We want you to have this small token, which cannot adequately express my . . . our fondness for you."

Vicente opened the elegant box, which contained a deep red ruby reflecting dark blood in the dim candlelight and set in a gold ring. *My love for you is more fiery than this ruby.* He dropped to his knees and kissed her hand with all the love and passion welling inside him.

"*¡Madre de Dios!*" Trembling, María placed her free hand against her breast and asked barely above a whisper, "Does it fit?"

Vicente reluctantly released her hand, rose to his feet, and slipped the ring onto the small finger of his right hand. "Perfectly, Your Majesty, and I thank you, although I would also have a lock of your hair. For pleasant memories of what was, the miracle of tonight, and to help me dream again and again of what might have been."

María stared at him surprised by his request. Then she smiled and nodded assent. "But we have nothing to cut it with."

Vicente produced a dagger from his sleeve. "Valencians come prepared for anything." He lifted María's hood and paused to admire her golden beauty and vivid blue eyes that shined on him, for him, and no one else. He cut a small lock from the back of her head, kissed it, and sequestered it in the box.

"What?" she said with mock anger. "No fair exchange?"

Vicente gave her the dagger, and she cut a curl from his forehead, which she kissed and placed in her cross.

"Yes, what might have been . . . in another time and place of our choosing. Even though we never wanted to marry that heretic, Charles Stuart, we still dream about the great deeds we could have accomplished had we become Queen of England with you as our Inquisitor General."

"As Holy Roman Empress, you may yet one day lead a great *reconquista* of northern Europe."

"Perhaps. But first, we must be a good wife and bear our husband many heirs." She seized his arm. "Don Vicente, what of you?"

Never let go of me.

"Olivares wishes to be rid of me until you depart for Vienna."

"We expected as much."

"I will go to my señorio and the city of Valencia for the first time in twelve years."

"Your beautiful Fragrant Coast. You still love it so. When do you leave?"

"This very night."

She gasped and squeezed his arm. Vicente placed his hand on hers.

Kiss her now or never.

Anticipating his intentions, María withdrew her hand and stepped away from him towards the panel. "And after you return to *la Corte*, will you become an Inquisitor? Sotomayor wishes it. Or, will you rise in the Church to become Bishop, a Cardinal, or even a General in your Order?"

"Whatever God wills."

"All the fashionable women of Madrid will want you for their confessor after we leave. Everyone at Court will flock to hear your sermons."

"I must pray and ask the Lord to guide me, and for you to forgive me, Doña María, my Queen."

"Forgive you for what?"

"For presuming to . . ."

"My Don Vicente," She said stepping back into her bedroom. Her eyes had never been softer, nor her expression so revealing of her heart before she closed the panel. "My Don Vicente, I assure you . . . it is no presumption."

Spain . . . a province that is not inclined
to take the point of view of reason.

Alonso de Palencia, 1459

PART FOUR
Vengeance, Schemes, & Dreams

Valencia, Madrid, and Barcelona, 1629-1633

Castile has made Spain, and
Castile has destroyed it.

Ortega y Gasset

Chapter 40
Sea Sprite

In the summer of 1629 after an absence of twelve years, Vicente approached the city of Valencia. Close to noon, the July sun blazed mercilessly as he rode through a palm grove onto a deserted strip of beach north of the city.

Here at last. All I have longed for during every vermin-infested moment, each bone-chilling cold day and night in Madrid. Clear blue sky. Turquoise waters. Sand of white gold. The invigorating fragrance of salt air.

Vicente dismounted and tethered his mule in the shade beneath the great palms. After he hid his weapons in one of the bags, he kicked off his sandals, ran across the broad expanse of sand, and plunged into the foamy surf. He removed his soaked robe and rubbed it against a nearby rock to free it from those hardier fleas and lice that had survived their salty bath. Then he dove back into the waves and swam until exhausted.

He carried his damp robe back to the palm grove and left it on stiff fronds to dry in the sun. He placed a small straw mat on the ground in the shade near his mule and laid out his midday meal of melon and citrus, coarse bread, and a skin of wine.

Near the end of his repast, Vicente saw a quartet of naked children burst out from the palms farther down the beach. He watched them frolic in the water until the tide carried one of the girls towards him. He put on his damp robe and retreated behind a tree.

She waded onto the sand brown as a *morilla* and on the threshold of puberty. Vicente almost laughed aloud when he saw she had a dagger in a scabbard tied to her left arm like any Gypsy wildcat.

She drew her blade and approached his mule. Satisfied that its owner was nowhere in the vicinity, she searched inside the bags. When Vicente stepped out from behind the tree to confront the girl, she moved back, heaped vile curses on his ancestry, and pointed her dagger at him.

He gaped at her curly brown hair and familiar green eyes. That nose. The shape of her face. It was as if he stared into his own reflection. "Is it not un-Christian for you to bathe, my child?"

She held his gaze and made threatening small circles with her blade. "I saw you swimming, Padre."

"Friar."

The girl was fearless and had no shame in her nakedness as she backed towards the water. "You say you're a friar, but I saw pistols and daggers in your bag."

He did not want her to go. "You are Brianda de Rocamora."

She stopped, her eyes narrowing. "I've never seen you before. How do you know my name?"

Although Vicente was overcome by an unexpected surge of paternal affection, he resisted the temptation to identify himself as her father. Happily, he saw nothing of Violante or the Anglesolas in his daughter. He modulated his voice to a tone that always inspired trust from those he confessed. "Years ago before you were born, I was acquainted with your family."

"Who are you?"

"In my Order, I am known as Fray Vicente." Brianda did not react to his name, which meant that Violante had not mentioned his existence to her.

"You speak our dialect. Maybe you tell the truth. But your bags are dusty. Where have you come from?"

An observant girl, he thought with fatherly pride. "I have traveled from Madrid." He glanced towards her companions still playing in the water. "Do your parents know you associate with Gypsies?"

"I also count thieves and assassins as my friends, so don't you try to harm me."

I would never harm you, my daughter.

"I left Valencia many years ago. Tell me about your family. Your parents, Alonso and Violante, are they still living?"

"Only my mother, and she is sick."

"What ails your mother, my child?"

"No one will tell me. I am not permitted to see her. Her room is always dark. I can speak to her only through a veil."

God, if you exist, do not send Violante to hell before I have my revenge. "Is that why you prefer not to stay at home?"

"I wanted to get out before my cousin came to visit. He expects to marry me. I hate the sight of him."

"But you cannot be more than eleven years old."

"I'll be twelve before the end of the year."

"What is your cousin's name?"

"José de Anglesola. He wants my title and lands. After I come of age, I will marry the man of my choice. Or no one."

Another Anglesola, murderers all.

The flames of vengeance burned within Vicente's heart no less than they had years before when he planned the assassination of Enríque de Anglesola. To protect Brianda, he would not hesitate to carve the presumptuous piglet José into thin strips of bacon; nor would he feel remorse if he had to exterminate everyone else from that misbegotten Anglesola brood.

"And does your mother want the marriage?"

"She hates the Anglesolas for stealing our wealth and murdering all our Suárez kin. And so do I." She cut the air with her dagger. "If I were a man . . . ."

"What did they do?"

"They control all the señorios next to ours. They cut off our water and poisoned our wells and springs because my mother will not give me to José. She says I am the last de Rocamora of Benetorrente and deserve better."

"No, there is another de Rocamora of Benetorrente. Your father's brother still lives."

"I don't believe you. If I had an uncle, my mother would have told me."

"Not necessarily." Without identifying himself, Vicente told Brianda how Enríque de Anglesola ambushed Don Luís, her de Rocamora grandfather, and the subsequent revenge carried out by her mysterious uncle.

Brianda again slashed at imaginary enemies with her blade. "I'd have done the same. I like my uncle even though we've never met. What is his name?"

Vicente changed the subject away from himself. "And there are more de Rocamoras in Orihuela, lords of señorios greater than Benetorrente. Heroic soldiers too. Some live in Madrid."

"Our eyes are the same color green." The girl shrewdly studied his features. "Perhaps you are the uncle you told me about?"

He reached into his bag and offered her a white linen shirt. "Cover yourself, Señorita Brianda, for you live in a kingdom of dangerous *pícaros*."

"I can take care of myself, and I still don't believe you're really a friar."

"I am, and are you a good Catholic?"

"No more than I need to be." She laughed, returned her dagger to its scabbard, and ran into the waves.

Vicente watched his daughter swim towards her Gypsy friends. He would claim her soon enough.

Chapter 41
La Samia

Before the sun lowered behind the western hills, Vicente passed through the gates of Valencia and continued towards the harbor unrecognized by friend or blood enemy. Although he had read reports of El Grau's reduced activity, the reality was much worse. Hulls of rotting ships filled the once-thriving port. A sparse few caravels were loading and unloading at the docks. Like the countryside, the ports of the Spanish Levant had continued to decline as a result of the Moriscos' expulsion twenty years earlier.

One aspect of El Grau had not changed. The usual layabouts, *pícaros*, and spies populated the waterfront. Because Vicente spoke their cant and knew where he was going, no one gave him trouble while he made his way through the filthy narrow streets and alleys to Don Lope's residence. His mentor had purchased the gambling house and bordello on each side and converted them to warehouses.

An urchin lookout scurried inside to alert everyone that a mysterious friar had arrived. In an instant, Yusef and several men and women who had worked at el Paraiso greeted Vicente. The Arab's hair had turned completely gray, the lines on his face more deeply etched. The men took charge of Vicente's mule and brought his bags inside.

Yusef led him into the back room where Don Lope slept on a narrow bed. Vicente's heart ached when he saw that the ailing physician was little more than a wispy-bearded skeleton.

"You have arrived barely in time,"

"What is he dying of?"

"Only Allah knows. His heart is strong. His mind is as keen as ever, but something is devouring him from within. No matter how much he eats, he loses weight."

Vicente could not bear to continue looking at what was left of the man he loved as a second father. "Is he in much pain?"

"We give him hashish and potions when necessary."

They went to another room where Vicente exchanged his robe for a pair of breeches. It was too hot to wear a shirt.

They sat a table laden with fruit and jugs of wine. Vicente selected an orange then discarded it. He had no appetite. "Where are Moraíma, Pablo, and Koitalel?"

"Pablo and Koitalel should be returning from Extremadura via Madrid sometime in August," Yusef said. "Moraíma is raising her daughter in a remote Catalan village near the French border."

"Why so far north?"

"The girl is fair and blond, like her father, His Majesty, and would excite much curiosity among the darker population of Valencia. Can you believe it? Philippa is almost six years old."

"Alas, time passes too quickly," Vicente said thinking of Brianda. He accepted a goblet of wine from Yusef and drank deeply.

"When must you return to Madrid?"

"I will remain in Valencia while Don Lope needs me and until I finish my business with Violante. What can you tell me about her?"

The Arab twisted his spade beard to a fine point. "She is a recluse. It is rumored she suffers from some disfiguring illness."

"God's punishment for her sins."

"By Allah, he does sound like a friar." Yusef made an exaggerated sign of the cross with his left hand. "Listen to me, my friend. Everything here in Valencia has changed for the worst. Your señorío . . ."

"I have heard that Benetorrente is now a desert, courtesy of the Anglesolas." Vicente picked up the orange again and quartered it with his dagger "I shall have my revenge."

"I expected you would. Blood feuds are still a way of life here in Valencia, a legacy of the Moors, which we Arabs understand as well." Yusef turned his head towards Don Lope's room. "The old man, he is awake."

Vicente went alone to his dying mentor. Although the physician was weak, his eyes emitted a potent life force. Overwhelmed by a sense of imminent loss, Vicente fought tears. He kissed the old man's cheek and brought a chair to his side.

"My son," Don Lope said barely audible. "I have refused to die until I saw you one last time. Let me look at you. Yes, you have become a man, but you never left Spain."

"I could not."

"Then what place have you made for yourself in Madrid?"

Vicente told him about Olivares, Sotomayor, Hombrecillo, and Ballebrera. He described his love for María, and for the first time in his life, he experienced the salubrious effect of a genuine confession.

"You never kissed her, never held her in your arms?"

"Never." He wiped drool from Don Lope's scarred chin and toothless disfigured mouth, mementos of the physician's years in the dungeons of the Inquisition.

"Nor told her of your love?"

"Not directly. It was too dangerous. María gave me no indication she would allow it."

"I fear for you."

"Why?"

"Physically, no one is bolder than you. Anglesola can attest to that from hell. But when it comes to making important decisions, you let events overtake you, the way Moriscos expect Allah or Kismet to guide them. You never took the *pícaro* road with Moraíma."

"I often regret it."

"You continue to reject my advice to go to Holland or England."

"Because I am a Spaniard."

"That is your tragedy. And mine. Listen to me. You are twenty-eight-years old. Forty comes more rapidly than thirty. Fifty in an eye blink. Before you know it, you will be too old, too set in your ways to risk leaving." He paused exhausted from his long speech.

"My vow to Rafal..."

"Meaningless. Yes, you gave him your word of honor, but where was his honor when he tricked you? You use it as an excuse to remain in Spain."

"Don Lope, I cannot leave and commit treason against Spain, nor can I live among Jews and Protestants. Although I do not believe in the dogma of any religion, I can live comfortably as a confessor at Court, especially if no one questions my certificates of *limpieza*."

"Then it should be easier for you to conform on the outside where there is no Inquisition and no *limpieza* and accomplish whatever you wish."

"The Cardinal-Infante is my friend. If he is allowed to go to war, he has promised to take me with him."

"Ay, Vicente, then you shall learn that one decent physician is worth more than a *tercio* of soldiers. Fight it all you may, one day you shall realize as I have known all these years... you are a born physician." Don Lope coughed spittle and blood, then closed his eyes. "I am weary. We will talk later."

The following morning, Vicente served Don Lope a brew of strong red wine, raw eggs and herbs. "Did you ever see a copy of my mother's genealogy? I now believe that you forged her certificate of *limpieza*." When the old man closed his eyes, Vicente feared he might die before answering. "I must know once and for all. Was my mother tainted?"

"Your father loved her so very much."

Because Don Lope whispered, Vicente had to place an ear close to his lips. "I beg you. Tell me the truth. You were their physician and confidante. Was my mother from a *converso* family? Was she a Judaizer?"

"I saw no evidence... still..."

Don Lope, do not die before you tell me.

"... your father knew the secret of your mother's origins. He almost told me once... something about Roquemaure in Languedoc." Don Lope gripped his blanket. "The pain."

Vicente summoned Yusef, but the old man rejected the Arab's offer of hashish and every other opiate.

"No more. I am dying." He pointed to a box. "Vicente... for you ... inside... a notarized document." He continued after Vicente opened it. "No forgery, this time. I leave you my medicines and disguises, books and jewels . . . all my gold and silver . . . paintings . . . a fortune worth tens of thousands in ducates. Take them . . . leave Spain on the next caravel. Accept your destiny. You were born to be a physician."

"Don Lope . . ."

"Use all that wealth well, my son."

"What about Yusef, Pablo, and Koitalel?"

"They will continue to run my enterprises . . . inherit these houses . . . other properties . . . tools of our trade . . . although they cannot forge documents as well as I."

"Only the ability to debase vellón." Yusef forced a smile for the dying man and wept.

"Vicente, promise me you will leave Spain."

"If Olivares fails."

"My boy, have you learned nothing from Cervantes' *Don Quixote* . . . or from empirical observation? Your love for the Queen of Hungary . . . the end of the *limpieza* . . . all windmills of your own impossible dreams. Your daughter . . . take her to new lands."

Tears streamed down Vicente's unshaven cheeks. He was about to lose the man he loved no less than his parents, the master who had made him who he was. He clutched Don Lope's hand as if to prevent Death from claiming him until he comprehended the futility of it all.

"Shall I give you the Blessed Sacrament of Last Rites?"

"No . . . after torture and the galleys . . . decided to be a ram, not a sheep . . . secretly returned to the ancient faith of my fathers . . . must recite *la Samia* . . ."

With his last breath, Don Lope whispered words Vicente had heretofore read only in manuscripts listed on the Index of Forbidden Works, heretical words:

"*Semah Ysrael* . . . Hear O Israel, the Lord our God, the Lord is One."

Chapter 42
Tío Vicente's Revenge

After burying Don Lope at sea, Vicente rode his mule through the Señorio de Benetorrente towards the house where he had been born and raised, scourged, drugged, raped, and exiled. Irrigation channels, wells, and springs were dry. Lifeless mulberry trees stood as grotesque sentinels over the parched landscape. The tenants had abandoned their small village. Their roofless houses and the small parish church were empty shells.

The graves of Vicente's mother, father, and brother had fared no better. They were untended and overgrown with weeds. He fought grief by replacing it with thoughts of revenge. Under the sleeves of his robe, he carried two sharp daggers and had concealed two loaded wheel-lock pistols beneath his saddle blanket.

Vicente dismounted and rapped hard on the great door of oak. After a long wait, an elderly lackey in faded threadbare blue and gold de Rocamora livery opened the door and scowled at him. "We give nothing to greedy friars."

"Take me to Violante."

"The Señora sees no one. Go away before I set the dogs on you."

"And are they as toothless as you, old man?" Vicente held the door open, seized the lackey's tattered doublet, and lifted him high off the ground. "How long have you served this house?"

"Please, put me down."

"Answer my question."

"I came here with the Señora in 'seventeen, and served her father before. Do I know you?"

He released the man and threw back his hood. "I am Vicente de Rocamora."

"¡Madre de Dios!"

Vicente brushed past the lackey and moved through the silent rooms. He was surprised to see familiar furniture, wall hangings, and relics of the True Faith in the same places he remembered. The patio garden once lush had become a jungle of weeds, wild flowers, and untrimmed bushes. The fountain and patio pool held stagnant algae covered water teeming with summer insects. Many of the *azulejos* were cracked or missing. The house and grounds crawled with vermin.

He entered the familiar *estrado* where he had received his sentence of banishment to Orihuela. It reeked pungently of mildew and ointments. Fine black gauze designed more to distort vision than to protect against mosquitoes divided the room.

The lackey followed him and pointed to a stool. "Sit there, and I entreat you, please do not part the veil."

Vicente preferred to stand at an angle with the entrance in full view. He did not intend to be shot in the back. He peered into the veil and saw an outline of a body reclining on a divan.

"Violante?"

"I am here, Vicente. Brianda told me about the friar with green eyes. Have you returned to take your revenge?"

"Yes." Her voice brought back vivid memories of a vulturine succubus. "Why do you hide from me?"

"I hide from everyone, even my daughter. God is punishing me for my terrible sins, sins I never dared confess to the priests."

Her fear and passivity surprised Vicente, who had prepared himself for a violent confrontation with the wicked shrew. "I also hear confessions."

"Is it true? I think you would lie to trap me."

"Have you not heard? In Orihuela, I entered the Dominican Order. In Madrid, I became confessor and spiritual director for the Most Illustrious Doña María, Infanta of Spain and now Queen of Hungary and Bohemia."

"I am not surprised. Even as a boy, you were very handsome and clever."

He ignored her remark. "I know what the Anglesolas did to the Suárez clan and to Benetorrente. Why have they allowed you to live?"

"Because I am half-Anglesola, and they expect me to die soon. May God help my daughter. I cannot protect her from the grave, and José de Anglesola is obsessed with Brianda."

"How can he be? She is but a child."

"And as you have seen a beautiful child,. He prefers his partners to be very young. After I die, he will manipulate the legal system to become Brianda's guardian, marry her, and take her land."

"I shall see him buried in it first."

"Yes, I am sure you will, and I expect you are going to take my life as well."

"Is there any reason why I should not?"

"I can think of none. But know this, Vicente. I have tried to achieve salvation through prayer and supplication, and through the love of God. If I confess all to you before you take my life, will you absolve me?"

Vicente preferred to send the witch to hell. But since God probably did not exist, whatever he said would be meaningless anyway. And like it or not, she was the mother of his daughter. "Yes, Violante, I can absolve you and prescribe proper penance."

"Then let us get on with it. I wish to confess to Almighty God . . . my testimony as a warning to others . . ."`

Vicente listened in anger to Violante's affirmation that she had used him to give her a child and in horror to her description of his brother Alonso's poisoning.

"Only the Lord giveth and taketh life," Vicente said through clenched teeth.

"I know that, and there is more."

Violante described her escapades involving adultery, sodomy, and sorcery, everything except bestiality. The woman's sole claim to virtue was her love for Brianda and desire to protect the girl from evil.

"And now I am dying slowly and painfully as punishment from God for my sins. Vicente, help me avoid the fires of hell. Absolve me. I know my body will die in agony, but my soul must be allowed to escape eternal damnation and punishments."

"How has God afflicted you?"

"*Mal frances*. Have mercy. Absolve me now, Vicente."

That she had the French sickness almost moved him to believe in a God of Justice. "I will absolve you if one condition is met."

"But you promised."

"And I will honor my promise when you give me my daughter. I want Brianda."

"Mother of God, Vicente. She does not know. I never told her. No one knows you are her father. If anyone found out, she would be declared illegitimate."

"Give me credit for brains, Violante. She need never know the truth. I will take her to Madrid, away from the Anglesolas and the feuds of Valencia. I have seen Benetorrente. She has no future here."

After Vicente described his powerful friends within the Alcazar, Violante said, "God is beginning to forgive me. Yes, my Brianda will have a better life with you in Madrid. But I must tell you she will have no dowry. Benetorrente is worthless. I have sold my jewels and dismissed nearly all my servants in order to survive."

"The entail of Benetorrente will again have value because I can guarantee a proper dowry for Brianda."

"Then it is right you take her, but only after I die."

"I expect to leave for Madrid in September."

"I beg you, Vicente, not before I die. Brianda is my one comfort. In spite of my sins, I have been a good mother. My death will come soon enough."

"I will take my daughter with me, Doña Violante, absolution or not. Your cooperation will make the inevitable easier for the three of us."

Violante sobbed behind the veil. "You are a hard man. You give me no choice."

"You were less generous to me." Vicente absolved her, then said, "God's will be done. *Mal frances* is penance enough. Now, I wish to see my daughter. Where is Brianda?"

"This time of day she will be where you first saw her."

At the palm grove by the sea, Vicente espied two armed *caballeros* on horseback lurking ahead of him behind the trees. The scum were ogling his naked daughter, who repeatedly dove into the waves unaware she was watched.

Vicente dismounted and took out his brace of wheel-locks that he had carefully wound and loaded with lead balls. He cocked the pistols, folded his arms, and placed them under his sleeves. He moved through the palms and stepped in front of the men. "Good morning, Señores."

One was still in his teens with the feral expression of a born killer. The older man matched descriptions given by Don Lope and Violante. José de Anglesola did indeed resemble his brother, Enríque, the murderer of his father, whom he had dispatched years ago.

Anglesola threw a coin to the sand. "Here's a quarto, Friar. Now be off with you." When Vicente did not pluck the vellón coin from the sand, the *caballero* snapped his whip. "Or would you prefer a stinging caress?"

The sun beat on Vicente's bare head. The sand reflected white heat. Because of the wavy glare, Anglesola's face merged with those of his kinsmen, the cowardly assassin, Enríque, and Bernardo, the vicious Dominican who had whipped him mercilessly.

Vicente pulled out the pistols from his sleeves and at close range shot both men between the eyes. Their horses bolted and carried them along the beach. Swimming beneath the waves, his daughter never heard the gunfire.

"Señorita Brianda," Vicente said in front of Violante's black gauze when his daughter entered barefoot in a yellow blouse and green skirt that reminded him of the carefree Moraíma and Gypsy girls of his youth.

She ignored him and went to the veil. "Mother, why is this friar here?"

"We have important matters to discuss, but it is difficult for me to speak. Please, Vicente, you tell her."

He placed his hands on the girl's shoulders and was pleased she neither tensed nor pulled away. "Brianda, you suspected it at the beach when you observed that we have the same color eyes. I think we have the same face. I am indeed your father's brother, Vicente de Rocamora."

Brianda flashed a smile. "I knew it." She stood on her toes to whisper in his ear. "I saw those pistols in your bag. You shot José and Felipe."

"You don't have to whisper. Your mother knows. They were planning to abduct you."

"I wish I'd seen you do it."

"Brianda, I want you listen to your uncle. He has made wonderful plans to take care of you after I . . ." Violante forced a cough to prevent herself from crying. "He will protect you and provide a dowry."

Vicente stood with Brianda close to the veil so Violante could hear everything. "My child everything your mother says is true, and more. You will have many servants, dresses made from the finest cloth, and jewels."

"A friar can do all that?"

"This one can, Brianda. For the past six years, I have been the confessor and spiritual director for Her Most Illustrious Majesty Doña María, Queen of Hungary and Bohemia and sister of King Philip. I also work for the most powerful man in Spain, the Count-Duke de Olivares. I have preached to Their Majesties, and at *autos-de-fé*. I can and will present you to Queen Isabel and find you a place in the house of some great lady."

"In Madrid?"

"Yes, in Madrid."

"I want to stay here in Valencia with my mother."

"Too dangerous. The Anglesolas will twist the law and force you to marry one of their numerous miserable brood or murder you if they fail."

"Your Uncle Vicente is right," Violante said.

"When do I have to go, Tío Vicente?"

"After I have educated and prepared you for your grand entrance. I must teach you Court etiquette, how to address the royal family, the nobility, and the clergy. You will learn to play the lute and guitar and have the use of great libraries."

"I can't read. And I don't want to learn."

He masked his disappointment at her lack of education. "But first, I will take you to El Grau to meet some colleagues of mine. They will be your protectors while you are still here in Valencia."

"You have friends at the waterfront? Then you must be the most unusual friar in the entire world."

Vicente initiated an intensive program to educate Brianda in the rituals and forms of address at Court. He introduced her to musical instruments, the game of chess, and the alphabet. The girl also learned the use of weapons and tricks of the *pícaro* trade from Yusef and his bandit gang. Like Vicente, she had a natural aptitude for manipulating cards and dice.

When Pablo and Koitalel returned to Valencia, they gave Vicente a letter from Ballebrera that summarized recent events. The situation in Italy was expected to be too unstable for María to travel safely until the end of the year, and Olivares had dispatched Spinola to take charge of the army there.

Vicente frowned when he read the next paragraph. Because of his friendship with Arce and Inquisitor General Zapata, during a visit to Madrid in July, Jacinto was appointed Familiar of the Holy Office, one of the youngest ever to achieve that honor and one of the very few to have the prerequisite of being married waived.

Vicente did not give voice to his dilemma. His enemies may have become too numerous and powerful. Should he take Brianda to Madrid or leave Spain with her?

Chapter 43
Natronai, Bodo, & Sep

During the next several months, reports of important happenings at the Alcazar reached Vicente. In October, Queen Isabel gave birth to a healthy son and heir, Baltazar Carlos, and at last in December, the Queen of Hungary was to leave Madrid.

After Violante breathed her last at the end of that same month and was buried in a quiet ceremony, Vicente and his daughter began their journey to Madrid with Pablo, Koitalel, Yusef, and a half dozen of their rogues. Because winter travel was difficult, they did not reach the city gates until the end of March, 1630. He left Brianda with his friends at an encampment outside the capital and rode to Ballebrera's new quarters, a modest room above a bootmaker's shop, which had barely enough space for a bed, chaise, table, and two chairs.

Ballebrera had just finished his *almuerzo*, a mid-morning meal of eggs fried in olive oil with onion, minced garlic, and pimento. He wore an orange and pale blue striped cotton Turkish robe and comfortable slippers. He had added more stomach to his powerful torso and was bald on top. His trimmed sides, great mustachio, and hairy chest had turned grey in contrast to his black eyebrows.

A diagonal of dust-filled sunlight angled through the open window over a frayed and stained russet mat. The room reeked of decay and human habitation, a steep descent from the Astórquia *Palacio*. At first opportunity, he would give Ballebrera sufficient escudos for accommodations more worthy of a de Rocamora and Knight of Alcántara.

They exchanged *saludos*. Although the wine was too warm, Vicente refilled his cup. He rejected the mushy fruit. A *tercio* of ants had staked out a claim on the bowl's contents in competition with a noisy swarm of flies that Ballebrera waved off with his horsetail swatter.

"And what are your immediate plans?"

"I shall know by tonight." Vicente moved his sandaled feet away from another column of ants marching towards the table leg. He took in the room with a sour expression and handed Ballebrera a bag of gold coins. "Don Lope left me a fortune. Have new clothes made in the latest fashion and find yourself a residence worthy of your name and station."

"A friar rich as a *poderoso*?"

"And most of my wealth will be preserved for Brianda and her dowry."

"Where is she?"

"A half-day's ride away."

"And the girl really believes you are her uncle?"

"Of course she does. Brianda calls me Tío Vicente."

"I look forward to meeting your . . . ah . . . niece."

"Brianda is also your kin."

"Does she resemble you?"

"We have the same color eyes and features."

"Then you should grow a mustache and beard. A strong family likeness could lead to some not-so-innocent speculations amongst your enemies and the clergy."

"You make sense as always."

"What are your plans for her?"

"I shall present Brianda to Queen Isabel. I'll scheme and do whatever I must to have her installed in the household of a Doña Somebody Important."

Ballebrera pulled on his mustachio. "It should not be difficult. Queen Isabel likes you. So does the Countess-Duchess de Olivares."

"I will need a carriage and a comfortable place where Brianda can refresh herself before we appear at court."

"I can arrange that."

Vicente had delayed long enough, and he broached the subject most dear to his heart. "When did the Queen of Hungary leave? Has she arrived safely in Italy?"

"She left Madrid the 26th December with a dowry of one-and-a-half million ducates plus traveling expenses, all of it a wedding gift from the taxpayers of Castile. As you expected, she took Quiroga as her confessor. Philip and the infantes escorted her to Zaragoza and stayed there until the middle of January before returning to Madrid."

"And from Zaragoza?"

"The Queen of Hungary traveled to Barcelona where she remains to this day."

"What? Still in Barcelona?"

"When the Queen of Hungary arrived at the port, she found neither galleys to transport her nor sufficient ducates to pay for the voyage to Naples. Of course she could not finance the journey with her dowry."

Still in Barcelona.

Vicente imagined María's mental state at yet further humiliation and physical inconvenience. He ground his teeth in frustration. He could have ridden north from Valencia to see her one more time before joining Brianda and his friends here in Madrid. Now it was too late.

In a rage over his missed opportunity, he ripped the chain from his neck, and threw his mother's cross against the wall. It fell to the floor and split open revealing inside a piece of paper. He picked it up and read two meaningless disconnected words or names, *Natronai* and *Bodo*, and what appeared to be an abbreviation for the Roman number seven, a month, or Septimania in France, Sep.

He kissed the yellowed paper. What message had his beloved mother sent him from beyond the grave?

In the evening after vespers, Vicente went to the Alcazar with a gift of rare books and manuscripts for Olivares from Don Lope's inventory. His heart ached when he glanced towards the king's courtyard and beyond to the apartments where María once lived. He sniffed for her scent of cinnamon. The air was foul, and an acute sense of depression overwhelmed him. Without her golden presence, the palace had become a rancid stone-vaulted void.

He found Olivares in bed going over reports and ordering his secretaries about. Papers covered his blanket, and documents filled the pockets of his robe. The count-duke still suffered from gout and other ailments, real or imagined, and palace physicians had just finished bleeding, worming, and purging him.

"Excellency, is there anything I can do for you?"

"God knows, I carry more weight on my shoulders than Atlas ever dreamed possible. I need to find six million escudos for the war in Italy, four million more for Flanders, two million for a fleet to defend Brazil, and a half million for Germany. Richelieu's army has marched into Savoy and taken Pinerolo. And Emperor Ferdinand blames me because the Queen of Hungary has yet to sail from Barcelona."

"Is Her Majesty in danger?" Vicente asked in the hope Olivares might send him to comfort María in Barcelona.

The Count-Duke dismissed the question with a wave of his hand as if she were of little consequence. He turned to the bag Vicente had placed on the floor. "Now then, what have you brought me?"

"Before he died, Don Lope told me of his wish for you to have these books and manuscripts. I have other gifts for Their Majesties and Royal Highnesses."

The rare volumes cheered Olivares. "Don Vicente, you have behaved in a most exemplary manner. Because the Queen of Hungary has departed the court, I can begin to make better use of your considerable talents. We will talk again when I am better. Until then, you may resume your unique position in the palace as confessor-at-large. I do not know who missed you the most, your little *bufónes* or the queen's ladies."

After Vicente left Olivares' suite, he had the good fortune to encounter one of Isabel's most flirtatious ladies-in-waiting in the corridor. He bowed respectfully. "Doña Juana-María, what an unexpected pleasure."

The plump young woman giggled behind her fan and exposed a coquettish eye. "How good to see you, Don Vicente. Everyone has missed your sermons. When can you confess me?"

"Immediately, if . . ."

"If what?" She fluttered her eyelashes

"If you will speak to Her Majesty and arrange an audience for tomorrow afternoon."

"Wait here." Juana-María hurried to the queen's apartments. She did not keep him waiting long. She returned with two ladies behind her. "Her Most Gracious Majesty will be pleased to see you tomorrow at the first hour after siesta. And now, Don Vicente, will you confess us? We have saved all our sins for you."

Chapter 44
Royal Conquest

At the end of a brisk sunny spring afternoon, Vicente and Ballebrera escorted Brianda to the Alcazar in a borrowed gilded carriage. They had covered the owner's coat-of-arms with the escutcheon of the de Rocamoras. The coachmen, Yusef, Pablo, and Koitalel wore livery of blue, gold, and silver.

For the royal audience, Vicente had Brianda dressed in a chaste black velvet guardinfante, a fine white lace ruff, and a plain gold necklace and cross under a black velour cloak trimmed in green silk selected to match her eyes. Like María and every other devout woman in Spain, she held rosary beads and a prayer book in her hands, which were warmed by black kid gloves.

He recognized the commander of the Spanish Guards stationed at the entrance to the Queen's Courtyard. "*Capitán* Gutierrez, please send your man to inform Their Most Illustrious Majesties and Their Royal Highnesses that Vicente de Rocamora has returned and brought them gifts to celebrate the birth of His Most Illustrious Highness, the Infante Don Baltazar Carlos. Her Majesty has kindly condescended to receive me and my party at the hour."

After the officer dispatched one of his guards to Isabel's apartments, Brianda showed how well she had learned her lessons. She gracefully stepped out of the carriage, took Vicente's arm, and looked neither right nor left as they entered the Queen's Courtyard, which bustled with its usual activities.

The crowd gaped when Vicente and his entourage arrived. With Yusef, Pablo, and Koitalel trailing behind them and carrying gifts, they walked towards the steps leading to the royal apartments, until Ballebrera pointed to a stall. "Look at that creature. Why, with glasses he could pass for Quevedo's twin."

The men stopped so that Brianda could watch a cloth merchant's monkey dressed as a *caballero* perform tricks for vellón coins. As they turned away to resume their walk to the Queen's apartments, Vicente heard his daughter cry out.

"What is it, Brianda?"

"Tío, who is he? I have never seen anyone so fair and handsome."

Brianda was staring at a slender clean-shaven young man garbed in shades of brown from the cap casually placed atop his shiny flaxen hair, to his breeches and boots. His suede hunting habit was tied at the waist and exposed his unpretentious beige golilla and the sleeves of his silver-embroidered doublet. With one tan chamois gloved hand, he held a German carbine. The other gripped the leash of his favorite hunting dog.

He gave the leash to one of his servants and hastened towards Vicente's party with his two agitated mistresses chasing after him as best they could in their cumbersome fashionable guardinfantes. Everyone he passed in the courtyard bowed deferentially.

Vicente recognized both María's former *menina* and the youthful wife of an elderly *grandee* and said to Brianda, "He is Cardinal-Infante Fernándo, brother of King Philip."

"Don Vicente, I am delighted that you have returned."

The men genuflected, and Vicente was proud of Brianda's curtsy.

Fernándo bade them rise, and he smiled at Brianda. "Who is this lovely girl?"

"Your Eminence, may I present my niece, Brianda de Rocamora y Suárez, Señorita de Benetorrente, kinswoman to the noble Ramón de Rocamora, Señor de Ballebrera, Knight of Alcántara. Brianda, His Eminence and Most Illustrious Highness, Cardinal-Infante Don Fernándo de Habsburgo y Austria."

Again, her curtsy was flawless, and she charmed him with a winsome smile. "I am honored, Eminence."

Fernándo's gaze lingered on Brianda while he introduced her to his out-of-breath paramours and said to Vicente, "And now tell me where you were going before our happy encounter."

"To present Brianda to Her Majesty Queen Isabel, Your Eminence."

"Indeed? Then let us do so."

The Cardinal-Infante peremptorily dismissed his unhappy mistresses. After he handed his servant the gun and ordered him to take the hound to the kennels, he led Brianda, Vicente, and Ballebrera through the Queen's Courtyard, up the stairs, and along the corridors past rows of Spanish guards to Isabel's suite of apartments. Yusef, Pablo, and Koitalel followed. At the massive doors, Fernándo told them to wait and went alone into Isabel's *estrado*.

"I believe Brianda has made a conquest," Ballebrera said.

Vicente also had seen the interplay and was delighted that his daughter's first ally at Court was no less a personage than the King's brother. He exchanged looks with his *pícaro* friends. Yusef ran a finger across his throat.

Pablo glanced at the lines of Spanish and German Guards along the corridor. "And so, here we are, deep inside the belly of the beast."

Fernándo reappeared with a broad smile and motioned for them to accompany him into Isabel's apartments. He escorted Brianda on his arm towards the platform where the Queen sat on a gilded chair upholstered in burgundy satin. This day, she wore a brocaded dress of small red rosettes outlined in silver squares against a black field. Although she had become matronly, her dark eyes and pretty face expressed her characteristic *joie de vivre*.

Her principal lady-of-the-bedchamber, the Countess-Duchess de Olivares, wore black attire because she continued to mourn the death of her only child. The Queen's coterie measured Brianda with narrow unfriendly eyes, specifically the women vying to be Fernándo's favorite.

After Brianda made an elaborate respectful curtsy, the Queen bade them rise, and the Cardinal-Infante took command of the introductions. "Most gracious Majesty, this lovely young lady is Don Vicente's niece, Brianda de Rocamora y Suárez, Señorita de Benetorrente."

Brianda performed another elegant obeisance, and impressed by her demeanor and beauty, Isabel beckoned the girl to the foot of the platform where several *bufónes* inspected her.

"The soil of Valencia must have rubbed off on you, Friar. You and your niece are brown as Berbers."

"I am most pleased to have returned to Court, Your Majesty. May I extend my belated congratulations on the birth of your son, His Most Illustrious Highness Infante Don Baltazar Carlos?" He snapped his fingers and Pablo brought forth an exotic lacquered ebony box from Asia. "And may I also offer this small relic in celebration of his birth?"

"You may indeed."

He followed court ritual and handed the box to the Countess-Duchess de Olivares, who passed it on to the Queen.

"You are always so charming, Don Vicente. My ladies have been accumulating many sins while they waited for you to return and confess them." She paused until their tittering stopped before she opened the box.

"It contains a sliver of bone belonging to San Vicente, who was martyred at Zaragoza in the fourth century," Vicente said.

"We thank you."

He held out his hand, and Yusef handed him another small box. "For you, Your Majesty, for all your kindnesses. I have it on good authority this vase was once part of the great Medici household, but lost when soldiers looted Florence." Yusef had told him that Don Lope acquired it from a *golondrero* who had returned with much booty from the Italian wars.

"My mother was a Medici," the Queen said as if remembering her childhood.

While Isabel admired the finely worked vase of swirling Venetian glass, Vicente snapped his fingers. Pablo stepped forward with a flat object wrapped in purple satin.

"I have brought this gift for His Majesty."

"You may give it to us," the Queen said. "His Majesty is away at his hunting lodge."

Everyone gasped when Vicente removed the cloth and displayed a portrait of a Venetian noble by one of Philip's favorite artists, Titian, which Don Lope had purchased from the same *golondrero* of insentient good taste.

"Why are you being so generous, Don Vicente?"

"I inherited them from a childless benefactor. Because of my vows, my way of life, I have no need of material things. And I have provided well for my niece's dowry."

Isabel waited for her entourage to finish commenting on his piety. "And is this the only reason why you requested an audience?"

"I wished to present my niece to you, in the hope, with your charity and considerable wisdom, Your Majesty might suggest the name of a household in which she may serve."

"She is pretty enough, and well-mannered. How old is your niece?"

"Twelve, Your Majesty."

"Almost thirteen, Your Majesty," Brianda said.

The Queen raised her fan so no one would see her smile. "But not of the *grandeza*."

"No, Your Majesty," Vicente said.

"Then she may not serve in the royal household."

"I did not expect so lofty an honor for my niece, but I had hoped to find a place for her in a noble household of pious Catholics. And although we are not of the *grandeza*, the lineages of de Rocamora and de Suárez are untainted by bad Jewish or Moorish blood. Brianda's family includes *hidalgos* and *caballeros*, royal bailiffs, and Valencian nobility, with a long history of service to the Crown like our kinsman standing next to me, Don Ramón de Rocamora, Señor de Ballebrera and Knight of Alcántara."

Vicente went on to name other de Rocamoras who had become Knights of Santiago, Alcántara, and Calatrava. He recounted the military exploits of Rafal and Francisco, and reminded everyone that King Philip had made the latter *primero* Conde de la Granja de Rocamora.

The Cardinal-Infante intervened. "And Don Vicente is too modest to speak of his own service to the Crown, with which you are quite familiar, Your Majesty," He faced her ladies. "Surely one of you can find a place for this lovely girl."

"Señorita Brianda is exceptionally talented for her age, Your Majesty." Vicente described his daughter's accomplishments in reading, the lute, and chess.

The Cardinal-Infante turned to Brianda. "Chess as well? Then, young lady, we shall have to play a match."

"At your pleasure, Eminence." She devastated him with a smile. "And at your peril."

He laughed and said, "Don Vicente, I like your niece's spirit."

The Queen rapped her fan for attention. "Señorita, why are you dressed in black. Is it modesty? Were you so advised by your uncle?"

Brianda sighed and cast down her eyes in the classic attitude of every statue of the Virgin and female saint throughout Spain, as Vicente had taught her. "Your Majesty, I am in mourning for my beloved mother."

"So am I still for my only daughter." The Countess-Duchess de Olivares stepped forward with a maternal expression that softened her scythic features. "Your Majesty, may I claim this modest child for my household?"

Vicente held his breath until Isabel consented. He had not expected Brianda to live within the household of the most influential woman in Spain after the Queen. He felt expansive and ready to burst because he had made the best possible choice for his daughter.

It could never have happened had he taken Brianda to foreign lands. Through her education in the Olivares household, with the sympathetic friendship of the Cardinal-Infante, and the innate kindness of Queen Isabel, his daughter would live like a princess at the Alcazar; and with a dowry of thousands of ducates, she might one day marry a Don Somebody of Great Consequence.

Vicente recalled Moraíma's prophecy that he would have three loves. Earthy, passionate, warm and fiery as the Valencian sun, the *morilla* had been his first. María would always be his unattainable idealized romantic love, chaste and pure as the snow on the Guardarrama Sierras. He had not expected the third to be the selfless love of a father for his child.

Chapter 45
Father & Daughter

Several weeks later during the mid-hour of siesta, Vicente walked alone through the fragrant gardens of the Casa de Campo. Lost in nostalgic thought, he neither heard the song of the lark, nor smelled the lush scent of spring flowers.

He passed the stone bench under the shade of great elms where María had confessed her trivial sins, confided her most secret yearnings, and ordered her ladies to bring him iced drinks. Two months earlier in February, she had at last formally wed her cousin Ferdinand, King of Hungary and Bohemia.

Vicente paused at the same vine-covered wall gallant naïve Prince Charles of England had climbed to woo his Juliet. Where was his Valencian boldness? He ought to have abducted Doña María and carried her off to a fragrant bower and bed of orange blossoms. And when the King and Olivares arrived with an army, they would have found him and his golden love entwined together in an eternal embrace to inspire *romanceros*, love stories more poignant than *Romeo and Juliet,* for all the ages to weep over.

He looked towards the bleak walls of the Alcazar and sang an old air:

"Once a maiden dwelt, fair, unknown,
   in a castle, tall, grim, gray stone . . ."

Vicente stepped back when the gate door opened. *Have I conjured my beloved María?*

Brianda entered the garden modestly dressed in black with a plain gold cross and chain hanging from her neck. A diaphanous lace shawl covered her hair and all of her face except for those mischievous green eyes. She carried a book of prayers, her rosary, and a large black silk and ivory fan she had inherited from her mother.

"You are not chaperoned, Brianda."

She removed the shawl from her face. "I had to see you, Tío. I can confess only to you."

Vicente sat beside her on María's bench. "What is it, my child?" At least as a cleric, he could always address his daughter paternally without arousing suspicion.

"Tío, I believe I may have sinned."

Vicente reached under his sleeve for his dagger, ready to kill the swine who had violated her. "You think? Don't you know?"

"Yes, it must be so. I am being punished by God."

Brianda blushed and hid her face behind the fan. Vicente immediately understood why. He had consoled many similarly frightened girls over the years, even María. Yet, he had never expected his own daughter, a wharf rat raised on the licentious docks of El Grau and by a lupine mother, to be ignorant of the inevitable onset of womanhood.

Vicente held Brianda's hands and explained more as a physician than a confessor what he knew of womankind's monthly rhythms and menses. ". . . and so you see, my child, the so called Curse of Eve has nothing to do with what you may have said or done. You have become a woman, and will bear children *after* you marry."

His explanation satisfied Brianda. "I like your new mustachio, Tío. You look more like a *caballero* than a Dominican."

Vicente had grown his stylish mustachio and goatee to divert attention from their uncanny and dangerous resemblance. He wished he could reveal himself to Brianda as her father, but it was essential for her to be known by all as his brother's daughter and forever be free from any accusation of bastardy or new-Christian taint. Before he died, however, Vicente intended to tell her the truth. By then, she might suspect as much. His daughter was no fool.

He saw that Brianda was becoming uncomfortable under his unblinking gaze and resumed his roles as uncle and friar. "Have you anything else to confess, my child?"

"No, Tío."

"Are you treated well by the Countess-Duchess?"

"She is very kind to me, but . . ."

"Yes?"

"Some of the other girls and ladies in her household flaunt their father's titles in my face. They claim superior lineage and ridicule me. They also say that I must be part Gypsy or Morisco because I'm so dark. It isn't true, is it, Tío?"

"Decidedly not. Remember this, Brianda, you are the Señorita de Benetorrente. You are descended from cousins of the Kings of France."

"They lived hundreds of years ago. My tormentors are the daughters and granddaughters of living *grandees* and *títulos*."

"That is their sin of pride. They are also guilty of the sin of envy, envy of your exceptional beauty and intelligence."

"You may be right, Tío Vicente. They are most unpleasant to me on those days I visit with Fernándo."

He had not needed to encourage his daughter's valuable friendship with the Cardinal-Infante. Several times each week, she played chess with the handsome young prince, who treated her as a younger sister. Even though Fernándo had a harem of beautiful mistresses, Vicente intended to watch them more carefully now that Brianda was nubile. He would have to find her a husband before she was led astray by her passionate Valencian nature or by dissolute and devious Court lounge lizards.

Years ago, Don Lope had shown him a copy of the brilliant letter Lord Cecil had written to his son. Vicente now applied the Englishman's advice to his daughter's situation. He placed his silver crucifix in Brianda's right palm and covered her hand with his. "I should have spoken to you of such matters sooner. Swear to me . . . swear you will follow the advice I give you this day."

"I so swear, in the name of the Father, the Son, and the Holy Spirit. You disapprove that I see Fernándo so often?"

"No, it is a good thing to associate with the powerful and influential. I have lived here at Court for more than ten years, and I have seen much. Are you willing to listen to my advice?"

"Yes, Tío."

"Never forget that your maidenhood is your most precious possession. But once lost, it is gone forever, unlike gold and land, which can always be recovered or replaced. No matter the temptations, you must resist the sweet arguments of handsome gallants on moonlit nights in perfumed gardens such as this one. You must keep your virtue, and surrender it only on your wedding night. Do you so swear?"

Brianda blushed and hid her face behind the fan. "Yes, Tío."

"I have other practical advice." Vicente released her hand from his crucifix. "Never trouble the powerful with small matters, nor ask for inconsequential favors. That will annoy them. Compliment Fernándo often, the Countess-Duchess de Olivares too. At unexpected moments, surprise them with many delightful yet inexpensive gifts. I will tell you when and which."

"On important occasions when you give any significant present, let it then be something they will see every day, so they will be favorably reminded of you. Daily, King Philip passes the Titian I donated to his gallery. Each moment the Count-Duke is in his library, he can see the rare volumes I have brought him. And I have not neglected the King's Confessor. Every night Fray António reads from the old illuminated Bible I gave him.

"So, always remember, my beloved niece, to advance in our ambitious court of intrigues you must be both humble and generous towards your superiors. Also, be familiar yet respectful towards your equals to enhance your reputation as a well-bred young woman. And to inferiors, show them kindness without familiarity. Then all will think well of you."

"It seems like a great deal of work."

"To be a successful courtier is a full time career and often requires natural talent more valuable than any learned skill or ability. I am still but a novice at it. Otherwise, I might have risen higher. And one final piece of advice. Your quick tongue is sharp as a Valencian dagger. Use it to defend yourself, but never sacrifice a *poderoso* or a friend to a pointed jest. Charm and gentle wit will take you farther."

"I promise. I'll do all you advise." Her expression brightened. "And whatever lies ahead for me, I can face it because I know you will always be close by to watch over me."

How he wanted to hug her. They were very much alike. Brianda had none of her mother's evil traits.

With Vicente's surge of paternal love and pride for his daughter came great anxiety. Ever since his night of love with Moraíma on their perfumed bed of orange blossoms, he had chased after the daughters of other men. Now his turn had come. He would have to devise clever stratagems to protect Brianda's virtue. And both their lives. If Jacinto and Tomás knew or at the very least suspected he was her father, they would not hesitate to inform Diego de Arce Reynoso, who would denounce him to the Holy Office as a fornicating adulterer. The ambitious zealot might even arrange on behalf of Jacinto and Tomás for Brianda to disappear in some remote convent or within the deepest bowels of the Inquisitorial dungeons.

That must never happen.

Chapter 46
The Flagellated Christ

Barely able to breathe because of the acrid mix of stale air and human waste, Vicente held a perfume soaked handkerchief to his nose and hurried through one of the insect infested secret passageways that had survived the remodeling and was used as an informal latrine by those privy to its existence. Despite recent renovations in the Alcazar, withdrawal rooms continued to be available only within the royal apartments. Everyone else still had to make do with chamber pots scattered along corridors and corners of antechambers, which were emptied at irregular intervals by night soil men.

Vicente opened the panel a slit to be sure no one was in the royal chapel and hesitated when he recognized voices.

Inquisitor General Zapata and Arce.

"First, I will remind the King that he was baptized Felipe Domingo after Santo Domingo, founder of our Holy Order. Then I shall demand a great *auto-de-fé* for the foul blasphemies committed by those Judaizing Portuguese in the Calle de las Infantas."

"For them and all the other Judaizing dogs," Arce said. "Every Portuguese is a Jew. All Spanish new-Christians too, despite their ostentatious displays of piety. We must rigidly enforce the *limpieza* statutes and cleanse Spain forever of everyone with even the slightest drop of Jew-blood."

"Olivares will resist, and so will Sotomayor, his cat's paw."

"The Count-Duke may have the royal confessor, but Your Reverence holds our King's conscience."

"Not completely. How I wish His Majesty would rid himself of Satan."

"Then we must do more than convince him to grant us an *auto-de-fé*," Arce said. "We should begin by collecting the Count-Duke's enemies with the same passion he accumulates his blasphemous books. With all due respect, Your Reverence . . . and we all wish you a very long life . . . we should also plan how to prevent Olivares from appointing Sotomayor as the next Inquisitor General."

"King Philip has great affection for his confessor. If Olivares wants Fray António to be Inquisitor General, His Majesty will assent."

"Then we must attack the Count-Duke and his Olivaristas precisely where they are most vulnerable . . . his *hombres de negócio*."

"The Portuguese."

"Exactly, Reverence. New-Christians all. Judaizers all. Those usurious swine and their agents have antagonized all classes. Everyone knows the Portuguese dominate banking, finance, and collection of royal rents solely to enrich themselves. Their numbers are growing. They pollute entire blocks of Madrid."

"I agree with you, Fray Diego, but we must proceed cautiously. The Count-Duke ferociously protects his cunning Portuguese bankers."

"But Olivares also knows he would be unwise to challenge the Inquisition over any documented case of Judaizing. With so many Jews coming and going freely at Court, surely it is a sign God is punishing Castile for its sinfulness," Arce lamented. "And prominent among them is that ubiquitous nuisance, Rocamora. It has been rumored that Sotomayor may succeed you one day and will groom him to be his successor."

Arce's mention of his name startled Vicente, who almost retched in the stifling atmosphere despite the scented handkerchief. *Clever dog. He thinks like a brilliant chess player and anticipates possibilities years in advance.*

"Fray Vicente is too young to be considered for Inquisitor General," Zapata said. "He is no more than thirty years old."

"If you have the long life we all wish you, and if your successor is Sotomayor, when the time comes, Rocamora will be old enough."

"I see no problem. There are worse choices. Everyone knows that Fray Vicente is the most pious . . ."

"A sham. He is not *limpio*."

"Not *limpio*, you say? His certificate . . ."

"A forgery. Of that, I am certain."

"So you and his enemies would like to believe, Fray Diego. Was he not confessor and spiritual director for our King's sister, Her Most Illustrious Majesty Doña María? Is not the unblemished Fray Tomás his cousin?"

"Unquestionably the de Rocamoras of Orihuela are *limpio*. But I have been reliably informed by his kinsmen that one cannot be certain of his mother's true origins, neither Olivares nor even Rocamora himself, I suspect."

Vicente's hand instinctively went to the dagger hidden under his sleeve.

"Have you any proof of his taint?"

"I am seeking documentation concerning his mother's family," Arce said. "*Limpio* de Rocamoras in the Kingdom of Valencia are making a thorough investigation of the matter. One is a Familiar of the Holy Office, the other the respected Dominican theologian, with whom you are acquainted. I expect them to present me with the damning proof that Vicente's maternal forebears were Jews. My informants are also investigating the circumstances of his niece's birth. Their physical resemblance is too uncanny to be an accident."

Vicente wanted to burst into the chapel and slit Arce's throat.

"Be careful, Fray Diego. If you are in error, you will lose all."

"I have alerted Juan Adán de la Parra, the Apostolic Liaison from the Tribunal of Toledo to *la Suprema* and the Court. Fray Adán and his spies will watch Rocamora's every move. By the time our *auto generale* takes place, we may yet have enough to roast him at the same *quemadero* with the other Jew-pigs. The scandal will cause great damage to Olivares and his allies."

"And guarantee you will be my successor?"

"You honor me."

"Fray Diego, do not rehearse your dance over my corpse just yet. I will prefer to believe that all you have suggested is the result of sincere religious zeal. It would be a grievous sin for you to destroy countless innocent lives solely to become Inquisitor General."

"Rocamora may be not so innocent. I believe he is a master of disguise, and as such, he fatally wounded my kinsman Don Rodrigo de Lograńo y Arce in a duel."

"Have you proof?"

"Not yet, but I have seen him teaching swordsmanship to the Cardinal-Infante."

"Hardly evidence. In my youth, I was considered one of the best swordsmen in Castile. This heat is wearying me, Fray Diego. Let us continue our conversation in my office over iced drinks."

Vicente lingered in the passageway no longer aware of its foulness as he planned how best to frustrate Arce and his spies. Unfortunately, he no longer acted for himself. Arce would not hesitate to get at him through his daughter.

Vicente entered Olivares' offices at a propitious moment. The Count-Duke was conferring alone with Sotomayor at the great desk in his study. He paid his respects and described all he had overheard except Arce's reference to his becoming Sotomayor's successor and the suspicion he might be Brianda's father.

"This *auto-de-fé*, which Zapata desires, is a terrible business."

Vicente had often heard Sotomayor discredit his rival. At age seventy-six, His Majesty's confessor believed time was running out for him to become Inquisitor General.

The Count-Duke did not offer Vicente a seat. "What do you know about the case of the *Cristo de la Paciencia*?"

"Only that several Portuguese have been arrested and accused of Judaizing and flagellating an image of our Savior, Excellency."

Olivares wrinkled his massive nose as if smelling rancid cheese. "It is a case with little merit, but one which Zapata and Arce are determined to transform into a major problem for us. Don António, bring him up to date."

Sotomayor adjusted his spectacles and looked at his notes. "Last summer, police of the Inquisition arrested two Portuguese immigrants on the Calle de las Infantas for suspicion of Judaizing. Inquisitors from the Tribunal of Toledo, which, unfortunately, still has jurisdiction over the Court and Madrid, questioned two children of the accused. After being fed delicacies and guided through a clever interrogation, the boy stated that he had seen his parents flagellate a statue of Christ. Then his sister confessed to having seen the same desecration."

"Everyone knows that testimonies of children less than eight years of age are null and void because they are too young to swear an oath," Olivares said.

"And the Inquisitorial Council of Madrid found their statements to be full of contradictions," Sotomayor said. "The case might have ended then and there, except that Fray Diego Arce y Reynoso pressured Zapata to order the parents tortured until they corroborated their children's story. A few months later, the accused Portuguese confessed that they had indeed flagellated an image of Our Lord, an image Who cried out in agony between lashes, 'Why do you mistreat me?' And afterwards, they burned it."

"An old wives' tale for the gullible," Olivares snarled. "We all know that Zapata dreams of presiding over one great *auto-de-fé generale* in Madrid while he is still Inquisitor General."

"Which may not be for long, given his failing health," Sotomayor said.

"Fray Antonio, do you believe they flogged a Christ?"

"Possibly, they may have, Fray Vicente, out of ignorance and hatred for our True Faith. The accused are poor and uneducated, most of them illiterate."

Olivares lifted his wig with a stick, scratched his head, and squashed a hair louse between thumb and forefinger. "Now, thanks to Don Vicente, we know for certain what we have suspected. Zapata's real intent is to use them to get at my bankers and financiers."

"Zapata is a tool of Arce, who expects to follow him as Inquisitor General," Sotomayor said.

Olivares did not reassure the royal confessor that he would succeed Zapata. "Unless I see absolute proof, my Portuguese are Judaizers only when I say they are. At this time, I cannot afford the sacrifice of even one of them, for then all the others will leave for Amsterdam and enrich our Dutch enemies."

He adjusted his wig and looked at Vicente who was still standing. "How would you divert attention from Zapata's demand for an *auto*?"

He reflected upon the most popular diversions excluding *autos* and *quemaderos*. At the slightest pretext, fabulous Court theatricals were given, followed by sumptuous meals and other entertainments lasting until dawn. Jousts, equestrian contests, and boar hunts took place almost daily in the Pardo woods. The public and nobility were addicted to bullfights.

Vicente visualized dozens of accused new-Christians being thrown to the lions in the Plaza Mayor. "We have had everything but a Roman circus."

Olivares slammed his fist on the desk. "Yes, a Roman fiesta. I can envision the entire panorama. The costumes. The animals. The drama. A spectacle beyond the wildest fantasy of any *madrileño*. But we will need an excuse for the occasion, which must take place as soon as possible. And I have it. Infante Don Baltazar Carlos will have his second birthday in October. We shall celebrate his birthday in the Imperial Roman style." The Count-Duke rose. "I must go to His Majesty and convince him to deny Zapata his *auto-de-fé*."

"I will bring *la Suprema* around," Sotomayor said as Vicente helped him to his feet. "And when I next confess His Majesty, I will also discourage him from consenting to Zapata's auto."

Because of Arce's threat, Vicente went out at night only in disguise and armed until one cloudy evening at the end of September. Upon sudden notice, Olivares sent him to deliver an important message to his ally, Villanueva, who lived near the Prado.

Alert to sounds and movement as he rode his mule through the narrow streets of Madrid, Vicente tensed when a two-horse carriage slowly approached him. Too slowly. As it came beside him, he noticed that dark curtains were drawn across its windows and a black cloth covered its coat-of-arms. Cloak and broad-brimmed hat obscured the coachman's identity.

A trio leaped out with drawn swords. Vicente dismounted from his mule, and the men advanced towards him from three directions. Their plan was to trap him against a high wall.

He removed his cloak and dragged it along the ground like a Roman gladiator's net. Instead of a long lethal trident in his other hand, he held his

dagger. It would be enough. These overconfident *matones* had not expected to face a Valencian master-of-arms.

"*¡Viva El Grau!*" Vicente shouted in gratitude for his practical education. He threw his dagger at the nearest assailant and struck him in the throat. With his cloak, he covered and confused the second *matone*. He stepped to one side in time to avoid a sword thrust by the third. Vicente seized the man's arm as he lunged and threw him hard against the wall. He picked up the dazed assailant's sword, plunged the blade deep into his vitals, and turned to face the surviving assassin who had freed himself from the cloak.

The *matone* looked at his two dead comrades, the sword in Vicente's hand, and jumped into the coach. Vicente caught a brief glimpse of someone else inside in the shadows. He saw a flash and heard a pistol discharge before the door closed again and the driver whipped his horses away at a gallop.

Vicente saw blood on the sleeve of his white robe. His left arm had been hit, nothing serious, a flesh wound. He pulled his dagger from the *matone's* throat, wiped the blade on the man's cape, and returned it to the scabbard under his sleeve. He removed the masks from the two dead men but did not recognize them. His assailaints were not of the Anglesola clan, nor Valencians.

Vicente retrieved his cloak, and returned to the Alcazar.

In the Queen's Courtyard, he had the good fortune to encounter Fernándo Cardoso, a physician from Portugal and unlikely friend of *alcalde* Quiñones. Vicente saw that he was carrying his bag of medicines and instruments and motioned for the physician to come with him to a torch lighted vestibule.

Cardoso inspected the wound, and treated it. "A minor scratch. How did it happen?"

Vicente measured the slight, swarthy young palace physician. "Not even a humble friar in royal service is spared violence."

Cardoso closed his bag. "The times we live in."

"What are you doing up at this late hour?"

"Don Juan de Quiñones is lying in bed on his stomach with a painful case of inflamed hemorrhoids."

The irony of the *alcalde*'s discomfort was not lost on Vicente. "Is he not the one who wrote that Jews have tails and menstruate through their anuses as a sign of God's punishment?"

Cardoso studied Vicente as if seeing him for the first time. "You should have seen the expression on our courageous *alcalde*'s face when I reminded him his affliction could be taken as proof of descent from a *converso*."

I wish I had been there.

Chapter 47

Beasts in the Arena

A pleasant autumn breeze wafted through the open windows and doors of a luxurious apartment with a balcony overlooking the Plaza del Parque, which had been selected as the site for Olivares' Roman fiesta honoring Infante Baltazar Carlos on his second birthday. Inside the great *estrado* he had requisitioned for his party, Fernándo played chess with Brianda. Vicente and Ballebrera stood nearby as part of the Cardinal-Infante's entourage of confessor, master-of-arms, hunting companions, servants, and two sulking mistresses.

They were drinking chocolate or flavored water and gossiping after a lavish meal of goats feet salad, aspic of capon, brain fritters with orange sauce, veal pie, stuffed artichoke bottoms, tender peas with bacon, assorted cheeses, and marzipan. Vicente selected a gold toothpick from a bowl of rose water and watched his radiant daughter. Her mantilla and deft use of fan gave her an aura of command. A gold necklace and cross broke the solid color of her black ensemble. She required no jewels. No emerald could rival the green of her eyes, which she used with devastating effect on the Cardinal-Infante.

Because Brianda had been out of the sun from the day they left Valencia, her skin had bleached to white gold. Unlike many girls her age, her teeth were straight and white, another family trait, and dimples further enhanced her captivating smile.

Her natural beauty contrasted with Fernándo's painted mistresses in their low cut, bare-shouldered guardinfantes. The two noblewomen nibbled on bits of scented unglazed white clay, a current fad, because they believed it enhanced a voguish pale complexion.

The Cardinal-Infante's Jesuit confessor, Jerónimo de Florencia, frowned with disapproval at their dresses. "Exaggerated to the point of folly. Look at them, Fray Vicente, their guardinfantes are so wide they cannot pass through church doors."

"Satan's design," Vicente never missed an opportunity to express pious platitudes. "It also allows them to conceal signs of pregnancy."

"Shocking. I had never considered so vile a deceit before."

Except for Vicente, Brianda, and Ballebrera, Fernándo and his entire entourage had succumbed to yet another fad rampant throughout la *Corte* and all Spain, the wearing of eyeglasses even if one had perfect eyesight. Everyone referred to spectacles as quevedos after the admired satirist Francisco de Quevedo who had made them fashionable.

Ballebrera preened in aqua and pale rose silk and velvet and selected a marzipan. "I cannot understand why it is considered elegant for men and women to allow their noses to bear the weight of quevedos, which also pinch the nostrils. They wear their spectacles all day long, though they read nothing, and remove them only when they go to bed." He paused and chuckled. "And one or two I know, not even then."

"Quevedo is fortunate he did not give his name to *servedumbres*," Vicente said, and Ballebrera's stomach shook with laughter.

Fernándo waved a scarlet suede glove. "Don Vicente, come closer and watch one of our rare victories over your prodigy niece."

Vicente found the Cardinal-Infante to be a natural tactician, tenacious on defense and bold on offense. They had fought often to draws and stalemates because he spent more time admiring Fernándo's collection of ornate chessboards and pieces than planning his moves.

Created in Augsburg, this particular set was a magnificent work of art sent by Holy Roman Emperor Ferdinand II as a gift when the boy was made a Cardinal. The ebony board was inlaid with ivory, silver, and mother-of-pearl. Each of the four corners had squares with allegorical figures representing the continents of Europe, Asia, Africa, and America. Between them along the edges, cartouches held intricate curvilinear scenes from mythology. The white squares on the playing field contained amusing caricatures of human activities, some portrayed by anthropomorphic animals. The pieces carved from ivory and serpentine represented two royal houses in contemporary clothes.

Playing the ivory pieces, Fernándo launched a reckless attack. "Exactly like war, is it not, Don Vicente?"

"Almost, Your Eminence."

"Almost? How is it different?"

"In chess, the terrain never changes, nor the climate. We do not worry about supplies, reinforcements, or plague, which kills ten times more men than our enemies on the field of battle."

"I always learn much from you, Don Vicente. ¡*Viva Jesús!* I have your king's knight, Señorita Brianda. I have already taken your king's bishop. I have twice your number of pawns and both my knights." After she moved a piece, Fernándo counter-moved without hesitation "Hah! You have lost your last bishop trying to protect your Queen's rook."

The de Rocamora rook and coat-of-arms. When would Rafal acquire his title?

The Cardinal-Infante became more ebullient with victory a few moves away. "Perhaps you are right after all, Don Vicente. I may be winning our match, but you have taught me another valuable lesson. I must never forget weather, terrain, supply and reinforcements. Ah, fittingly with a bishop. Check, Señorita Brianda."

When the Cardinal-Infante acknowledged his applauding entourage, Brianda without a moment's hesitation took his bishop with her knight. "Checkmate, Your Eminence."

He stared in disbelief at the board, and Ballebrera whispered in Vicente's ear, "Was it an illusion? Did she move her piece when no one was watching?"

"Brianda does have nimble fingers. A gift from her father."

Fernándo stood, raised Brianda to her feet, and bowed. "I humble myself before fair Hippolyte. Perhaps we ought to raise an army of Catholic Amazon warriors to confound the heretic Protestants."

As the entourage dutifully laughed, a great fanfare of horns announced the start of Olivares' Roman circus. The Cardinal-Infante took Brianda's arm and led her outside to the balcony next to Their Majesties, Infante Baltazar Carlos, and the Count-Duke. Vicente, Ballebrera, and other selected favorites followed to take their places behind Fernándo and Brianda. His mistresses struggled and complained when they were unable to pass through the door because their guardinfantes were too wide.

The pageant began with a parade of horse-drawn caged beasts from all continents. Next came a procession of performers dressed in costumes as Roman gods and goddesses, vestal virgins, and soldiers wearing shining armor and animal skins as legionnaires and barbarians. All saluted Philip and Isabel in the Roman style. After elaborate sets and tableaux had been pulled into the temporary arena, the entertainers mimed mythical events and engaged in battles and jousts between Roman Legions and Carthaginians, Persians, Gauls, and Goths.

Vicente focused more on the interplay between the Cardinal-Infante and Brianda, who was still two months away from her fourteenth birthday. *Fernándo is infatuated with her. My own daughter. Amazing. She uses her fan with all the devastating effect of the most experienced courtesan.*

Vicente intended to have another fatherly talk with Brianda and reprimand her for ignoring his advice. She was playing a dangerous game. She must never arouse a prince, and then deny him. If she submitted to him, she would be ruined.

The roar of the crowd brought his attention back to the arena floor. Olivares had arranged an event no Spaniard had ever seen, a battle between animals. Every known beast, large and small, was pitted against a different creature: Tiger against bear; rhino versus bull or greyhound, lion, jackal, and boar.

He turned away disgusted. Olivares' grand fiesta was no different from the vicious treatment meted to dogs, cats, and donkeys by Spaniards of all classes.

"Don Vicente, which, in your opinion, is the most dangerous beast? Bull, lion, or perhaps the wild boar?"

Vicente scanned the plaza, the faces of Philip and Isabel, members of the clergy, nobles and commoners alike. He remembered similar expressions at the *autos-de-fé* and *quemaderos* of Judaizers, blasphemers, and *alumbrados*. "The most dangerous beast is the crowd, Your Eminence, always the crowd."

"Don Vicente, to your many accomplishments you must add a new title, Philosopher."

The crowd roared louder when the keepers threw all surviving animals into a general melee. The *madrileños* were delighted when a bull, the great symbol of Spanish manhood, gored or trampled all that challenged it and intimidated the rest. The magnificent glistening black beast charged across the plaza as if he was the lord of the arena and all Spain. Even when goaded by lackeys in wooden armor, the other animals refused to attack the bull or fight each other.

King Philip motioned for a guard to hand him his harquebus. He adjusted his cape to free an arm and took aim. The entire arena became silent in anticipation. When the great bull passed under his balcony, he shot the beast. It fell to to the plaza floor, and the crowd hysterically cheered their expressionless King.

Vicente expressed his true reaction to His Majesty's dispatch of the bull one afternoon several weeks later when he walked with Ballebrera along a poplar shaded lane in the Prado. "The bull deserved to live. And Philip would have been more heroic if he had jumped into the arena with cape and sword and faced it *mano a toro*."

Ballebrera held a slim volume. "All you say is true, but so wondrous a feat cannot be passed over in silence. His Majesty's unerring aim has produced over a hundred verses by poets, nobles, and courtiers. They run the gamut of genius from Lope de Vega to poetaster amateurs like Quiñones. Most astonishing of all, in record speed for Spain, within three weeks of the fiesta, all poems were published in this single volume, with a preface describing the event by Royal Chronicler Don José Pellicer de Tovar. I can recite the title only if I take a second breath."

He showed Vicente the title page: *Amphitheater of Philip the Great, Catholic King of the Spanish Realms, Sovereign Monarch of the Indies, East and West, always August, Pious, Felicitous, and Supreme, Containing the Eulogies Which Have Celebrated the Fate He Has Dealt The Bull, in the Agonal Celebration of the 13th of October, 1631.*

"And that is merely the first salvo *ad nauseum*. These verses effusively compare His Majesty to every mythical and Roman hero."

Vicente listened to Ballebrera read several of the poems aloud until he could take no more. "It seems every sycophant has competed to surpass all their previous hyperbolic laudatory imagery to flatter our monarch."

"And to enhance or at worst maintain their positions at Court."

Vicente took the book of poems from him and thumbed through its contents. "And why not you?"

"I tried, but my tears of laughter so drenched the paper I gave it up."

Vicente shook his head at one poetic effort. "The physician Cardoso has been superbly góngoric. Did you know His Majesty sends forth rays of light like a Christian Apollo?"

"Not bad. I have been expecting to read how our King pees pure nectar and evacuates attar of roses."

"But I will concede one point. For a physician, Cardoso has a flair for the fanciful and knows exactly what to praise. After he describes the bull's blissful death at the hands of so great a King, he announces that Philip's shot augurs victories in war against all enemies."

"Because he is Portuguese, Cardoso must work harder to solidify his position at Court. Perhaps, you ought to have written one as well."

"Alas, this unfortunate friar can only create poems affirming love and life, not allegories celebrating death."

Chapter 48
An Unexpected Clue

After Easter Sunday, 1632, Olivares sent Vicente to Seville and Cordoba on yet another spying and book-finding mission. Siesta was a time when he could be most productive without being disturbed. While the clergy slept, he searched through the most arcane volumes in the Cathedral of Cordoba's extensive library to find those the Count-Duke coveted and to research new subjects for his sermons. He intended to answer questions posed during a recent theological debate. Which is worse? Who is sent to the lowest level of hell? A Jew who converts and then Judaizes, or a Christian who accepts Judaism?

Vicente also looked in vain for documents that would confirm his mother's *limpieza*. In Seville, he feared that he had discovered a paternal *converso* ancestor or kinsman when he came across the name, Moses ben Samuel de

Roquemaure, who had converted to the True Faith in 1358. On further reading it became obvious that the *de* meant he came from Roquemaure and was not of the *sieur's* family because he Castilianized his name to Juan de Aviñon, from Avignon. Moses-Juan must have been a prominent physician, for he had written the *Sevillana Medicinae*.

Vicente opened a worn, dust-covered volume and perused through it until he came to a description of the polemical correspondences between Paulus Alvarus and Bodo, known as the Apostate. Bodo. The name leaped from the pages. Bodo, the same name on the scrap of paper hidden in his mother's cross.

His heartbeat accelerated in anticipation of a great discovery about his ancestry. He had a clue at last. And more. Other sources in the library also mentioned Bodo: The ninth century *Annales Bertiniani* by Prudence, Bishop of Troyes, and the *Epistola seu liber contra Judaeos* also titled *Liber Epistolarum*, by Amolo, Bishop of Lyons.

Vicente read that Bodo had come from a noble Germanic family of pure Alamannian descent. He was educated for a clerical career after Charlemagne defeated the Alamanni, Saxons, and other northern barbarian tribes and converted them to Christianity by the sword.

Bodo was educated for the church at the court of Charlemagne's son, Emperor Louis the Pious, also known as *le debonnaire*. While still a sub-deacon, he was the subject of a gushy poem of praise composed in eight distiches by the ecclesiastic scholar poet, Walafrid Strabo, a fellow Alamanni tribesman who addressed him fondly as "my little blond green-eyed lad."

Bodo had green eyes. So did my mother. So have I, which I have passed on to Brianda.

Vicente returned to the document and read that Bodo became one of Emperor Louis' chaplains and favorites. In the year 838, at age twenty-five, he asked permission to make a pilgrimage to Rome. Emperor Louis did more than grant Bodo's request. He provided him with a substantial entourage and many gifts for the Pope.

Bodo never went to Rome. Instead, he headed south to Vic in Catalonia, known as Asona in his time and inhabited by Jews. The Christian sources were very specific about what happened in OAsona. Bodo converted to the Jewish Faith between eight and nine in the morning before the Vigil of Ascension Day, the twenty-second of May, and took the Hebrew name Eliezer. Vicente shuddered when he read that Bodo also underwent the barbarous practice of circumcision.

Bodo-Eliezer sold his entire entourage of Christians into slavery, except for a nephew who also converted. He then married a Jewess, whose name was not recorded among the documents, and let his beard and the hair on his head grow long. When Emperor Louis heard of Bodo's apostasy, he refused to believe what his Deacon had done, but soon the scandal spread throughout France, the Empire, and the Church.

Vicente paused to reflect and draw some logical conclusions, which created more questions. Something unusual must have been going on at the court of Emperor Louis the Pious to cause Bodo's departure and conversion. Then as now, Jews were despised throughout Christendom. If so, what would have caused a deacon of aristocratic barbarian origins, untainted by Jewish blood, and the Emperor's favorite, to convert to a despised religion and change his life so drastically?

Vicente concluded that one motive might have been an intense hatred of Christianity. Bodo was of the Alamanni. He may have given only outward conformity to a religion forced upon him and his tribe after defeat in battle. Another might have had something to do with the unnamed woman he married.

He returned to the documents and encountered another surprise. After his conversion, Bodo wore armor and carried weapons. How was it possible? In Bodo's time, the Muslims did not rule Asona, and Jews were forbidden to bear arms in Christian lands.

Bodo moved on to Zaragoza and then to the Caliphate of Cordoba where he became an anti-Christian polemicist and was challenged to a literary duel by Pablo Albar, a Cordoban Christian of Jewish descent known in church records as Paulus Alvarus.

Vicente turned to a tenth century manuscript of their debate that had been preserved in the archives at the Cathedral of Cordoba. Only tiny portions of Bodo-Eliezer's replies were extant because Christian zealots had erased or destroyed the rest of the manuscript. As a result, the surviving correspondence was one sided. In essence, Albar cited specific Hebrew prophecies and historic events to prove his conclusion: Jesus must inevitably be recognized as the true Messiah.

Vicente was disappointed to read that Bodo disappeared sometime after the year 847. In addition, he failed to find the name or word Natronai in any of his readings. He now believed, however, that Sep, the third word on his mother's scrap of paper, was an abbreviation of Septimania, as Languedoc was called when Bodo lived and where Roquemaure was located on the Rhone River.

Bodo and Sep. Was the original home of the Rocamoras connected somehow to Bodo? A further search through more dusty tomes brought Vicente no closer to learning what his mother was trying to tell him from beyond the grave.

Was she descended from Bodo?

Am I?

Vicente believed the documentation of his mother's origins, if it still existed, should be found in Roquemaure. If he went there and learned the truth, would he be able to face it?

Whatever the truth, Vicente felt a kinship with Bodo. Like himself, the apostate must have been forced into the Church. Later, Bodo wore armor, as Vicente believed he would and ride to battle with His Eminence, Fernándo.

Vicente timed his return to Madrid in early July after Zapata presided over his *auto-de-fé generale* on one of the hottest days in memory. Arce's blood boiled at an even higher temperature. Olivares had finessed the zealot and the Inquisitor General when he influenced the Holy Office to serve a main course of poor and illiterate Portuguese Judaizers, with the usual side dishes of several dozen bigamists, blasphemers, and sorcerers, a total of forty unfortunate souls.

Events moved swiftly after the *auto generale*. Authorities leveled and burned the house where the alleged desecration of the Christ took place, and the site was given to the Capuchin Friars to build a convent. Lope de Vega commemorated the event with a 101 stanza poem he titled *Sentiments at the Offenses Done unto Our Good Christ by the Hebrew Nation*.

Of greater significance, the twelve-hour *auto-de-fé* further enfeebled the eighty-two year old Inquisitor General, and Olivares encouraged his immediate retirement. He replaced Zapata with Sotomayor, but failed to rusticate Arce to a remote monastery. The bigot had powerful allies in the Church who schemed successfully to make him Bishop of Palencia. As one of Sotomayor's presumed heirs apparent, Vicente expected more trouble from Arce and other rivals.

Within the same month the King's brother, Infante Don Carlos, died of fever and a weakened condition caused by his addiction to vices prevalent at Court. At one of the palace *mentideros*, Vicente overheard several new-Christian Portuguese gloating that God had slain Don Carlos as revenge for the *auto* on behalf of all those of Jewish blood.

If that were true, then God has made a poor choice, for He allowed Death to take the most ineffectual, mentally limited, least consequential Habsburg of all.

Chapter 49
The Cardinal-Infante Commands

"Tío."

Brianda was the first to greet Vicente when he entered Fernándo's *estrado*. She sat opposite the Cardinal-Infante at a small table and chessboard by a window, chaperoned by the Countess-Duchess de Olivares' most disagreeable *duenna*.

A father's suspicion consumed Vicente. Fernándo's harem of mistresses, his confessor, and hunting companions were absent. Had Brianda and the Cardinal-Infante deliberately color-coordinated their clothes? She wore a neck high brown velour dress with ruff and gloves of beige lace, Fernándo his brown and silver hunting costume.

The loss of a brother had not affected his good nature and enthusiasm. "Again, Señorita Brianda has bested me. I was too rash. A good lesson learned. Chess is excellent training for war. Plan many moves ahead. Be prepared for all possibilities. Learn how your opponent thinks. Although who can ever understand the mind of a woman?"

Brianda flashed a flirtatious smile for him. "I trust the journey through its maze is always delightful in the attempt, Your Eminence."

"Indeed it is." He kissed her gloved hand and made a polite gesture for her to withdraw. After Brianda curtsied and left, the Cardinal-Infante led Vicente to a table where he had spread out a map of Europe. "Here is the chessboard upon which the future of Spain will be decided."

"Remember, Your Eminence, there are more than two players at the gaming board of Europe."

"With Buckingham dead, the English count for little." Fernándo tapped his finger on the Duchy of Mantua. "Even Italy is a minor matter. Cardinal Richelieu's intent has always been to draw the bulk of our forces into that morass to ensure our defeat in the Netherlands and the Emperor's in Germany."

He moved his hand upward to the Imperial lands. "The great danger is here. Richelieu, aided by Sweden and the German Protestant princes, intends to crush Austria so that France can dominate Europe. Unfortunately for us, his plan is succeeding. The Imperial army regularly suffers defeat. It lacks the discipline and pride of our own Spanish army. Their best general, Count Tilly, was killed last April. Their most powerful general, Count Wallenstein, is unreliable and may decide to carve out an empire for himself."

"If only the Marqués de Spinola had not died in Italy."

"There are other, perhaps greater generals, waiting to prove themselves. The Count-Duke and I agree. We must support Emperor Ferdinand to prevent his complete defeat." Fernándo swept his hands westward to the Netherlands. "As you know, our spies have informed us that Prince Frederick Henry of Orange made a secret agreement with Richelieu to split the Spanish Netherlands. It now seems that he has had second thoughts and has come to a significant conclusion. Brussels must never fall into French hands. Orange now fears that Cardinal Richelieu's grandiose ambitions will include a conquest of the United Provinces. Therefore, he is determined to preserve a buffer between himself and the powerful French."

Vicente appreciated the irony that the Protestant Dutch, enemies of the Catholic Habsburgs, had become the guarantors of Spain's control of Flanders against the aggression of France. Dynastic ambition had replaced religion as the cause of war. *Raison d'Etat* had replaced religious solidarity during war.

"Our governor of the Netherlands, Archduchess Isabella, believes that Orange is prepared to make a peaceful settlement with us. The Dutch Prince may be sincere, but we know that French agents are working behind his back to arouse the war party in the United Provinces."

"A most complex situation, Your Eminence."

"Not for long. His Majesty and the Count-Duke have at last listened to me. I shall be appointed Viceroy, Governor of the Netherlands, to succeed the Archduchess. It may take many more months, but I shall leave for Barcelona, and from there embark for Milan to raise a great army and march through Germany to the Netherlands." He seized Vicente's shoulders. "For how many years have we shared our boyhood dreams of soldiering? Now the time has come. For both of us. Don Vicente, come ride with me. Give me the benefit of your wise counsel, strong sword arm, and your acute mind, for you will also be my cipher master."

Vicente could barely contain his joy. His dream to soldier for the Crown had become reality, and a Prince of the Blood had commanded him to serve. "Your Eminence, I must tell the Count-Duke and His Reverence. As you know, I have been serving at their pleasure."

Fernándo drew a sword from a scabbard hanging on the wall and lunged at an imaginary foe. "They will give you no trouble. In fact, I have a message for you from Sotomayor. He requests that you attend him at his *palacio* after vespers."

"Your Reverence."

Vicente entered the great antechamber of the Inquisitor General's residence known as *El Espíritu Santo*, which faced the Plaza Santo Domingo. Although the streets that opened onto it on all four sides had proper names, each was known as *calle Inquisición*.

Vicente genuflected and received permission to sit. Sotomayor appeared ageless despite his thick spectacles. "Always remember, Fray Vicente, waging war is not proper work for a true son of our church."

"There are precedents, Your Reverence."

"You are referring to those Bishops of centuries past who fought against pagans and infidels with mace and chain."

"And the warrior Pope, Julius II. I confess to you that I hear the martial blood of my ancestors calling me."

"Of course, Fray Vicente, and neither you nor I can overrule one who is both Cardinal and Infante. Life has many surprises, setbacks, and great rewards. After His Majesty ascended to the throne in 1621, I was disappointed not to be chosen Inquisitor General. And now I am just that at the advanced age of seventy-seven."

"But stronger in body and mind than men twenty years younger."

"I prefer to think so. And to think ahead. I have told the Count-Duke that we should begin to groom one who shares our views to be my successor."

"You still have a long life ahead of you, Your Reverence."

"And it may take all those years to overcome our opposition, barriers, and lies."

Because he had overheard Arce and Zapata in the royal chapel, Vicente was prepared for what might be coming next. His expression was all innocence when he asked, "You have a candidate, Your Reverence?"

"I have. One who is renowned for his piety, whose sermons inspire congregations to serve our Lord, whose brilliant imagery reduces sinners to tears and contrition. Fray Vicente, I cannot prevent you from accompanying His Eminence. However, if you survive this war with an unblemished soul, I shall prepare you to succeed me as Inquisitor General."

"Your Reverence." Vicente dropped to his knees and kissed the hem of Sotomayor's robe. "I am truly honored. Overwhelmed. But have you discussed it with His Majesty, who must approve me, the Count-Duke who advises King Philip, and His Eminence who has commanded me to ride with him?"

Sotomayor motioned for Vicente to rise and return to his chair. "I have mentioned my plans to no one except the Count-Duke."

"What was his reaction?"

"He will speak with you about it tomorrow. Do your utmost to gain his support."

Vicente met with Ballebrera that night and shared a bottle of brandy in his room while he told him of the Cardinal-Infante's command. "And so at last, I shall ride to war as a soldier of the Crown, as I had hoped the day you and Jerónimo dashed my dreams."

"You have not done so badly since. I must tell you this, Vicente. War will not be what you expect. It is more than drums, horns, colorful flags, and shining armor. More than a glorious cavalry charge. The blood, the torn bodies." Ballebrera shook his head, drank his brandy, and poured another.

"I am aware of all that."

"You have described for me more than once the tortures of the Inquisition you witnessed, and we both have seen the *quemadero*. Believe me, you will experience more than fighting. You will have a glimpse of hell that, if you survive, will haunt you to the grave." Ballebrera raised his goblet, "Neither drink nor the charms of a beautiful woman can obliterate the memory of those horrors."

"Like you, I am a de Rocamora, of the warrior caste."

"I know that I cannot change your mind, and as you said, the Cardinal-Infante has commanded. Still, it may not be wise for you to leave Madrid. Your enemies at *la Corte*, in the Church are many and growing. They will become stronger and more effective while you are away."

Vicente shrugged and drank his brandy. "I have no control over that."

"And what about Brianda?"

"I will speak with the Countess-Duchess de Olivares. If necessary, I shall place her in the Convent of the Barefoot Carmelites until my return."

"A wise decision, of which I am sure His Eminence will approve."

"Yes, he cares for her as he would his own sister."

Ballebrera lapsed into silence and Vicente took the opportunity to describe his discovery of Bodo. "Have you heard his name mentioned before?"

"Never, as I told you the day you found those names in your mother's cross."

"But what are your thoughts?"

"I have none, except to wish you well in battle and survival without serious wounds."

Ballebrera's lack of interest disappointed Vicente. His kinsman obviously did not want to pursue the matter. It was the same whenever he wanted to discuss his mother's origins. In each instance, Ramón's eyes gave him away.

What is he not telling me? And why?

The following day, Vicente found Olivares at the edge of the Prado near the Monastery of San Jerónimo where he was supervising the building of Buen Retiro, the Good Retreat. The King's new pleasure palace, begun the previous year on the Count-Duke's property, was to be set in the midst of lush gardens, shaded groves, and a network of lagoons.

Olivares took Vicente aside. "You interest me, Friar. Everyone wants you. Your kinsman, Don Ramón, has told me that you have always yearned to be a soldier."

"Then I have your permission, Excellency?"

"Friar, I find it inconvenient to lose so valuable a servant. Still, your absence from Spain for a few years can work to both our advantages. You will be far from enemies who have tried to harm you. Therefore, you have my . . . His Majesty's permission to accompany the Cardinal-Infante to war, with one specific instruction. You will send coded reports directly to me at frequent intervals. Describe everything of importance he says, does, and plans."

"As you command, Excellency."

"Now then, regarding the office of Inquisitor General. Sotomayor was precipitous, too precipitous. It is more than your lack of years."

"Excellency, I have never aspired to be Inquisitor General."

"I wonder." Olivares tapped his walking stick on the ground. "Nevertheless, Sotomayor will support you to be his successor after you return, if he is still alive. And so may I, provided your *limpieza de sangre* is unassailable."

Chapter 50
Betrayal

Early in September, Vicente received word to meet the Cardinal-Infante in the palace armory. He found Fernándo dressed in black gilded armor and holding a marshal's baton. Flaxen curls framed his pale handsome face and a ferocious blond mustachio covered his upper lip.

"Don Vicente, my aunt, Archduchess Isabella, has written sound advice that I have taken to heart. She suggested I exchange my scarlet robe and biretta for armor, because Cardinals as governors have an unsavory reputation in Brussels."

He took Vicente's arm and led him closer to the forges where sweaty armorers hammered out swords, breastplates, and moines. The din forced them to raise their voices, and Vicente stepped back from the great heat, flying sparks, and thick smoke.

"If a Cardinal, why not a friar as well? Master Armorer, make a suit for Don Vicente, one befitting his rank of captain."

After the armorers removed the Cardinal-Infante's leg and arm guards and breastplate, they dressed him again in his robe and measured Vicente close to the forges. He was so soaked with sweat his muscles and veins glistened in the firelight as if he had been molded from bronze.

"I see that you are fit enough for our march to Brussels. After you have been measured, let us take cool refreshment in my apartments."

"Thank you, Eminence, but I promised to confess my niece."

"I know, and she is waiting for us."

Brianda stood alone in Fernándo's *estrado* dressed all in white. Pearls decorated her silk guardinfante and ivory fan. Her white mantilla, ruff, and gloves were of the finest lace. Vicente thought she was more beautiful and radiant than any bride on her wedding day. Then he realized that Brianda was unchaperoned and wearing an expensive gift from Fernándo, an emerald necklace. He barely contained his rage at their betrayal. He would never be able to arrange a decent marriage for his daughter. He ought to slay them both. Vicente reached under the sleeve of his robe. Lucky girl. Fortunate prince. He was not carrying his dagger on this dark day.

Brianda saw his distress. "Eminence, I wish to confess to my uncle. May we be left alone?"

After the Cardinal-Infante withdrew, Brianda sat on his carved, embroidered armchair as if she were his lady of the house. "You are angry, Tío."

Vicente wanted to shake Brianda and slap her face. "Angry? Yes. Shamed too. And played false."

"But I followed your advice better than you expected. Fernándo did not seduce me. I set out to beguile him."

Vicente studied his daughter anew. Had he been wrong about her? Was she like Violante after all? He began to believe so when she described how she had worn Gypsy clothes and danced chaconnes and zambras for the smitten prince.

Brianda clutched her cross when she saw the murderous look in his eyes. "Believe me, Tío. I swear. I have loved Fernándo, my golden Adonis, since the day you presented me at Court. I wish you were not so pious a friar. Perhaps if you had ever loved a woman, you would understand."

If I ever loved a woman? Are we de Rocamoras of Benetorrente fated to love only unattainable Habsburgs?

Vicente modulated his voice. "Fernándo is royal and a Cardinal. He can never marry. He has ruined you."

"No, not ruined. It is my symbolic bridal dress. I wanted to tell you first because I love and respect you as if you were my real father."

Vicente almost dropped his mask of clerical rectitude. "What are your plans?"

"We will leave for his hunting lodge in the Pardo woods. I have agreed to become Don Fernándo's mistress. He has forsworn all others for me. He loves me as much as I love him."

"For how long, Brianda, one brief season of summer?"

"Forever."

"And after you have his child?"

"My Fernandiño is not cruel like King Philip. He has sworn a solemn promise. He will never banish me to a convent."

Vicente pulled at his mustachio and remembered Moraíma's naiveté. "Royals are fickle. He is more likely to discard you."

"Then, if necessary, I can always make a marriage with some noble. Don't look at me like that. I will have been mistress to the Viceroy of the Netherlands, brother of the King, son of a long line of Kings. Surely, you have seen how the *grandees* preen when their wives, sisters, and daughters are chosen for the King's bed. Then they receive their expected appointments or expensive presents." Brianda snapped her fan. "Those pompous dukes and counts of the *grandeza* are no different from the pimps of El Grau."

And now I shall appear as one of them.

Calmer now, Vicente considered the merits of her situation. What were Brianda's realistic alternatives? Spinsterhood or marriage to a minor title at best, most likely someone effete and degenerate. On the other hand, as Fernándo's mistress, she would have protection from calumnies regarding her bloodline. If she gave birth to the Cardinal-Infante's child, his grandchild would carry the royal blood of the Habsburgs. Not an unpleasant outcome.

"Then, Brianda, you will be accompanying Fernándo on his march to the Netherlands."

"Yes."

"I wish you would reconsider. If battles are lost, or if epidemics and plagues ravage the camps . . ."

"We will not lose any battles, and have you ever known me to be ill?" Her face clouded. "But I do so worry about my Fernándiño's health and stamina."

"Then you must be mother as well as mistress." Vicente stood over Brianda and made an exaggerated cross. "You have my blessing. And I absolve you of all sin in the name of the Father, the Son, and the Holy Spirit. May His Eminence bring you all the joy and happiness I wish for you."

Brianda stood, hugged Vicente, and shouted her joy, which brought the Cardinal-Infante to the doorway, diffident in manner, until he saw both of them smiling.

"My uncle has given me his blessing."

"But at the request of a favor, Eminence."

"Name it."

"I ask permission to leave for Barcelona ahead of you."

"Granted."

Now he would have more time to seek evidence of his mother's origins in the north of Spain.

Chapter 51
Barcelona

During his circuitous journey to Barcelona through Aragón, Spanish Roussillon, and the north of Catalonia, Vicente found no evidence of his mother's family in church libraries, parish records, civil documents, and on gravestones. Were it not for the war, he would have sneaked into French Languedoc and gone to Roquemaure in the same pursuit.

Vicente entered Barcelona on a chilly February morning wearing doublet, hose, boots, plumed hat, and cape. To discourage human predators, he did not hide his weapons as he rode through the bustling narrow hilly streets and to the top of Mont Juic. At the great lighthouse, he took in its commanding view of the city, the thriving port below, and the dark waters beyond. The King and Olivares had already arrived in Barcelona. So had Fernándo and Brianda, and he could see the Cardinal-Infante's ships in the harbor.

Vicente galloped across the field past a group of officers drilling a company of pikemen to Ballebrera and an old soldier he recognized. They were watching masters-of-arms instruct a line of recruits in the drill of loading muskets, adjusting aim to compensate for the wind, and firing at dummy targets. *Rafal.* He ought to have expected the Cardinal-Infante to summon one of Spain's most experienced commanders in the wars against the Dutch.

Accompanying the sixty-one year old Rafal was his third son now a strapping young man of twenty. Built more like Ballebrera, Juan de Rocamora's short legs supported the muscular torso of a taller man. He was swarthy, with a dark mustachio and fashionable goatee, lively brown eyes, handsome masculine features, and a genial mien so unlike his older vicious brother, Jacinto.

Vicente greeted his kinsmen. Rafal looked him up and down with no change of expression. "Vicente? Dressed as an officer? Legs planted in two worlds, it seems. What brings you here to Barcelona?"

"The same service as you, Don Jerónimo. His Eminence, Don Fernándo, has commanded me to accompany him on this great adventure."

"Yes, I remember. If you could have had your way, you would have soldiered for the Crown."

"We can always use another de Rocamora in the heat of battle," Juan said. "Gaspar would have come as well, but someone had to be left behind to look after the family estates."

Ballebrera waited to speak until the recruits fired a volley, which tore apart several of the targets. "You may come to regret your decision, Vicente. I repeat, war can be a nasty business."

"That is something I will have to experience myself. Don Jerónimo, I believe that after this campaign, the Cardinal-Infante will recommend you for a title."

"If you are truly intent upon going to war, perhaps you should spend some time here and become proficient with the weapons you are carrying."

"Now is as good a time as any, Don Jerónimo, to show you my skills."

When two officers ended their exercise in swordplay nearby, Vicente called out to one and challenged him. Without the restrictions of his woolen robe, he applied what he remembered of *la destreza* and easily bested his opponent, after which, he showed Juan clever tricks with sword and dagger.

"Friar. You have all the skill of a *golondrero* and not unlike that of the mythical Señor de Algorfa."

Vicente turned to Jacinto, who tapped a coiled black whip against boot and spur. The wound he had given him distorted his once perfect feminine features. A thick scar ran across his cheek from ear to mouth and twisted his lips in a permanent sneer of undiluted malignancy.

Vicente returned his sword and dagger to their scabbards and fixed his eyes on Jacinto's disfiguring scar "I have learned the necessary skills to deal with criminals from all castes."

"Friar!" Jacinto snapped his whip at a rock near Vicente's feet. "You ought to care more about my father's title."

Vicente did not flinch. "You and I, we have exhausted the subject. At least I am serving His Majesty and Spain in war, unlike those cowards who posture as *hidalgos* in their remote *señorios*."

"So have I waged war against Judaizers, blasphemers, sorcerers," Jacinto paused and sneered at Ballebrera. "And sodomites."

Ballebrera's mustachio bristled like the quills of a porcupine as he reached for his sword. Rafal stepped between them, gripped Jacinto's arm, and pulled him towards the barracks with Juan following.

Ballebrera recovered his equanimity. "Now tell me everything, Vicente. Did you find any documents concerning your mother's family during your travels?"

"Nothing."

"Perhaps it is better if none exist."

The tone of his comment chilled Vicente. It was not the first time Ballebrera had implied his mother might indeed have been tainted.

Vicente would have preferred to sit by a fireplace at an inn and drink local brandy to warm his innards on this blustery afternoon atop Mt. Juic. Instead, he stood with Juan apart from Jacinto, who was sulking, and watched Ballebrera and Rafal prepare to mount their horses.

Rafal spurred his Andalusian, but Ballebrera lingered and exposed his *hábito* to humiliate Jacinto. "We are all looking forward to tonight's activities. The Count-Duke has promised a great feast and much entertainment."

Jacinto mounted his horse. "Yes, why should you not add dining with Jews to your other vices?"

"The day you speak those same words to the Count-Duke's face will be the day you might become a man."

"And on that day, Olivares will be finished."

Vicente, Juan, and Ballebrera walked away from Jacinto who followed them on horseback snapping his whip.

Vicente tightened his back muscles. All senses were alert while he made light conversation. "Don Juan, I have not had an opportunity to ask your father what he thinks of His Eminence."

"He says the Cardinal-Infante was born to be a soldier and is a natural leader. His Eminence has shown my father the greatest respect. He has appointed him to his Council of War and made him *Maestro de Campo de Infanteria*. You were right, Don Vicente. When the Cardinal-Infante sees how great a soldier my father is, surely he will convince the King to award him his title." Don Juan hesitated at the stables and looked down towards the city. "I wish I could be at . . ."

"The Council of War?" Vicente finished for him.

"No, to gaze once again upon His Eminence's mistress." Vicente gaped at him horrified that Brianda had been mentioned within Jacinto's hearing. "I saw her yesterday in the palace gardens walking with the Cardinal-Infante. Never have I seen beauty so exceptional."

Jacinto rode closer. "Unfortunate *galanteo*, to wear the horns even in your dreams."

When Juan reached for his dagger, Ballebrera held his arm. "Cool your ardor, for she is beyond your reach."

"If Jacinto were not my brother . . . ." He turned to Vicente. "Perhaps after His Eminence discards her for another . . ."

"You would make her your mistress?"

"My wife. Have you seen her?"

"I am her confessor."

"You are? Then, do you not agree? Is she not the most beautiful woman in all Spain?"

"Have you heard her name spoken?"

"No, but surely she must come from an important family."

"Indeed she does," Ballebrera said. "The most important of all. Tell him, Vicente. In the name of God, tell him."

He lowered his voice. "The Cardinal-Infante's mistress is my niece, the daughter of my long-deceased brother, Alonso. Her name is Brianda de Rocamora y Suárez, la Señorita de Benetorrente."

"Then we are cousins."

Jacinto edged his mount between Vicente and Juan. "Friar, how well you pimp your flesh and blood."

No self-imposed restraints this time. Jacinto had gone too far with the insult to Brianda and himself. No objections from Ballebrera and Juan when Vicente drew his sword and cursed like a Morisco. "Product of swine vomit and dog droppings. Be ready to die here and now."

Jacinto backed his horse several sword lengths from Vicente and snapped his black whip. "I understand you have been making inquiries about your friends."

"If you know anything . . ."

"Oh, but I do. The Arab pig who called himself Yusef died in his personal *quemadero* when we cornered him at his warehouse in El Grau. I burned an entire block to get him."

"Butcher."

"But I have good news about your other bandit accomplices. The Morisco you call Pablo escaped my ambush in the mountains beyond Elx. His whore of a sister has also disappeared. But be assured, I shall find them both." Jacinto snapped his whip again. "Oh, yes, the African you called Koitalel.

Although we cut him to pieces during the ambush, there was enough left of his tough hide to make this excellent whip."

Vicente pulled it from his hand, but before he could thrust with his sword, Jacinto galloped away laughing. Enraged, he leaped onto his horse and chased him down Mt. Juic and into Barcelona. Neither man gave thought to the citizens and venders' stalls in their way.

Vicente closed to a couple of lengths behind Jacinto and followed him into a narrow alley where he ran into a fusillade of gunfire. His horse reared and threw him. He recovered his sword and drew his dagger ready to take on the quartet of *matones* desperately reloading their muskets. They dropped their weapons and scattered when Ballebrera, Juan and several soldiers charged into the alley.

"Vicente, were you harmed?"

He held up his hat. "A hole here and another two in my cape. Kismet has other plans for me it seems."

"Better than Athena is to have Dame Fortune as your lover."

"I should have expected an ambush. Jacinto will never fight me m*ano a mano*. I must find another way."

And Jacinto is not my only enemy. He mentioned Algorfa. That means he has allied himself with Arce.

Back at camp, Vicente threw the whip into a nearby fire where grooms were warming their hands. He said brief prayers and final rites as flames charred the abomination into ashes.

"Your final purification, old warrior. And you, clever Yusef, who died fighting the infidels, may you be feasting and wenching in your garden paradise."

He would be unable to protect Pablo, Moraíma, and her daughter while he soldiered for the Crown. They would need all their wiles to survive.

Ballebrera stood beside Vicente. "I wish you had killed the swine."

"I expect there will be another time."

"I should have finished him the day he murdered Doña Xímena."

"And I would not have prevented you. Since then, I have learned that it is better to make a mistake through strength than one through weakness." Vicente thought of María. "I often regret more that which I have failed to do than the things I have done."

Juan came over to Vicente. "You know the practices of the Court. If His Eminence finds other women to warm his bed, what will happen to Brianda?"

Despite his rage and grief, Vicente could not suppress a smile. He imagined his daughter shoving her dagger deep into Fernándo's ribs or gouging the eyes of her rival. He also believed His Eminence, as a man of honor, would not casually discard Brianda. If he did tire of her, he would give her compensation, at the very least a dowry for a worthy knight. Vicente did not voice his thoughts to Juan. He could think of no finer young man for his daughter, but Rafal and Jacinto would create insurmountable obstacles. Brussels was close to the United Provinces. If Brianda fell from favor and Fernándo did behave badly, he might take her to Amsterdam or even to England as Don Lope had counseled so many times.

Chapter 52
The Soldiers' Friar

In August of 1633, Vicente sat alone with Brianda at a wooden table under a vine-covered trellis in a vineyard above a meadow near a Romanesque villa that the Cardinal-Infante had confiscated for his temporary headquarters outside the city of Milan. They were enjoying a midday repast of cheeses, fruits, and freshly baked bread. Broad and deep terra-cotta bowls were filled with cold water and cooled glasses of different colored wines, from pale straw to rich gold, pink rose and deep reds to lush purple.

Vicente wore black breeches, boots and a white linen shirt. Brianda had also dressed for the heat in a loose green and white striped cotton skirt and white blouse. The bright Italian sun had darkened them both during these lethargic hot summer days.

Vicente had not expected so much interminable waiting and boredom. Six months had passed before the Cardinal-Infante could create his army of twenty thousand Spaniards. By then, Swedish General Horn had blockaded Breisach, which controlled the upper Rhine, and prevented Fernando from marching into Germany. If the siege could not be lifted soon, they would be forced to wait until after the spring thaws of the next year before the Cardinal-Infante could march his army through the Val Telline.

"There he is," Brianda said when Fernándo rode into the field below ahead of his commanders and their aides.

"I must compliment you, my child. It seems you have successfully diverted His Eminence's attention from the ladies of the Milan Court."

"My only rival is the siren song of war. Tonight my Fernandiño will sleep in an ordinary tent among his men. Yes, soldiering is his first love, but not his only love. After tomorrow's mock battle and conferences with his commanders, he will return to my bed. And look, Tío, I also see Juan. He is so gallant and attentive to me. And very handsome too."

"Take care. I think you tease him too much."

"I cannot resist. He blushes so easily. I mean him no harm."

"Juan loves you."

"As a cousin, a friend."

"No, you bear the responsibility of being his first love."

"Do you think he finds me desirable because of my status as Fernándo's mistress?"

"In spite of it. Juan loved you at first sight before he knew who you were."

"Did he? Then I shall keep his love."

"Brianda, that is a most sinful and selfish attitude."

"Tío, I am not a fool. Fernándo is a man, and, like all men, one day he will choose other women. If you were not the most pious of friars, you would understand."

"Enlighten me then."

"How many women do you think have let him know they are willing to share his bed?"

"Here in Milan? Dozens."

"And over the years?"

"Beyond my ability to add."

"It is not his fault. As I said, men are what they are. And so are women. He attracts them the way a flame draws moths."

"Seriously, Brianda, you must treat Juan with more restraint."

"That is what I have been trying to tell you. If I did not love Fernándo, I think I might be able to love Juan. And one day, if I am replaced by someone younger and prettier, why should I not encourage him to court me? You have assured me of a dowry worthy of a *grandee's* daughter. Fernándo would be generous too."

"Let us hope so. For now, I pray that you will have a long life together."

Brianda's confession of interest in Juan impelled Vicente to risk speaking to Rafal. In the evening, he went to the soldiers' encampment where he heard their confessions, absolved them of their sins with good humor, and gave fitting, tolerable penances.

Except for his impatience to end this long period of waiting, he had adapted well to army life because it was a society similar to the docks of El Grau. Cunning counted as much as strength, and here one was judged not by lineage, but by his ability to survive and thrive in the rough, often brutal environment.

The men called him the Soldier's Friar. He spoke their coarse language and dialects and implied that he had committed the same transgressions before taking his vows. He also earned their respect because of his exceptional skill with weapons and talent for winning at knucklebones and cards when he wanted to emphasize the evils of gaming.

As Vicente passed two sentries at the outer perimeter, he saw a mob of several hundred soldiers in a clearing where cauldrons steamed with the evening meal. They surrounded a belligerent, drunk, and shirtless red-bearded recruit, who stood head and shoulders taller than any other man and twice as wide. He held a centuries old double blade battle axe. A pair of tough Lombard veterans who had tried to subdue the rufic giant lay unconscious and bleeding at his feet.

Vicente stopped a safe distance from the enraged colossus, whose body was covered with so much hair he looked more like a red bear than a human. If Olivares had seen this man, he would have added him to the great animals of his Roman fiesta.

Juan arrived with a squad of musketeers supported by a dozen pikemen. "Don Vicente, I thank God you are here. As you can see, we cannot restrain this ogre with our bare hands. We can't sweet-talk him either because he does not understand Spanish or Italian. If we don't tame him, we will have to shoot, or else he'll destroy our army before we ever go to war."

"Where is he from?"

"Switzerland."

"His name?"

"As best I can pronounce it, Karl Stauffacher."
"What provoked the fellow?"
"Gambling losses and drink. Claims he was cheated."
"Do something," a soldier shouted.
"If anyone can, it will be our Fray *Capitán*."

Vicente faced a pair of difficult choices. To walk away would be cowardice in the soldiers' eyes, and he would no longer have any influence over them. To fight the brute might well lead to his own early death. Vicente cautiously approached Stauffacher and spoke to him in what German he knew. The Swiss raised his great axe, shouted curses, and charged. Vicente timed his sidestep, and used Stauffacher's momentum to throw him. To everyone's relief the man lay on the ground unconscious.

While the soldiers cheered Vicente, Juan ordered his men to chain the Swiss. No individual soldier could lift Stauffacher's weapon.

"An elegant move, Don Vicente." The Cardinal-Infante had arrived with Rafal and a half dozen other senior officers. This evening Fernando wore a burgundy velvet doublet, short cape, and gloves trimmed in scarlet and gold. His broad-brimmed hat held a scarlet plume. The Cardinal-Infante's spurs were gold, as were the jeweled scabbards for his sword and dagger.

Rafal's sober black and gray garb contrasted with those of the flamboyant prince and the other commanders. "You did not learn that trick from our masters-of-arms."

"My school was on the docks of El Grau. My strength comes from faith in our Lord."

"Perhaps you will teach it to our men."

"Perhaps, Don Jerónimo." He preferred to keep such hand-to-hand tactics to himself. Too many of these soldiers after military service would become *golondreros*, and assault and rob the weak along the roads and streets of Spain.

The Cardinal-Infante stood over Stauffacher. "We must win him over. He might be worth an entire *tercio*. And so are you, Don Vicente. He turned to his commanders and said, "Now I shall walk among my men, see to their needs, and raise their spirits."

Vicente moved closer to Rafal. "I must speak with you alone."

"After I have made the rounds with His Eminence."

Vicente heard a groan and bent to speak with Stauffacher. After an intense exchange with the Swiss, he ordered Juan's men to release him and called out to Fernándo. Because Vicente had bested him, the Swiss giant had begged to be baptized and received into the Roman Catholic faith.

The Cardinal-Infante, his commanders, and the entire camp gathered to watch the sacrament. After the baptism, Fernándo gave Stauffacher to Vicente. "I suspect you are the only man he will obey."

Vicente intended for Stauffacher to watch over Brianda until they went into battle. After the congregation disbanded, he walked with Rafal to a rise at the outer perimeter for their private conversation. The old soldier was impatient to get back to his men.

"Well, what is it?"

"I believe Juan is enamored of Brianda. If she were not the Cardinal-Infante's companion, would you accept her as a wife for your son?"

"Never." Rafal lowered his voice to a harsh whisper. "I believe she is your daughter. Nothing can convince me otherwise. Therefore, she may be tainted no less than you. More to the point, she is illegitimate."

Vicente momentarily panicked. Who could have told him? Not Ballebrera. And no one else knew for certain, not even Jacinto. It had to be the close facial resemblance of father and daughter.

"Don Jerónimo, I have always respected and admired you. I am disappointed that you have accepted calumnies spread by my enemies without hearing my side. Let me emphasize this. My brother, Don Alonso, may God let him rest in peace, is named Brianda's father on her baptismal certificate. I can show you the papers."

"I have no interest in reading forged documents. I remember that your friend in El Grau was the most gifted forger in all Spain. To the point, you and the girl have identical features and the same unusual green eyes. Was she not born a few months after you came to Orihuela?"

"Coincidence. I was but a boy then."

"With a man's body." Rafal looked towards the Cardinal-Infante's tent. "Have no fear regarding my silence in this matter. I will not tell His Eminence. It would humiliate him, destroy you and your daughter, and I want no scandal attached to my name."

"I repeat, Brianda's baptismal certificate is no forgery." Rafal did not respond. Further arguments would be wasted on him. "Will you tell Juan?"

"Only if necessary. The fewer who know your shameful secrets, the better."

Vicente watched him walk down the rise to the camp. If Rafal, who essentially meant him no harm, believed the worst, then he could expect both Court and Church to give credence to every rumor spread by Arce and his minions.

Brianda must never return to Spain.

Chapter 53
Through the Val Telline

Not until the following spring could the Cardinal-Infante's army move out towards the Val Telline. With Stauffacher as her escort, Brianda sat on a spare mount atop a hill beneath snow-peaked mountains to watch the procession with Vicente. All wore heavy cloaks except the fierce Swiss who thrived in his native Alpine weather.

Unfortunate charger. You must bear the great weight of that human mountain.

Below, the Order of March had been arranged for the *tercios* to be deployed in battle formations to counter any surprise attack. The first six companies consisted of alternating lancers and harquebusiers, followed by six more of mounted musketeers, and the last seven alternating between pikemen and cuirassiers.

Next came the artillery and logistical support, the latter a long column of military baggage and supply carts pulled by mules. Every company had its own chaplain, physician, surgeon, and apothecary. So did each *tercio*.

Behind the army, Brianda's empty gilded coach led a train of privileged wives and mistresses riding in carriages of lesser equipage. Bawdy whores followed them in colorful, ribbon-festooned covered wagons.

A great city on the move brought up the rear. Thousands of men, women, and children rode in wagons; others pulled carts; most walked and carried all their possessions on their backs. They included astrologers and fortune-tellers, clergymen, pawnbrokers, peddlers and merchants, barber-surgeons, smiths, and servants.

Juan rode up to the hill and with great panache tipped his plumed hat to Brianda. He twisted his mustachio and sneered at the mass of humanity. "Look at them. Like rats who overpopulate all of Europe. They outnumber our soldiers by two, perhaps three-to-one, and it will be five-to-one before we face our first battle. My father despises them. Like mercenary armies, they live off the land. Creeping parasites all. Avoid them, Doña Brianda."

"And, Don Juan, do you avoid the *mujeres perdidas*?"

His face turned red at her mention of the camp prostitutes. He gasped for air as words failed to come.

Vicente felt compassion for Juan. No artifice. Honest and direct. No capacity for quick verbal repartee. *She baits him to dizziness, yet he comes back for more.*

Juan found his voice and pointed at a surgeon's wagon. "And stay away from those butchers. Better to let a clean wound heal by itself."

Vicente agreed with him. Most army surgeons were charlatans no better than Gypsy fortune tellers with their fake cure-alls. The rest were tradesmen: Cobblers, barbers, even hog and horse gelders. Filthy men, each one of them. They sawed bones, lanced ulcerated sores and boils, and cauterized wounds with tools of their true trades, which they also used to stuff food in their mouths, and with hands that wiped behinds and touched water only by accident.

In Barcelona and Italy, Vicente had collected many of the same salves and tinctures Don Lope had used. He had brought others with him from Spain and was confident that he would remember how to apply them if necessary.

"So soon?" Brianda asked when the great procession stopped to encamp for the night. "It is still a good hour before sundown. Don Juan, how long will it take us to cross the Alps?"

"We should be in Swabia by next month."

Juan's optimistic prediction proved to be false. Their progress around the Swiss Confederation consumed several months. It might have taken longer had the Swedish Marshal, Gustavus Horn, succeeded in taking the fortress of Überlingen, which guarded the southern shore of Lake Constance along the route of the Spanish march. The town held out for four weeks, and Horn broke off the siege to join his ally, Bernard, Duke of Saxe-Weimar. The two Protestant generals decided it was essential to destroy the Imperial army before the Spanish arrived. Unfortunately for their cause, their pestilence ridden and inadequately supplied troops were unable to outflank King Ferdinand. By then, the Cardinal-Infante's army had passed through Überlingen, and into the eastern edge of the Black Forest.

While the Spanish army encamped on high green ground in Swabia between Freiburg and Rottweil, Fernándo summoned Vicente to sup with him and Brianda in front of his tent. "Don Vicente, rread this letter, which you might find of interest."

Vicente moved closer to the torches and almost gasped aloud when he read who had written it. In the letter, María described how she had pleaded with her husband and father-in-law to allow her to journey and meet Fernándo, her favorite brother, until they relented. She had crossed the Danube accompanied by her confessor and ladies. One of the Emperor's palaces near Ülm was to be the site of their meeting.

Aware of Brianda's intense gaze, Vicente concealed his emotions. "Your Eminence, I pray nothing happens to Her Majesty, for the enemy army is too close by and the peasantry is in revolt. She also risks exposure to epidemic."

"All that and because she is four months pregnant with her second child are the reasons why the Emperor ordered her to stay at Linz. As if anyone who calls himself human can command my sister." The Cardinal-Infante giggled like a little boy. "Don Vicente, prepare to ride with me tomorrow. And how surprized she will be to see her brother and former confessor together in the garb of soldiers."

Vicente was speechless. He had hoped but never expected to see María again.

After their meal, Brianda asked Vicente to confess her. She lit a solitary candle inside her tent, and they sat in semi-darkness on thick cushions atop Turkish rugs. Outside, Stauffacher and his battle-axe would discourage eavesdroppers.

"Tío, your face. When you read the Queen of Hungary's letter. Never before have I seen you lose your composure so."

Vicente preferred to change the subject. "What is it you wish to confess?"

"First, I think you need to confess to me. The Queen of Hungary is said to be as beautiful as Don Fernándo is handsome. Intelligent and devout. Qualities you most admire. Am I wrong to believe that when you were her confessor you had strong feelings of affection for her?"

"Brianda . . ."

"You would have been alone with her more often than anyone, even her brothers. I have heard *murmuraciónes* that she was very fond of you."

"Her Majesty went to her husband chaste." He regretted his voice sounded so forced.

Brianda kissed his cheek, and Vicente was amazed at his daughter's sudden transformation from girl to woman. He would never confess to anyone all he had felt and experienced with María.

"You need not say anything more, Tio. It was thoughtful of Fernándo to invite you."

Vicente pulled at his goatee. The Cardinal-Infante had not written María that her former confessor was accompanying him on the campaign.

How will she react to seeing me without a warning?

When he attempted to rise, Brianda held on to his arm. "Wait, I do have something to confess." In the flickering candlelight, her downcast eyes and serene expression suggested the Madonna. "I am four months with child."

Vicente looked at her stomach. He had never observed that Brianda was pregnant because her guardinfante and cloak concealed her contours. Astonishing. His daughter, soon to be seventeen, was going to make him a grandfather at thirty-three. Like Moraíma's daughter, his grandchild would be half-Habsburg.

"Are you pleased, Tío? Say you are, and will you bless me and my child?"

Vicente kissed Brianda's forehead and blessed her. "I look forward to baptizing your child. But now you must go to a safer place."

"I will not leave Fernándo's side."

"Does he know?"

"Yes, and have no fears on my behalf. He will not sentence me to life in a convent."

"How can you be sure?"

"Because Fernándo is clergy and can never marry, he will have no jealous Queen to appease."

Chapter 54
Reunion

Hat and plume, cape and gorget, doublet, hose, boots, and gloves, Vicente was all in black except for his white ecclesiastic collar when he rode with Fernándo and a company of a hundred and fifty men towards Ülm on the Danube. Brianda stayed behind to avoid an expected snub.

On the eleventh of August surrounded by her ladies of honor, the Queen of Hungary received the Cardinal-Infante at the front steps of the Ülm palace. She wore an elaborate guardinfante of gold-trimmed black velvet and silk and a mantilla. Her attending ladies also dressed in the Spanish style to honor Fernándo. A confessor and other clergy stood nearby.

After exchanges of formalities and warm greetings between brother and sister, the Cardinal-Infante said, "We have a surprise for you." He turned to his escort and beckoned one of the officers. "*Capitán*."

Vicente dismounted and advanced towards the Queen of Hungary. At his first sight of her in more than four years, he felt familiar love and affection, and then concern. María's face was wan and drawn. Deep shadows ringed her blue eyes. He stood before her. Their eyes met and held. As he was about to kneel, María whispered his name and collapsed in his arms. Everyone present believed Her Majesty's fainting spell was the result of her condition and the difficult journey.

During the first day and night of their visit, the Queen of Hungary spent all her time conferring with Don Fernándo. Not until the end of the second day did she summon Vicente.

They met in a secluded corner of the palace garden, which stirred memories of pleasurable days in the Casa de Campo, although he saw no palm, poplar, or cypress, nor any shade-giving great elm. Alien spruce and oak lined the paths. Even the birds sang a different tune.

For their meeting, Vicente discarded his armor and wore plain doublet and hose. María awaited him on a marble bench in the same black ensemble. She held both fan and rosary in her lap and clutched the great golden cross hanging from her neck. Two of her ladies waited out of hearing at the far end of the garden.

How will she receive me? Is our last meeting as vividly etched in her memory as in mine?

After Vicente genuflected, the Queen of Hungary commanded him to sit beside her. As he did so, she arched a silky blonde eyebrow and looked him up and down. "No woolen robe? No silver crucifix? Instead, we see mustachio and beard. We do not recognize our former confessor and spiritual director."

"His Eminence commanded me to ride with him to war, but you will always have first call for my services, Your Majesty."

María sighed. "With all our titles, we still miss the way you addressed us as *Alteza*."

"I pray you are happy and content, Your Majesty . . . *Alteza*," ," ," he added drawing out the 'e' with all he felt for her.

High color consumed her cheeks and she pursed her lips to avoid a spontaneous response. "I love my husband, and he loves me."

How could he not? Vicente was gratified she had dropped the imperial we for the more personal I. *Alas, premature.*

"We have so much work to do for the Empire. God's work. Spain's work. All for our True Faith."

He dared not risk offending her with further use of *Alteza*. "My Queen, all agree that you are the one person most responsible for drawing Spain and the Empire closer. In Madrid, I have read reports. They confirm that from the day of your marriage to King Ferdinand, you have been the dominant influence in his life."

"Spoken like a courtier. Tell us, Don Vicente. Are you content to be merely a fashionable confessor to the *grandeza* and Satan's servant for the rest of your life?"

"No, but I say in all truth, like His Eminence, I too have always wanted to soldier for the Crown."

Her expression hardened, the blue of her eyes became glacial. "Perhaps he wants you to watch over his mistress?"

"You know who she is?"

"They say she is your niece."

"They speak the truth, but I assure you, my Queen. I did not foist her on His Eminence."

"We know that. We are amazed that our brother is loyal to one woman. But then, we are told she is exceptionally beautiful. Dark, like you. With green eyes, like you. With Valencian cunning and temperament, like you. Was your brother also of dark complexion?"

"He was blond and fair, but Doña Violante, her mother, was dark."

She raised a hand to silence him. "We wonder. Did you grow your mustachio and beard to stifle gossip about your close resemblance?"

"I wish protocol would allow Your Majesty to receive her. My niece, Brianda, is lovely and charming."

"And we are told she is skilled at music, chess, and other diversions. Our brother has repeatedly sung her praises. She has indeed enchanted him. We wish her a safe easy delivery, and a healthy child."

Vicente allowed himself the luxury of imagining Brianda conversing with María. Impossible in a reality of *punctilio*, precedence, and bloodlines where queens and mistresses never met. Still, he preferred to believe they might have become friends within the limitations of royal protocol.

He offered María an embroidered box containing a fashion doll he had intended to give Brianda. "For Your Majesty's birthday next week."

"You remembered."

"I shall never forget."

She indicated for him to place her present on the bench between them. "We shall open it after we return to Linz." María waited until after her ladies brought a small table and served chocolate and cold water. "And you, Don

Vicente, you must return to Spain and counter your enemies' calumnies if you wish to follow Sotomayor as Inquisitor General."

"I prefer to be a soldier."

"Tell us that after you have experienced your first taste of battle." She touched her stomach. "Although dynastic survival requires we produce a son, if our next child is a girl, she will marry our nephew, Infante Don Baltazar Carlos. Is His Highness as handsome and intelligent as everyone reports?"

"Yes, My Queen, and with a natural majesty and ability to command."

"We shall write His Majesty, King Philip, this. If we do give birth to a girl . . . and when Her Highness arrives in Spain, we recommend you to be our daughter's confessor and spiritual director, as you were ours, even if you have become Inquisitor General by then or risen high in the Church. Perhaps we should not tell you. His Eminence, the Cardinal-Infante, intends to offer you the Bishopric of Antwerp or some other one of those impossible to pronounce Flemish cities."

"So he has said to me, but most of all, I wish to return to your service."

She blushed again and fanned herself. "Do you not think we would have sent for you if it were possible? Here, in the Empire, Jesuits and Capuchins are in favor. To be a Dominican at the Imperial Court, why that would be almost as abominable as being a Protestant heretic." María placed her fan on the bench and sipped her chocolate. "Is Satan still as powerful as ever?"

"He is, and the Count-Duke has given His Majesty King Philip the great gift of Buen Retiro. When I left Madrid, construction had just begun, but I saw the plans. The main building will have many well lighted rooms built around several courtyards. There will be a great theater, game preserves, a wooded park with cascades, lakes, and grottoes. Good Retreat is an appropriate name for it."

Her eyes misted as she turned her head to the southwest towards Spain. "We often think of the Casa de Campo. The garden was our *buen retiro*."

"The great elms are lonely and weep rivers of tears in memory of you."

"Still a poet."

They reminisced about the times they shared. "The highest moment of my life has been to serve Your Majesty."

María abruptly picked up her fan and pointed it at him. "Then we command you. After our two armies meet, watch over our husband, His Majesty, and our brother, His Eminence. They must triumph and survive their great battle against the heretic Protestants."

"I so promise." He removed his glove to display the silken blue ribbon and the ruby ring she had bestowed upon him during their final secret rendezvous in the Alcazar. "And this time I wear your favor to conquer more than language."

Her voice softened as she dismissed him. "Then we ask one more thing of you."

"Anything, on my life ."

"Your life, yes. Take care of yourself as well, Don Vicente. Please, for me, do take great care."

Chapter 55
Nördlingen

At the end of August during a night encampment, the Cardinal-Infante finished dictating dispatches to Vicente in the torchlight outside his tent. He was about to confer with Rafal and the other commanders when an Imperial officer galloped to them and dismounted. He gave the man permission to speak.

"Your Eminence. There is a change of plans. Instead of heading west along the north shore of the Danube to link up with your army, King Ferdinand has decided to attack Nördlingen five leagues northwest of Donauwörth. The town has a strong Swedish garrison capable of launching a surprise flank attack, and its commander has prevented the burghers from surrendering. When I left His Majesty, our big guns were bombarding the city walls."

"Then, we shall move out to meet him there."

"We must first find, then annihilate the armies of Horn and Saxe-Weimar," Rafal advised. He turned to the officer. "Where is the enemy?"

"Deploying in the hills and woods a short league away from Nördlingen, which is why my King has not stormed the town."

"Have Horn and Saxe-Weimar attacked?"

"No, Eminence."

"What are they waiting for?"

"The surrounding countryside is unable to supply even one army. At first, the enemy believed hunger would force us to retreat without fighting, which they prefer to avoid."

"Avoid pitched battle? But why?"

"Our armies are almost equal in size, and the terrain is broken and difficult. The Protestants' insignificant reinforcements are poorly equipped and hungry."

"What are their numbers?"

"About twenty-two thousand men against His Majesty's fifteen thousand."

"And I have twenty thousand." Fernándo faced his commanders. "Our combined armies outnumber the enemy. Prepare your men. At first light we force-march to Nördlingen. Remind them to keep their powder dry. Don Jerónimo, stay with me. Don Vicente, bring me the dispatches as soon as you have encoded them."

After Vicente completed his tasks for Fernándo, he carried a polished ebony box to Brianda, who rested in her tent. "Tomorrow, we march to our first battle. I am not pleased to leave you behind unprotected. Stay as far away from the battlefield as possible, my daughter." He tried to make his last words sound priestly.

In an eyeblink, deadly steel flashed in the candlelight. "I can take care of myself."

"You may need more than a dagger." He opened the box. "I have brought you a brace of wheel-lock pistols. Be careful with them. They are loaded and ready to fire."

"Tío, I worry more about you and my Fernandiño. Look after him. I shall say prayers for you both and for Juan too until the battle is won,."

On the morning of the fifth of September, Vicente sat on his charger with Stauffacher at his side among the Cardinal-Infante's escort and the King of Hungary's general staff at a command post on a hillock close to the southern side of the walled town of Nördlingen. Vicente was dismayed when he had a closer look at The Emperor's son. Ferdinand was short with dark hair, mournful brown eyes, poor teeth, and undistinguished features. He had not expected María's husband to be so ugly and tried not to imagine what she must have gone through on her wedding night.

Below, dust stirred as the Habsburg armies faced west on the flat terrain. Their right flanks extended northwards almost to the banks of a Danube tributary; their left flanks brushed against densely wooded rolling hills; and to the south, forested heights protected the rear.

Royal flags, battle standards, and regimental pennants jutted up towards the cumulus. Sunlight breaking through the clouds reflected off the polished armor and weapons of the Spanish and Imperial soldiers who numbered twenty-five thousand foot and thirteen thousand cavalry.

Tercios were organized into typical Spanish squares forty men wide and thirty-eight deep behind a row of artillery pieces. Several lines of musketeers stood in front of the pikes with smaller squares of three hundred harquebusiers at each of the four corners. Musketeers and harquebusiers rested their matchlock weapons on stands. Each man carried a powder flask for priming and a bandolier.

"The muskets are reasonably accurate up to four hundred paces," Juan said to Vicente. "They fire a lead ball that can shatter bone." Pikemen braced their poles in the ground against their feet and drew their swords. "On command, they separate two arms' length apart when under artillery fire. To defend against infantry, they close until there is only an arm's length of space between each man. Then they mass shoulder-to-shoulder to present a solid wall of pikes against cavalry."

Fernándo pointed with his telescope. "Here comes the cavalry to protect the flanks. How well they ride."

"I prefer to use cavalry only for skirmishes and to chase enemy fleeing the field," Rafal said, forever an infantry commander.

The Protestant army, now estimated to be sixteen thousand infantry and nine thousand horse, was nowhere to be seen. Scouts reported that Horn and Saxe-Weimar had taken positions about a league to the southwest beyond the hills in scattered woods and knolls.

As if making an opening chess move, King Ferdinand sent an advance guard of Imperial German troops to occupy the nearest hill ahead of their left flank. Its northern slope facing the valley was relatively smooth, and his men would have a clear line of fire over the enemy's only possible route to Nördlingen.

Not to be outdone, the Cardinal-Infante ordered a small contingent of musketeers to secure a hill farther to the left. After he saw their flag raised on the crest, he said, "Now let them try to advance against us."

Vicente's mouth was dry in anticipation of his first taste of warfare. Sweat soaked his body beneath black armor. The moine weighed heavily on his head. He believed he could smell fear in the breeze wafting towards him from the men of both armies.

He hoped to follow Ballebrera's advice and sustain a cool situational awareness. Ramón had described how men needlessly died because they became confused and disoriented amidst the din and violence of battle.

The opposing armies did not engage that day because summer thunderstorms drenched the field of battle. After a light supper, Vicente accompanied the Cardinal-Infante to a conference with the King of Hungary. The Imperial field marshals and generals pressed the royal commanders to set up defensive formations in front of the town and let the siege run its course. They believed they were hearing more thunder in the distance until a messenger arrived. Saxe-Weimar's troops had taken the farther hill where Fernándo had sent his musketeers.

Without further consulting their generals, the Cardinal-Infante and King Ferdinand reorganized their armies into stronger defensive positions facing west. Imperial infantry and artillery manned the front lines from riverbank to the hills. Vicente watched the Imperial troops deploy, a total of forty-five hundred cavalry and more than fifteen thousand infantry. From left to right, he recognized the two German regiments and a Neapolitan *tercio* with ten artillery pieces. Behind them on the left ready to reinforce where necessary and beat off any surprise attack from the town garrison, were a Spanish *tercio*, two smaller Neapolitan *tercios*, and an Imperial regiment supported by nine Spanish cavalry squadrons. Another seven squadrons of Italian and Imperial cavalry covered the right flank. Behind them, Generals Gallas and Leganéz commanded a reserve corps of five *tercios,* one of them led by Rafal, two Burgundian regiments, and another Italian *tercio*, supported on the left by a thousand Imperial cavalry and two companies of the Spanish cavalry guards.

At daybreak, the two Ferdinands and their staffs were on the hillock above their armies when Saxe-Weimar's soldiers took up positions opposite them on the field of battle. At the sound of gunfire, all turned to the hill on their left. Vicente shared their frustration when they could not see the action on the other side.

Vicente would later learn from prisoners of war what happened next. To create an element of surprise, Protestant General Horn chose a difficult route of attack on the second hill held by Ferdinand's Germans where it was most densely covered with trees, but a Swedish colonel led his cavalry ahead of the infantry in an all-out charge up through the woods towards the center of the entrenched defenders. Although the Germans raked Horn's cavalry with concentrated musket fire, the Swedish infantry courageously pressed forward unsupported by horse. The violence of their attack caused the Imperial troops to break without defending the ridge and run down the northern slope of the hill.

Then God, as the Spaniards expected He would, joined the Catholic side. When the Swedes overran the forward Imperial entrenchments, a store of gunpowder abandoned by the Germans exploded in their midst. Blinded by smoke while advancing through trees in full leaf, the Swedish soldiers could not see who was friend or foe. Unaware they had routed the Germans, the two brigades of Horn's infantry mistook each other for the enemy and fought against themselves.

When his aides cheered at the confusion of their enemy on the hill, the Cardinal-Infante turned to Vicente. "Tell Don Jerónimo to move out with a *tercio*, reorganize the fleeing Germans, and recapture that hill."

"Yes, Your Eminence."

He pointed at the giant Swiss. "And take your personal *tercio* with you."

Vicente and Stauffacher galloped down the hillock to Rafal, who sat on a great Andalusian charger behind the Spanish regiments. "Don Jerónimo. You have been given the honor of retaking the hill."

Rafal issued orders to his officers. Every man in the *tercio* shouted *¡Viva España!* and advanced in battle formation to the left towards the hill as the two armies exchanged artillery fire.

Vicente and Stauffacher spurred their horses behind Rafal and Juan. He gripped the reins in one hand, and held his carbine in the other. All his senses concentrated on their objective.

Demoralized and confused, the Swedish infantry fled before the disciplined Spanish advance, and within the hour Rafal's men controlled the summit. Jerónimo raised the standards of Spain and his *tercio*, and Juan waved a flag bearing the arms of Rocamora.

Before Horn could organize a counter-attack, Rafal deployed his *tercio* in an even more unassailable defensive position supported by the regrouped Germans. At the same time, he ordered several companies of musketeers to open fire on Saxe-Weimar's cavalry on the Protestant extreme right flank in the valley below.

In front of Nördlingen where his outnumbered and malnourished Protestant infantry faced the main Imperial and Spanish armies, Saxe-Weimar used artillery to prevent the Cardinal-Infante from sending more troops to support Rafal. When he ordered cavalry feints to keep the Spanish and Germans off balance; two mercenary regiments of horse fled the field because they were unable to retaliate against Rafal's musketeers shooting at them from the heights.

Horn, the other Protestant general, sent both horse and foot soldiers up the hill against the Spanish position. When the Swedes came into view and prepared to open fire, Rafal's first line of disciplined musketeers dropped to their knees on command. The enemy's shot passed over their heads. Before the Swedes could reload, the Spaniards stood and fired as one. The drill was repeated as if a stately court dance.

The deafening intensity of musket and artillery fire, the shouting and cursing of men to sustain their morale, the screams of pain, and the whinnying of maimed and dying horses became one sustained demonic roar of battle. The Swedes retreated and left their dead. Horn reorganized them, and they attacked again. One company of Protestants broke through only to be gutted by the push of Spanish pike.

Rafal left the summit and used his authority to shore up a weakening section of Germans on his left flank. A trio of Swedish lancers isolated Jerónimo and shot his horse. Jerónimo was thrown to the ground, and a cavalryman lowered his lance to impale him.

Vicente charged through the trees towards Rafal and fired his carbine at the lancer. As the Swede fell off his horse, he smashed the butt of his weapon against the head of another cavalryman. He turned in time to see Stauffacher decapitate both the surviving lancer and his mount in one sweeping blow with his two-headed battle-axe. Rafal climbed onto the back of Vicente's horse, and they galloped to his command post at the summit.

Juan looked at his father. "Are you unharmed?"

"I lost my favorite charger."

Vicente dismounted. "Take mine."

Rafal settled in the saddle. "You saved my life, Don Vicente. You have proven to be a soldier after all and do honor to our name."

Don, he said. The great soldier has at last come around to accept me as Don Somebody.

"I have counted at least a dozen assaults," Vicente said after they beat back another attack by the Swedes. "They seem more determined each time. Why do they continue this madness?"

Rafal removed his moine and wiped his brow. "Experience in war teaches us that a bit more effort often turns the tide of battle."

During a respite, Vicente borrowed Juan's telescope. He scanned the field in front of Nördlingen where relays of horse-drawn carts rushed fresh ammunition to the Imperial artillery exchanging relentless volleys with Saxe-Weimar's big guns. Next, he focused on the hillock where the King of Hungary and the Cardinal-Infante sent couriers to their commanders below with orders to strengthen perceived weak points.

A captain standing between the two Ferdinands was shot. Despite pleas from their generals, the royal cousins refused to withdraw to a safer command post.

His troops too decimated and fatigued to be effective in the afternoon heat, Horn ordered a retreat. Rafal then moved his regiment farther down the smooth side of the hill and concentrated all his firepower on Saxe-Weimar's men in the smoking valley below.

The Cardinal-Infante saw the change in tactics and made an instant decision. From the crest of the hill, Vicente and Rafal watched Fernándo and the King of Hungary ride down the hillock to their armies. The Cardinal-Infante's charger reared on its powerful hind legs when he raised his marshal's baton to signal an all-out attack.

Shouting *¡Viva España!* and *¡Viva Santiago!*, the *tercios* broke out of their defensive positions ahead of the Imperial troops. Hot Spanish blood boiled over. Musketeers and pikemen rushed towards the Protestants behind their cavalry.

Rafal raised his sword and led his spirited men down the hill towards Saxe-Weimar's disintegrating right flank. Vicente leaped upon a dead officer's mount and followed Juan and Rafal into the valley with Stauffacher behind.

Before the Spanish breached their defenses, Saxe-Weimar's army broke ranks. With Fernándo's cavalry on their heels, the Protestants scattered and ran broadside into Horn's Swedes crossing behind them.

Vicente charged past Spanish pikemen and musketeers who shouted oaths and obscenities as they butchered winded stragglers and dispatched helpless riders trapped under spent horses. At the western end of the valley, Habsburg cavalry regiments cut off the Protestant escape. The *tercios* caught up and joined in the slaughter.

Vicente succumbed to the *furor hispanicus* when he chased after a group of Saxe-Weimar's musketeers fleeing towards the riverbank. He hacked and slashed left and right until he could no longer lift his sword arm.

Chapter 56
Aftermath of Battle

Horn was captured. Saxe-Weimar fled. The remnants of the Protestant armies surrendered. So did the garrison at Nördlingen. The Cardinal-Infante and the King of Hungary decreed under Laws of War that the town would not suffer pillage, rape, and destruction because the Swedish commander had prevented its citizens from opening its gates to Ferdinand.

At day's end, Fernándo still in gilded black armor rode through the silent battlefield with Vicente and Rafal among his escort of commanders and aides. The stench from thousands of dead men and horses was overpowering. Black ravens and other avian predators circled over them. Like maggots on rotten meat, camp followers searched the dead for booty.

Sunset turned the sky blood red, as if a sanguinary pagan god of war drank a toast to their victory. Vicente chose to take in the gruesome scene as a whole rather than stare at individual remains of humans and horses.

carpeting the ground and littering the banks of the tributary. He could not, however, shut out the agonized screams and cries for help from the wounded, nor ignore the bloodstains on his armor from the men he had slain.

Comrades and loyal women searched the battlefield for friends and loved ones. They comforted those whom the physicians could not attend. Many more would die from their wounds. If Stauffacher was worth a *tercio*, a good physician and competent surgeon might well be equal to an army.

Vicente had much to be thankful for. He had survived the battle unscathed. Rafal and Don Juan had minor powder burns and harmless scratches. *A glorious and fortunate day for the name de Rocamora.*

The Cardinal-Infante asked Rafal to give him a detailed account of the one phase of the battle he had been unable to see and shook his head in amazement at Horn's blunders. "How many enemy dead?"

"More than seventeen thousand, Your Eminence, and we have taken four thousand prisoners, including the town garrison. Nearly all of them, mercenary officers and men, have gone into the Imperial service."

"And our losses?"

"Our combined Spanish-Imperial forces lost two thousand dead and twice as many wounded."

Fernándo crossed himself and led a solemn prayer. He thanked God, Savior, Santiago, and other pertinent saints. He said for all to hear, "This day has seen the greatest Spanish victory since Lepanto where we defeated the Turks and saved Europe for Christendom."

"And that was at sea, Your Eminence," Vicente said. "This is our greatest land victory since the days of the *reconquista*."

They accompanied the Cardinal-Infante to his temporary headquarters. Although a nearby manor had been confiscated for his comfort, he insisted it be used as a hospital for the wounded and made use of a small farm instead.

After an informal supper during which he wrote letters and Vicente encoded messages, Fernándo summoned his commanders and their staffs for a meeting in the torchlight outside the farmhouse. He called out Rafal's name, beckoned him to step forward and said, "You and your *tercio* held the hill, which enabled us to win the day."

"Our Spanish soldiers are the best in the world, Eminence."

The Cardinal-Infante led them past a pile of more than fifty enemy standards to a covered wagon filled with booty taken from the field. He snapped his fingers, and two officers brought out a life-size image of the Virgin. Protestant vandals had removed its eyes. Spaniards who saw the desecrated Mary cursed and promised vengeance.

Fernándo touched an eye socket as if he expected to feel the Virgin's tears. "Don Jerónimo, I give you the honor of taking this mutilated image of Our Holy Mother and all these captured standards to King Philip in Madrid." He signaled for Vicente to bring him the letters and gave them one-by-one to Rafal. "I have written a report of our victory, to which you can add specific details when His Majesty questions you. And be sure to give him this, my personal recommendation that he grant you a title for your victories and selfless services to the Crown."

Rafal kneeled in gratitude, and Fernándo turned to Vicente. "Go this night to Brianda, and tell her of my great victory. I will see her on the morrow. Until we reach Brussels, I want you and your Swiss Alp to stay at her side."

Chapter 57
Brussels

The Swedes evacuated southern Germany. The two Ferdinands split their armies and swept through the towns and cities of the Palatinate and the Rhineland. In December, Fernándo entered Brussels as a soldier at the head of his army dressed in cloth of scarlet and gold and carrying the sword of his Burgundian great-grandfather, Emperor Charles V.

Vicente rode with Brianda inside her luxurious gilded carriage. He found Brussels to be yet another gloomy northern city, its cathedrals, churches, and buildings so different from the warmer Romanesque and Moorish-inspired architectural styles common throughout Spain. Vicente had see Brianda react similarly but for a different reason. She crossed herself and drew the drapes of their carriage whenever they passed a cathedral, as she had done in every other city and town in the Germanies. She feared her baby would be born as deformed as those misshapen gargoyles lurking between jagged spires on the threatening stone facades.

The Viceroy's palace contained a superb collection of tapestries, bejeweled gilded reliquaries, and paintings by Peter Paul Rubens and other renowned artists. The walls of Brianda's suite held several magnificent allegorical tapestries in gold and silver thread, jeweled colors illustrating biblical and mythological scenes, and more paintings by Flemish masters.

Harsh weather at the end of the year brought a welcome respite from battle. Vicente settled into a routine of encoding dispatches for Fernándo and watching over his daughter.

The arched windows of Brianda's suite steamed to an opaque gray because the sitting room was well heated by a fireplace and braziers. Nearing the end of her ninth month of pregnancy, she reclined on a chaise bundled under heavy winter clothes and a goose-down quilt.

Vicente and Juan came to keep her company. Brianda craved much attention, which was why he always invited the young officer to come with him, except when she needed to confess. Each visit was an adventure for the young man who was unfamiliar with the emotional state of women in late pregnancy, and he often left her suite in complete confusion.

Besides her maids and servants, two others attended Brianda. After making extensive inquiries among the palace women of all classes, Vicente had summoned Kaatje, a robust no-nonsense Flemish midwife in her thirties with a reputation for ensuring successful deliveries. Kaatje slept in his daughter's suite with orders to notify him the instant she went into labor.

That command was all the more important because Fernándo, who meant well, had sent Brianda one of the physicians he had inherited from his late aunt, Archduchess Isabella. Jorge Álvarez was a pretentious *hidalgo,* a filthy ignorant old man of the type who had so poorly attended Hombrecillo's wife, the unfortunate Doña Inéz.

These past months, Fernándo had seen little of Brianda. Vicented could not fault the Cardinal-Infante for his extended absences. Fernando was less the boy now with no time for chess and cards. He spent long hours reorganizing the government and making plans to deploy his forces against both the French and the United Provinces before fighting resumed in the spring.

Vicente had read reports describing how the overwhelming success of the Habsburgs had motivated the German Protestant princes to sign a treaty with King Louis XIII, who promised them twelve thousand soldiers and a half million *livres* in return for their guarantees allowing freedom for Catholics to worship openly. The Germans also ceded Alsatian towns and gave France control of the bridgehead at Strasbourg. In a separate agreement with the Dutch, Cardinal Richelieu offered a subsidy to the United Provinces so that they would continue the war in the Netherlands and prevent the Cardinal-Infante from attacking France.

Vicente frowned at a painting of Mars and Venus near Brianda's carved and canopied bed. During the late stages of Brianda's pregnancy, Fernándo had taken a Flemish mistress, a docile fleshy blonde of the type idealized by Rubens. Vicente had guaranteed death to anyone who informed his daughter of her lover's infidelities.

Brianda cried out and spread her arms in welcome when Fernándo entered her suite. He demonstrated his great affection for Brianda when he kissed her lips, felt her belly, and held her hand. "We all pray it will be a boy."

Álvarez pulled on his wispy gray beard stained with food and grease. "Your Eminence, I could tell you the infant's gender this very day if I knew certain facts."

"Indeed? What facts?"

"I need to know if you consumed hot and dry foods before conceiving, and the phase of the moon at that time."

Fernándo gave Álvarez a cold look for his lèse majesté, and Brianda pleaded with him, "Stay with me tonight. It has been weeks since we played chess."

"I advise against it," Álvarez said. "And I must ask you a delicate question, Your Eminence. Have you and Doña Brianda been abstaining? Such excesses harm the development of the fetus. There is truth in the adage, 'Who plows the field too much when seeds are sown, will spoil his own work and make it overthrown'." He pointed to a small tray holding rich Flemish cheeses and freshly baked bread. "So will powerful spices and noxious vapors given off by spoiled cheeses and rotten eggs."

The old man's tiresome prattle annoyed Fernándo. He kissed Brianda's hand again, wished her well, and left despite her entreaties for him to stay. Álvarez and the midwife also withdrew.

Brianda gazed at a steamed window as if she could see through it and the night sky to an unseen faraway place. "Tío, will my child ever know the sun and warmth of Valencia? Will any of us ever see the Fragrant Coast again?"

"I often pray so." Vicente gestured for her servants to bring a table, chessboard, and chairs to the chaise. "I miss most the abundance of sweet melons and other fresh fruits, and swimming in the cool transparent sea on unbearably hot summer days."

"Oh, so do I."

"Swimming?" Juan gaped at them horrified. "But that is un-Christian."

Vicente occupied one of the chairs and set up the pieces. "Alas, it is a malaise which afflicts certain members of our family. Ramón often went to the Moorish baths of his señorio before they were destroyed."

"Which explains his softness."

"That was uncharitable, Don Juan. Ramón was a valiant soldier and is an honorable man."

The young man blushed. "You are right. I was not thinking. Doña Brianda, perhaps you will teach me how to swim one day."

"If your thick head does not cause you to sink to the bottom." She tapped Vicente's left hand, drew the black chess piece, and gripped his fingers. "Tío, promise me . . . promise you'll be with me at the birth of my child."

"I promise."

Brianda beckoned him to come closer and kissed his cheek. "If God blesses me with a son, I shall name him Vicente."

He turned his head so she would not see his eyes water.

Chapter 58
Childbirth

"Don Vicente. Wake up." Juan shook him.

"What is it?"

"Doña Brianda is in labor. The midwife says it is a difficult birth."

Vicente leaped out of bed, dressed, and picked up his box of salves and tinctures. "Where is His Eminence?"

"In the chapel praying. He gave orders not to be disturbed until after the baby is delivered."

They hurried through the chilly corridors, Juan told Vicente that Brianda had been lonely and went to the Cardinal-Infaand nte's apartments where she caught him in bed with his mistress. She lost her temper, then her balance, and fell, which precipitated a birth crisis.

Stauffacher stood guard at the doors to Brianda's suite. Vicente ordered him and Juan to stay outside and rushed into the room. In a blood-soaked chemise, Brianda was strapped to a birthing chair, the seat shaped like an oversized horseshoe, which gave the midwife easy access to her uterus. Blood-stained pillows and cushions used to change her position and a porcelain basin filled with bloody water lay on the floor beside her chair.

Álvarez and the midwife were arguing. A filthy priest Vicente had never seen before held a curved metal baptismal syringe. The opening of the nozzle was shaped like a cross for added sanctity. As commonly practiced, if Brianda's baby died *in utero*, the priest was prepared to insert the syringe up her vagina and give the unborn child last rites to save its soul.

Vicente dropped his box, knocked the syringe from the priest's hand, and pushed the protesting cleric out the door. When he returned to Brianda, physician and midwife were attending her once again. His daughter's skin was abnormally white, her body drenched in sweat.

"She is in pain," Kaatje said. "Give her a cloth to bite on."

Álvarez shook his head. "No, it might prevent air from getting to the infant in her womb."

Fear left Brianda's eyes when she saw Vicente. He kissed her moist forehead. Both hands were so tightly clenched that her nails dug into the palms. When she opened them, she appeared to have stigmata.

"Help me, Tío. Help me."

"My sweet Brianda, I shall keep my promise and stay with you until your baby is delivered." Vicente took the physician aside while the midwife reached under his daughter's chemise to encourage the child's birth. "What happened?"

"The labor was induced by extreme activity, which I clearly forbade. It's not my fault."

He seized the physician's shoulders. "A million curses on you, man. What is your diagnosis?"

Álvarez backed away. "Not good. She has been in labor for several hours. If it lasts beyond two or three days, we can assume the child is dead. If it lodges in the birth passage, a surgeon will have to amputate the arms and legs *in utero* to free it."

"What is the baby's condition?"

He shrank under Vicente's hard gaze. "It is lodged in the pelvis and needs to be turned."

Vicente called to the midwife, "Is it still alive?"

She withdrew her hand from Brianda's vagina and wiped it on a bloody towel. "Yes, so far. I'm doing everything possible."

"So am I," Álvarez said. "After she went into labor, I gave her a cup of broth. Later, I purged her to accelerate the contractions. That did not work, so I ordered her to be overfed followed by inducements to vomit."

When Vicente gave the midwife tinctures of myrrh and aloe to use as poultices and laves if Brianda's vaginal walls tore, he frowned at the typical instruments of birthing on a nearby table. They could as well have been forged for the dungeons of the Inquisition: Sharp knives; midwife's shears for cutting the umbilical cord; a catheter; and heavy hooks to help turn an infant if it was in an awkward position or to extract the body if it died *in utero*. Missing were *strappado*, rack, and hot pincers.

There has to be a better way to deliver babies. "Can you not stop the bleeding? Is there no blood for her to drink, to replenish what she has lost?"

"Don Vicente, blood ebbs and flows through the body like the tides of the ocean while the heart mixes it with a divine essence inhaled through the lungs. As long as she continues to breathe . . ." Álvarez turned his hands palms up in a gesture of resignation.

To save his daughter, Vicente would have given her his own blood. Anyone's. He stared at one of the young servant girls. He was almost desperate enough to follow the vile example of Innocent VIII. In 1492 the ailing Pope had three young boys sacrificed in the belief he could regain his health by drinking their blood.

Vicente prepared himself for the worst. Summoned all too often to give last rites, he was familiar with the struggle to extract a baby without tearing the mother to pieces. Some births lasted three, up to five days. The longer it took, the less likely both mother and child could be saved. During those times, he had been first a detached scientific observer, and then as the attending cleric he offered comfort, prayer, and hope. Now, he had been forced to witness the suffering of his own flesh and blood.

He winced at each scream from Brianda while Kaatje continued to induce birth. He had seen too often how the hands of a midwife could be the most damaging instruments of all. When they reached into the womb and seized the baby's ears or put a hand in its mouth and to pull, they often caused irreparable damage to the mother and mutilation of the infant.

In El Grau, Don Lope had told his midwives to use the safer more efficient podalic method when the baby was in an abnormal position. He would instruct them how to insert their hands in the uterus, take hold of one or both feet, and turn the baby into the correct position for it to be born. When necessary, the midwife pulled from under its jaw, or turned the fetus at the shoulder, which more often than not saved both baby and mother.

Vicente knew the importance of observing the progressive dilation of the cervix to gauge the progress and tempo of the labor. He had observed how a torn and detached placenta during a breech birth could smother an infant, if it had not been strangled before by the umbilical cord. Caesarians were seldom performed and never on a live mother. Even then, if a woman died before giving birth, midwives and physicians generally chose to pull and extract the infant by hooks through the birth passage.

For a mother to give life, she risked her own. Familiar with gaming, Vicente knew all too well the unfavorable odds Brianda faced. From what Don Lope had told him and his own experiences giving last rites, at least one in four women died during or immediately after giving birth.

Brianda screamed when the midwife adjusted several cushions under her buttocks and Vicente again searched through his medicines. He mixed saffron and anis seed into a mild sedative, which he ordered Kaatje to give Brianda. The midwife, over the physician's objections, prepared warm wine to soothe her inflamed and traumatized organs.

Kaatje ordered the servants to bring more towels and rags to staunch Brianda's hemorrhaging. "If this doesn't work, we will have to force-feed her again to increase her strength. And give her diluted brandy. It will accelerate her contractions better than your purges did to make her vomit." She turned to a servant. "Prepare melted butter." The midwife saw Álvarez' blank look. "I use it as a lubricant to ease the emergence of the infant." Again, she inserted her hand into Brianda's bloody womb.

Vicente stood beside her. "What do you feel?"

"I cannot tell."

"Feel for the nose. Feel for the hair. Find the head and bring it down."

Kaatje thrust her arm deeper into the birth passage almost to the elbow as Brianda screamed for God to end her life and give her peace. After long seconds, the midwife withdrew her blood-smeared limb and attempted to block the flow of blood with more towels.

Vicente pushed Álvarez aside. "Did you turn it?"

"I think so."

"Woman. Do you not know a head from a rump?"

"I think it may be dead."

"Then deliver the child now, dead or alive. Save my daughter . . . the mother."

His eyes locked with Brianda's. He knew she had heard and understood. He also saw that she was dying.

Kaatje removed the baby, turned her back to Brianda, and showed it to Vicente. That it was a boy gave him no comfort. He was a silent baby, blue all over and covered with blood, strangled by the cord of birth around his pathetic little neck.

My grandson.

"My baby," Brianda said weakly.

Vicente wiped his daughter's brow as the midwife carried the infant to the other side of the curtain. "It is a boy, perfectly formed."

"I want to hold my son."

"After Kaatje washes him."

Vicente carried Brianda to her bed. With the baby out of her womb and the medication beginning to work, she suffered less pain. The midwife returned with salves and more towels to stop the bleeding and covered

Brianda with blankets. A tearful servant girl placed the washed and swathed dead infant on the bed beside its mother.

Vicente kneeled at Brianda's bedside and ordered everyone else to the other side of the curtain. She put one arm around her baby, reached out for Vicente's hand, and said in the Valencian vernacular, "I always suspected."

"Do not talk. Save your strength."

"No, I am dying. I'm content to know that you, my father, so happy to at last call you my father . . . you watched over me, and loved me."

"Brianda . . ."

"And be kind to my little Cardinal. He also loved me."

"I would give my life so you may live."

"You gave me life. That is enough, except my last wish."

"Name it."

"Tell me how you became my father."

"It is a long story."

And one she would never hear. With tear filled eyes, Vicente looked down at Brianda, pale and virginal in eternal sleep, her hair spread out on the great satin pillow as a dark nimbus of death.

He kissed his daughter one last time and picked up the syringe the priest had dropped. He baptized his dead grandson and recited last rites for both Brianda and Vicente de Habsburgo y Austria Rocamora Suárez, whom he absolved of all sins in the name of the Father, Son, and Holy Spirit.

Then, to his great surprise, he caught himself sincerely praying for their immortal souls and not merely reciting those same words he had uttered pro forma countless times before. Had the deaths of Brianda and stillborn Vicente caused a transformation in his theology?

From young manhood, he had embraced the Averroistic position that denied the concept of an afterlife. Now, he felt a great emptiness, as if parts of his own soul had expired this day with Brianda and his grandson. Was the human soul then immortalized through offspring? Not an unreasonable proposition, but what happened to the souls of those who died without issue, or too young?

Enough! His self-dialogue was beginning to resemble one of those theological exercises so beloved by the monastic orders. To dwell on the nature of the human soul might well alter his view of God and the cosmos. Or lead to madness. He shifted his thoughts to more immediate considerations.

When Vicente parted the curtains, Juan cried out Brianda's name and hurried past him to her bedside. He dropped to his knees and pressed her hand against his cheek.

Vicente found Fernándo praying alone at a *prie-Dieu*, dressed not as warrior or Governor of the Netherlands, but as a Prince of the Church. He kneeled behind the Cardinal-Infante and silently cursed the God who murdered innocent women and children with the same brutality as the most vicious mercenary. He scowled at statues, icons, and the stained glass illustrations in the arched windows. He heaped equal wrath on God, Savior, Virgin, and assorted saints. Their successes were negligible. A prayer that appeared to be answered was merely the result of random chance. Worse odds than wagering at cards or knucklebones. Empirical observations convinced him that only improved medical practices would result in more successful childbirths and elimination of subsequent puerperal fevers.

"Brianda?" Fernándo asked turning to Vicente.

"She did not survive, Eminence, nor your son."

He looked upwards. "God has punished me for being too happy. My son . . . he was baptized and given last rites?"

"Yes."

"That is good." The Cardinal-Infante stood. "I will see them now."

On their way to Brianda's rooms, Vicente said, "Your Eminence, I request permission to leave your service after their burial."

"Don Vicente, a great part of me wishes for you to stay and accept a bishopric and be my trusted advisor, my Gray Eminence, as the Jesuit Father Joseph is to Cardinal Richelieu. Yet, I must confess, I do prefer you go. You would always remind me of Brianda. Know that I loved her."

"I know, Eminence."

"And what will you do in Spain?"

"Serve Church and Crown as needed."

"If my advice is asked, I will support you to replace Sotomayor as Inquisitor General, although I would be happier to recommend you to be commander of the King's palace guards."

Vicente thanked him without enthusiasm. He left the Cardinal-Infante and invited Juan and Stauffacher to his quarters where they tried and failed to get drunk on the strongest *eau de vie* in the Spanish Netherlands.

"Juan, I shall leave Brussels after the funeral."

"I thought you might. I will prepare letters for my father."

Vicente embraced Stauffacher. "You are your own man. Go home to Switzerland, or better yet, watch over Don Juan. I prefer to travel alone."

The Swiss was too overcome with grief to speak, and Juan swallowed hard. "I loved Brianda. I will never love again."

"You are still very young," Vicente said. "There will be other women."

"Not for marriage. Who would marry this soldier, a poor third son?"

Vicente realized an irony of life. With Brianda dead, he would at last inherit Benetorrente. *Capitán* and Señor, dreams of youth now ashes in his mouth. He said over Juan's protests, "I shall make you heir to Benetorrente."

Chapter 59
Antwerp

What is left for me in Spain? Who is left for me in Spain?

In deep mourning for Brianda and his stillborn grandson, Vicente left Brussels and rode northward instead of heading south to Spain. After witnessing his daughter's painful death, the pull to become a physician had never been stronger. But not in Spain. He could never study medicine in a land where the profession was condemned as a new-Christian predilection.

He decided to follow Don Lope's advice and go to the United Provinces, land of freethinkers and tolerance. On the way, he intended to stop in Antwerp. Perhaps his mentor's kin might still be living there.

Vicente found Antwerp to be another grim Gothic city even though the snow pack was clean and the winter sun blazed above frozen canals and the Scheldt River. No date palms. No fields of melons or groves of orange trees. No translucent turquoise sea.

Antwerp was familiar to him on paper because of reports he had read in Olivares' office. After conquest by Spanish troops in 1585, the city had lost its dominance of the wool market to France, England, and the United Provinces.

Yet, as he rode through the crowded streets, he saw evidence of great prosperity. Antwerp was still a center of diamond cutting and glass. It had the best printing and publishing houses in Europe. Its luxury goods of tapestries and lace were in great demand throughout England and the Continent. An efficient network of canals allowed ship captains to bypass blockades and sustain a thriving seaborne trade and uninterrupted commerce with Spain's enemy, the Dutch of the United Provinces.

After making discreet inquiries in Flemish and Spanish as needed, Vicente located the house said to belong to a family named Fernández y Vega.

He dismounted, tethered his horse to a nearby post, and went up a half dozen steps to the dark green, waxed oak front door. He glanced at the shiny decorative copper plate covering the keyhole, lifted a heavy brass knocker shaped in the form of a bull's head, and rapped.

He held his breath in anticipation. Were they cousins of Don Lope? If so, would they remember the physician after all these years and admit kinship?

A girl on the threshold of puberty opened the door. She was dressed in black wool, her skin almost as white as her clean collar and bonnet. Her inquisitive hazel eyes were so thickly lashed she appeared to be using paint.

"Tell your master *Capitán* Vicente de Rocamora wishes to speak with him," he said in Castilian." He repeated his request in Flemish while the girl stared at him.

She did not speak and she led him into a formal reception room. Subdued light filtered through the colored glass and fine leaded panes of the sash-windows.

After the girl left, Vicente stepped closer to the unlit fireplace of the great room and wrapped his cloak around his chilled body. The intimate symmetry of the room interested him. An enormous table and cupboard dominated the undecorated heavy oak furniture. The high-back wood chairs had low, leather covered seats and cushions. A Venetian mirror framed in a crystal border of glass roses hung on a wall opposite the cupboard. The cleanliness of the otherwise unadorned walls, ceiling of white plaster, and Italianate blue and white diamond tiled floor raised his hopes. So did a pleasing aroma of freshly baked bread. If he had indeed come to a home of Judaizers, perhaps they had a secret bath.

"*Capitán* de Rocamora?"

A short sickly man with a graying reddish beard entered the room. His immaculate black attire was padded to keep him warm. His fine Walloon lace collar was freshly laundered. His hat covered what Vicente suspected was a balding head.

"I am Don Jaime Fernández y Vega," he said in Portiñol. "What is your business?"

Vicente saw nothing in the man's features to suggest consanguinity with his beloved mentor. Fernández' eyes and unhealthy coloring betrayed symptoms of recurring fever and ringworm.

"I pose no threat."

"Why should I feel threatened? Although, I do not usually receive a surprise visit from a *capitán* in His Majesty's army."

"I am originally from Valencia. As a boy there, I was mentored by the physician Don Diego Fernández y Vega, also known as Don Lope."

The man glanced towards his other rooms. "I do not know the name."

It was Friday, the eve of the Jewish Sabbath with sundown less than an hour away, and Fernández' nervousness aroused Vicente interest. *Fresh bread and clean collar. Yes, I may have entered the home of Judaizers.* "Before Don Lope died, he told me I should seek his kin if I ever visited Antwerp."

"We are not the only family of that name."

"Perhaps our kin in Amsterdam or Rotterdam would know," said the girl who had let him in.

Fernández frowned at her intrusion and became distressed at her mention of family in the United Provinces. "Leave us now, Teresa."

Vicente thought the girl's composed manner was mature far beyond her years. He stepped in front of her. "Where are your cousins, Señorita Teresa?" When Fernández gestured for her to be quiet, Vicente turned to him. "I assure you, Don Jaime, I am no spy for the Inquisition. Let me also tell you about Don Diego Fernández of Valencia. He was physician to my parents. He served time in the galleys after torture and confession to Judaizing. He was reconciled. His *sambenito* still hangs in the Cathedral of Valencia. Don Lope mentored me when I was a boy and taught me much. I was present at his death. With his last breath, he recited *la Samia.*"

"*The Shemah?*"

Fernández gave his daughter another sharp look and again commanded her to withdraw from the room. The girl did not move.

"Are you also a Judaizing new-Christian, *Capitán* de Rocamora?"

The man who spoke brushed past Teresa as he entered the room. Like Fernández his curly graying beard was longer than current Spanish fashion. Although he was dressed in the Dutch style with a broad-brimmed hat shadowing most of his face, Vicente recognized him.

"Don Martín."

Martín Pinto approached Vicente and squinted at him through thick spectacles.

"You know him?" Fernández asked.

"He arranged my escape from Spain." Pinto went on to describe Vicente's service to the Habsburgs and his activities on behalf of Olivares and Sotomayor.

"A filthy Dominican." Fernández picked up a metal poker from the fireplace. "And he said he was not a spy for the Inquisition. He must not leave here alive."

Pinto took his host's arm. "Put it down, Don Jaime. We have nothing to fear from Fray-*Capitán* Vicente. His enemies say he has new-Christian blood . . . from his mother."

"Not proven."

"Torquemada, that fiend from hell, also was part-new-Christian."

"Don Jaime, I can assure you, he is no Torquemada."

"Then why has he come to my home on the eve of our Sabbath? Surely, he will denounce us to the Inquisition."

"I was unaware Judaizers lived here," Vicente said. He looked anew at Pinto, whose tone of voice and posture were those of a man used to being obeyed. Although it was Fernández' home, Olivares' financier was in command.

Pinto took hold of the poker and returned it to the fireplace. "We are in no danger from this man. He tells the truth about Don Diego Fernández, who was his mentor and very generous benefactor."

Pinto invited Vicente to sit, and Teresa covered the windows with heavy drapes. Vicente loosened his cloak and selected the chair closest to the fireplace when he saw she was going to light it. Pinto and Fernández sat opposite him. The headstrong girl refused to leave the room and stood behind her father.

Pinto blew on his spectacles to clear them. "It is almost sundown, our Sabbath. Don Vicente, will you dine with us."

Fernández sprang to his feet. "Don Martín, are you mad? He is a Dominican."

"Let me assure you again, Don Jaime. He will not denounce us."

When Vicente stood, Teresa stepped forward and took his arm. "*Capitán*, come and welcome the Sabbath Bride with us."

The Jewish Sabbath meal took place in a large ground floor room at the back of Fernández' home. Vicente removed his cloak and put his weapons aside in deference to the Jews' sensibilities. He instantly adapted to one of their rituals and washed his hands. *And why not a Sabbath bath later as well if Fernández has a tub?*

For the first time, Vicente experienced customs shunned by every Spaniard who wished to appear old-Christian and *limpio*. Pinto told him to keep his hat on when they sat at a long table covered with freshly laundered linen. Wine cups and plates of fine silver were decorated with the Star of David or Hebrew letters. Fires had been kindled and candles lit throughout the house before sundown, to be extinguished on the morrow at sundown after the Sabbath.

During a preliminary benediction, Teresa and Pinto's wife lit ceremonial candles in elaborate silver holders on the table. Vicente knew enough Hebrew to recognize the word Adonai, one of the names Jews called their God.

"*Mi dios, la alma que me diste tu la criaste limpia y tu la formaste* ... Lord, the soul which Thou didst place in me is pure; it was Thou that didst create and fashion it . . .

"*Bendito el sol, bendito el día, bendito se a aquel guarde señor que lo cria, bendito el angel que lo guía, benditas las aguas sobre las aguas, bendita la fuente ... Santo, Santo Dios de Sabahot.* Blessed sun, blessed day, blessed Lord that watches over his creation, blessed angel who guides us, blessed waters over waters, blessed its source . . . Holy, Holy God of Sabbath."

Vicente believed that he knew much about Jewish practices from reading and common Spanish beliefs. If he had appeared during their Holy Days, he would have heard them recite the same prayer Don Lope had uttered: *la Samia*, the heretical, Judaizing "Hear o Israel, the Lord our God, the Lord is One". And then, after reciting from their prayer books, they faced east towards Jerusalem, stood on tiptoe, and took three steps back as if wishing to raise themselves higher. He was not sure why. Probably to get closer to their God.

He suppressed a sudden perverse impulse to laugh when he imagined the reaction of Arce, Jacinto, and Tomás were they to see him enjoying a Jewish Sabbath meal.

The meal was a mix of taste sensations created by Pinto's wife and Jaime's daughter, with an absence of dairy products. Small round flat breads common to peoples of the Levant and great loaves with a slightly sour taste whetted his appetite for more. A steaming broth, which contained parts of chickens, scalded his mouth, and a pungent white sauce atop a ball of minced fish caused his eyes to water. He preferred small fillets of a salty fish marinated in vinegar and assorted spices. Familiar couscous and saffron rice accompanied a lamb and vegetable dish.

Each time Teresa entered to serve the men a new course and replenish their wine, she stared unblinking at Vicente. She ate in a separate room with Pinto's wife, children, and widowed sister-in-law.

During dinner conversation, Fernández described how his wife and two sons had died of fever several years earlier and more. "Yes, *Capitán*, in answer to your question, my grandfather and Don Lope's father were brothers. We have not lived in Iberia for several generations and are the last of our family to reside in lands controlled by your King."

"Why do you?"

"The necessities of business. We are also obligated to provide a safe house for our persecuted brethren, like the Most Illustrious Don Martín, and help them escape to the New Jerusalem in Amsterdam and other cities of the United Provinces. Will you also go to Amsterdam?"

"I have considered it."

"To return to the faith of your mother's people?"

Vicente saw no harm in confessing his true beliefs. "Regardless of the facts of my mother's origins, old- or new-Christian, I am a freethinker."

Fernández gasped horrified, and Pinto said with surprising humor, "At least his Church could not convert him, Don Jaime. Perhaps the Law of Moses may yet be written upon his *tabula rasa*."

Chapter 60
The Challenge

"Don Jaime, I cannot thank you enough for your hospitality and for inviting me to share you Sabbath meal."

"My house is honored to have had so noble a guest."

Vicente went to the women, kissed the hand of each, and thanked them for preparing the delicious repast. He did not express disappointment he would have no bath.

"Before you go, I wish to speak with you alone," Pinto said.

"As you wish, Don Martín." Vicente gathered his weapons and cloak and followed Pinto upstairs to the front room."

"Don Vicente, please tell me your true impressions of the Count-Duke. Do you think, if he can outlast his enemies, will the King give him the authority to allow Jews to return to Spain?"

"If the Count-Duke had his way, he would abolish the *limpieza*, the Inquisition, and the Index of forbidden works."

"That is good to hear. I believe our Lord God has plans for you and meant for us to meet this Sabbath."

Vicente accepted some tobacco from Pinto after they sat by the fireplace and lit his long clay pipe. "Go on."

"Sotomayor has plans for you to become his successor."

"Why am I not surprised you know that?"

"With the support of Olivares and Sotomayor, you can thwart Arce and perform great services for our people."

"You do not understand. My rivals in Valencia would denounce me with lies. Among them are my own kinsmen. Jacinto is a Familiar and has already murdered to have his way. Tomás is a pitiless Dominican who also aspires to be Inquisitor General. They prefer to believe that I am tainted through my mother."

"Be that as it may, many men of influence will support you. Certain *poderosos*, both new-Christians and old-Christian sympathizers, agree that you are the best and only man to replace Sotomayor."

"Why should it matter to you in the safety of your New Jerusalem?"

"I still have family in Spain and Portugal. We believe that if the Count-Duke's policies come to fruition, we will be able to return and practice our religion openly and proudly in Spain. You have said as much."

"I spoke to you of Olivares' desires, not the reality of the situation in Spain, which you refuse to accept. Like Don Quixote, you Judaizers tilt at the windmills of *convivencia* and *esperanza*. Why not also demand that your Jewish faith become the religion for all Spain while you await your messiah?"

Pinto ignored Vicente's sarcasm. "As Inquisitor General, you would be able to end all arrests and denunciations of new-Christians and abolish the *autos-de-fé* for condemned Judaizers. You could go farther. Influence the King to abolish the *limpieza* statutes and reverse the decree of 1492 that expelled all Jews from Sefarad."

"You want too much," Vicente said. "Be satisfied if Olivares succeeds in abolishing or even modifying the *limpieza*. Practicing Jews will never be welcome in Spain."

"Abolition of the *limpieza* and the freedom to worship as Jews are inseparable."

"I repeat, the former is a remote possibility, and the latter a distinct impossibility."

"If all you say is true, then you will always live in fear of exposure in Spain. I plead with you one more time. Seize your opportunity to accomplish great deeds."

"My mother's origins, my enemies are determined and relentless."

"Then they will attempt to destroy you no matter what you choose. Is it not preferable to be an aggressive ram rather than a docile lamb? If you have enemies, earn them."

"That I have accomplished better than most."

"Think again of the authority you would have as Inquisitor General," Pinto pressed. "Only the King and an exceptional favorite like Olivares wield more influence and power throughout Spain. You could mold the mind of the young Infante. The unacceptable alternative is Arce or another as bigoted. Then, neither the greatest soldier, nor the most august prelate will be safe from denunciation."

"I will have to think about it. Perhaps it is best that I do not return to Madrid."

"What? Where would you go? If you were to follow his advice, you would have to leave Spain forever."

But can I leave Spain? Honor requires I search for my friends Moraíma and Pablo and see to their safety although the pícaro road no longer entices me. All other paths lay within the Church if I continue to live in Spain. With the Cardinal-Infante's recommendations, I might indeed rise to bishop. Better yet, if I cannot heal individuals in Spain as a physician, then why not cure all Spain within the Church? Yes, I shall follow Sotomayor's route, become confessor and conscience of the future King of Spain, and after that, Inquisitor General.

Pinto broke into his thoughts. "After you return to Madrid . . ."

"Your assumption . . ."

". . . my associates will be in touch with you. Do you remember the physician, Fernándo Cardoso?"

"Yes."

"He is prepared to be your good friend."

Vicente preferred to avoid Portuguese new-Christians. He put out his pipe and stood. "I am ready to leave, Don Martín."

"Consider all I have said. If Arce becomes Inquisitor General, thousands of new-Christian families will leave Spain. Do not fight your destiny." Pinto looked towards the front door. "Because it is the Sabbath and there are no gentile servants, you will have to see your own way out."

Strange customs, these Jews have.

After Pinto left the room, Teresa appeared with a large cloth bag. She gave the parcel to Vicente and escorted him to the front door. "Here, *Capitán*. I have included bread, cheeses, and nuts. Eat sparingly. There is word of a great famine spreading throughout the Rhineland."

"Thank you, Señorita."

"We shall meet again, Don Vicente."

Does the girl have second sight like Moraíma? "How can you be so sure?"

"Because I have chosen you."

Vicente would not laugh or tease her. She was too serious with a natural serenity seldom found even in adults. Teresa was not yet a woman, shapeless in her padded dress, features still undefined, so unlike Brianda at the same age. He held back tears and envied Fernández, whose daughter lived.

"Child, I will soon be thirty-four. I am old enough to be your father."

She gestured for Vicente to open the door. "It matters not. Know that I shall wait for you. One day, we shall meet again. In the new Jerusalem. In Amsterdam."

"Señorita Teresa . . ."

"No, remember me not as Teresa. My true given name is Abigail, daughter of Moses. We dare not use our real names in Antwerp because our family in the United Provinces and in the Venetian ghetto follows the Law of Moses."

Vicente opened the front door and wrapped his cloak tighter when the frigid night air cut through his garments. "Then your family name is not Fernández y Vega?"

"Only in Spanish and Portuguese lands." She pointed to the brass knocker. "Everywhere else, it is Toro."

Chapter 61
A Season in Hell

Vicente was not yet ready to live among Jews in a bleak northern city. He decided to return to Spain, the land he loved with a passion equal to all he had felt for Moraíma and María. His conversation with Pinto had much to do with his decision as well. The thought of Arce and his ilk triumphing was intolerable.

Vicente pushed his mount to its limits of endurance and hurried through the nightmarish Rhenish landscape. He allowed himself no time to grieve for Brianda and his grandson. He needed all his energy and wits to survive in a hell not even Lucifer or Dante could have conceived, a hell created by ordinary men.

During his journey through snowy wastelands and devastated villages, Vicente saw depredations by roving bands more vicious than those committed by the *golondreros*. He came upon peasants with infected hands in bloody bandages, victims of extortionist soldiers who had jammed their fingers or thumbs into barrels of pistols and fired them when not enough money or food was forthcoming.

He passed children wailing over the mutilated body of their dead father, a Protestant. People told Vicente that after the man surrendered his meager wealth, a mercenary had twisted a cord around his head until the eyes popped.

He prevented a pair of drunken mercenaries from forcing "Swedish drink", liquefied human and animal waste, into the mouth of an old man who refused to tell where his granddaughters were hiding. He was too outnumbered to stop another atrocity outside of Strasbourg. The soldiers' mania for gambling had found an outlet in a fiendish game of chance. Prisoners were tied in long rows behind each other, and mercenaries wagered on the number that could be penetrated by one shot.

During the winter months of 1635, the greatest famine in living memory was taking place from Lorraine to Württemburg. Vicente witnessed the starving cook acorns, goats' skins, and grass to make soup. Markets he passed sold skinned dogs, cats, and rats. The alternative was cannibalism.

Under a doleful dark gray sky and wrapped in his great black cloak, Vicente rode along a snow-covered road towards a Spanish held garrison town north of Breisach. Near the outskirts, he encountered a group of skeletal feral women in rags fighting off dogs and ravens for the raw meat of a dead horse. The crones turned towards him with darkly ringed crazed red eyes, their mouths and jaws dripping blood. He needed no further motivation to spur his horse towards the safety of the town.

Inside the walls, Vicente galloped into the main square where a company of beleaguered soldiers faced a savage mob of several hundred malnourished inhabitants. The troops ordered the unruly townsfolk to disperse with curses and threats.

Vicente took out his carbine and rode closer to support the soldiers as they advanced with pikes, swords, and muskets. A few shots scattered the townsfolk into the dark narrow streets. Only then did he see a pair of naked corpses in the bloody snow by the gibbets. Great chunks of their flesh had been cut away.

Afterwards, he sat with the garrison officers by a roaring fireplace at their headquarters in a shabby inn. They consumed great amounts of brandy as they waited for a huge pot of stew to finish cooking.

Vicente raised his bottle in a salute to their commander, Coronel Hernándo de Rivera, a leathery Castilian with uncut hair and untrimmed beard. "It is good to see Spanish faces and hear our noble language spoken in this Godforsaken land, Coronel."

"And I thank you for your help, *Capitán*. This damn famine. Those poor devils. So crazed by hunger. As you saw, the moment we hang the criminals, they cut down their bodies and attempt to devour them on the spot."

When Vicente described the feral women he had encountered, the men were not surprised. "This town is typical," another officer said. "Throughout the Rhineland and Lorraine, guards are posted at cemeteries. Otherwise, thieves will rob the graves and sell the flesh of the newly buried as fresh meat."

Rivera lit his long-stem pipe and moved his feet closer to the fireplace where the flames almost licked his boots. "Our magistrates are punishing crimes that were unimaginable until this winter. And everywhere, people live in fear of being killed and eaten by those maddened with hunger. Near Wertheim, fresh human bones were discovered in a pit, fleshless and drained of marrow. Yesterday, a woman confessed she had devoured her own child. And where are you headed, *Capitán*?"

"Through the Val Telline to Italy, and then on to Madrid."

"Sunny Spain. How I envy you."

"Avoid Munich," one of the officers said. "A plague that began among our troops has taken ten thousand lives so far. The Four Horsemen do indeed rule in Germany."

Rivera turned in the direction of a scraping noise, threw his dagger across the room, and impaled a huge brown rat against the wall. "Got the bastard."

An officer went over to the squealing rodent still alive and dangerous. He slit the rat's throat, skinned it, and set it on a spit over the fire. After the carcass was browned, he chopped it into small bits and tossed the meat into the stewpot.

Vicente decided not to share their meal. Where rats thrived, so did plague. He recalled what Don Lope had taught him about the habits of rats. They preferred inns and the shops of butcher, baker, and weaver, which afforded food and warmth, and avoided smiths and coopers because they disliked noise.

Vicente felt a sudden chill when the front door of the inn opened. Two soldiers herded in more than a dozen frightened young women and girls who might have been attractive had not been so undernourished. Their feverish eyes focused not on the men but on the steaming pot of stew.

Rivera forced them into a line and ran his riding whip across their dirty faces and frail bodies. He selected the youngest, then turned to Vicente. "Your preference, *Capitán*? They'll do anything for a small cup of stew."

"Not tonight, Coronel."

Rivera laughed nastily. "Perhaps then, you'd rather have a pretty boy?"

"This night I prefer to romance my bottle of brandy."

As had happened on so many other nights after he left Antwerp, sleep did not come to Vicente. The cause was not the rowdy laughter and screams coming from the rooms upstairs, nor fear of a knife in his back. He could not shut out the sounds of the howling wind outside. Or was it Brianda begging him to stop the pain? Wherever he looked, at the shifting mist on the windowpanes or the swirling smoke in the fireplace, he saw the frightened faces of the soldiers he had killed at Nördlingen.

Overcome by grief over his daughter's death and consumed by guilt for having slaughtered men in battle who could no longer harm him, Vicente finally broke down and sobbed until his guts ached.

Before dawn, he read the Cardinal-Infante's letter for the first time. Fernándo had asked King Philip to appoint him to a command in His

Majesty's Spanish Guards and included an unexpected recommendation for his membership in the Order of Santiago.

Vicente tossed the Cardinal-Infante's letter into the roaring fireplace and watched it burn to ashes. At almost thirty-four years of age, the man said farewell forever to the boy who had dreamed of serving as Soldier for the Crown.

One of the calamities which must be considered with the greatest attention and grief is to see Spain filled on all sides with Jews, enemies of our Holy Catholic faith.

Royal Chronicler, Don José Pellicer y Tovar, 1639

PART FIVE
To Become Inquisitor-General
Madrid, 1635-1643

I hold strongly to this: that it is better to be impetuous than circumspect; because fortune is a woman, and if she is to be submissive it is necessary to beat and coerce her. Experience shows that she is more often subdued by men who do this than those who act coldly. Always, being a woman, she favors younger men, because they are less circumspect and more ardent, and because they command her with greater audacity.

Niccolò Machiavelli, Il Principie

Chapter 62
Queen's Gambit

Once again wearing the robe of his Dominican Order, Vicente entered Madrid on a June morning in 1635 and arrived at the Alcazar a good hour before siesta. He reported to Philip in Velázquez' studio, where the King was accompanied by Isabella and Infante Don Baltazar Carlos with his dwarfs and dogs, attended by the Count-Duke and Countess-Duchess de Olivares, and surrounded by his usual entourage of courtiers, ladies, and *bufónes*. Velázquez was adding finishing touches on yet another painting of the King, who sat on a cushioned throne-chair by the easel. He portrayed Philip in gilded armor as a contemporary god of war on a magnificent rearing charger.

In contrast to his costume in the portrait and those of his courtiers, the King as usual wore simple elegant black, the only aspect of his appearance that had not changed. Had a three year absence from Court given Vicente a more accurate perspective? Philip looked less regal than he remembered, a living caricature of Velázquez' idealized majestic and spiritual portraits hanging everywhere on the palace walls. The King's cheeks were heavy not lean, the great jaw more deformed, his neck fatter and shorter, the eyes dull and baggy. His Majesty's pale face had all the expression and charm of a death mask. Velázquez' ability to flatter His Majesty with paint explained why the artist had received the prestigious rank and position of Assistant of the King's Wardrobe.

Vivacious Queen Isabel also had gained weight, which was exaggerated by a great ruff pushing up her double chin and a wide brown guardinfante decorated with gold thread and yellow flowers. Ill-favored women like the Countess-Duchess de Olivares seemed never to change or age.

When the *bufónes* greeted Vicente, they brought back memories of his great friends, Hombrecillo and Inéz. The void of their loss could never be filled, and a tableaux of images and voices from the past assaulted Vicente: Sancho's biting wit, Inéz dressed in miniature as the Infanta, the day he presented Brianda at court, and that auspicious moment of María's subtle smile meant for him alone as she sat for her portrait.

Barely concealing his emotions, Vicente genuflected before Their Majesties in the stifling, overcrowded studio and presented letters to Philip from Fernándo. After the King read them, he commanded Vicente to describe all he had seen.

Philip appeared less than delighted with the Cardinal-Infante's great victory at Nördlingen. Vicente understood why. The King wanted to command an army in the field and was consumed with envy over his brother's military victories. Was that why His Majesty did not react when he emphasized how Rafal's tactical acumen and great courage helped save the day for the Catholic cause? Philip gave not the slightest indication that Don Jerónimo had ever appeared at Court with the captured standards and the mutilated Virgin.

After Vicente related the Cardinal-Infante's visit to María, Philip said to Isabel "Yes, our niece, Infanta Doña María Anna, shall wed our Infante Don Baltazar Carlos."

María has survived childbirth. If only my Brianda had.

Isabel beamed at her handsome son. "And our grandson could well inherit both the empire and all lands belonging to Spain."

"That is exactly the hope expressed by Her Most Illustrious Majesty, the Queen of Hungary," Vicente said.

Isabella pointed her fan and flashed a malicious smile at Olivares. "Don Vicente's account of His Eminence's victory at Nördlingen has convinced us. Don Diego Velázquez must memorialize that glorious day and create a panorama of the battle for the Hall of Realms at Buen Retiro."

Philip stroked his massive jaw. "Commence work on it immediately."

"And, Don Diego, confer with Don Vicente," Isabel said to the artist, "for he was an active participant."

Vicente appreciated the clever Queen's motives. In April, France and Sweden had signed an alliance specifying which German lands each was to receive upon victory. Richelieu intended for France to have the natural boundaries of Rhine, Alps, and Pyrenees. In May, Louis XIII had declared war against the Emperor and Philip IV of Spain, his brother-in-law.

A great painting commemorating the Cardinal-Infante's victory would intensify the King's envy of his brother and inflame his desire to lead an army against Spain's enemies. Once Philip left Madrid, Isabel would rule as regent, surround herself with Olivares' enemies, and at last rid her husband of the Count-Duke.

Vicente's narrative of Fernándo's martial feats and the Queen's suggestion of a major painting to immortalize the victory at Nördlingen put the King in a foul humor. He ended his sitting, dismissed everyone except Olivares, and summoned his Council of War.

Before Vicente withdrew, the Count-Duke took him aside. "Report to me after siesta. I have many questions."

Ballebrera embraced Vicente at the *mentidero* in the Queen's Courtyard. "When did you return?"

"This morning. I reported directly to His Majesty."

"Almost three long years. How I have missed you."

Vicente stepped back to look at Ballebrera, who wore a flattering beige and scarlet ensemble. "You have not changed, I am pleased to say."

"But you. . . lines on your face have been added to mustachio and goatee. Your eyes are older."

The words came out with difficulty. "Brianda, my daughter, she died giving birth. Her baby too."

Ballebrera crossed himself. "I had not heard. I am truly sorry."

"I do not wish to speak of it. Can you tell me why Jerónimo has not received his title?"

"There is nothing more he can do. His Majesty properly received him when he arrived with the enemy standards and other trophies of war. At present, Jerónimo is in Orihuela."

Vicente no longer cared if Rafal was made *conde* or *marqués*. For the second time that day, he recounted the battle of Nördlingen. After he gratified Ballebrera with details of the significant part played by Rafal and Juan in the victory, Vicente made sure no one could hear them. "I almost went to Amsterdam."

"Perhaps you should have."

"Are you suggesting that I should not have returned?"

"Who can say with certainty? You will always be in danger while you live in Spain. Your rivals continued to plot against you while you were gone. Now that you have returned, that queer triumvirate of Arce, Tomás, and Jacinto will become more active in their endeavors to destroy you."

"I would be surprised if it were otherwise. But why did you use the word, queer?"

"Their hatred of you is their bond otherwise they would be at each other's throats. Tomás and Arce both want to be Inquisitor General. Tomás believes that Jacinto is quite capable of eliminating Francisco and all his heirs. Then, in accordance with our family agreement, the Lord of Rafal would inherit the title and lands of Granja de Rocamora and also my señorio. Arce despises Jacinto for his vices, and he hates himself for needing his services."

"I should have killed the pig in Barcelona and avenged Yusef, Koitalel, and your Duchess."

"And Rafal would have had you executed on the spot."

"Any word of Pablo and Moraíma?"

"None, I regret to say. And what are your immediate plans?"

"I will know tonight. Olivares commanded me to be in his offices after siesta, and I have been summoned to Sotomayor's *palacio* after vespers."

"Good. They may confirm rumors I have heard repeated in the *mentideros*."

"Such as?"

"The Count-Duke's enemies are convinced that his real goal is to bring back all the new-Christians and Jews who fled to the United Provinces, Italy, and the Ottoman Empire."

Their fears and Pinto's esperanza. "His enemies have been spreading those rumors for years," Vicente said.

"Nevertheless, a large number of Portuguese of dubious faith came to Madrid during the years you were away soldiering. Did you observe any tension between His Majesty and the Count-Duke?"

"No, but then, stone carvings of all the saints have more changes of expression than our King. Still, His Majesty lets everyone know that he wants to lead an army against France, which Olivares opposes."

"Understandable, Vicente. Philip is thirty years old and wants to make his own mark on the world. And you too should go for the great prize. Seize kismet by its balls and crush them to your will. Become Inquisitor General. You must do all you can to prevent Arce or Tomás from following Sotomayor."

"Arce, Jacinto, Tomás. Tell me, Ramón, how does one stop making enemies?"

"In death, only in death."

Chapter 63
Carpe Diem, Carpe Fortuna

The Count-Duke's bandaged gouty foot rested on a cushioned ottoman. He lifted his black wig with a gold-capped stick and felt his scalp for lice. "Friar, I was sorry to hear of your niece's passing. Certain problems have arisen, and you may be the most qualified man in all Spain to deal with them. Sotomayor has been working at cross purposes with me."

"I thought he was your ally."

"He is, but although Sotomayor is almost eighty and enjoys superb physical health, his forgetfulness, lassitude, and reluctance to make decisions allow the regional tribunals of the Inquisition to function more aggressively than I want. I need someone who is loyal to me close by his side, a man who will watch out for my . . . our mutual interests."

"What would you have me do?"

"Denunciations and arrests of new-Christians have increased. Arce and his minions hope to squeeze just one confession of Judaizing from any poor devil and implicate my financiers in some heresy, and me as well. The Bishop of Palencia is pressing Sotomayor to prepare an *auto generale* of my new-Christian financiers while at the same time spreading rumors that the Inquisitor General is too soft to hold office. I must protect my Portuguese. The Crown needs their wealth and financial acumen."

"I cannot believe Sotomayor would condone an *auto-de-fé* of the innocent. He prefers saving souls to presiding over torture and the *quemadero*."

"The old fart also believes a secretariat of Dominicans sits in heaven to deal specifically with Spanish affairs. Now here is what I want from you. If any of my financiers are at risk, I give you authority to deliver all incriminating documents to me at once or destroy them if you cannot. And remember this, Friar. You serve my interests before those of Sotomayor."

"As I did while acting as Doña María's confessor and spiritual director. And, if I may speak freely . . ."

"Go on."

"I could serve your interests even more as Infante Don Baltazar Carlos' confessor and mold him to your way of thinking."

Olivares squinted at Vicente. "In time, Friar, in time. He is still too young. For the moment, I want you to tell me everything Sotomayor does, says, and plans."

"Your Reverence."

In the Council Chamber of the *Inquisitorial Palacio,* Vicente kissed the hem of Sotomayor's robe and received permission to squat opposite him on an uncomfortable stool. The Inquisitor General sat atop a burgundy velvet cushion in a high-back armchair.

While Sotomayor sipped a clear broth, Vicente studied the old man's features. His sparse snow white hair, his once majestic beard and mustachio now wispy, shrunken red-rimmed blue eyes behind spectacles on a massive nose, face and neck more wrinkled than a prune, all made him indistinguishable from countless men and women of advanced age. Sotomayor had lost his face and many of his teeth. His voice, however, still had the timbre of authority.

"Fray Vicente, I have summoned you for several reasons. I want to tell you that I am delighted you have returned and you have my condolences and prayers for the soul of your niece, may she rest in peace."

"Thank you, Your Reverence."

"Now then, I want to alert you. Arce makes no secret of his intentions to remove me as Inquisitor General and to destroy you as well."

"Yes, he is relentless. Has the Holy Office completed its investigation into my family's origins?"

"Your paternal de Rocamora family has been certified as *limpio* many times over, and we have found nothing to contradict your mother's certificate of *limpieza*. However, I have been told by more than one source that Arce has ordered his own investigation into your background."

"He will find nothing, of that I can assure you, but he might create forgeries to prove I am tainted."

"What you say is possible from so ambitious a man."

"Then if you would advise Their Majesties that I should be the Infante's confessor."

"No, no, no. Too precipitous. Much too precipitous. You are but thirty-four years of age."

And, therefore, capable of having a long reign as your successor.

Chapter 64
Buen Retiro

On a sunny late afternoon in the middle of June, 1636, Vicente ambled with Ballebrera through the grounds of Philip's pleasure palace. "I can understand why His Majesty prefers Buen Retiro to the Alcazar."

"So do we all." Ballebrera flicked an annoying insect off the *hábito* of Alcántara that covered his velvet and satin doublet of fawn brown. All his harmonized clothes and accessories were of the latest fashion, and he had come to prefer his falling lace Walloon collar to the *golilla*.

Buen Retiro had well lighted spacious chambers and galleries for the King's vast art collection. An imposing statue of Philip dominated the forecourt.

Outer wings opened onto other courtyards, plazas, and lush formal flower gardens leading to long avenues lined with statuary, elaborate fountains, and terraced pools linked by canals. On Buen Retiro's extensive grounds one could linger in secluded groves, pavilions, and bowers ideal for adulterous liaisons. At E*l Estanque*, The Reservoir, an enormous lake had been created for water festivals with a landscaped island in its center and a stage where elaborate productions were presented and watched from gondolas or small decorated boats.

Ballebrera stopped to admire a marble statue of a naked young athlete sculpted in the classical style. "Such wonderful symmetry."

They heard their names called and saw Quiñones and Cardoso approaching. Vicente thought them to be an odd pair of friends, an *alcalde* persecutor of new-Christians and a Portuguese physician of dubious ancestry and suspect faith.

Quiñones and Cardoso continued to make names for themselves at l*a Corte* as dabblers in assorted arts and sciences. Both men had published discourses on the recent eruption of Vesuvius, which took tens of thousands of lives. And, during the nine days of funereal solemnities following the death of Lope de Vega the previous twenty-seventh of August, *alcalde* and physician were among the literary giants and a multitude of lesser poetasters who had written and recited panegyrics honoring the colossus of Spanish literature.

The four men walked towards the Hall of Realms, their boots and sandals stirring gravel on the pathway. Whenever they paused to inhale fragrant flowers along the statue-lined avenue, the loquacious Quiñones gave them unasked for lessons in botany.

"Don Vicente, are you as comfortable in your woolen robe as you were in soldier's doublet and hose?" Cardoso asked.

Vicente touched his silver crucifix and said for the *alcalde* to hear as well, "You should take into consideration the weight and restrictions of armor. But physical comfort is irrelevant, when souls must be saved and nourished."

"Don Vicente, you are absolutely right," Quiñones said, "and all of us were impressed with your sermon this morning. No one is more eloquent when preaching the terrible punishments in hell awaiting sinners, heretics, and blasphemers for all eternity."

Despite Quiñones' surface amiability, Vicente marked the *alcalde* as Arce's man and thought it wise to be circumspect and reticent in his presence.

Quiñones confirmed his wariness. "Our Most Illustrious and Reverend Lord and Bishop of Palencia, Don Diego de Arce Reynoso, and I supped last night with your kinsmen, Don Tomás and Don Jacinto."

"I am sure the conversation was stimulating and illuminating." Vicente was pleased how nonchalant his own voice sounded.

I should have been an actor.

They entered the Hall of Realms, filled to capacity with courtiers, clergy, and knights who anticipated a new unveiling. In their eagerness to see everything, several young nobles climbed atop the massive statues representing Spain's legendary heroes. All agreed that Velázquez had outdone himself when he designed the gallery. Between the large windows, his assistants had hung enormous canvases portraying every celebrated victory of Spanish arms from the glory days of the *reconquista* and Lepanto to his own masterpiece, *The Surrender of Breda*, and Zurbaran's *Relief of Cadiz*.

Sotomayor, Arce, Tomás and other clerical notables made one horn of a crescent facing yet another massive painting temporarily covered by gold and vermilion satin bearing the royal coat-of-arms. The men and women of the *grandeza* gathered on the other side in rows by rank. The most important palace officials stood in the center, with a space in their midst reserved for Their Majesties, the Count-Duke, and their personal retinues.

Quiñones left them to stand at the head of the *alcaldes*. Farther back toward the middle of the noisy restless throng, Vicente and Cardoso separated to take their places along with other clergy and physicians, minor palace administrators, and those of lower rank. Ballebrera joined his fellow Knights of Alcántara.

Vicente saw Rafal and Jacinto among the Knights of Santiago. The old soldier had not completely recovered from a fever that had swept through Orihuela and claimed Francisco's family at Granja de Rocamora, leaving only a granddaughter and Tomás.

If only Jacinto were one of the dead.

A fanfare of horns announced the arrival of Their Majesties and Infante Baltazar Carlos followed by the Count-Duke and Duchess, their retinues, and the *bufónes*. Olivares wore his *hábito* of Alcántara and the gold chains, spurs, and keys of his royal household functions.

The King and Queen led their gentlemen and ladies-in-waiting to the open space in front of the covered painting where Velázquez genuflected obsequiously. After the artist was given permission to rise, he snapped his fingers. Liveried assistants on each side of the canvas pulled golden cords, which parted the drapes.

A collective cry of awe, then approval filled the great hall. *The Battle of Nördlingen* was larger by half than any previous painting, and Vicente believed it to be Velázquez' masterpiece, superior in every way to *The Surrender of Breda*. In the foreground wearing gilded black armor and astride his rearing Andalusian charger, the Cardinal-Infante dominated the action and pointed his marshal's baton towards the battle as if ordering an attack. Velázquez had placed the King of Hungary behind Fernándo in the minor role of an observer. A significant part of the canvas showed the Spanish *tercios* in victorious battle against the Protestant armies.

Vicente's eyes moved to the upper left side of the massive painting where Spanish troops repelled a charge. He recognized Rafal portrayed at the crest on horseback and Juan at his side. One of the banners raised on the hill identified Jerónimo's *tercio*; another was the standard of Santiago; and a third bore the familiar blue, gold, and silver coat-of-arms of de Rocamora. Vicente could not have been more pleased. Velázquez had painted faithfully his description of the battle and honored their family name for all to see, for all time. The artist had given the de Rocamoras immortality.

The Royal Chamberlain whispered in the King's ear, received a nod, and rapped his gold and jeweled stick of office on the marble floor until silence prevailed. Philip moved closer to the painting and pointed to its upper left corner. "We recognize our loyal servant, Don Jerónimo de Rocamora y Roda, hereditary *Primero Marqués* de Rafal."

The Chamberlain's voice resonated throughout the hall. "The *Marqués* de Rafal will remove his hat before addressing His Majesty and remain bareheaded until he returns to his place."

Jerónimo removed his hat, stepped forward, kneeled, and said after he received permission to rise, "Your Majesty, words cannot express my deepest gratitude and affection."

The King stared at Rafal in silence, and the Chamberlain motioned for him to return to his place. As the newly made *grandee* put on his hat, Philip turned to discuss technical features of the painting with Velázquez.

Vicente pushed through the crowd to Rafal, who was surrounded by cheering knights of Santiago. Honor had been satisfied. Jerónimo had become both *marqués* and *Grandee* Third Class. Although Don Francisco was the first de Rocamora to be granted a title by a King of Spain, Rafal would be superior in rank.

"*Marqués* de Rafal. How proud I am to address you thus, Don Jerónimo." No thanks for him, all Vicente received was a slight nod of acknowledgement. Don Lope had been proven correct again.

Ballebrera also congratulated his kinsman, and Vicente saw Jacinto nearby preening and swaggering as if he were already the Second *Marqués* de Rafal. To judge by Jerónimo's frailty that unfortunate day loomed near.

When Arce and Tomás offered congratulations, Ballebrera said for all within hearing, "You accomplished it at last, Don Vicente."

Jacinto stepped from behind his father. "He deserves no credit. It was Tomás' piety and the Bishop of Palencia's influence that brought my father his long overdue title, not this friar's pathetic and futile efforts."

"You demean your father's exceptional heroism in battle, his great military victories, and long years of service to the Crown," Vicente countered, all too aware that Rafal believed his son.

"Friar." The Bishop of Palencia's dour expression was hard as granite. He beckoned Vicente to come closer. "You will appear tomorrow for matins at San Tomás and afterwards attend ceremonies confirming the appointment of Fray Tomás de Rocamora as Dominican Provincial General for the Kingdom of Aragón."

"And there we shall find a suitable monastery for you to spend the rest of your life in solitary meditation and penitence," Tomás said.

"Perhaps you should tell the Inquisitor General of your plans for me, *cousin*," Vicente countered.

Tomás flinched at the reminder of their kinship, and Arce held Vicente's arm to prevent him from leaving. "You are playing a dangerous game, a game you will lose in the end, Jewish swine."

"You have no proof of any taint, for none exists." Vicente removed Arce's hand. His forceful grip brought tears to the bishop's eyes. "And remember this. Your Most Illustrious Reverend Self has much in common with swine, for they also are uncircumcised."

Chapter 65
Vicente's Comedia

The war against France had not been forgotten. Between frivolous entertainments calculated to distract the King from taking command of an army, Olivares flattered him as a great military leader. He influenced Philip to send for experienced generals who had participated in the recent campaigns and discuss with them how best to build a new army of forty thousand men capable of invading France.

At his desk in Olivares' office, Vicente finished and sealed a personal note of congratulations to María, who had at last become an Empress when her husband, Ferdinand III, was elected King of the Romans, Holy Roman Emperor.

Vicente reflected upon his place in Spain and if he would become Inquisitor General. As the protagonist of a real *comedia*, he would be wise to assess the roles fate had assigned to other players.

Any one of three powerful men could make him Inquisitor General. How to cast them? Were they friend or foe? Motivated by enlightened self-interest or fear? Or whimsical as the gods of the Greeks?

Inquisitor General Sotomayor's one consistency was his reluctance to name a successor for fear of instant removal. Olivares too had become unreliable. He would sit alone for days in a dark room and then act with incredible energy. His moods swung from unprovoked tantrums, to euphoria, and then to deep depression.

Olivares had failed to appoint him confessor for the seven year old Infante Baltazar Carlos. That office had been the stepping-stone to Inquisitor General for both Aliaga and Sotomayor. Instead, the Count-Duke supplied the Infante with numerous inconsequential confessors.

Vicente had searched for ways to bypass Olivares and Sotomayor and deal directly with His Majesty, whom he served well on several occasions, but Philip either ignored his presence or tolerated it with frigid formality.

Two strong women had important roles to play in his *comedia*. María had recommended to Their Majesties that he should become confessor for Infante Baltazar Carlos and become Inquisitor General. Isabel had praised his work at the orphanage, yet she no longer asked him to confess her.

A well-constructed play needed dramatic conflict and antagonists. Vicente knew that his chief rival was the Bishop of Palencia, Diego de Arce Reynoso. No less dangerous, the elegant and gregarious Inquisitor Juan Adán de la Parra was welcomed in homes of the *grandees* and *literati* because of his charm, wit, and skill in poetic jousts. The latter's visceral hatred of Jews could be attributed to more than Castilian old-Christian prejudice. When de la Parra was a young man struggling to make his mark in Madrid, Góngora and other writers presumed to be tainted had ridiculed his efforts at poetry.

Jacinto, Tomás, and all other bigoted old-Christians would do everything and anything to prevent him from rising to Inquisitor General. Vicente included Quiñones as an adversary despite their surface friendship.

A formidable wall constructed of inertia and aggressive opposition.

Vicente listed his allies of varying abilities and faithfulness. Ballebrera had become ineffectual, and Cardoso, for all his scheming, had yet to achieve a significant position at Court.

Vicente's most influential partisan, Jerónimo de Villanueva, had aged noticeably. Although very much in the King's favor and still Olivares' closest friend, the *Protonotario* of Aragón lived under repeated threats of arrest. The Inquisition refused to forget his involvement in the notorious San Plácido affair, with accusations of sorcery and fornication, and rumors of his Jewish origins had not abated.

The Portuguese new-Christians were his most numerous allies, but so far they had been more passive than active. Vicente had learned much about their backgrounds from relevant Inquisitorial dossiers. Most had siblings and kin who lived as Jews under assumed names in the Venice ghetto, Ottoman Empire, and the United Provinces.

They included Rodrigo Méndez de Silva, who had been appointed one of His Majesty's Royal Chroniclers in 1635, and Royal Financier Manuel Cortizos de Villasante, Knight of Calatrava and rumored to be the wealthiest man in all Spain. Vicente related most to twenty-nine-year old Manuel Fernández de Villareal. Fernández was a restless man of many talents: Army captain; poet; writer of tracts; and successful in assorted financial enterprises. He had taken it upon himself to become Vicente's sword and protector.

Vicente's most eccentric ally was Pedro Zapata de Callosa, Fourth Count de Avilés. The twenty-five year old handsome blond noble was an old-Christian related to the former Inquisitor General and other important families of Castile and Murcia. Zapata lived off and with a wealthy widowed cousin and had become Ballebrera's inseparable friend of late, which did not surprise Vicente. The young man's fair complexion and delicate features aroused male aesthetes.

Vicente mused about Zapata's cousin, Catalina Bustamante de Faxardo. Was she the motivating force behind the young sybarite's support of his candidacy?

Not a well constructed comedia. An imbalance favors the antagonists. Unless changes are made, the protagonist will face defeat.

High comedy or low tragedy?

Chapter 66
Catalina

An hour before siesta, Vicente waited in the antechamber at the Zapata de Callosa *palacio* not far from the abandoned Convent of San Plácido to confess Doña Catalina, who had inherited a great fortune accumulated by her

Murcian family in New World trade. She had come to Madrid the previous summer one year after the death of her husband and soon presided over the most stimulating literary salon in the capital.

Catalina was the one exception in his routines confessing the fashionable, serving Olivares, preparing orphans for their first communion, and giving fatherly attention to boys close in age to his grandson, had the infant lived.

Of all the women Vicente confessed, Catalina intrigued him most. She was a *tapada* beauty in her twenties, unattractive of face and form, but skilled in the use of veil and cloak to reveal only her seductive eyes. Like everyone else in Madrid, he was captivated by her charm, wit and exceptional intelligence.

The servant returned to tell Vicente that Catalina awaited him in the family chapel. He knew the way and passed alone through luxurious rooms, more antechambers, and across a tiled patio to another wing of the *palacio* and the most ostentatious private family chapel he had seen in Madrid. It was filled with golden jewel encrusted crucifixes, reliquaries containing hairs and bones of saints and pieces of the True Cross, elaborate chalices, and a stained glass window representing the Resurrection. Cloth of vermilion silk highlighted with designs in gold thread decorated the baldacchino.

Catalina kneeled at her *prie-Dieu*. A black lace shawl covered her head.

Vicente froze in the chapel doorway when she recited a prayer loud enough for him to hear.

"*O Alto Dios de Abraham, Dios fuerte Israel, tu que a toda criatura abriste camino y fonte alce meus ollos au monte donde vendra mi ayuda, mi ayuda, mi ayuda, es al señor Dios que crio el cielo y la tierra y el movimento, en tu pie ni dormira, el que te guarde de aquel, que guardo a Israel guardete el señor de todo mal guardara, tu alma, tu vida guardara, tu entrada guardara, tu salida desde aoro para siempre de los siglos. Amen.*"

"O, High God of Abraham, God sustain Israel, Thou who opens the way for every creature, and lift mine eyes to the mountain from where Thou came to help me, help me, help me, Lord God who created the sky, the earth, and all that moves, not even Thy foot sleeps, who Thyself protects that which will protect Israel, protect the Lord from all evil, Thy soul will protect Thy life, will protect Thy gate, Thy departure from now through all the centuries. Amen."

After she finished, Catalina stood and faced Vicente. "Now you know. Now you know all, Friar. I am a Judaizer."

"You deliberately let me overhear your prayer and discover your secret. Why?"

"One moment."

Catalina brushed past him, closed the chapel door, and locked it. Vicente inhaled the unmistakable scent of a woman in heat. Her black dress was no protective guardinfante. The material was lighter and clung to the contours of her body, and her heavy breathing made him aware of her breasts for the first time, large gourds for so short a woman.

Vicente had encountered various Bustamantes, Faxardos, and Callosas when he lived in Orihuela. Their *limpio* status had never been questioned. "I thought you came from old-Christian families."

She toyed with the gold cross hanging from her neck. "So everyone believes, and it is absolutely true of my late husband's family. Most of my own flesh and blood were indeed old-Christians, untainted by Jews, Moors, and whatever else. One branch, however, was descended from the Jews of Orihuela who converted *en masse* during the massacres of 1391, and they never forgot the faith of our Israelite ancestors who now call out to me."

"Does Don Pedro know that you have Judaized?"

"No, my cousin is and always will be a devout Catholic."

"Why have you told me all this?"

"To test you. To be sure of you."

"For what purpose?"

"My cousin and the others believe you are the best man to replace Sotomayor as Inquisitor General."

"Which is no secret."

"I have studied you. I find you to be clever and shall I say . . . Machiavellian?"

"You flatter me. How do you know I will not send for the inquisitorial police?"

"That is the essence of my test. Is it not better for me to know who you are now instead of placing false hopes in your candidacy to become Inquisitor General?"

Catalina moved closer to Vicente until their bodies touched. Her dark hair and swarthy coloring, her full purple lips, sharpness of nose, and fire in her eyes reminded him of Violante.

"What advantage is there to my not denouncing you?"

"Unlimited financial support and influence."

"I thought I had that."

"Too much so. My brother and his *poderoso* friends have allowed you to be too much your own man. We need to exert more control over you."

"I submit only to the authority of Their Majesties, His Reverence, the Inquisitor General, and his Excellency, the Count-Duke."

"Even so, if you do not denounce me, you violate the law."

"Then you are forcing me to have you arrested."

"And I will name you as the one who introduced me to the Law of Moses, a fornicating sorcerer who seduced me into the false faith. My penalties will be minor compared to yours. Perhaps none at all. Arce, de la Parra, and all your Valencian enemies would pay any price to destroy you."

Vicente studied the woman's expression. He believed she would indeed carry out her threat. "I have never denounced anyone to the Holy Office, nor shall I do so now."

"I thought as much."

"Then the matter is settled. I do not denounce you as a Judaizer, and you continue your work behind the scenes to make me Inquisitor General."

As he turned to leave, she gripped his arm. "There is more."

"What else do you want of me?"

"I know I am not like those pale, sickly blonde old-Christian girls with their blue veins and delicate appeal. Nor, can I dance and expose myself like those Gypsy sluts you men slobber over." Catalina removed her shawl, mantilla, and combs, and let her hair fall past her shoulders. She stood where chapel candles illuminated her face. "Are my eyebrows too thick? I would pluck them for you." Off came her dress. She faced him in a white diaphanous linen shift. The nipples of her large breasts pressed through the sheer material, which exposed the matted dark forest of her delta. "Are my arms and legs too hairy for you? My mustache a distraction? I would wax them off for you in the Moorish custom. Yes, Vicente, my full price for keeping silent is to possess what you have denied all the others, what I have desired ever since I became a woman. You may have me on demand. Any time. Anything you want." Her shift fell to the floor. She pressed against him. "And you will do the same for me."

Vicente believed he could prevent Catalina from making good those threats if he rejected her. He was not certain if he wanted to, having been aroused several times earlier in the day by attractive women who let him know he was welcome to share their beds.

On the chapel carpets and in her bedroom, they fed their voracious carnal appetites until she was sated and he was exhausted.

"Be here at the same time tomorrow. I must confess my sins to you, receive penance, and absolution."

And begin the cycle all over again.

Catalina had ended his drought unexpectedly and, to his surprise, pleasurably. She also had taught him a great lesson he had never before considered or chanced. External beauty meant little in the dark with a passionate woman.

Chapter 67
The State of Art

"It would have been better to gather inside," Ballebrera said walking with Vicente, Fernández de Villareal and Méndez de Silva along a tree lined path towards the lagoon theater in Buen Retiro to attend the premiere of a new play.

A florid sunset had not alleviated the steamy heat of an unseasonable late September day. Insects swarmed about them as Madrid suffered from a vexation of voracious mosquitoes.

Now that Brianda no longer lived, Vicente had no fear that their identical features would lead to the only logical conclusion. His was the only clean-shaven face among flaring curled mustachios and elegant beards of varying colors.

Ballebrera waved his hand to ward off more flying insects and held a silk handkerchief to his face. "I do not know which is worse, the insects or the bad air."

"*Mal aria*, the Italians call it," Vicente said, sweating under his white woolen robe. Algae, scum, and insects covered the stagnant waters of Buen Retiro, and he longed for those delightful summer days when María offered him iced drinks in the shade of the cloistered Casa de Campo.

Fernández tried to grasp an insect buzzing at his ear. "How is it that the mosquitoes do not bother you, Vicente?"

Méndez brushed another away from his cheek now flushed from the heat. "Yes, why do they leave you alone? I refuse to believe it is a result of prayers or your renowned piety."

"I have repeatedly urged all of you to use the ointment I prepared." When Vicente was a boy, Don Lope had taught him how to fix a fine paste repellent against mosquitoes and other bloodsucking insects.

Ballebrera raised a perfumed lace cuff to his nose. "But the odor is so foul, which is why we prefer to walk upwind from you, that is, if there was a breeze."

Méndez asked through his scented silk handkerchief. "What are the ingredients?"

"A garlic base . . ."

"Of course," Ballebrera interrupted. "It cannot matter for a friar, on whom the odors of unwashed sanctity predominate."

Fernández walked beside Vicente. "Have the censors explained why they rejected your play?"

"No, nor have they returned it to me."

"What was the story?" Méndez asked.

"A variation of Tarquin and Lucretia set in a contemporary confused world where appearances deceive and lead to *desengaño*, a world where to dream is to live, and to live is to dream."

"Tarquin and Lucretia? But that old tale has been done so many times."

Ballebrera defended Vicente against the royal chronicler. "As everyone knows, all stories have been told over and over. It is for the writer of each generation to incorporate the old, yet make it new and true for his times, as Vicente has done."

Fernández tapped the hilt of his sword. "Did you include plenty of *espada* and *capa* like in the dramas of Lope and Calderón?"

"Swordplay and cloak? All that and more. There are mistaken identities. Facades built upon facades. Honor more valued than life itself."

"We look forward to seeing it performed in spite of the censors. Perhaps one evening at Doña Catalina's salon."

"Yes, she has read it and made valuable suggestions."

Ballebrera glanced about to make sure no one except his companions could hear him. "So tonight, instead of Vicente's masterpiece, we must suffer through another of those dreadful *comedias* written by one who calls himself *un ingenio d'esta Corte*, a wit of this court, His Majesty's preposterous *nom de plume*."

"It is more than royal pretension," Méndez said leering. "The King delights in casting his own plays so he can bed all the comely actresses, as we all wish to do. At least the theater directors are clever enough to obscure his lack of talent with fantastic sets and spectacular effects."

Ballebrera made an exaggerated cross. "May God spare us this night from bands of trumpeting angels, Apollos in flaming chariots, and repugnant cupids flying across the stage. How the theater has degenerated. Great acting and brilliant dialogue are things of the past."

"Alas, Ramón is right," Méndez said. "Even Calderón must include volcanoes, seas filled with ships, and castles suddenly appearing on stage at the touch of a magic wand. How much farther can things go?"

Vicente touched his silver crucifix when they passed several *títulos* and their ladies. "Without Church controls, we might see actual blood shed, nudity, and coupling, and worse abominations on stage."

"That is the least of our problems," Méndez complained. "I am unhappy with your lack of progress, Vicente. You should have been accepted into the Holy Office by now."

"Because of Arce's insistence, their investigators find excuses to look into my mother's background."

"That they can find no evidence her family ever existed causes them to prolong the search," Méndez said. "We should create additional forgeries. I can assure you they will be so perfect His Majesty would wish them for himself. If one honestly traces his lineage back to Ferdinand the Catholic's great-grandmother, the Jewess, Raquel Enríquez, la Paloma de Toledo."

"I insist on seeing those forgeries before you turn them over to the Holy Office," Vicente said.

Méndez flinched when a mosquito buzzed him. "Of course, and we will not present them until we formally offer your candidacy. The less time we give the reactionaries, the better."

Fernández swept a finger across his throat. "We can always arrange for Arce to have an accident."

"A sweet thought, but there are my cousin Tomás, Inquisitor de la Parra, and countless others. Too many for us to eliminate."

Loud laughter and cries distracted them when revelers ran along a parallel path leading from a ballroom. Showing no regard for rank, they chased surprised strollers along promenades and across lawns and pelted them with perfume filled eggshells. Callosa came to them reeking of scent, a wreath of flowers on his uncovered head. The handsome young blond said between bursts of laughter, "You should have seen it. They passed out baskets of eggshells filled with perfume to each of us, and Queen Isabel threw the first one at the Countess-Duchess de Olivares. That gave all of us license to pelt each other. As you can see, the silliness has spilled outside."

Ballebrera waved goodbye to his comrades and left with Callosa before they reached the theater. Vicente observed someone all in black beckoning him from the woods with a familiar signal. He told his friends they need not accompany him. When he caught up with the man, they embraced.

"Pablo."

"Old friend."

Chapter 68
A Mother's Dream

Pablo's physical appearance shocked Vicente. H, who offered condolences for the death of his friend's wife and children in Jacinto's inferno. The Morisco's face was lined from years of deprivation and suffering. What was left of his hair had turned white.

"Tell me about Moraíma and Philippa."

"Later, Vicente. First, Jacinto has let it be known he will pay well for your death."

"So have others, the Anglesolas, and perhaps even my cousin Tomás. Certain rivals have hired assassins to prevent me from becoming the next Inquisitor General."

"You? Inquisitor General? What a wonderful defeat for our enemies should it come to pass. How close are you to the prize, and how can I help?"

"Nothing may happen until we find corroborating proof my mother was truly *limpia*. But tell me, my friend, what has brought you to Madrid?"

He led Vicente to a nearby carriage with a driver and two coachmen typical of Valencian brigands. After they settled inside, Pablo pulled the shades and rapped for the driver to move out. "We cannot stay in Catalonia. Either it will explode in revolt, or the French will invade and be welcomed as liberators. Blood will flow there in any case, and women will be violated. As you know, we have no sanctuary in Valencia. Aragón also is denied us for the same reasons, thanks to your kinsman, Tomás. May his crotch be infested with ten thousand fleas. So, why not survive in the belly of the beast?"

"You could have gone to Andalusia, Extremadura, or even France."

"Moraíma insisted we come to Madrid because she heard rumors that Philip intends to legitimize the bastard son he sired with la Calteróna."

"Juan José de Austria."

"So grand a name? Then the rumors are true."

"Only rumors so far."

"In any case, she has convinced herself that when the King sees their daughter he will legitimize Philippa too."

"Impossible. Our enemies will denounce Moraíma as a *morilla* and use her to destroy me. Pablo, she must leave Madrid."

"You tell her that."

They arrived at a walled house and went into a small cluttered *estrado* where Moraíma awaited them. Dressed in plain black and carrying cross and rosary typical of devout women found everywhere in Spain, Vicente's first great passion had become plump and matronly with graying hair. Yet, her attraction was still strong with those seductive eyes, full lips, and unblemished skin.

After they embraced and kissed, she said, "You have not changed, Vicente. You must have discovered the secret of eternal youth."

"And so have you."

"You are very kind to say that." Moraíma guided him to a plain chair, sat opposite him, and held his hands while Pablo stood behind her. "Tell me about Philip."

"He has not changed. His passions are hunting, theatricals, and collecting paintings,"

"And mistresses?"

"Mistresses and bastards, with exaggerated swings of the pendulum from wild debauchery to periods of extreme piety And how is your daughter? When may I see her?"

Moraíma took him into an adjacent room where her daughter slept. Vicente gasped. Twelve-year old Philippa was all Habsburg, with flaxen blond hair, pale complexion, and a pouting lower lip.

"I know you see not my daughter but your beloved Infanta."

Moraíma was right. In sleep, Philippa could have been María's twin. No one at Court would doubt His Majesty's paternity.

She roused her daughter. "Philippa, I want you to meet an old friend of mine."

Philippa opened pale blue eyes and sat with her mother's help.

He bowed to the girl. "Señorita Philippa."

When she looked at Vicente, he first thought that she was still groggy after being awakened from a sound sleep. Then his blood froze during an attempt to make small talk. No, not María, not the Cardinal-Infante, nor even King Philip. Philippa most resembled her paternal uncle, and like the unlamented Infante Carlos, she was slow of mind.

Moraíma, who refused to see Philippa's limitations, commented on the girl's innate shyness. After they returned to the *estrado*, she asked, "Now, what do you think of my daughter?"

"Her likeness to the Habsburgs is uncanny."

"That is why I have come to Madrid, to ask you to do for my daughter what you did for yours. Present her at Court. Once Philip sees my Philippa he will . . ."

"Vicente," Pablo interrupted, "tell her it is impossible."

"I am not mad, as my brother believes and probably told you. I must arrange for Philippa's future."

"Leave Spain, go even farther north where fair blondes are as common as grains of sand."

"Leave Spain for northern lands colder than Catalonia? Even you who should leave, Vicente, even you have not yet taken that step. Now, I ask you again. How do we present Philippa at Court, and when? It must be soon. We have so little time."

"My success on your behalf depends upon others. I must think about the best way to approach them."

"That is all I ask."

Vicente took out his mother's cross. "You said I would have three great loves, and so I have. You, María, and Brianda, my daughter. Perhaps you can see more of my future."

"What is it you want to know?"

He pressed the cross into her hand. "Influential men are backing me to succeed Sotomayor as Inquisitor General. Will that come to pass? Can you see anything like that in my future?"

She closed her eyes and frowned. "It is a near thing. It depends upon the outcome of important events and the actions of others. Nothing you can do will affect it either way. Do you want to be Inquisitor General?"

"I must, if I wish to live the rest of my life in Spain. And, there is more I need to know." Vicente gripped Moraíma's hand. He recited the names he found inside his mother's cross. "What do they mean?"

"Nothing. I see nothing. No. Wait. There is something . . . someone else. Not your daughter. I never saw . . . never spoke of a father's love. There will be another."

Vicente was astounded. Did Moraíma see Catalina as his third love? Impossible. He respected the woman's keen mind, enjoyed fulfilling her physical demands, even felt affection for her. But never love as he had known it with Moraíma and for María.

"Who will I love? When will I meet her?"

"I cannot say. I can see no more." Moraíma opened her eyes and thrust the cross into his lap. "Promise me, Vicente, promise me that you will arrange for Philippa to be presented at Court."

"I will do all I can," he said knowing that he could do absolutely nothing for her.

Chapter 69
A Business Proposal

Vicente and Catalina lay entwined in bed under the sheets. Her mouth and tongue were everywhere. She had made good her promises. She had waxed her facial and body hair for him, and she risked washing frequently.

Vicente made love with Catalina more often than in all the years since his days and nights at el Paraiso. Their liaisons took place during her confession time in a secret, windowless bedroom adjacent to the chapel.

"You are insatiable, Catalina. You should take many more lovers."

"Would you prefer it?"

"If they were guaranteed to be free of *mal frances*."

"Beast. You are, God-willing, my only and last lover. I will share you with no one. What do you think of that?"

"You leave me with no energy to think," he said when she placed him inside her yet another time.

Afterwards, Catalina cuddled against Vicente and toyed with his chest hairs. "My love, if you had to flee Spain . . ."

"Flee Spain? Never."

"Even if it is proven you are not *limpio*?"

"An impossibility."

"Humor me, Vicente. Where would you go, what would you do? Become a merchant?"

"I come from a long line of *caballeros*, soldiers, and landowners. I can never be a merchant. Honor has more value for me than mere money."

"Mere money? God have mercy on you. No wonder some of your supporters see you as a dangerous romantic."

"Then let them find a better man to replace Sotomayor."

She sat unashamed of her nakedness. "Listen to me, Vicente. If it should come to pass that you fail to become Inquisitor General . . ."

"I shall not fail . . ."

". . . and we must flee one day, you would no longer have to be a Dominican. You would be free to marry me."

"Marry?"

"I know your thoughts, Vicente. You do not love me yet. But I know you feel affection for me."

"Then you also know how much I admire your intelligence and wit."

Catalina held his hand. "I have seen how your eyes soften in the presence of children. I am certain a bond would develop between us after we married and had our own offspring. I sometimes hope that you do not succeed Sotomayor. My wealth would be enough for us to live well anywhere in the world."

"What wealth would there be if you must flee?"

"Even my cousin Pedro does not know. What I now confide will prove my complete trust in you. I have sent many ducates to my factors in the United Provinces. My investments have tripled in stock ventures and more than tenfold in tulip futures. In Amsterdam with my financial resources we could become both husband and wife and business partners. Live grandly."

"Tulips? Flowers? And what are futures?"

Catalina explained how she bought and sold shares and traded in paper without ever accepting the goods. "The inflated price of any single tulip bud doubles and trebles by the week, even by the day."

Vicente understood the concept of creating paper fortunes through speculation. "It is unethical and immoral to inflate prices without ever intending to take delivery of the tulips."

"Spoken like a virtuous Catholic cleric."

"Like the sorcerer alchemists, you dream of turning mere paper and flower bulbs into gold."

"Great fortunes are made that way. And you can be part of it with me, Vicente."

"I told you. I can never be a merchant. Not in Spain, not anywhere."

She silenced him with a kiss. "We shall discuss your future another day. In the meantime, since you still fancy yourself a *caballero*, ride me. Ride me hard."

Chapter 70
Bad Eggs

Vicente faced unwanted company on the bench across the table from him while he ate a modest mid-morning meal of coarse bread and soft boiled eggs sweetened with powdered sugar in the ecclesiastic feeding room at the Casa de Tesoro wing of the Alcazar. Inquisitor Juan Adán de la Parra prided himself as having the finest blond mustachio in all Madrid, and Giovanni Malatesta, a Veronese with the pink face of a malignant cherub, was one of the Papal Nuncio's secretaries. These days, Vicente often found himself in the company of the Inquisitor, who watched his every move and listened to each word he spoke.

"Fray Vicente," de la Parra said, "I have heard you performed the Holy Sacrament of Marriage between Cortizos de Villasante's niece and a cousin of Méndez de Silva."

"Yes, at the Cathedral of San Felipe de Real."

"It is said that never has Madrid seen such ostentatious piety. Their oriental display of wealth and luxury in the presence of poor, honest Spaniards. The arrogance, the unjustified pride with which these Portuguese go about Madrid . They aspire not only to equal our *grandees*, they wish to surpass them. These Portuguese are secret Jews, all of them. Like chameleons, they create false lineages and assume old-Christian names like Guzmán, Mendoza, Zúñiga." De la Parra looked meaningfully at Vicente and added, "Méndez and Villanueva. Through their actions, they expose the fiction of their nobility and truth of their origins."

"So I have observed," Malatesta said.

"And they beguile His Majesty away from important affairs of State with the help of Olivares, the second King of Spain. As we all know, these sinful frivolities are caused by the malignant influence of Jews. And always through their writings." De la Parra sneered at Vicente. "A pity the censors have forbidden your play to be performed. *Comedias.* No proper man of the Church would write such drivel."

"Surely, you have not forgotten that the clergy educates through drama, as in the *autos sacramental*, our religious plays. Cervantes died a Franciscan. Góngora and Lope de Vega were priests. You and I, we write poetry. Perhaps one day I too may join my colleagues and gain entry into the Order of Santiago."

"You are indeed presumptuous and arrogant, a characteristic more typical of Jews."

Vicente laughed in his face. "Then perhaps I should take lessons from you, Juan Adán. You must be the greatest spiritual alchemist of all to have changed the virtuous gold of benign humility into the leaden sin of malicious mendacity."

"What was the subject of his play?" Malatesta asked.

"Tarquin and Lucretia. And, I am proud to say, I was responsible for censoring it."

Vicente was not surprised. "It was my only copy. If you return it to me, perhaps I can improve . . ."

"I believe it accidentally fell into the fire." De la Parra forced a yawn. "No great loss to literature, though."

Malatesta tore a piece of bread with the gusto typical of his countrymen. "During my short time in Spain, I have observed that the Portuguese seem to have all the money."

"Their day will come," de la Parra said, "because we know their real identity."

"Jewish dogs," Malatesta growled as if reciting a catechism.

"Padre Giovanni, with all due respect, I believe it is a mistake to call Jews dogs." When the Italian looked at de la Parra in surprise, the Inquisitor said, "Have you not observed, and you especially, Fray Vicente, that Jews share identical characteristics with swine?"

"I suppose that is why Jews are forbidden pork. It would be the same as eating the flesh of their brothers," Vicente said to lighten the conversation.

No one laughed and de la Parra continued, "You see, if someone beats a dog, the other curs either run away, or they attack their fellow mutt. If you throw a stone at a pig, and it grunts, all the other pigs grunt in support. It is the same with Jews. When a Jew is arrested, all the others offer to pay for his release and squeal without surcease until they succeed."

"Yes," Malatesta agreed, "the Jews are for each other wherever they live, and for no one else."

Vicente cried out in agony and gripped his stomach. Priests and friars watched him struggle to his feet. He staggered away from the table and out of the Casa de Tesoro. Courtiers, tradesmen, and gossips milling about the Queen's Patio ceased their activities and gawked at him when he moaned and dropped to his knees.

The pain in his gut was intense, like nothing Vicente had ever experienced. He vomited dark green slime and evacuated a stream of loose, inky bile. He retched and excreted until his guts and bowels felt as if they had been turned inside out with nothing more to give.

"Don Vicente."

He forced open his watery eyes and saw Cardoso kneeling beside him before he fainted.

Cardoso again.

Vicente awakened in bed at Ballebrera's apartment, and the physician forced him to drink a concoction of thick fruit cordial mixed with herbs.

Ballebrera sat beside his bed. "Among the living at last."

Cardoso wiped Vicente's mouth. "He will be all right after a few days rest and proper nourishment. Don Vicente, Dame Fortune adores you. Because I was in the Queen's patio, I was able to see what you passed at both ends and make an instant diagnosis."

"What poison did they give me?" Vicente rasped.

"One of the soft boiled eggs you ate was seasoned with more than sugar. It was powdered arsenic, a typical Italian method of poisoning," Cardoso said. "Olivares has mentioned the attempt on your life to the King. His Majesty is outraged that a murder has been attempted within his own palace, and he has placed Quiñones in charge of the investigation."

Vicente coughed before speaking. "Little good that will do. Undoubtedly, the *alcalde* is also involved."

"I disagree," Cardoso said. "But I will concede this point. If Quiñones suspects Arce and de la Parra were behind it, nothing will come of his investigation. He has told me it is impossible to learn who poisoned your eggs in the kitchen. Coincidentally, Malatesta left for Rome within the hour of your poisoning."

Vicente forced a laugh, which he regretted because of his sore innards. "My enemies must be convinced that my chances to replace Sotomayor are improving."

"They are, which should give comfort to our mutual friends."

Vicente's partisans paid brief visits while he was bedridden. Many women, whom he confessed, came with gifts and sweets. Several ladies brought messages of comfort from the Queen and the Count-Duke. Sotomayor sent a palace priest to inquire about his health.

Catalina prudently waited three days to call on Vicente. After she saw that he had almost recovered, her concern gave way to impatience. "I need to confess, as soon as possible."

Chapter 71
Spain's Bloodiest Sport

Ballebrera used Vicente's arm and a walking stick for support and sat the moment they entered Catalina's *estrado*. They were the first of her guests to arrive.

She had not succumbed to the current female fad for daring décolletage and received them in a modest black dress. She wrinkled her nose at Vicente. "Must you always wear that foul-smelling ointment?"

"It keeps me free of insect bites."

"If I heeded your advice, no one would attend my salons," Catalina said as she fended off night-flying pests with her black silk and ivory fan. "Will this heat never end?"

Everyone in Madrid suffered from the unseasonable October weather, which had brought bad air and fevers, some intermittent, others malignant and fatal. Deaths had increased to epidemic proportions throughout the capital, and Vicente had been summoned all too often to give last rites. Physicians were useless. The epidemic would run its course unchecked.

Recurring fevers and chills weakened Ballebrera. Catalina and Callosa had recovered from their recent bouts with tertian fevers but might suffer relapses at any time. The Royayas also had not been spared. Moraíma and Pablo were bedridden, and Philippa's fair complexion had been marred by fresh insect bites and healing scabs.

Throughout it all, Catalina continued to draw many guests to her salon. She often chose to be the only woman present, a Queen Bee attended by a swarm of men influential in the government and church, playwrights, poets, artists, and members of the knightly Orders, each selected for his charm and wit.

The *estrado* began to fill with Catalina's other guests. She had invited many of Vicente's partisans, both overt and covert. The latter included Juan Pérez de Montalván, priest and Notary of the Holy Office, and great friend and disciple of the late Lope de Vega.

Miguel de Silveyra, a *tabaquero*, brought samples of tobacco and snuff flavored with musk, amber, bergamot, and orange blossom. Vicente relished his occasional smoke from a long-stem clay pipe.

When Méndez lit an enormous rolled Cuban leaf in the shape of a candle, Ballebrera said to Vicente, "How inelegant. It looks as if he is ingesting a turd."

The last to arrive, Cardoso, Cortizos, and Fernández entered the great room together. Fernández had recently published *El Chatálogo Real de España* in honor of Infante Baltazar Carlos' eighth birthday, to which Vicente had contributed sonnets.

They gathered around Cardoso to ask questions about the fever and to compare losses of family and friends to the epidemic. Despite a long list of patients, the physician had found time to write on many subjects. Everyone praised his *Utilidades del Agua y de la Nieva*, a treatise on the medicinal use of water and melted snow, which he had dedicated to the Count-Duke, whose coat-of-arms were engraved on the title page.

Ballebrera could not resist a friendly jibe. "Is it not dangerous to write on the subject of water, Don Fernándo? Fascination with it may lead one to be suspected of impure origins?"

"Every Spaniard appreciates *agua muy rica*. And water is the symbol of purity," Cardoso said. "As the Psalmist writes, 'the pure of hand and heart shall ascend the mount of the Lord.'"

"A pity the Psalmist failed to emphasize the necessity of a washed body for salvation," Ballebrera lamented.

The conversation shifted to the war against France. The stakes were high. The victor would dominate Europe. French armies had taken Landrecy and la Chapelle, swept through Luxembourg and the Franche-Comte, and came close to annihilating a Spanish army invading the south of France. Richelieu's persevering ally, Saxe-Weimar, who escaped capture at Nördlingen, occupied Alsace. The French navy had seized the islands of St. Marguerite and St. Honoré.

"Victory or defeat in specific battles means little to poverty-stricken idle Spain," Montalván said. He looked at a great gold, jeweled encrusted crucifix hanging from a central place on the *estrado* wall. "Our Holy Mother Church has not been spared either. The Count-Duke is appropriating the ecclesiastic revenues of Toledo and other cities."

Cortizos lit his pipe. "Olivares has tried every known scheme to raise more money and invented others. Only peace can save us. The Crown is unable to finance its armies."

Vicente added what he knew about the royal finances to Cortizos' bleak assessment. "And this very day, His Majesty wrote the Cardinal-Infante that Spain is bankrupt. His Eminence would have taken Paris last year if the Prince of Orange had not attacked his exposed rear with an army of thirty thousand."

Silveyra sniffed bergamot snuff and sneezed. "What will happen in Flanders?"

"In his letter, King Philip advised the Cardinal-Infante to dress his household in plain cloth and live frugally on beef and mutton, with an occasional fowl or partridge."

"While Buen Retiro glitters," Montalván moralized.

Catalina experimented with a long rolled leaf of tobacco, coughed, and waited for her eyes to stop watering.

"What is the subject for tonight's *juego*, most illustrious muse of muses?" Méndez called out to her.

"I am undecided, but the prize is a gold laurel wreath."

Vicente never ceased to be amazed how literature and poetry obsessed Spaniards of all classes. Competitions were held in the smallest, most remote villages. Philip himself presided over the Palace Academy. Rich and influential *grandees* and ladies of intelligence and charm like Catalina held sway in their respective salons. After the participants read their most recent compositions, they belittled their rivals' efforts and abilities and dueled in literary jousts with verbal thrusts and parries of impromptu verse and song.

Ballebrera forced an exaggerated sigh. "Not the hunt, not the *corrida,* not the procession of penitentes, not even the *quemadero* . . . without question the destruction of literary reputations is our most violent blood sport."

"Of course it is," Vicente said. "Everyone in Spain believes himself to be the greatest poet who has lived, is living, or ever will live. As many of you can attest, the most notable is unable to survive by pen alone. Without a generous patron, without income from a benefice or sinecure, all creative men must in the end demean themselves. Thus perishes their honor."

Méndez said, "That is because all writers prefer fame to honor and loyalty. To receive praise for a mot or elaborate phrase is more desirable than keeping one's word or performing some noble deed."

"Alas, poor Spain." Ballebrera smiled. "Populated only by shallow poetasters and versifiers, each eternally seeking a rhyme."

"And a publisher," Fernández added.

"But can anyone understand their intended meaning?" Catalina asked. "They ignore all rules of style. Their bombast is mixed with irrelevant Greek words and confused Latinisms. They place the noun miles away from its adjective, and the subject ten lines apart from its verb."

"Perhaps Vicente can tell us their meaning," Fernández suggested. "Is he not Olivares' most valuable master of ciphers?"

"Even I cannot decipher complete chaos. Is it so difficult to write I love you clearly and simply?"

"What? And lose one's reputation?" Ballebrera bowed towards Fernández. "Did not our friend here deliberately write an absolutely meaningless sonnet which was published and acclaimed?"

"And which has since convinced me that I am indeed a very deep and brilliant man."

"Spain would prosper more if Crown and Church would forget about purity of blood and instead establish a *limpieza de lingua* before our pure Castilian tongue is destroyed," Méndez said.

"Perhaps satire is the cure," Callosa offered.

"Parody and satire are insufficient medicines to rid Spain of its rhyming pestilence," Ballebrera said. "Poetasters and versifiers see only their rivals as the subjects of ridicule, never themselves. They continue to flaunt their meaningless metaphors, preposterous parallels, and absurd allusions, and tear at each other's reputations like rats in a sack."

Vicente puffed on his pipe. "Perhaps I should advise the Count-Duke to draw new laws to regulate poets,"

"With wording such as this," Méndez said and continued sonorously, "Know that being aware of the great confusion and damage which have up to now beset those who make our rhymes and verses and the excessive number of those, who without fear of God and their own consciences, compose, write, and make verses by stealing and plundering the styles, ideas, and manner of writing of their elders, not to mention adapting *centos* borrowed from other people and committing all sorts of frauds and trickeries in their verses . . ."

Ballebrera raised his arm in a Roman salute after Méndez ran out of breath. "Hail Bombastus Prolixus."

"My turn," Catalina said over her guests' laughter. "Being desirous of remedying this state of things, those present command and ordain . . ." Catalina thought for a moment. "What shall we ordain?"

"Let each of us take turns, and I will go first," Ballebrera said. "Obviously, from this night, all poets must write in Castilian, without introducing words from foreign languages."

Fernández spoke next. "Those who introduce extravagant statements and hyperboles in their verses shall be deprived of their status as poets, and, in the case of repetition of the offense, shall have all their verses confiscated."

Montalván continued the satire, "The oldest poets must assume the task of giving alms in the form of sonnets, songs, roundelays, ballads, and all other verse to inferior poets, and collect from the streets all those who have lost their senses through reading *The Solitudes* by Don Luís Góngora."

Silveyra relit his pipe and added to the decree, "Poetry in the Moorish style shall be baptized within forty days on pain of being exiled from the kingdom."

Cortizos passed his turn to Vicente who said, "Each poet who enters the service of a grand señor may be justly allowed to die of hunger."

"Nor should any poet be so bold as to speak ill of his fellows more than twice a week," Callosa decreed.

"Enough. Please." Catalina wiped her eyes after she recovered from her fit of laughter. "It is time for our *juego*."

She summoned servants to rearrange the chairs. Her *mayordomo* called everyone in the *estrado* to attend her and Callosa in a manner mocking Court ritual. As hosts, they sat on throne chairs facing their guests, who were given ribbons of green to honor the two passionate defenders of the color, Cardoso and Fernández. Both brilliant men could be as trivial and góngorically sulfurous as any poetasting dilettante in Madrid.

Catalina pointed her fan at Vicente. "Shall this evening's question be which of the senses is most important? Or, shall we decide when is vice a virtue and virtue a vice in matters of love? Or still yet, which is the greater? Love between man and woman, or man and money?"

Vicente bowed towards her. "Let our own muse inspire the course of our poetry."

That was what she expected to hear. Catalina clapped her hands, and a servant brought her a guitar. She plucked a tune, and sang extempore:

> "Is it better to believe sweet lies
> offered by a faithless lover;
> than one cold awful moment discover
> bitter truth revealed by surprise?"

After acknowledging her guests' applause and shouts of *brava*, she passed her guitar to Vicente for him to offer the first response. He sang without hesitation:

"Pain caused by virtuous veracity
cannot be overcome and mended;
but happily never-ended
is the deceit of sustained mendacity."

"How wicked of you," Catalina said over the approval of her guests. She took back her guitar and countered:

"Is Aphrodite, of perfect beauty,
the goddess you choose to honor?
asks the Muse of her loyal troubadour,
Or to Athena's wisdom do you offer fealty?"

Instead of applause, silence filled the room. Callosa had gone into convulsions.

Cardoso hurried to the young noble and touched his forehead. The physician's diagnosis stunned all. "Fever, malignant."

Chapter 72
Bad Air

Death everywhere.

Callosa succumbed a few days after collapsing at Catalina's salon. The great fever continued to ravage Madrid, and December was a month of devastating losses for Vicente. In the Royayas' small bare *estrado*, he closed little Philippa's eyes forever and covered her emaciated body with a sheet. Pablo, great friend of his childhood, barely survived and had begun a slow recovery.

Vicente went to Moraíma who slept peacefully because of the potion he had given her. She was pallid and wasting away with circles around her eyes as black as her hair. She would not last the night. He kept vigil at her side and blocked her line of vision to Philippa's corpse should she open her eyes. He relived their glorious night on a bed of orange blossoms, his first sight of *la Hermosura* dancing at el Paraíso, and her sweet voice. Memories and dreams, those had become his realities of choice.

Moraíma awakened in pain. "My Philippa, has she improved?"

Vicente prepared a new mix of opiates for her to drink. "She no longer suffers from fever. She sleeps peacefully."

"God is merciful." Moraíma attempted to move but was too weak. "I must see her, hold her."

"Let her be. She needs rest to recover her strength."

Moraíma sank deeper into her pillow. "Yes, you are right. Have I much time?"

"Only God knows."

"And Pablo?"

"He sleeps."

"Ay, Vicente, a terrible end to our lives. We were born to suffer."

"And to know joy. We have shared moments of earthly paradise. You have loved and been loved by a King, and I have had adventures I never dreamed possible."

"Yes, you are well placed at Court. My Philippa . . . you will be her guardian . . . present my daughter to her father . . . get him to acknowledge her. You promised."

Vicente placed the opiate to her lips. "Drink, drink deeply, my *encantadora*."

"Some enchantress I must be in my condition."

"You will always be *la Hermosura*. The most beautiful of all women." He wiped her chin.

"Yes, Vicente, it has been a great adventure." She gripped his robe. "But I'm afraid."

"Death is a threshold we all must cross."

"Not death. It's afterwards. Will I spend eternity in Allah's paradise, or face the eternal damnation preached by such as you?"

"No, Moraíma, God will summon you to sing your songs with a choir of angels."

She never heard him.

Pablo awakened when Vicente came to his bedside. "My sister is dead?"

"Yes."

"Better if I had joined her. My wife and children burned to death by Jacinto, my sister and niece gone. I have nothing to live for."

"You are young enough to begin a new family."

"So they may die as well?"

"There is always vengeance."

Pablo sat up with sudden energy while he listened to Vicente's plan to destroy Jacinto and his specific role. "A brilliant scheme, my friend and better than any medicine you could have given me."

After they buried Moraíma and Philippa, Vicente ricocheted from grieving to grieving. Catalina took to her bed, ill from more than fever. She was exhausted dealing with Callosa's relations: Bustamantes, Faxardos, Riquelmes, and countless other strangers from Murcia who, with their lawyers, laid claim to her estate according to their interpretations of centuries old *mayorazgos*.

She lapsed into delirium after receiving devastating news from her factors in Amsterdam. The tulip market had collapsed and her other stocks were worthless, all of which reinforced Vicente's belief that paper speculation was unethical and dangerous.

Catalina never regained consciousness. Vicente gave her a pro forma Holy Sacrament of Last Rites and recited, as he knew she would have wanted, *la Samia*, the same last words Don Lope had uttered. Only then, did he realize how much he had lost: A good friend, a stimulating conversationalist, and a passionate lover.

The epidemic of fever continued, and Ballebrera was bedridden. Once a broad-shouldered bull of a man, he lay shrunken under his hábito of Alcántara, which he wore over his bedclothes. His great mustachio drooped and merged with his untrimmed gray beard.

During the months while Ballebrera declined, Vicente was overworked as preacher and sought after as a fashionable confessor, all too often giving last rites, while serving Olivares as spy, courier, and code master and Sotomayor as best he could.

As Moraíma predicted, Vicente's acceptance into the Holy Order and rise to be head of *la Suprema* continued to be delayed by events even beyond the control of the men who could make him Inquisitor General. The fickle fortunes of war, the domestic political situation, and Philip's unpredictable conscience overwhelmed Olivares, even though he was still the most powerful man in Spain.

The King was furious with the Count-Duke for allowing Sotomayor to harangue him and interfere with his carnal pleasures, specifically those regarding a beautiful novice nun. Relations between His Majesty and Olivares further worsened when Isabel, not the Inquisitor General, stirred Philip's conscience and reawakened his inconsistent paternal feelings. She gave birth to their second healthy child, a girl baptized María Teresa.

After the arrival of the new Infanta, the King rode the great swing of his emotional pendulum from lustful obsession to extreme morality, prudery, and an ostentatious piety worthy of a Portuguese new-Christian.

Influenced by Isabel, he castigated the Count-Duke for leading him astray at San Plácido and in front of courtiers blamed him for permitting the intolerable insult of French armies invading and occupying Spanish soil.

Continuing to suffer from gout and headaches, the Count-Duke gained weight to the point where he could not mount a horse. As always, he went from days of inertia to periods of intense activity when he worked through the night, but his state of mind became more unpredictable. In what Vicente thought to be a great error of judgment, Olivares summoned Quevedo from exile to propagandize for him.

Vicente's prescience was born out several weeks later when he carried a package into Olivares' offices. The Count-Duke sat at his desk surrounded by his most trusted advisers, the *sinagoga*, as they were derided by his foes: Villanueva; the Count-Duke's indispensable personal secretaries, José González, António Carnero and Jerónimo de Lezama; the Protonotarios of Flanders and Italy; and the Secretary to the Junta de Ejecución, and his confessor, Hernándo de Salazar.

"You bring us good news, Friar?"

"Interesting news, Excellency, and bad news."

"Let us hear the interesting news first, for perhaps favorable events will overtake the bad."

"We have received a coded message from one of our spies in Paris. His Majesty's sister, Anne, Queen of France, has given birth to a healthy male heir."

Olivares raised his great eyebrows in surprise. "How is it possible? Everyone knows that Anne and Louis have not shared the same bed for more than thirteen years. But, continue your astonishing fable, Friar."

"It seems that on the fifth of December of last year, the King of France paid a visit to his mistress, Louise de la Fayette, at the Convent of the Visitation. Afterwards bad weather prevented him from proceeding to St. Maur. He had no choice but to spend the night instead at his Louvre Palace. Because Louis had not been expected, his suites were not prepared. Queen Anne, who was in residence at her apartments in the palace, presumably invited him to stay with her. A warm meal, a fireplace, some heady wine . . . and nine months later . . . *voila*. An heir."

"A pretty tale, Friar, but I would wager my entire fortune the infant may look more natural wearing a biretta than the crown of France."

Every man present understood the Count-Duke's reference to the Queen's rumored lover, Cardinal Mazarin, as the probable father. Over their laughter and ribald comments, Olivares said, "And now, Friar, what is it you have so carefully wrapped? Another rare manuscript for me?"

Vicente handed Olivares his package. "I wish it were, Excellency. Unfortunately, it is my bad news. Quevedo's latest calumny."

He had read the manuscript. Disillusioned by more than Olivares' dictatorial rule, the satirist believed the Count-Duke had betrayed the True Faith, corrupted traditional values, and tarnished Castile's glory with flawed, immoral policies.

The title of Quevedo's savage attack against Olivares was *La Isla de Los Monopantos*. He had named the governor of the island Pragas Chincollos, an obvious reference the Count-Duke's converso ancestor, Lope Conchillos, secretary to Emperor Charles V. He also had used his barbed pen to condemn Olivares' reliance on sycophantic ministers, incompetent venal relatives, and Jews in the guise of new-Christians, who prospered as Castile grew poorer.

The Count-Duke read the pages aloud and cursed after each devastating sentence. Tension permeated the room. All knew that Olivares dreaded and forbade any public reference to his own alleged partial-Jewish origins. And there it was in print. Written by Spain's greatest savage wit. For all his enemies to read.

And theirs.

With a deliberate lack of subtlety in his satire, Quevedo's asserted that Jews held all the important offices in Spain.

Olivares threw the manuscript across the room "If I cannot have his head, I will forever rusticate the treasonous swine."

That evening Cardoso arrived at Ballebrera's apartments to examine him at Vicente's request. "Is it true Quevedo has been exiled to his home in San Juan Abad?"

"Yes, but the Count-Duke has been unable to prevent copies of the satire from being distributed throughout Court and capital."

"And the breach between His Majesty and the Count-Duke?"

"Mended for the time being." He did not think it prudent to tell the physician that the King was again bedding the beautiful novice nun.

Cardoso did not fully understand Vicente's response. "If all is well between the King and his *privado*, we should press ahead more aggressively for them to remove Sotomayor."

"Be cautious. Because Olivares is relentlessly attacked by the reactionaries, His Majesty could very well try to appease them by selecting Arce, de la Parra, or Tomás."

"God forbid."

"Is there nothing more you can do for Ramón?"

"Give him raw eggs in wine and plenty of water. Always plenty of water. If he does not . . ."

He choked on the words. "I know. Last rites."

Vicente watched over Ballebrera until he awakened in the middle of the night. He gave Ramón the wine and eggs Cardoso prescribed. Ballebrera swallowed with difficulty and motioned for Vicente to come nearer.

"Jerónimo, he still lives?"

"I have heard nothing to the contrary."

"May he survive his own recurring fevers in Orihuela and outlive Jacinto. You helped win him his title. Honor was satisfied." Ballebrera gripped Vicente's hand. "I must confess . . . confess what I never told you about your parents."

"My parents? What about them?"

"More wine. No eggs." Ballebrera drank and the Rioja gave him the strength to continue. "Your father . . . he went to Roquemaure in 1598, after the peace with France."

"And he married my mother in Catalonia on his way back to Valencia."

"No, not in Catalonia . . . married in Roquemaure."

Vicente resisted seizing Ballebrera's shoulders. "Why did you not tell me sooner?"

"What he learned in Roquemaure changed him drastically."

"What did my father learn?"

"He spoke of it only once . . . to Jerónimo's father . . . and mine . . . severed family connections." Ballebrera's voice became a faint whisper. "Answers in Roquemaure . . . what day is it?"

"Tuesday, not yet sunrise."

"Where?"

"Your bed. We were speaking of my parents."

"Jerónimo . . . he will be Señor de Ballebrera . . . the *mayorazgo* . . . should be yours . . ."

"You must tell me more about my parents and Roquemaure."

"Dreamed I was a youth again at the Moorish baths ... my loves. Fair Yolanda . . . dead so young. Beautiful Alfonsito, and my gorgeous Miguel, so perfectly formed. Axa, my lovely *morilla*, to bathe again with you in *agua muy dulce*." Coughing bought Ballebrera a moment of reality. "Give me the Holy Sacrament of Last Rites."

Vicente absolved him of all sins in the Name of the Father, Son, and Holy Spirit. "About my mother . . ."

Alta y delgada	Tall and slender
blanca salada	fair and charming
pensado en ti	thinking of thee
me muero de amores	am dying of love
desde que te ví.	since I saw thee.
Ai, busco	Oh, I search
a la blanca salada	for the fair charming one.

"Ramón, my friend . . ."

"Farewell, Vicente. And so I die to the tune of a bad air," Ballebrera punned with his last breath.

Chapter 73
Disintegration

Forgive me, Don Fernándo, for deserting you.

Vicente's bleak mood matched the gloomy dark afternoon in Buen Retiro's Hall of Realms. He stood before Velázquez' painting celebrating the Cardinal-Infante's victory at Nördlingen. Weakened from long hours given to administrative detail and physical exertion in the field, the Cardinal-Infante had sickened and died of fever in Flanders the previous year, too young at thirty-two years of age.

Vicente was still no closer to becoming Inquisitor General. While Philip fornicated and both Olivares and Sotomayor clung to power, he observed events with serene detachment as the Spanish Empire teetered on the precipice of complete disintegration.

Resentful of Castile's dominance and Olivares' punitive taxes, the Catalans revolted and pledged allegiance to Louis XIII of France. Inspired by the Catalans and encouraged by the French, the Archbishop of Lisbon and a party of nobles elected Duke Juan de Braganza King of Portugal, João IV de Bragança in their language, and declared independence from Spain. King João then encouraged Olivares' cousin, Gaspar Pérez de Guzmán, Ninth Duke of Medina-Sidonia and the grandest *grandee* in all Spain, to establish an independent Andalusian kingdom in alliance with Portugal. The brother of Portugal's Queen Luísa, Medina-Sidonia headed the senior branch of Olivares' family, and all of Andalusia acknowledged him and not Philip as their true ruler.

Olivares' enemies expected him to fall at any moment. Some believed he was mad because he had made his twenty-eight-year old bastard, Enríque Felipe de Guzmán, his principal heir and thus alienated each grasping cousin, brother-in-law, and nephew he had raised to high office. Fearing he would be removed as Inquisitor General if Olivares fell from power, Sotomayor also tried to ingratiate himself with the Queen. Still, the old man would not name a successor.

The reactionaries gained influence and power. They blamed the loss of Portugal and Catalonia on all Portuguese living in Spain, ending each sermon with the same inflammatory condemnations and admonitions: "Portuguese and Jews are one and the same. Santiago will not deliver Castile until the last of His Majesty's Portuguese advisors are driven from Court."

Vicente saw many strangers at Buen Retiro and the Alcazar. Some were sly, others hard and pitiless. Jacinto and several Anglesolas lurked about Madrid as well. Alert to assassination, Vicente prudently wore armor and carried daggers under his robe.

Like Olivares, he also had lost many supporters. Fernández de Villareal, the best of them all, left Spain to support his friend, King João. After Philip elevated Méndez de Silva to the Royal Council and Cardoso to the position of Royal Physician, they became the King's men and Olivaristas no longer.

Then the Count-Duke surprised everyone by crushing the rebellion in Andalusia. Medina-Sidonia was exiled and his great wealth confiscated by the Crown. Although Olivares regained his influence over Philip yet another time, events and his own decisions conspired against him.

Isabel at last persuaded Philip to lead Spain's armies. Fearful of leaving the king alone and under the influence of others, the Count-Duke decided to accompany His Majesty to war. He also convinced Philip to require every *grandee* and important titled nobleman to join the royal entourage, thus removing his most powerful enemies from the capital for the duration of their absence.

Vicente thought that would have been a brilliant move if Olivares had not placed his brother-in-law, the Count of Castrillo and *Mayordomo Mayor* of the Palace, as head of the government. Castrillo had been the most resentful of all when the Count-Duke made his own bastard son principal heir.

Olivares ordered Vicente to remain in Madrid and send him coded messages. Vicente's reports of Castrillo's actions should have been sufficient cause for the Count-Duke to remove his brother-in-law from power. Castrillo made a great show of accepting the Queen's advice at Council meetings and praised her courage and wisdom in front of the Court at every opportunity. He understood what the Count-Duke would not and what Vicente believed to be Olivares' greatest blunder of all: Isabel had become the real ruler of Spain.

With Philip and Olivares in the field, the war continued to go badly for Spain. The French took Perpignan in September, and the entire province of Roussillon became theirs for all time. Monzón, Aragón's ancient capital, fell next. Subsequent reports from the battlefield could not be kept secret. Spanish generals quarreled. Unpaid, ill-fed soldiers deserted by the thousands. Philip blamed Olivares for the defeats and distanced himself from the Count-Duke. After Lérida fell to the French, the humiliated King decided to return to Madrid.

Murmuraciónes swept through Court and capital that the Count-Duke was finished and Sotomayor would be replaced as Inquisitor General. Although a few loyal Olivaristas clung to the slim hope that the Count-Duke could regain His Majesty's confidence, like proverbial rats, the rest deserted his Ship of State.

Vicente's supporters now w shut him out of their homes and lives. They attended Isabel and Castrillo or attached themselves to other households of powerful *grandees* and officials who hated Olivares. Cardoso became Quiñones' appendage. Whenever Vicente encountered his erstwhile partisans and friends in the courtyards and corridors of the Alcazar, they avoided from him.

By the time Philip and Olivares returned from the war at year's end, the Count-Duke's offices no longer bustled with councilors, *títulos*, greedy relations, secretaries, and supplicants. Only a few grim men worked at their desks.

Olivares was attended only by Villanueva, Carnero, and Salazar when Vicente came to pay his respects. Wrapped in a black cloak, the fifty-five year old Count-Duke slouched in his chair next to a brazier, eyes vacant, and mouth flaccid. For more than two decades he had been the greatest man in Spain and the principal actor on the European stage along with his antagonist, Cardinal Richelieu. Gone were Olivares' *hidalgo* pride, sense of Spanish honor, and boundless energy. He appeared older than his years, bent and shrunken, a deflated bladder.

"Tragic, so very disappointing," Olivares commented to no one in particular. "In spite of the large armies we assembled, His Majesty did not return from Aragón with the glory we all expected. But without Richelieu to guide France, we shall yet reverse our fortunes. The King is still dependent upon my advice and guidance."

Vicente told him what the others would not. "Excellency, you should know that the most powerful nobles oppose you. The Dukes of Infantado, Medinacelli, Híjar, and Osuna. The Counts of Lemos, Paredes, and your own kinsmen the Haros."

"No, never the Haros. The others, though . . . yes, you are correct, Friar . . . they smell my blood, but I shall prevail over the Queen. My epitaph must not read that I was thwarted by a mere woman."

The Count-Duke had again underestimated Isabel's intelligence and determination. At this very moment, the Queen was conferring alone with Philip. She continued to do so well into the night. Because no one was privy to their discussion and decisions, rumors ran the gamut from Olivares' dismissal and arrest to his regaining the King's favor.

Chapter 74
A Dantean End

During that same evening, Vicente received interesting news from Genoa where the Dominican Provincials had convened. Tomás de Rocamora would have been elected Master General of the Order if Pope Urban VIII had not intervened and used his influence to ensure that Miguel de Mazarin, a cousin of the French Cardinal, became *Maestro del Sacro Palacio*. He mused over Tomás' near success while he walked along the silent archways of the King's patio after matins. Deep in thought, he failed to notice that torches had been snuffed and no guards stood at their regular stations.

In the dark corridor outside María's former apartments, Vicente passed a hooded Dominican. Too late, he realized the false friar wore boots and spurs, not sandals. A blow to Vicente's back pushed him into a stone arch. The *matone* cursed in the Valencian idiom and stared at his broken blade, which had snapped at contact with the armor under his intended victim's robe. Recovering quickly, Vicente pulled out a pair of daggers and chased after his assailant. Boots were faster than sandals. The *matone* ran to his mount in the Queen's patio where a second horseman fired a pistol at Vicente and missed.

Before they rode away, Vicente recognized the second man, whose prominent scar ran from mouth to ear. He could put if off no longer. The time had come to avenge Yusef, Koitalel, and Jacinto's murder of Xímena that had prevented Ballebrera from becoming Duke of Astórquia.

Vicente could not begin to guess how and why such monsters posing as humans were born. Don Lope might have had the answer.

Many times, Vicente had imagined how he would take his revenge against Jacinto. In his youth, it would have been *mano a mano* with sword, dagger, whip, or pistol. As he matured, he decided that a duel with those weapons would make the swine's death too easy and swift. Jacinto was a coward, cunning and dangerous, but no match for him. Vicente then began to create in his mind tortures worse than those he had seen in the chambers of the Inquisition and read in Dante's *Inferno*. He had considered taking Jacinto to a secluded house and applying the most horrible of Quiñones devices or giving him his own *quemadero*, a slow roasting while impaled on a spit. Only during the past year had he come to an inspired decision, for which part of his wealth had been used to good effect. Pablo had been reporting Jacinto's routine, and this night, Rafal's eldest son would pay fittingly for all his vile crimes with usurious interest.

Vicente darkened some of his teeth with black wax and added a long scar, similar to what he recalled of Fray Bernardo's, running from the top of his forehead to his jaw through an eye he covered with a leather patch. Then he donned the clothing of a *matone*, adding a brace of pistols, sword, daggers, and whip.

He rode first to an appointed rendezvous in the Prado where he met with Pablo and quartet from Yusef's old band. Although the men had survived Jacinto's fire, each had been disfigured. He also had hired a trio of *golondreros*.

"Pablo, has everyone gathered at the villa?"

"Yes, my friend."

"Then let us make haste. But remember, Jacinto must be taken alive."

Vicente led them to the *garito* where Jacinto and his henchmen preferred to drink, gamble, and whore. They entered individually and in pairs, mingled with the rowdy patrons and women, and selected the best tactical positions for their attack.

Vicente recognized the man who had attempted to murder him at the Alcazar playing knucklebones. "Pablo, that one is mine."

"I do not see Jacinto."

"He is probably abusing some unfortunate girl or pretty boy in one of the back rooms." Shrill screams pierced the din. "Yes, the swine is there. Now, let us do this swiftly."

Rocamora

Vicente stood behind his quarry and signaled. The Valencians and *golondreros* dispatched Jacinto's men with their daggers, and he slit the *matone's* throat.

Vicente reassured the whores and other patrons that no one else would be harmed and ordered his men to guard the door and windows. With Pablo and two Valencians, he burst into the back room where Jacinto was dripping hot wax on the breasts and genitalia of a young girl he had tied to a bed.

Vicente swooped on him like an avenging angel and with one blow knocked him unconscious.

"Truss him. We will take this poor child with us."

Vicente wrapped the girl in a blanket, lifted her onto his horse, and led his band and their prisoner to the villa he had purchased as a disguised Señor de Somebody. Several dozen men, women, and children welcomed them. Each carried mementos from Jacinto: burns, scars from his whips, breasts cut off, castration, and other deliberate mutilations. Vicente had collected as many victims as he could find and kin of those the creature had murdered. He deeded the villa to the Valencians to use as a hospital and sanctuary for Jacinto's victims.

They stared at Jacinto with hatred, palpable feral hatred. By now, Rafal's son had regained consciousness. His eyes expressed fear, justifiably so.

"Do you know who I am, dog?" Vicente said.

"A *matone* hired by my enemies. But listen to me. I can pay much more than your employer."

"Oh, you shall pay, Jacinto, pay for all your crimes. Yusef, Koitalel, Doña Xímena . . . and all the others."

"You, Vicente?"

"Yes, and Pablo too. You shall die knowing that you failed to murder me, die knowing that you shall pay for all your sins without absolution. No last rites for you. If there is no hell for criminals like you, then also know that I have created this hell on earth for you." Vicente turned to Pablo and Jacinto's victims. "Take your time. Whatever you do, take your time with him."

Pablo embraced Vicente. "After we finish with the swine, come with me, and return to the Fragrant Coast."

"No, old friend. I have made an irrevocable decision. To become a physician, I must leave Spain forever. *Adios.*"

Vicente left the villa satisfied when he heard the first of what he expected to be many prolonged screams.

Chapter 75
Exeunt Vicente

Vicente received an unexpected summons to appear before the Queen. Still wearing armor and daggers under his robe, he passed through a gauntlet of pages, flirtatious ladies, scheming courtiers, and hostile clerics all milling about her outer rooms. Attended only by an elderly, hard-of-hearing *título* and an ancient duenna, Isabel sat on a gilded throne-chair between lit braziers atop a carpeted dais decorated in vermilion and gold silks and damask. Under a fur-lined black cape, she wore a plain black velvet dress to symbolize her mourning over the evils suffered by unfortunate Spain as a result of the Count-Duke's policies. The thirty-nine year old Queen's aura glowed more brilliantly than King Philip's pallid monolithic presence ever had. Purposeful energy removed removed years from her attractive features. Her dark eyes were bright and alert. Restricted by Court *punctilio* from the day she married Philip in 1615 and thwarted by Olivares' relentless misogyny and dominance over her husband, she was no longer the giggling mischievous Queen.

Isabel beckoned him to come closer. "Don Vicente, we have had little contact these past years."

"My duties, Your Majesty, and to my regret."

"And your aspirations. We have been aware of attempts to make you our son's confessor, as a first step to your becoming Inquisitor General of all Spain."

"Alas, this humble friar has been but a servant to the ambitions of others."

"We have always appreciated the vulnerability of your position."

"Thank you, Your Majesty."

"And certain palace schemers believe your Queen also can be used as their cat's paw to power. They forget we are the daughter of Henry IV and the Medicis."

"I have never underestimated Your Majesty."

"We know." Isabel removed several sheets of paper from the folds of her guardinfante. "These are pages from letters sent by Her Imperial Majesty, Empress Doña María." The Queen paused to watch his reaction. "She writes that she remembers you fondly."

Although Vicente could not slow his heartbeat, he used all his acting skills to say in a detached tone, "And I cherish my memories of Her Imperial Majesty. She is well, I trust."

"Yes, she is well. The Empress has often suggested that we use our influence to make you Inquisitor General of all Spain."

He knew better than to ask the Queen if she would permit him to read María's letters. He spoke without revealing the powerful emotions he felt, "When she was still Infanta of Spain, Her Imperial Majesty often expressed her wish for me to be her Torquemada."

"Yes, she confided the same to us when we were young." Isabel's eyes softened. "We always looked back with some amusement at the Prince of Wales' clumsy courtship." She crossed herself. "May God protect King Charles and our sister Queen Henrietta María, and ensure they prevail against their treasonous Parliament."

Vicente also crossed himself. "Amen."

"Over the years, we intercepted the letters of condolence and congratulations that you attempted to send the Empress. Cleverly phrased, Friar, but to a subtle mind, shall we say they reveal a certain depth of feeling?" Vicente did not insult the Queen's intelligence with a protest, and she continued, "We do not want any chronicler or vile *mumurador* to suggest you may have been her Mazarin."

"Nor have I given them any reason to."

Isabel set each page afire in the brazier to her right as she spoke. "We were so close when we were young, like sisters. We pray her daughter will be exactly like Doña María, for Infanta María Anna will marry our son."

"My sincere wish as well." Vicente watched each page brown, curl, and blacken into ashes. *What had she written?*

"But you shall never be her confessor. We cannot permit it. Have you asked yourself why we have kept you at a distance all these years? Why we never requested you to be our son's spiritual director?"

"I have, Your Majesty. May I presume to ask why?"

"The choice was not ours because . . ." She leaned forward and continued softly, less regal, ". . . because His Majesty envied you for being closer than he could ever be to his own sister. He has resented you since that day in Velázquez' studio when Doña María smiled for you alone, a smile any *galanteo* would have died for. Can you imagine what His Majesty would have done had we selected you to be our confessor and spiritual director after she left Madrid?"

Vicente had never considered the possibility that the world's greatest monarch could envy a mere Dominican friar. He had come to believe that Philip barely acknowledged his existence because His Majesty considered him too inconsequential. Instead, he had the distinct and unwanted honor to be the Planet King's significant object of dislike.

"His Majesty also was jealous of your friendship with the Cardinal-Infante."

"Was the Count-Duke aware of His Majesty's prejudices against me?"

She dropped the final page of María's letter into the brazier. "Of course he was. That is why Olivares never moved to have you replace Sotomayor. Nor did he ever intend to." Isabel shook her fan at Vicente. "You should have gone on to serve the Cardinal-Infante in the Netherlands. He might still be alive if you had been there to ease his burdens with your talents and friendship."

"That sin lies heavily on my heart."

"It was and is a mistake for you to not to leave Spain. We summoned you to convince you of that reality, Inquisitor de la Parra has stationed men at each of the tower gates leading from the city to identify you for assassins. Arce has alerted Familiars in Castile, León, and Vizcaya, should you take that well traveled new-Christian land route to France. Tomás de Rocamora has his men waiting to imprison you in some desolate monastery should you pass through Aragón. You must leave Madrid. All Spanish soil. At once."

Shaken by the Queen's revelations, Vicente spoke from his heart. "Your Majesty has advised me to flee Spain. I am a Spaniard. For what bleak country shall I leave our sweet land of cypress and palms, the fragrant coast?"

"Then stay and die a Spaniard. We have done all we can for you, Friar." Isabel glanced at the ashes in the brazier. "And for her."

Vicente also looked one last time at the charred remains of María's letters. His heart overflowed with pride and love for his beloved *Alteza* because he knew that she would always remember him and, he presumed to hope, in her deepest heart of hearts reciprocate all he felt for her.

The twenty-third of January, 1643, was a perfect day to disappear from *la Corte* and Madrid. Despite the foul weather, the streets overflowed with rabble. Yokels and riffraff poured into the capital from the countryside. Cathedral and church bells rang to celebrate Olivares' fall from power and rustication to one of his estates.

No one paid attention to yet another ragged filthy old hunchback crone, lame of foot, with twisted features, hairy wens, and black gaps between discolored teeth. Vicente used a crooked stick and foul language as he pushed through the rowdy crowd. He bore the heavy weight of a hollow hump on his back filled with gold escudos and the precious gifts he had received from María so very long ago.

Although eager to escape his enemies, he tarried to watch a triumphal procession led by Philip, Isabel, Infante Baltazar Carlos, and the Duchess of Mantua. Their destination was the convent Church of the Barefoot Carmelites to give thanks and prayers for a new and glorious day. Satan had been defeated.

Castrillo and other relations of Olivares who had deserted him followed the royals, and behind them the Royal Councils; the *grandeza* and lesser *títulos*; *la Suprema*, Inquisitors, and palace clergy; knights of the Military Orders, civic dignitaries, and guild masters.

Powerful emotions overwhelmed Vicente. He had never seen a royal procession without the Count-Duke preening in all his glory. For twenty-two years, the greatest man in Spain had determined the course of his life. In the end, his and Olivares' successes were as evanescent as the Cardinal-Infante's victory at Nördlingen.

I have lost my place in Spain. At age forty-one can I make another? And where?

Vicente recognized Cortizos riding with the Knights of Calatrava, Méndez with the Royal Councilors, and other erstwhile supporters as the grand cavalcade proceeded through the noisy city. How long before they also would be arrested or flee into exile?

His self-control at the sight of Arce, Tomás, and de la Parra marching in the clerical ranks astonished him. He had no desire to leap out of the crowd and slit their throats as he had done on that Shrove Tuesday in 1617, when as a fifteen-year old boy he had sent to hell the dog who murdered his beloved father.

Vicente decided that to live a long life would be the sweetest revenge of all.

Thousands of *madrileños* were shouting:
"Satan is dead."
"Philip is King of Spain at last."
"Isabellas have always saved Spain."
And I must save myself.

PART SIX
To the New Jerusalem
Roquemaure, Prague, and Amsterdam 1643

Farewell land of my birth,
Fragrant coast of orange blossoms,
Farewell to fruits and melons,
Ambrosia of land and sea.
Farewell palm trees, cypress and pines,
And to Moraíma, first of my loves.
Farewell to my lost friends,
And María, my beloved enchantress
And my hopeless dreams.
Farewell forever my Spain!
Impossible ideal.

Vicente de Rocamora
fragments of a poem no longer extant

Chapter 76
Rock of the Moors

Land of my progenitors.

In the summer of 1643, Vicente stood amidst rows of ripening grapes near the small Romanesque *Abbaye* de St. Roch. The abbey dominated a slope above Roquemaure and the Rhone River in a valley between dentated limestone hills and cliffs covered by groves of silver olive trees and abundant vineyards. Vicente saw church spires, castle ruins, and the river port below where Hannibal floated his elephants on rafts across the Rhone. There in the eighth-century at the apex of their conquests, the Moors built a fortress and bridge and gave Roquemaure its name, Rock of the Moors.

Vicente took in the view, and reflected upon the events of the past six months. Escape from Spain had been easier than he expected. Foul weather, chaos in Aragón, and his skill with disguises enabled him to elude spies and assassins and pass through French lines.

Along the coastal route through French Roussillon and Languedoc, he mixed with the population without arousing suspicion. Their languages were almost identical to Catalan and akin to the Valencian dialect.

Because the Inquisitions of Spain and France cooperated and informers and blackmailers lurked everywhere, he wore the costume and false face of a veteran in one community, a notary or country bumpkin in the next. During the Rhone Valley leg of his journey to Roquemaure, he assumed the identity and swagger of a *golondrero* and added a vertical scar along his left cheek and a leather eye patch.

For the first time during his adulthood, Vicente enjoyed a *pícaro's* life freed from all duty and obligations like the boy he had been who played on the beaches of Valencia and roamed the docks of El Grau so many years ago. He dallied in towns and villages to feast, drink, and wench at leisure. He bathed in rivers and swam in the salt waters of the Mediterranean where he physically and metaphorically washed away the foul odor and dirt of clerical sanctity, and more. His future no longer depended upon the fortunes and whims of others: Rafal's quest for a title, Olivares' promises, Sotomayor's reluctance to name a successor, and a jealous monarch. From now on, only his actions and choices would determine his fate.

Earlier in the day when he arrived at Roquemaure, Vicente had gone to the parish church to seek baptismal records and other documents concerning the Seigneurs de Roquemaure. That was where Abbé Pierre de Taurelle approached him. A portly, genial man about sixty years of age, Taurelle had a neatly trimmed mustache and goatee as gray as the full head of curly hair under his straw hat. His creased and discolored face revealed a man who indulged in the excesses of dissipation. Heavy lids and dark pouches left only narrow slits that obscured the color of his eyes under the shadow of his hat. The Abbé informed Vicente, who had given him a false name, that what he sought lay in the archives of the Abbey of St. Roch and invited him to visit for a midday meal as well.

Voices from a nearby outdoor table distracted Vicente when the frères sat for their repast. The Abbé came over to him, lifted his wide-brimmed straw hat, and wiped his moist brow with the sleeve of his beige linen robe.

"We shall sup alone after the brothers finish. Let us walk now." He guided Vicente through rows of vines and said, "Tell me the truth. Who are you really, and why do you seek information about the Seigneurs de Roquemaure?"

"I told you who I am."

"I spoke to you in Latin, and it was in the language of a cleric you replied. I believe you can see out of that eye. Excellent disguise. Your repugnant scar is quite realistic. I ask again. This time in the vernacular of Languedoc. Who are you?"

Vicente stared into eyes green as his own and chanced a truthful reply. "I am Vicente de Rocamora, Son of Don Luís, descendant of Pierre Román, son of the Seigneur de Roquemaure, who Castilianized his name to Pedro Ramón when he fought alongside King Jaime the Conqueror. I have come here to learn more about the origins of my lineage."

"And you have fled Spain. Wait, sheath your knife. Have no fear for your life. Certain news travels quickly. I have been anticipating your arrival ever since word came to me that someone was making inquiries about the original Seigneurs de Roquemaure. And here we are. Tell me, Vicente, what has motivated a prominent court cleric to leave Spain? Olivares' downfall? Were you denounced to the Holy Office as a Judaizer? Or both?"

"Personal vendettas."

"And suspicion you might be a new-Christian?"

"Only suspicion. I have seen no proof the blood of Jews flows through my veins."

"And so, you were almost Inquisitor General of all Spain."

"Almost is still the widest of chasms."

"What a prize it would have been for you. And how did you manage to escape Spain and travel this far through France? Did you use any of the safe houses in Narbonne, Montpelier, and Arles?"

He is astonishingly well informed.

Vicente thought himself to be a shrewd judge of men. He twirled an end of his mustachio and leered. "I preferred the softer, more welcoming sanctuaries in the arms of the nymphs of Languedoc."

The Abbé laughed heartily. "You most definitely belong in my Order."

Why do I trust you? Is it because your eyes are green as my own, my mother's, and Brianda's?

After the frères retired to take the Languedoc equivalent of a siesta, Vicente sat alone with Taurelle under a vine covered trellis. Novices served them an abundance of freshly baked breads, cheeses, and fruits, accompanied by terra cotta pitchers of wine. He placed his buckler and sword on the bench. He took off his hat and doublet, loosened his blouse, and removed the eye-patch and scar.

Taurelle's beige linen robe was soaked through with sweat. He used his horsetail swatter to brush away flying insects buzzing around their bowls of food. An occasional breeze wafted the lush scent of flowers past their table.

The Abbé poured a deep purple wine into two oversized crystal goblets. "A man can easily adapt to our little patch of paradise, live happily here, and die exquisitely, either drowned in wine or worn to exhaustion by the lusty wenches of Languedoc and Avignon."

Vicente touched glasses with Taurelle and took his first sip. "Better than any wine I have had in Spain or Italy."

"Like our women, our Rhone wines are of many varieties, all of them delicious." Taurelle pressed tongue against palate and licked his lips. "Excellent. Although this vintage will be softer, more voluptuous when it matures, I generally prefer my wine to be youthful, piquant and flirtatious, like the sweet young maids who benefit from my experienced mouth."

"How young?"

"That depends upon the vineyards where they flower. Many wines mature and age to sour taste too soon. Others test a man's patience and develop slowly."

Vicente recalled his own recent debauching through Languedoc and thought of a theme for the literary jousts he used to attend. "Wine and women. Which is the metaphor for the other?"

"Interchangeable. And, perhaps you might prefer an ecclesiastic metaphor as well." The Abbé lifted a bunch of grapes and bit into them as a latter day Bacchus. After wiping juice from his jaw, he raised his glass to the sun and intoned as if celebrating mass, "It has been said that in its youth our wine takes on the bishop's purple. As it matures, it ages to a cardinal's crimson. My greatest delight is to taste both wines and girls while they are still developing. There is much to be said for the sweetness of youth. Yet, one must not sample either too soon or too late."

Vicente did not wait for Taurelle to refill his goblet and poured for both of them. "Which wine are we drinking?"

"The Rhone's very best. It comes from a castle town across the river built around three hundred years ago by the second anti-Pope of Avignon. Jacques Duese, Bishop of Fréjus, took the name John XXII and created a magnificent vineyard at his castle, Chateauneuf du Pape."

"In Spain, John XXII is so accursed we were forbidden to speak or write his name because he is said to have been a sorcerer."

"Lies spread by his enemies. John XXII was a Pope ideally suited to the temperament of our land. He composed many a drinking song." Taurelle's baritone boomed off-key:

> *Je veux vous chanter, mes amis,*
> *Ce vieux Chateauneuf que j'ai mis*
> *Pour vous seuls en bouteille,*
> *Il va faire merveille.*
>
> *Quand de ce vin nous serons gris,*
> *Venus applaudira nos ris.*
> *Je prends a temoin Lise,*
> *La chose est bien permise!*

I will sing for you, my friends
About this old Chateauneuf
I have bottled for your souls.
It will work wonders.

When this wine makes us tipsy,
Venus will applaud our laughter.
I take Lise as my witness,
The goddess permits our carousel.

Vicente would not presume to guess how many Lises the debauched Abbé had comforted. Not only did he trust the man, he had taken a strong liking to him, and the wine as well. Too much so. He felt heavy lidded and lethargic, ready for a siesta.

"With all due respect Abbé Pierre, I am impatient to learn the history of my family and continue on my way. Those castle ruins below your abbey, is it there my ancestors, the Seigneurs de Roquemaure, once lived?"

Taurelle pushed away his empty plate, patted his belly, and bellowed for the novices to serve more wine. "No, that castle is where the first anti-Pope, Clement V, died in 1316 after eating his physician's cure for a stomach ache, a plate filled with ground emeralds."

"Obviously too rich a meal for him."

"*Quelle drôle.*"

After the novices brought them more pitchers of wine, Taurelle lit his long clay pipe and another for Vicente, who luxuriated in a smoke of savory tobacco, closed his eyes, and imagined Ballebrera in the Abbé's place. Like Ramón, Taurelle indulged in all pleasures of the senses. What a pair they would have made debauching throughout Madrid together.

Good food, an abundance of wine, and witty conversation had not diverted him from his objective. "You said you had information."

"I have." Taurelle encouraged Vicente to let him refill his goblet. "But what have you been told of your origins."

"As you already know, through my father, I trace descent from Pedro Ramón de Rocamora, a son of the Seigneur de Roquemaure. I know nothing of my mother's family. Doubts were raised about the authenticity of her surnames and her certificate of *limpieza*." Vicente showed Taurelle the paper he had discovered in his mother's cross. "Sep is obviously Septimania. Bodo is documented in church histories, but this third word or name, Natronai . . ."

The Abbé raised a hand to silence him. "To understand the significance of Natronai and Bodo, you must first learn a suppressed history." He smiled in anticipation of Vicente's reaction. "After siesta when we are both refreshed, I shall do for you exactly as my uncle did for your father in my presence many years ago."

Vicente leaped from the table. "You knew my father?"

Taurelle gestured for Vicente to calm himself and lower his voice. "When Luís visited Roquemaure, I was a young man of less than twenty years. My uncle, Jean de Taurelle, was Abbé then. You and I, Vicente, we are kin."

Chapter 77
The Nasim of Septimania

After siesta, Vicente followed Taurelle along narrow winding stone stairs below the ground floor. At the bottom, the Abbé unlocked a heavy oak door.

It opened into a dark windowless chamber. He lit candelabra and sconces until the room was illuminated to a brightness approaching daylight. Bound in protective leather, manuscripts and documents filled shelves and covered tables.

Taurelle seated Vicente at a sturdy oak table. "You know Latin and Greek of course, having been educated for the Church, but can you read Hebrew?"

"Adequately."

"And you are reasonably fluent in French." Taurelle put on his spectacles and collected specific manuscripts and documents from the shelves. He placed them on the table in two stacks and stood over Vicente. "Most of what you will be reading is in Church or legal Latin, much in Hebrew, some in the old language of the Franks. They are a mix of Church and Court annals, legal documents from *mayorazgos* as you call them in Spanish, decrees, lawsuits, and a series of epic poems, the *Chansons de Geste*. The earliest documents date from the reign of Pepin, Charlemagne's father."

He unrolled a centuries-old map of the region. All provinces, towns, rivers, and landmarks had been written in Hebrew. He handed Vicente a thin manuscript. "My late uncle, may he rest in peace, and I organized this account with references to corroborate these documents. It will be your guide through the maze of truth, lies, and legend." The Abbé tapped the top of one stack. "The Church has been successful in its attempts to establish a false history. You will have many questions. Save them for when we sup tonight. I leave you now."

Well into the evening, Vicente read, translated, and searched for places on the map. He spoke two words aloud at almost every sentence: "Incredible, unbelievable."

Taurelle's narratives began with a description of Pepin the Short, King of the Franks and son of Charles Martel, who turned back the tide of Arab conquests at Tours in 732. Pepin had ambitious goals: subdue the rebellious counts in the south, drive the Ummayad Muslims out of Frankia and Spain, renew the Roman Empire, and obtain Divine Right to succeed the Biblical Kings of Israel. The last objective resulted from his extensive contact with Jews who were numerous and prominent throughout the kingdom.

Those who followed the Law of Moses had thrived in the land of the Franks because of a fortuitous confluence. The Church's authority was not yet supreme in Frankia. The kings' aggressions were dynastic rather than religious. Many of their subjects came from barbaric tribes recently converted to

Christianity by the sword after defeat in battle and had not yet been indoctrinated by the Church to hate the Jews.

In those days, the Septimanian port city of Narbonne was active, the community thriving, and the majority of its population Jews. In return for Pepin's pledge of autonomy and a prince of their own, they surrendered the city to him in 759. At their request, Pepin sent to Baghdad for a *nasi*, an exilarch or prince of the Jewish exile from the Bustanai clan, whose authority derived through descent from the Royal House of David. The *nasi's* name was Natronai.

Vicente paused. He looked at the scrap of paper left by his mother and turned to a document in Hebrew, which stated that Natronai was the *nasi's* Persian name, El-Makhir his Hebrew-Biblical name.

In 768, Pepin gave Natronai the Frankish noble name of Theodoric and granted him an extensive independent domain in Septimania, the Toulousain, and what lands the *nasi* could hold and take from the Muslims in Roussillon and northern Catalonia. After Natronai-Makhir-Theodoric became Pepin's vassal, the King's legal lordship over a Davidic prince and the Jews thus enabled him, in his mind, to claim his right to Biblical succession.

Pope Stephen III and the Frankish Church protested the establishment of the Jewish princedom, but to no avail. Pepin further solidified his alliance with the Jews when he gave his sister, Alda, daughter of Charles Martel, as wife for the *Nasi* of Narbonne.

At night when they supped alone, Vicente asked Taurelle, "Did Natronai's wife, sister of a Christian king, convert to the Law of Moses?"

"We do not know for certain, although based on the subsequent actions of Natronai's son, it is likely. He gave his first born the name Isaac. Isaac married Guiburc, a pagan aristocratic woman who did accept the Jewish religion. According to traditional Christian history and legend, Isaac is known as Guillaume, Guillherme, Guillermo in your Spanish, the First Count of Toulouse. He became the second *Nasi* of Narbonne. In him flowed the blood of two great lineages, David of Israel and Arnulf of the Franks. Two mighty houses. Houses of our blood."

Vicente occupied his days and nights in the library translating countless manuscripts and decrees. Parchments were brittle. Much of the legal and Church vocabulary was archaic and presented problems of syntax. He also scrutinized the documents for evidence of forgery. He knew how to identify falsely aged paper, ink, illuminations, and seals.

He compared the narratives with the conflicting documents. Church forgeries frequently gave themselves away with contradictions and inconsistencies. Nevertheless, a coherent and intriguing story emerged. The first two *Nasim* of Septimania, Natronai-Makhiri-Theodoric and his son, Isaac-Guillherme, served Pepin and his son Charlemagne well in war. By 791, the *nasim* extended their principality across the Pyrenees to include the seacoast of northern Catalonia, also known as the Spanish March. Their exploits were celebrated in epic poems known as the *Chansons de Geste*, in which Natronai was known by a fourth name, Aymeri, based on the Arabic spelling of his name, Al-Makhiri.

Frankish Court annals often supported the narratives. Vicente stared in amazement at two decrees. One *privilegium* had the added authority of illiterate King Charlemagne's mark. It granted "the status, dignity, and power of the Jewish principate in southern France on both sides of the Pyrenees". The other stated: "Charlemagne designed, out of love for Prince Makhir, good statutes for the benefit of all Jews living in Narbonne."

More Jewish and Christian documents from the eighth and ninth centuries proved, despite later forgeries to the contrary, that a contemporary Church council in the presence of a Papal Nuncio endorsed *Nasi* Natronai-Makhir's right to all possessions.

After Natronai died, Isaac-Guillherme became the second *nasi*. He was Charlemagne's emissary to Haroun al-Rashid in Baghdad, established a Jewish academy in Narbonne, and led the Frank army that captured Barcelona.

According to Church history and the *Chansons*, however, Guillherme-Isaac defended Christianity against Islam, became a monk, and founded a monastery. Those same sources also mentioned his fluency in Hebrew and Arabic and unintentionally revealed that he scrupulously followed the Law of Moses. A typical example was his un-Christian habit of washing hands before each meal. Additional evidence of his true faith appeared in an epic poem written by Ermold Niger, who dated the major events of Isaac-Guillherme's campaign against the Arabs according to the Jewish method of chronology.

The more Vicente learned about the exceptional warrior, diplomat, and scholar, the more he admired him. According to the second *nasi's* contemporaries, Isaac-Guillherme could deliver a fatal blow to a man's throat with the cutting edge of his palm. As the most influential prince at the courts of Charlemagne and his successor, Louis the Pious, also known as *le debonnaire*, Guillherme-Isaac sparked a great interest in the Law of Moses among a number of literate Alamanni, Saxons, and Franks whom Charlemagne had converted from paganism to Christianity by the sword.

Isaac-Guillherme was followed as *nasi* by his son, Bernard of Septimania, who married his cousin and Charlemagne's daughter, Dhuoda. Marquis of the Spanish March and later chamberlain to his brother-in-law when he became King Louis, Bernard was the most powerful man in the realm. By then, Septimania was mentioned in court documents as a kingdom in its own right.

Outraged that another Jew had been raised so high, Bernard's rivals referred to him as *naso*, which they derived from *nasi* and used as a derogatory reference to his prominent nose. Bernard's fall came as a result of dynastic reasons not connected to religion.

Some of the recently converted and not yet completely christianized pagan nobles, preferred Bernard to be their king, and by blood he was descended from Charles Martel and Pepin. They believed Bernard had more ability than either Louis or his son, Charles the Bald. Charles won the power struggle, and after he became king executed Bernard on the pretext he had committed adultery with his mother, Queen Judith. Bernard's oldest son also was executed a few years later; another was ambushed, thus terminating the direct male line of the *nasim* of Narbonne.

On the female side, Bernard of Septimania's sister had married a Jewish warrior noble named Solomon, who became Fourth *Nasi* of Narbonne, Count of Roussillon, Conflent, and Cerdagne, and Marquis of the Spanish March. Upon Solomon's death, all lands and titles went to his son, Bernard-Makhir d'Auvergne, who recaptured Barcelona and received royal appointment to rule over Aquitaine. While serving as Fifth *Nasi* of Narbonne, Bernard-Makhir received homage from German Jewry after King Charles the Bald became Emperor and died in battle during the reign of King Charles the Fat.

With the death of Bernard-Makhir d'Auvergne, the heyday of the warrior Jewish Princes of Septimania came to an end. The Church's strength increased, and the *nasim* became merely symbolic leaders within the weakened Jewish community. At the same time, Septimania entered a period of prolonged instability caused by feudal wars, Christian heresies, and pestilence. In the thirteenth-century, many Jews chose conversion over death or exile when King Philip Augustus expelled them from French soil.

Vicente closed the last page of the final manuscript Taurelle had laid out for him. He was dissatisfied, his expectations unfulfilled. Not once had a Seigneur de Roquemaure appeared. Nowhere did he find evidence his lineage derived from Bodo, who had not been mentioned, or the *nasim* of Septimania.

His temples throbbed. Tired eyes watered. Too often during his research, he misread the numbers three, five, and eight. He seemed to be holding pages farther from his eyes in order to see the writing more clearly. Had the time come for him to wear quevedos?

Vicente confronted Taurelle the moment he entered the library. "Abbé, I have patiently read about the Jewish princes of Septimania. I have gone blind pouring over Church forgeries and distortions. Interesting and enlightening. But what have they to do with me?"

Taurelle snuffed the flickering candles and took his arm. "It is late. Time to sup, enjoy more fruit of the vines, and then retire. Tomorrow, Vicente, I will tell you all you desire to know."

Chapter 78
Tainted Blood, Royal Blood

The Abbé selected a quill, dipped it in a bottle of ink, and created in elegant script a genealogy chart of the first five *nasim* on a large piece of parchment. He left a big space beside and below Bernard-Makhir d'Auvergne, the fifth and last great *nasi* of Narbonne.

"I have omitted the daughters and younger sons of the *nasim*, who married the nobility and petty royalty of Septimania, Provence, the Toulousain, and Aquitaine." He added more lines and names to the chart. "A female descendant of both Bernard of Septimania's sister and Marquis Solomon married a nephew of Louis VIII, whom the King made Seigneur de Roquemaure after the annexation of Languedoc in 1229." Taurelle wrote *extinct* on the chart. "The original French de Roquemaure line died out during the Black Plague, about a century after Pedro Ramón left for Spain."

"Then who presumes to be the current Seigneur de Roquemaure?"

"The son of a wealthy peasant now uses our once proud name. His father outbid my family and purchased the title from Henry IV, who sold thousands of them to fill his empty treasury. No kin of ours, I thank God."

Incomplete. The saga is still half-told. Where is my mother's family? How does Bodo fit into my lineage, if at all?

Taurelle continued, "Now to Bodo, the Apostate. As is written in Church histories, he married a Jewish woman after submitting to circumcision and converting to the Law of Moses. Not mentioned in those same documents is the fact she was a daughter of Bernard of Septimania, who had planned a royal marriage for her.

A connection to Bodo at last?

"A younger son of Bodo and Bernard's daughter returned to Septimania to serve Bernard-Makhir d'Auvergne. He married one of the Fifth *Nasi's* daughters. His descendants through a family named Tauros had a daughter who wed the first Seigneur de Roquemaure."

"Yesterday, I read an eleventh century viscountal judgment on behalf of Tauros, Hebrew of Narbonne. I should have seen the connection immediately. Tauros, Taurelle."

"When Philip Augustus ordered all Jews to convert, go into exile, or face death, our forebears chose conversion and changed their name to Taurelle. A few, however, continued to follow the Law of Moses in secret."

"And my mother?" Taurelle did not reply. "And you?" More silence. "Then, tell me, how did my parents meet?"

"Uncle Jean introduced Don Luís to my father, a wine merchant residing in Avignon. Living with us was a beautiful seventeen year old cousin and ward, whose parents had died of the plague in Catalonia when she was a small child."

Vicente watched the Abbé write a beloved name. "My mother."

"And my cousin, Gabrielle. It was romantic love at first sight for both of them. Avignon often does that to men and women. My uncle married your parents in our chapel."

Vicente tensed. Had his own father submitted to circumcision like Bodo and converted to the Law of Moses? "In what religion were they married?"

"In the True Faith of course."

"Then there was no wedding according to the Law of Moses?"

"No, your father was a rationalist interested in blood and lineage, not faith." Taurelle's eyes became unfocused with memory. "The antecedents of my lovely cousin, Gabrielle, had observed the Law of Moses in Catalonia from the time of their forced conversion to Christianity more than two hundred years ago. She was but three years old when her immediate family died, too young to be instructed in religion."

"And when she lived with your parents in Avignon?"

"We were like brother and sister. From the day Gabrielle wed your father, I have searched in vain for another like her."

Vicente could not recall anything from his childhood to indicate his parents had Judaized, nor had he ever heard the slightest hint of their true origins. "Why didn't my mother and father tell me?"

"I cannot speak for them. Perhaps they believed the truth would have made you restless in spirit. According to your idiotic *limpieza* statutes, Gabrielle was completely tainted." The Abbé handed Vicente the chart. "Study it, memorize it, and burn it. Should you wed and have children, for the sake of your family, never tell them of our secret. With pride in blood will

Genealogy of Vincente de Rocamora

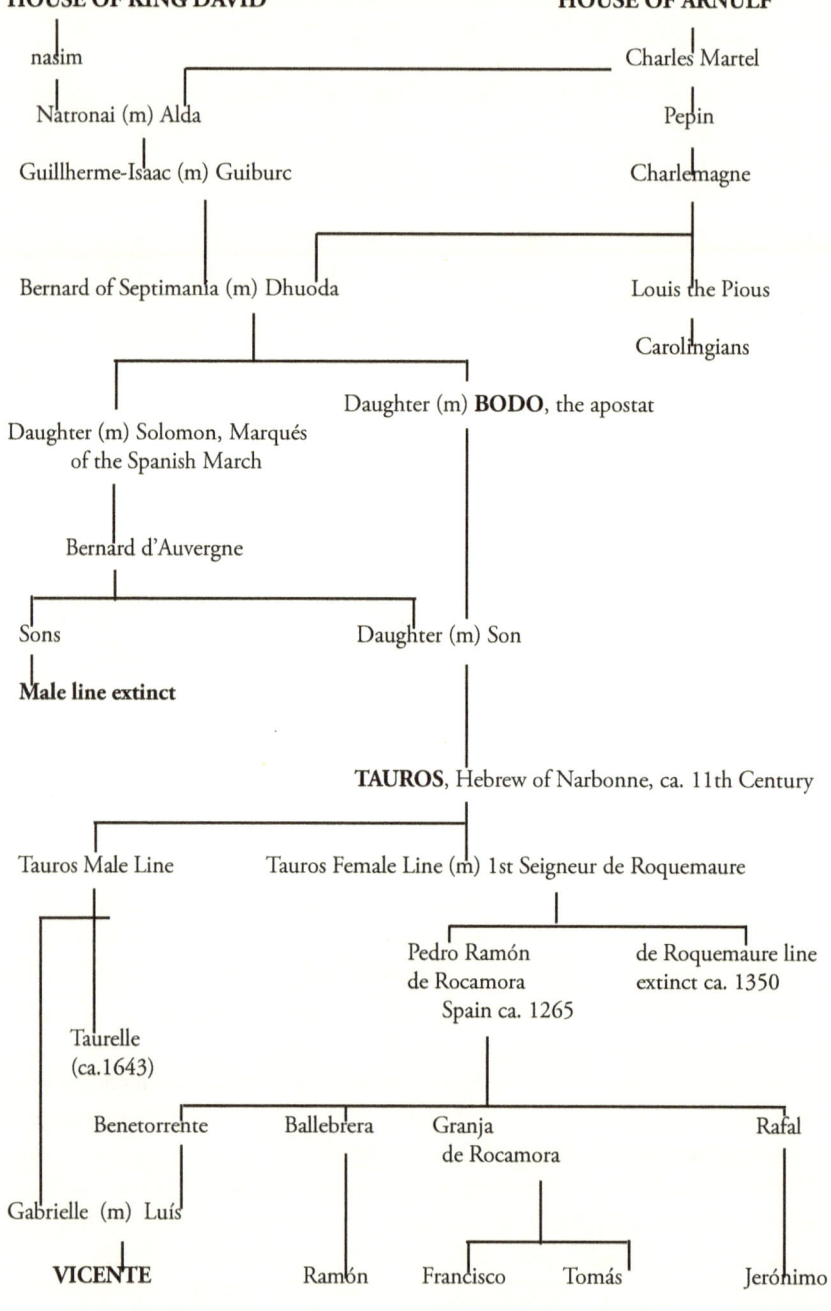

come only unhappiness. To speak or write of our genealogy in the Christian world guarantees accusations of blasphemy and treason."

Vicente read the chart from top to bottom and felt no shame he was of one-half new-Christian blood. Instead, he laughed until his innards hurt.

So what if the blood of David and Charlemagne flowed through his veins. Taurelle was right. No Christian would believe it. Would any Jew? He could tell no one.

How Ramón might have appreciated the irony, Brianda too, if she had but known.

And you, Doña María, my golden love, how would you react?

Vicente searched for Taurelle and found the Abbé in the wine cellar, naked and rump-up playing the beast with two backs on a straw mat with a sturdy young peasant girl. He turned his candelabrum away from the rutting pair and went behind the vats to a table where he sampled wines until they finished.

After the Abbé saw the girl out the side door, he sat with Vicente and raised his goblet of wine to the candlelight. "Young, but rapidly maturing. Lush and full-bodied. The girl too. There are countless wenches like her. Tomorrow I shall introduce you to . . ."

"I leave on the morrow."

"So soon? Let me dissuade you. Stay for the harvesting of the vines. It is the best time of the year. Festive and pagan. You must experience the delights of trampling plump juicy grapes inside immense open barrels in the company of succulent country girls."

Vicente toasted his lecherous cousin. Neither Velázquez nor Rubens could have adequately portrayed Taurelle romping satyr-like among the fleshy nymphs of Languedoc and Avignon.

"There is a local proverb," Taurelle said. *"Quau se lèvo d'Avignon se lèvo de la resoun.* Whoever leaves Avignon takes leave of his senses."

"I have made mistakes before."

"Let me assure you, Vicente, in Languedoc and Avignon, it matters little if one is descended from Jews. The authorities are relatively uninterested in those who may have what you Spaniards foolishly call tainted blood. Outward conformity is all the authorities require. No one cares how you worship in the privacy of your home. You can become king of a small domain if you stay here and marry a rich widow, preferably one with a vineyard."

"I have no desire to imprison myself in marriage or in this valley. The Rhone has its own beauty, but the hills are closing in on me. I prefer a sweeping beach with a limitless horizon of sea."

"I also know of a hot young heiress to make you forget the outdoors."

"I am forty-two, too old to begin a family."

"Nonsense. Only two things improve with age, wine and a lover. You still appear to be virile enough to plow new fields where you can spread your seed and make up for lost time."

"It cannot be in France, which has become too unstable a land since Louis XIII died this past May. Because your new King, Louis XIV, is a mere boy of five, civil war is likely to begin before the dust settles. That is why I have, to my regret, decided against going to Paris and visit my old friend and ally, the Portuguese Consul, Manuel Fernández de Villareal."

"Yes, your description of the situation in France is correct. But Avignon is not France. It is not ruled by a French King or regional nobles. It is a Papal enclave governed by a Cardinal-legate."

"Which could be overrun at the slightest provocation."

"I see I must work harder to convince you to stay. Perhaps I should have told my wench to send you her nubile friends to change your mind."

"You may do so for tonight. I shall leave tomorrow."

"Vicente, you are a most difficult fellow. Very well then, let us consider your lesser options. If not Languedoc or Avignon, Italy has the climate, language, and culture most suitable for a Spaniard."

"That is true, but I would always be looking over my shoulder for assassins or denunciation. If I declared myself to be . . . to follow the Law of Moses, which I have no desire to do, I would be forced into a ghetto and end up wearing a red cap to mark me as a Jew not a Cardinal."

"Surely you are not considering one of the Mediterranean communities within the Ottoman Empire?"

"No, the Turk is too unpredictable and savage to trust, his religion oppressive to unbelievers. One mistake, and they would behead me, or I might be flayed alive, drawn and quartered, my skin stuffed with straw and attached to the city gate for all to see and ridicule."

Taurelle poured more wine. "You have proven my point. Roquemaure and Avignon are the best possible choices. Let us toast my sweet land of carnal pleasures."

"I will concede that it is very much like the beloved Valencia of my youth," Vicente said when they touched cups. "Your Rhone Valley has an abundance of sensual delights, delicious wines, passionate women, a menu of rich widows, and, most important of all, your friendship. Yet I prefer to live openly with no secrets, judged only by my own actions and accomplishments, not my Jewish blood."

"And where is this mythical paradise?"

"Amsterdam."

Taurelle pretended to shiver. "Too far north and cold for me. Too austere, those Dutch Calvinists. The men believe their cocks are to be used for making babies and pissing, nothing else. I have been told that the Iberian Jews who live there are no different. And how happy do you really think you can be in Amsterdam? You have walked among Kings and Queens, served the greatest men in Spain, worked at the highest levels of Church and State. Will you be content to deal with the ordinary day-to-day pettiness of a burger's life?"

"As a merchant or tradesman? Definitely not, but at least in Amsterdam a man can become what he chooses to make of himself."

"You know less about the world then you think. Throughout the United Provinces, men are concerned only with acquiring wealth through hard work, through marriage, or through inheritance. Furthermore, Amsterdam is infested with spies for the Inquisition. So why not stay here, wed a rich widow, and enjoy the sweetest of lives in a pleasing climate?"

"Regretfully, I must bid farewell to Bacchus and all your lusty daughters of Venus. As I said, on the morrow, I leave for what the Jews call the New Jerusalem where I can best answer my true calling and become a physician."

Unless Empress María were to summon me.

Chapter 79
Empress María

Have you no word for me of my former confessor, Don Vicente de Rocamora?

Empress María could not voice her question during a formal audience in her suite at the Prague Palace. She listened in silence while Diego Muñoz de Castro, emissary from the Spanish Court, offered greetings and gifts from her brother, King Philip IV.

Attended by her physician, ladies, and liveried servants, the Empress reclined on a divan close to the warmth of a roaring fireplace. A sable cap covered her tightly braided golden hair. Her frail body was swathed in woolen and fur garments under a down-filled purple satin quilt embroidered with the Imperial arms in thread of gold surrounding the black two-headed Habsburg eagle and red and white shield. Atop the quilt, her gloved slender hands clutched rosary, crucifix, and prayer book.

María was unwell. After almost fourteen years, her thin Spanish Habsburg blood had yet to adjust to the more severe weather of Imperial lands. Her Spanish constitution was susceptible to all the ills brought on by the damp air and draughts penetrating the rooms and corridors of her palaces and hunting lodges.

Before Muñoz left to meet with her husband Emperor Ferdinand III and the Imperial Council, María ordered him to return afterwards for a second private audience. Then she accepted a steaming broth from Immanuel Bocarro Francês y Rosales, her gray-bearded physician who had come from Hamburg to serve the Imperial family and in time to save her life from a virulent fever.

Bocarro's calming presence and soothing voice seemed to heal as well as his prescriptions. The physician was short, balding, of small stature, with dark intelligent eyes behind thick spectacles. A man in his fifties, he was reputed to be one of the greatest physicians in Europe. He had attended the Archbishop of Braga, King João of Portugal when he was still Duke of Bragança, the Commander of the Portuguese Order of Santiago, and the Crown Prince of Denmark.

Bocarro also was a man of diverse accomplishments. The ever inquisitive Emperor had installed the physician within his circle of intimates because of his brilliance in astronomy, astrology, and mathematics and despite or because of a friendship with the heretic Galileo.

After the Empress dismissed Bocarro, her ladies attempted to amuse her with music, gossip, and commentary on the latest styles, which reminded her of those elegant fashion dolls Don Vicente had given her on each birthday so many years ago. María had been thinking much about the panorama of her life ever since she lay close to death. She cherished many fond memories of her former confessor and spiritual director.

Where has he gone? Is he still alive?

María reluctantly accepted the reasons why Don Vicente could not have accompanied her to the Empire in 1629. The Imperial Court favored Jesuits and Capuchins over Dominicans, and from the Spanish side, Philip IV and Olivares feared Rocamora's potential to become more Mazarin than Torquemada.

The Empress thought of her older sister, Anne, whom she had not seen since the day of her marriage to Louis XIII in 1615. The previous May, after both Louis XIII and Cardinal Richelieu died, Anne became Regent for her five year old son, Louis XIV. Over the past decades, rumors had linked Anne to many men including Buckingham and now Richelieu's protégé, Mazarin. The Sicilian Cardinal's influence over Queen Anne was so strong he had become de facto ruler of France, and so notorious, he was alleged to be the natural father of Louis XIV, a canard first spread by Olivares' agents.

María believed the relationship between her sister and the Cardinal was similar to that which she had shared with her own confessor and spiritual director. She had convinced herself that Anne and Mazarin were confidants, perhaps best friends, as she and Don Vicente had been within the strict limitations of *punctilio* and rank. If her confessor had accompanied her to the Empire, María believed there would have been no rumors of impropriety.

She dreamed about Don Vicente as her most devoted *caballero*. First, she saw him as her gallant of the grilles, to amuse, flatter, and serenade her had she never married and ended her days in a convent. Then she pictured him as the hero of her private *romancero*, who carried her away from the Alcazar for a brief moment of bliss before they died in each other's arms as Romeo and Juliet.

María opened her eyes surprised she had slept. It was dark outside. Candlelight reflected off the misted windows. Her principal lady approached and informed her that the Spanish emissary was waiting outside.

"Summon him."

Muñoz entered, kneeled, and at the Empress' command sat facing her divan. She waved for her entourage to withdraw and studied the emissary before she spoke. Muñoz was a slight, austere Castilian dressed all in black with a modest collar. María expected the punctilious courtier to ingratiate himself in the hope that she would report favorably about him to the King and advance his career. According to *murmuraciónes*, he aspired to be a member of King Philip's Royal Council.

The Empress initiated a conversational pavanne. "What news and gossip do you bring us other than formal greetings, Don Diego?"

Muñoz related in detail how Philip IV had truly become King of Spain in the nine months after Olivares was rusticated to a remote estate in León. "All of the Olivaristas have been removed from office and many arrested."

While Muñoz spoke, María dwelled on her dynastic concerns and congratulated herself for fulfilling her father's deathbed request. She had become an empress and produced heirs for both branches of their dynasty. Her brother's fourteen-year old son and heir to the throne of Spain, Baltazar Carlos, would marry her daughter, María Anna, soon to be nine. Her son Ferdinand would inherit the Empire.

The reports Muñoz sent from Spain could not have pleased María more, with one glaring exception. No one, not Their Majesties Philip IV and Isabel, nor her former *meninas*, nor any Spanish emissary and cleric had volunteered information about the circumstances of Don Vicente's disappearance.

Muñoz concluded with undisguised glee, "With the removal of Olivares and Sotomayor, Spain has returned to its true course. Under Arce Reynoso's leadership, *la Suprema* has instructed the Valencian Tribunal to rescind Olivares' policies and forbid Jews from Oran from setting foot on Spanish soil. And now, those arrogant despicable new-Christians who have been infesting Court and Kingdom will be receiving all they deserve."

"Does the Inquisitor General intend to drive out from Spain all those with the slightest drop of Jewish blood, regardless of their devotion to our Faith?"

"Of course, Your Majesty. One drop of Jewish blood is enough to pollute."

"Santa Teresa too?"

Not knowing how to respond, Muñoz gaped at her.

Although María believed all heretics and infidels were damned for eternity, she never embraced the Castilian concept of tainted blood. She had agreed with Olivares' policy on that particular matter, also supported by Inquisitor General Sotomayor. If new-Christians were proven to be devout Catholics they should suffer no penalties for their Jewish origins. Had not the Church made Teresa of Avila a saint, she whose grandfather had been born a Jew? If Don Vicente had tainted blood, it must be so slight as to be inconsequential, like that of her own, if, God Forbid, old rumors were true concerning the Jewish origins of her ancestor eight generations ago, Raquel d'Enríquez, the White Dove of Toledo, great-grandmother of Ferdinand the Catholic.

"Now then," María said in her most casual tone, "have you any news of Vicente de Rocamora?"

The emissary was reluctant to speak until he saw her expression. Determined Habsburg jaw. Blue eyes cold as a tarn in winter. "Forgive me, Your Imperial Majesty, but I am forbidden to mention his name or speak of him."

"Are we Empress or not? We command you. Tell us what you know about our former confessor." When Muñoz did not reply, María gripped her crucifix. "If you refuse to answer our questions, we swear by all that is holy our next message to His Majesty, King Philip, our brother, will end your career and ruin your entire family for all time."

Muñoz needed several moments to recover from the intensity of her attack. "Your Imperial Majesty, his own de Rocamora kinsman, Don Tomás, with the cooperation of Inquisitor General Don Diego de Arce Reynoso . . . they are expunging his name from all records, clerical and lay."

"Why should they do that?"

"They believe him to be tainted. His mother may have been of new-Christian origins."

"Old news, typical of slanders by the envious."

"Worst of all, he may have Judaized."

"We refuse to believe so vile a calumny. Are you telling us he Judaized in Spain?"

"Not in Spain, but it is said he may have gone to the Jewish community in Amsterdam."

She crossed herself and clutched her prayer book. "Don Vicente a Jew? Impossible. We knew him better than anyone. He was the most pious and spiritual of all men. He preached at *autos-de-fé* when Jews were condemned. He sermonized against them each Lent and Easter. In our own chapel."

"I heard him preach myself," Muñoz said to reestablish himself in her good graces. "Truly, no one was ever more eloquent."

"And did he not have a certificate *of limpieza de sangre*? Did not *la Suprema* approve his certificate? How else could he have become a royal confessor? Our confessor. Sotomayor himself chose Don Vicente to succeed him as Inquisitor General. Our brother, the Cardinal-Infante, may God grant him eternal peace, offered him a bishopric. Don Vicente could have and should have risen to the highest pinnacle in the Church."

"All you say is true, Your Imperial Majesty, but rumors of forgeries surfaced after you left Spain."

"Lies by envious rivals. Never proven."

"That may also be true. Still, as your Imperial Majesty must know, King Philip and Queen Isabel never considered him suitable to become Inquisitor General or confessor for His Highness, Infante Baltazar Carlos."

"They saw him as an Olivarista, an ally of Satan. But know this. Before Olivares, he was always first and foremost our loyal and devoted servant. No, we refuse to believe without proof that Vicente de Rocamora has Judaized." María tapped her fingers on her prayer book while she thought. "He is in Amsterdam among the Jews, you say?"

"So I have heard. If it is true he has Judaized, it would be a great humiliation and insult to our True Faith and a most grievous embarrassment for our Court. If true, you can well imagine why the Inquisitor General and

Rocamora's untainted kinsman would expunge his name from all records, as even Olivares also has been effaced from Velázquez' painting of Infante Baltazar Carlos at the Riding Academy."

"We must hear it or read it from Don Vicente in his own words, not from the lips or forgeries of his enemies. We cannot conceive of so great a betrayal." *Not he to whom I confessed and confided my most private thoughts.* "If he is in Amsterdam, how best can we get a message to him?"

Shocked by her request, Muñoz gulped for air like a fish out of water until he was able to speak. "I think one here at the Imperial Court may be able to help."

"Here? At Court? Who?"

"Your physician."

"Bocarro? What has he to do with Don Vicente?" She had almost said *my* Vicente.

"Imperial Majesty, as you know, I am a Familiar of the Holy Office. When he lived in Amsterdam about twenty years ago, spies of the Inquisitorial Tribunals of Madrid and Lisbon reported that Bocarro may have revealed himself to be a Judaizer. There, he went by the name Jacob Rosales."

María's demeanor and tone of voice became identical to what had provoked Olivares to refer to her as *that block of ice*. "Be very careful how you answer us. Are you accusing my physician, Bocarro, of Judaizing?"

"I would not presume to say for certain."

"As we thought. More innuendos."

"But Your Imperial Majesty . . ."

"Enough."

María dismissed Muñoz and sent for Bocarro. While she waited for the physician, she reviewed her conversation with the emissary. She could not imagine her Vicente as a filthy Jew. It was obvious that he had fled Spain because he had too many enemies and no powerful friends there. He would not be safe in France and Italy, lands hospitable to the Inquisitor General's agents and assassins. With England in the throes of civil war, the Germanies devastated by plague, famine, and war, the United Provinces would be a logical destination, although not necessarily a permanent sanctuary for Don Vicente if she could find a way to invite him to serve her.

There must be a way.

When Bocarro entered, María dispensed with *punctilio* and beckoned him to take a seat beside her divan. She thought it unnecessary to ask Bocarro if he had Judaized. Her husband's decision to invite the Portuguese to the Imperial Court as their physician and include him within his most intimate circle of friends was proof enough against Muñoz' unsubstantiated rumors.

"Is Your Imperial Majesty feeling better?"

"Yes, your broth and medicines have helped, as always." She raised a hand to prevent him from speaking. "Don Manuel, have you any knowledge of the Spanish Dominican, Vicente de Rocamora?"

"I believe I have heard his name mentioned over the years."

"He was our confessor and spiritual director in Spain." Bocarro did not comment or react. "You have lived in Amsterdam, we are told."

"Many years ago, I passed through that city on my way to Hamburg."

"Do you still have friends there?"

"From time to time, I am in contact with certain respected scholars."

"Have you heard if Don Vicente has Judaized in Amsterdam?"

"I have heard no such rumor."

"We have, and we must know if it is true. Is it possible to send a message to Amsterdam and make inquiries, discreetly of course?"

"Yes, although there would be difficulties for Your Imperial Majesty should it be intercepted."

"He taught us a code, which has confounded all who have seen it."

"There is one to whom such a message can be delivered."

"Name him."

"He is a scholar respected by all Christians. He knows everything about everyone in Amsterdam. Rabbi Menasseh ben Israel."

"A rabbi?" María crossed herself and imagined her confessor under the pernicious influence and lies of contemptible Jews. No, she should credit him with more faith and intellect. He would resist their attempts to proselyte him to their false religion. Rather, her eloquent preacher would be more likely to convert the Jews to the True Faith.

"Is there no one other than this Jew you mentioned?"

"Trust me in this matter, Your Imperial Majesty."

"Very well then. Write the rabbi and instruct him, without naming us, to give our coded message to Don Vicente if he should be in Amsterdam."

"As you command, Your Imperial Majesty."

"We shall prepare our letter immediately. How soon can it be delivered?"

"Because of the war, the route must be indirect. The condition of the roads will also cause delays. It may take months."

"No matter," she said dismissing Bocarro with a wave of her hand. "We must know."

The Empress rose from her divan and went to the window overlooking the palace garden. Because of mist, night, and candlelight, the glass had become a mirror. María gazed through her reflection and saw herself amidst the scented spring flowers of the Casa de Campo, the gardens of the Alcazar, sitting once again with Vicente on their favorite stone bench under the shade of a great elm. Don Vicente, her pious and eloquent "Torquemada" who, she had believed, would have helped her purge England of the Protestant heresy had she wed Charles Stuart.

María recalled their conspiring to thwart the Prince of Wales' courtship, her confessing to Don Vicente, his inspiring sermons and instructive penances. He had anticipated and understood her moods better than anyone before or since.

She recalled his intense green eyes and handsome clean shaven features when he was her confessor. What might she have said to him that summer day in the Casa de Campo if the Prince of Wales had not leaped from the garden wall and interrupted her confession? And oh, what could have happened the night of their meeting before she left Spain forever?

María relived each perilous moment of their rendezvous more than fourteen years earlier. They had exchanged locks of hair. She had gifted him with a ruby ring.

His eyes had spoken eloquent poetry.
If he had taken me in his arms.
If I had said all that was in my heart.
He had given every indication he wanted to kiss my mouth.
And if he had.

Tears came to María's eyes. She crossed herself and prayed: *Blessed Virgin. Forgive my sinful thoughts. I love my husband and children. I have fulfilled … am still fulfilling my duty to my family, dynasty, and the Empire.*

But, oh, my Vicente, do you also remember me?

Chapter 80
Cornucopia

María

I send this letter to you, my love,
On the wings of a milk-white dove,
Sweetened with cinnamon water,
And scented with spring flowers
From our lost Garden of Eden.

> I remember the golden sun of your hair,
> The soft May-blue sky of your eyes,
> The blooming pink rose of your lips,
> The perfectly matched pearls of your teeth,
> And the dulcet nightingale song of your voice.
>
> Do you hear me call your name in the wind,
> Taste my tears of remorse in the rain,
> Hear my heartbeat in the distant thunder,
> Echoing your dainty footsteps
> In the corridors of memory?

Vicente had felt a need to put on paper a poem he had composed years ago but dared not write. He dreamed of what might have been and thought about how best to send it to Empress María with a plea that he might still serve her.

He returned to reality, left the table, and inspected his room yet again to be certain that his imagination was not playing tricks and he was indeed in Amsterdam. He had arrived on a morning in October and had chosen to lodge in a home run by a respectable widow who let rooms by the month on a canal street with a name he could not yet pronounce like a Dutchman.

Vicente ran his hand along the shiny chest of drawers and bedpost. No dirt, not even a speck of dust. The porcelain washbowl, ewer, and chamber pot had been scoured to mirror clarity. He bent to smell the freshly laundered bedding and saw no vermin on the down quilt, sheets, or pillowcases. Downstairs, a servant girl was washing his spare clothing.

More than the land of Erasmus, rational thought, and tolerance, Vicente found the United Provinces to be antipodal to Spain in every way. When not obscured by gray mist, Dutch light was softer than the glaring sun that baked the Peninsula. It gently illuminated the Netherlands' palette of lush green fields, yellow haystacks, carpets of vivid flowers, red brick villages, and beige gold dunes.

The low-lying Dutch towns he passed through had been built on flat ground surrounded by long brick walls and earthen ramparts, marked by windmills, a few turrets, church belfry, and rooftops. No castles, villages, monasteries, or fortresses perched high atop sere craggy mountains as in Spain.

Absorbing warmth from the fireplace, Vicente faced the mirror in shirt, breeches, and boots, and studied his reflection. He looked many years younger than his forty-two despite a few gray hairs. No man was in better shape.

Ten months of traveling on foot and horseback had toned his body to youthful musculature, quickness, and endurance.

He put on his doublet, burdened with all his coins and jewels sewn into it, then his cloak and hat, and went downstairs to seek out the landlady. He found the heavyset gray-haired woman in her immaculate kitchen where copper pots and pans blazed like a galaxy of suns.

"*Mevrouw* Cornelia, please prepare hot water for me tonight. I wish to bathe."

She did not look up. "At what time?"

Vicente almost said, *after Vespers*. "At sundown."

"At half past the hour of five," she corrected him.

He would have to purchase a timepiece. These Dutch regulated their lives by clock, not church bells.

Cornelia served him breakfast, and he questioned her about life in Amsterdam. His landlady seemed to be obsessed with money and complained about the cost of everything. He learned from her a broad picture of relative wealth. A skilled worker earned about three florins a week. The annual wage for a schoolmaster was two hundred, a university professor eleven hundred, municipal physicians close to two thousand, and a municipal official five thousand. He would have to find out on his own what a beginning physician earned.

Vicente left the rooming house for a walk to familiarize himself with the city that had been built on marshes where the Amstel River emptied its waters into the Zuider Zee. Semi-circular manmade canals spread out like a fan from the harbor, stock exchange, and municipal buildings. At first impression, he had equated Amsterdam's cleanliness with his own idea of paradise. He saw no ordure and human filth on cobblestone streets or on the canal quays and parks lined with oak and linden trees. Houses and windmills glistened from continual scrubbing, scouring, burnishing, rubbing, mopping, and washing. Silver, copper, and bronze nails, hinges, and knockers on their lacquered door-fronts sparkled.

Vicente noted how the rows of the identical and narrow two-story brick houses contrasted with the somber and enigmatic residences in Spain, whose owners disdained trade and commerce and were secluded from the world by high walls and narrow, grilled windows. The typical burger's home was separated from the street by gratings over a narrow ditch. Vaults at street level had small leaded glass windows with canopies of wood covering the frontage to protect craftsmen from the elements while they worked. He was appalled that these homes had been constructed to allow their tradesmen to deal in business from the street. Shamelessly, for all who passed by to see.

Above the canopies were the windows of the first story. *So much glass, so little privacy.* The second story had either a great single casement window or a door between smaller windows and eaves if the merchant desired to receive merchandise hoisted from the street. The roofs had steep side panels, which formed pediments on top of facades and also contained dormer windows embellished with square shields extending on both sides.

No siesta for the industrious Protestants. Fleets of ships anchored in the harbor waited turns to dock at the busy waterfront where fishwives screeched louder than the seabirds and hawked their husbands' catches of the day. Along the canals, Amsterdam's warehouses opened onto the street and water's edge where laborers unloaded boxes, barrels, sacks, and tuns. In homes between the warehouses, artisans, shopkeepers, and merchants plied their trades.

During his walk, Vicente discovered two blights he had not observed at first: Citizens regularly dumped huge amounts of rubbish into the canals; and the docks reeked of residue left by chandlers, salt refining houses, and fish markets. El Grau, Barcelona, and Amsterdam. All waterfronts were the same.

He strolled over foot bridges, which could be raised and lowered, and arcaded fixed spans that took him into fashionable districts where goods from all over the world were sold. He browsed among bookshops, stationers, and purveyors of charts, maps, sextants, and other nautical necessities. He passed hardware, dye, ironmonger shops, and apothecaries with precious and arcane curatives from the eastern end of the Mediterranean.

At the canal known as The Belt, Singel in the Dutch language, Vicente stopped at the market where farmers and flower growers delivered produce by barge and coastal packets. He went out of his way to look at boxes of spectacular tulips. Their flaming primary colors dazzled his eyes. Others no less brilliant were irregularly striped: Red and pink on white; lilac and purples on white; red or violet on yellow. Their names matched their pigmented glory: Viceroy, Admiral Pottebaker, General Bol, Semper Augustus.

And all Catalina had ever seen of these beauties was worthless paper.

Continuing on his walk, Vicente succumbed to enticing aromas and sampled delicious pastries, breads, and cheeses. He roamed through shops filled with fine fabrics, Nuremberg porcelain, Italian majolica, Delft faience, Lyons silk, Spanish taffeta, and Haarlem linen bleached to blinding whiteness.

Amsterdam seemed not to be a city but the largest market ever created by man. A consumer's cornucopia.

He often made eye contact with flirtatious young women. What had those laughing girls said as they passed? He wished he could understand all their comments, especially when they used their local idiom. His ear had not yet adapted to the Dutch language, and he would have to expand his vocabulary.

Vicente believed he would never starve in Amsterdam should he ever run out of money. The Dutch were as addicted to gambling as cleanliness. In the taverns, he watched men wager at cards and other games while they drank and smoked. On the streets he saw them betting on every conceivable probability. He also paid attention to prices offered by tradesmen and merchants.

The Amsterdam equivalent to the Spanish escudo was the gold sovereign, worth fifteen silver florins. One florin equaled twenty stuivers, an odd name for a coin, and a stuiver was worth sixteen penningen. Vicente spent eight penningen for a tankard of ale. Awful tasting bile, he thought. In the bakeries he saw a heavy loaf of rye priced at seven and-a-half stuivers.

For the first time in his life, he would have to keep an accurate ledger. He no longer had income from clerical duties and benefices. Vicente felt his doublet weighing heavily. He could not continue to carry so much wealth on his person. He had been told the regulated Wisselbank would be the safest place for it, which seemed no different to him than entrusting strangers with his coins and gems.

The strong north wind cut through his clothes like an icy knife. He would need sturdier garments for the coming winter. He wrapped his cloak around his body and visited shops that sold men's clothing. Shirts averaged about a florin; a house gown ten; plain coat, vest, breeches about thirty. Doublets of black velvet adorned with black silk facings cost many times more.

Vicente inspected a small house offered for sale at three hundred florins, the equivalent of twenty Spanish escudos. He learned from his inquiries that speculators subdivided homes into apartments and let them at exorbitant prices, some for as high as two thousand florins a year. He would have to speak with *Vrouw* Cornelia. She was gouging him at five a week for one small room.

Vicente calculated he had enough escudos to live comfortably without working for about two years if he was careful, more if he would sell the embroidery, triptych, ruby ring and jeweled gold cross María had given him. *As if I would part with them.* He expected to be established as a physician before need overcame sentiment.

Because the sun was about to set, Vicente decided to wait until the following morning to make his first appearance in the district where most Spanish and Portuguese Jews chose to live. This evening he intended to soak his body. No more icy rivers or cold seas in winter. A tub filled with hot water would be ocean enough.

Chapter 81
Jews

At daybreak, Vicente stood on Houtgrachtstraat off Jodenbreestraat, Jews Broad Street, and marveled at the first active Jewish house of worship he had ever seen. Its architecture was not oriental or exotic in any way, but typical of Amsterdam. The wide three-story sandstone building had small casement windows between pilastered columns and molded curvilinear detail covering its facade and gables. To his surprise, the synagogue door was wide open and unguarded.

He watched and listened to the citizens of Amsterdam as they walked past. No vicious mob formed to attack the Jews. No malicious comments directed against them. No hostile glances towards the building. But then, he was in Amsterdam, not Spain.

Vicente walked up the three front steps of the synagogue between ornate wrought iron benches with space for two and went through the open door into a bare vestibule with stairways on each side. The unadorned anteroom contained a tap, soap and towel.

More cleanliness. Jews washed their hands before they entered their houses of worship. So did Vicente before he negotiated the stairs.

He hesitated at the top. Impressive silver chandeliers hung from ceiling beams. Grilled galleries ran along both lengths of the synagogue.

Under the gallery to Vicente's right, a bearded scholar and a pale boy bent over a book at one of the tables used for studying or praying. Beneath the gallery to his left were five rows of wooden benches where more than a dozen men sat and swayed in prayer. Each wore a long fringed shawl that fell from hat to waist. Each had a peculiar black strap wrapped around his wrists and between the fingers, and another around the forehead.

The synagogue's wooden floor planks squeaked at each of Vicente's steps. The worshipers glared in his direction, then resumed their praying. Across the room, the man and boy also stared at him.

Aware he was being watched, Vicente went to the middle of the synagogue. He stopped at a raised platform about a meter above the floor surrounded by railings, benches, and candles flaming in glass lamps. He assumed it was the pulpit where their rabbis taught and preached.

No bleeding statues. No Virgin, Savior, saints, or biblical tale represented in stained glass. Nothing in the synagogue to suggest myth and superstition. A rational and reasonable religion, the Law of Moses seemed to be, contrary to the Church's teachings.

Vicente turned to walk towards a cupboard at the far end of the synagogue, and the man who had been reading at the table rose and blocked his way. He put a finger to his lips, took Vicente's arm, and escorted him out of the synagogue. The pale boy, whose dark curls hung past his ears, carried the book and followed at their heels like an eager puppy.

They stood by a young linden tree in a small park across from the synagogue. An hour into daylight, the streets were filled with noisy tradesmen, shoppers, and an occasional fancy carriage. The aroma of fresh bread wafted in the breeze.

The man had a dignified bearing and honest eyes. Physically, he was ordinary: Typical graying mustache and beard; slight physique and less than average height. He dressed plainly.

Definitely a scholar. Most likely the boy's teacher.

"I see you are a stranger, Senhor. Can I be of help?"

Vicente was pleased to hear an Iberian tongue spoken in a foreign land, even if it was Portuguese. He replied in Spanish, "Yes, Señor. I arrived in Amsterdam two days ago."

The man switched to adequate Spanish. "For good or for ill?"

"I am neither spy, informer, nor assassin."

"Then whom do I have the honor of addressing?"

"Vicente de Rocamora." He was tempted to add *de las casas* David y Arnulf.

"De Rocamora?" He moved closer to Vicente and studied his face. "The same man who was confessor to King Philip's sister, now Empress María? The Dominican who might have become Inquisitor General of all Spain?"

Vicente had expected his reputation to precede him. "I am that man. And how are you addressed, Señor?"

"I am Menasseh ben Israel, one of the rabbis at our synagogue, Kahal Kadosh de Talmud Torah, the Holy Congregation of the Talmud Torah."

"And I have heard of you, Don Menasseh."

Vicente had learned much about the thirty-five year old rabbi from the Inquisitorial dossiers of both Portugal and Spain. Born Manuel Dias Soeiro, he had been brought to Amsterdam by his father, who then converted to the Law of Moses, took the name Joseph ben Israel and changed his son's name to Menasseh. According to informers, the rabbi approached every immigrant and visitor from Portugal and Spain. If they had the slightest trace of Jewish blood, he persuaded them to come back to the faith of their fathers, as he and his family had done.

Although a rabbi, Menasseh also had a printing press. He published prayer books in Hebrew, and his own plays and treatises in several languages. His *Conciliador,* published in Latin, had made the Jewish religion more understandable and acceptable to Protestants. The rabbi's sermons were so stirring that Dutch Christians came to the synagogue to hear them.

The boy coughed to bring attention to himself, and Menasseh said, "Don Vicente, this is my most brilliant pupil, Bento . . . Baruch d'Espinoza, who is studying for his bar mitzvah to come in two years."

Vicente acknowledged Bento. Then he noticed several men enter the synagogue wearing shawls and carrying prayer books. "How many Jews live in Amsterdam?"

"More than three hundred families, mostly Portuguese and a few Spanish. Not a significant number. Amsterdam has a population of well over a hundred thousand. Now, please tell me, Don Vicente, why have you come to Amsterdam?"

"Because it is the only place on earth where one can have Jewish blood without suffering penalties."

"Yes, for the most part what you say is true. Dutch Protestants generally receive us with interest, curiosity, and even esteem. As in no other place in Europe, they give us the freedom to worship as Jews, in Hebrew, to live where we choose, to print our books, and to dress no differently from them. Here in Amsterdam, you will find no cap, badge, or outlandish clothes to identify and humiliate us, and no Inquisition to hound us. But know this. The magistrates have passed laws that forbid Jews to proselyte, and they deny us entry to nearly all their guilds."

Vicente was grateful he had encountered the gregarious rabbi, whose reputation for garrulousness had reached Spain. He intended to feed on every bit of information possible, even if they stayed as rooted as the lindens in the park soil.

"Don Vicente, there is something else you should know. Many *poderosos* and rabbis in our community are unreceptive to those who flee Portugal and Spain solely because of their Jewish blood and come here for sanctuary without embracing the Law of Moses. Did you Judaize secretly in Spain?"

"No."

"But you were denounced to the Inquisition."

"No."

"No? Then why did you leave?"

"I was an Olivarista, and the new Inquisitor General is a bigot who intends to enforce the *limpieza* statutes to their full extent and beyond. Although no one could produce proof, all my enemies believed my mother was tainted."

"Was she?"

"Yes."

Menasseh frowned and pulled at his beard. "But you are still a Christian who has come here out of convenience, not to return to the religion of our forefathers."

"Those of us born in Spain and Portugal, even you, Don Menasseh, we have all been baptized and raised as Catholics. And yes, I preached and confessed penitents as a Dominican. I found much that is positive in the Church. But still a Christian? I suppose so. I have not accepted another faith."

"May I assume that in time you will be ready to follow the Law of Moses?"

"First, I must learn what it is."

"And study Hebrew."

"I read Hebrew fluently."

"Excellent, your education as a Jew will be much easier. Now, to more practical matters. Who will speak for you in our community?"

Vicente did not intend to commit to Menasseh's alien religion. He had come to Amsterdam to live freely as a man of Jewish blood without converting to another restrictive faith. Yet, the rabbi's presumptuous enthusiasm was so ingratiating he decided to play along. He should be able to associate with these Iberian Jews and learn from their physicians without submitting to the Law of Moses.

"I was unaware one needed references in order to enter your Jewish community, Don Menasseh."

"We must always be alert for spies of the Inquisition who wish to learn the names of our families still living in Spain and Portugal."

"I repeat, I am no spy."

"Then I must ask, is there anyone who will vouch for you in Amsterdam?"

Vicente recalled the names of those he had helped flee Spain. Many had gone to the Ottoman Empire and the Venetian ghetto. "Martín Pinto."

"Don Abraham, you mean. He passed away last month."

Vicente almost crossed himself. "May he rest in peace." He remembered the name of a man he had met once and casually at the Astórquia Palacio. "Pedro Aranha knew of my association with Martín Pinto and his friends before he left Spain."

"Alas, he died a broken man about five years ago. He lost all in the great tulip fiasco."

"So did a good friend of mine who foolishly invested in that immoral scheme."

"I see that we will have to rid you of the Catholic prejudice against trading in stocks and commodities. Can you name anyone else?"

"No, those I helped escape the Inquisition are unaware of my services."

"Anyone in Hamburg?"

"Again, no."

Menasseh stared at Vicente as if trying to read his mind. "I believe you. Come with me. I must officiate at a *berit milah*, the circumcision of Don Daniel Touro's firstborn son. He will welcome you. Yes, everyone there will welcome you to our community."

Chapter 82
The Family Touro

The Touro home was situated in the middle of a row of identical and narrow two-story brick houses owned by prosperous diamond and coral merchants. Vicente followed Menasseh to a waxed oak front door painted dark green with a shiny decorative copper plate protecting the keyhole. The rabbi lifted a heavy brass knocker shaped in the form of a bull's head Vicente had seen before in Antwerp and rapped twice. Then he and Bento kissed their fingers and touched the Hebrew letters of a small metal cylinder attached to the doorframe.

"Don Menasseh, what is that ritual?"

"Every Jewish home has a mezuzah on the front door. It contains a piece of rolled parchment inscribed on one side with scriptural passages from Deuteronomy and the Lord's name written on the other. It is a reminder of our faith in God."

Vicente chose not to offend Menasseh by voicing his skepticism. He saw no difference between reverence for a mezuzah and genuflecting before cross and holy images.

A young woman opened the door. A white linen cap covered her hair. Clothed in black wool and plain falling collar, she gave Vicente a thousand-sun smile of welcome, as if she could not have been happier to see him, as if she had been expecting him.

Menasseh made the introductions. "Senhorita Abigail, this man is Don Vicente de Rocamora, recently arrived from Spain. Don Vicente, Senhorita Abigail Moses Toura."

"Welcome to my uncle's home, *Capitán* de Rocamora. We have met before in Antwerp."

"Señorita."

The shapeless child has blossomed into a spectacular flower.

Vicente's eyes lingered on each of the young woman's attractive features: Pouting kissable pink lips, and fair skin without wens, mustache, or moles; hazel eyes expressing a lively spirit, keen intelligence, and thickly lashed as if she had applied Egyptian kohl. She evoked memories of Moraíma's earthy appeal and María's serene regal demeanor.

And her name: Toura, Toro, Taurelle, Taurus. Are we also kin?

Abigail led them upstairs where family and guests had gathered in the great room above the ground floor. She flashed Vicente another warm smile before joining the other women.

Vicente appreciated the fine furniture and colorful Turkish rugs scattered over the shiny slate blue and ivory white tile floor. Above the doorway, a silver curvilinear plaque had an inscription in Hebrew. He was impressed by several large paintings with biblical themes and puzzled when he saw the new mother sitting in a canopied bed.

"What is a bed doing in the *estrado*?"

"In Dutch homes, it is customary for the master's bed to be in the great room." Menasseh took him to the men, "I have brought an important guest who has just arrived from Spain. Don Vicente de Rocamora."

All the men wore hats and expensive velvet doublets, breeches and silk hose of somber colors broken only by falling snowy white lace collars. A disheveled artist was sketching them, and Menasseh identified him by one of those impossible Dutch names, which Vicente heard as *Rimbrand*.

Daniel Touro, a portly merchant in his late thirties, welcomed Vicente and introduced him to his brothers, Judah and Eliahu, and to a dozen or so men and adolescent boys all of whom had patriarchal or scriptural names.

Menasseh next presented Vicente to the first of two men not related to the Touros. "This is our illustrious Don Ephraim Bueno, son of the equally esteemed and departed Don Joseph Bueno, who was physician to Prince Maurice of Orange."

Vicente saw through Bueno's kindly face and marked the graying physician as suspicious and inflexible.

Menasseh turned to the second man, who was taller, wider in girth, and no less guarded. "And another of our community's shining lights, Don Jacob Barossa."

Vicente had read Barossa's Inquisitorial dossier. Born in Castile, he had been known as Diego de Barros when still a professing Christian and student of natural sciences, medicine, botany, and astronomy.

"Don Jacob is one of the *parnassim* of Talmud Torah."

"*Parnassim*?" Not only Dutch, he would also have to adjust his hearing to spoken Hebrew.

Menasseh next led Vicente to the women with Bento trailing after them. "A *parnass* is a warden and judge of the community."

Although the women dressed alike in black attire with elaborate freshly laundered white collars, their fashionable wigs or linen bonnets differentiated them. Attended by female relations, the mother sat against fine yellow satin pillows in the freestanding carved bed under a sumptuous gold trimmed cobalt blue silk canopy. She wore a sable fur stole to warm her shoulders. Clothed in lacy white linen, her son slept in the crook of her arm.

The youngest children played or crawled close to their mothers. Dressed as miniature adults, they reminded Vicente of the Court *bufónes*.

Abigail introduced him to the women. "My aunts, Doñas Rachel Toura, Leah Toura, Ribcá Toura . . . and my cousin, Senhorita Sara Toura, daughter of my father's brother, Don Eliahu, who is visiting from Rotterdam. Everyone, Don Vicente de Rocamora."

Sara stared unblinking at Vicente. She was slight of build, with sharp swarthy features and kinky blue-black hair. Her velvet dress and fancy lace collar were of the most expensive materials. Her dark eyes and predatory expression reminded him of Violante.

He bowed to the women and faced the new mother, "My congratulations, Doña Rachael." He turned to Abigail. "Don Menasseh told me. My condolences for your father's passing."

"My Uncle Judah has been generous. I am living in his house until I marry."

Sara stepped between them. "That may be forever. No man will wed a girl with so little dowry." She moved closer to Vicente. "Anyway, Uncle Judah will not allow her to marry so easily. She is too valuable. She mills and polishes his diamonds better than anyone in Amsterdam."

Abigail held Vicente's gaze. "I know whom I shall marry. I have already chosen him."

A small boy ran into Vicente's leg and fell. He lifted the toddler and coaxed him out of crying by making the same coin reappear from different parts of his face. He returned the boy to his mother where Tía Ribcá, a wrinkled old woman, pressed an amulet into her hand. "Take this and ward off the evil eye."

Ribcá's superstition contradicted Vicente's assumption that the Law of Moses was rational. It seemed these Jews were as superstitious as Christians. He returned to Menasseh with Bento still at his heels. "Are incantations against the evil eye part of your rites of circumcision?"

The rabbi frowned at Bento when the boy snickered. "Ribcá comes from Morocco where they believe Adam's first wife, Lilith, appears after the birth of a child as a female demon with a hag's face, long hair, sharp talons, and wings. That amulet supposedly prevents Lilith from harming the newborn infant and its mother."

"Silly nonsense, is it not, Don Vicente?"

"Bento, you must never . . ."

Menasseh's reprimand to the boy was stillborn when he saw a young man lead an elder into the great room and seat him in a chair by a small table at the far end. The newcomer wore a skullcap and had the majestic flowing white beard of a biblical patriarch. "Don Vicente, he is Rabbi Abraham Abulafia, recently arrived from Salonika and the *mohel* who will circumcise the infant."

"*Mohel?*" Vicente winked at Bento. "It seems I must also become Rabbi Menasseh's pupil."

Chapter 83
Berit Mila

"Don Vicente," Menasseh said, "the ceremony will begin shortly, so your lesson must be brief. Do you know why every male Jewish child is circumcised?"

"I have never believed it was intended to mark Jews as different. I have seen African slaves who had been circumcised according to tribal rites, and those who submit to Islam also practice the custom."

"The *Shulchan Aruch*, the traditional Code of Jewish Law, states that circumcision is the most fundamental and important commandment of the entire Torah." Menasseh opened his bible to Genesis and showed Vicente relevant passages. "The religious significance of *berit milah* is derived from God's commandments for Abraham to remove the blemish of his foreskin, to circumcise his son Isaac eight days after his birth, and all male children thereafter. *Berit* means covenant, that binding unbreakable relationship of love between God and Abraham. *Milah*, the ceremony of circumcision, symbolizes the continuation of the covenant from one generation to the next. At the end of the *berit milah*, the infant formally receives his Hebrew name."

"Must mature males who come from Spain and Portugal also submit?"

"Without question. *Berit milah* is the only spiritual entrance to our covenant with God. A Midrash tells us that our unbroken observance of the mitzvah of circumcision was one of the four reasons why we were redeemed from slavery in Egypt. And the Talmud tells us that Jerusalem fell to the Romans and the Temple was destroyed because Jews failed to circumcise their sons."

"Why would not cutting off an earlobe or piercing it do as well as a symbol?"

"That would be a mutilation. Circumcision removes a physical blemish." Menasseh cited passages from Jeremiah, Ezekiel, Leviticus, and Exodus to explain spiritual blemishes such as uncircumcised heart and ears, and in the instance of Moses' stuttering, uncircumcised lips. "It applies not only to man. Leviticus states: 'When you enter the land of Israel and plant any tree for food, you shall regard its first fruit as the foreskin. For the first three years the tree shall be uncircumcised for you, its fruit not to be eaten. In the fourth year, all its fruit shall be set aside for jubilation before the Lord; and only in the fifth year may you use its fruit . . . that its yield to you may be increased: I the Lord am your God'."

"If it can be done to a man at any age, why is the male infant always circumcised on the eighth day?" Vicente asked.

Menasseh saw that the *mohel* was not yet ready, so he continued, "It is also written in Leviticus that after a woman bears a child, she is in a severe state of impurity for seven days. The mother's blood is filthy, socially disruptive, contaminated, and associated with death. Only on the eighth day, does she enter a lesser state of impurity. At that time, the male child is removed from his mother's contamination by the spilling of his own blood during his *berit milah*. Then, his blood becomes clean, unifying, and symbolic of God's covenant. The ceremony of circumcision thus removes the infant male from the realm of death and marks his passage from the impurity of being born of woman to the purity of life in a community of men."

Once again, limpio, limpieza de sangre. Obsession with purity of blood. Are all religions, all peoples the same after all? Have I come to the Jewish community of Amsterdam for naught? These Spanish and Portuguese Jews are no different from the old-Christian Castilians. Their religion too. Blood as symbolism. Their ritual of circumcision, and the wine of a Catholic mass.

"But, also know this," Menasseh said, "circumcision is not a rite into manhood. Only Bar Mitzvah makes a Jewish boy of thirteen a man in the religious community. He cannot be a complete man, however, until he marries."

"Don Menasseh, if circumcision is so special, why did not God create all men without foreskins?"

"Interesting point," Bento said.

"Abraham pretty much asked our Lord God the same question in *Genesis*. 'And God replied, I am The One who said, Enough.' Because God commands circumcision, the committed Jew must observe it. Therefore, all questions become irrelevant. You cannot be a Jew or bring yourself into the covenant without being circumcised according to ritual."

"Even if others believe you to be a Jew and mistreat you because of it?"

"Even so."

"Rabbi." Bento tugged at Menasseh's sleeve when Daniel brought soap, towel, and a basin filled with water to Abulafia.

"We are ready to begin," Menasseh said to Vicente with a twinkle in his eye. "I expect Bento here will be delighted to answer your questions during the ceremony."

Two of the Touro males placed elaborately carved straight back chairs with thick burgundy and gold silk cushions opposite Abulafia. Judah sat in one of them with a clean fine linen pillow on his lap.

"If either of the infant's grandfathers were alive, he would be *sandak*, the godfather," Bento said. "As the oldest male of the family, Don Judah will be *sandak* today, and he has been given the added honor of holding the baby during the *Milah*."

"Why not the father?"

"See how nervous Don Daniel is? If he faints or even shakes at the wrong moment, tragedy can occur. That is why Doña Rachel cannot be allowed to witness the ceremony. She might cry out or scream at the instant the *mohel* cuts her son and may cause him to make a mistake."

"Who will sit in the other chair?"

"It is the chair of Elijah. When weak-willed King Ahab was influenced to abolish circumcision by his wicked Phoenician wife, Jezebel, Elijah appealed to God on behalf of the Israelites. And the Lord intervened to restore the observance of *berit milah*. Therefore Elijah is present at all circumcisions as a witness to our enduring loyalty, a symbol of our commitment to keep Israel alive."

"How many circumcisions has Don Menasseh performed, Bento?"

"None. He is not trained to be a *mohel*."

Vicente looked at Abulafia. Could his veined gnarled hands wield a steady knife?

The baby screamed and cried when one of the men took him from his mother's arms, wrapped him in restraining cloths, and handed him to Daniel. The women and their smaller children remained at Rachael's bedside. All the males stood with their backs to the women. The artist known as Rimbrand sketched the scene.

After Daniel Touro brought his eight-day old son to Abulafia, all chanted:

Berukhim atem kehel emunay. Ubarukh haba beshem Hashem. Yeled hayulad yiheye besiman tob.

Vicente's hearing had not quite adapted to their Hebrew and he caught only a few words without understanding their meaning.

The rabbi-*mohel* held the infant. He intoned what sounded to Vicente like a blessing over its crying, and placed the baby on the linen pillow in Judah's lap.

Daniel also receited blessings, and all sang:

Baruch HaBa B'ahavah, we welcome you . . .

Vicente was beginning to understand as they spoke:

"You are your parent's dream realized, and their hopes fulfilled . . .

"You are the latest and best chapter in the unfolding lives of your mother and father . . .

"You are brand new . . . a symbol of today and tomorrow; your life is a new clean slate upon which events and people will leave their impression . . .

"You are a bridge over which we who welcome you can gaze from this day into future days, from our generation into yours . . .

"You are the newest link in the endless chain of our people's history . . .

"*Baruch HaBa B'ahavah* . . . we welcome you to life with love."

Abulafia invited the Prophet Elijah to come and give both him and the baby support and strength. He washed his hands in the basin, dipped each of his tools in an engraved silver flagon of wine, and held them over a candle flame. The *mohel* then dropped to one knee and adjusted the crying infant's position on the pillow in Judah's lap. He exposed the baby's penis and between thumb and forefinger, stretched the foreskin to its limit, and pulled it through the small loop extending from one of the instruments.

Vicente winced when Abulafia cut and intoned over the baby's screaming, "Blessed art Thou, Lord our God, King of the Universe, Who has sanctified us by Thy commandments, and commanded us regarding *milah* . . . Who has sanctified Thy beloved from birth."

All responded with "Amen."

Daniel recited, "Blessed art Thou Lord our God, King of the Universe, Who has sanctified us by Thy commandments and commanded us to bring our son into the covenant of Abraham our father."

The men responded, "As he entered the covenant, so may he attain a life of Torah, mitzvah, and go to the wedding canopy."

Marriage.

Vicente turned to Abigail. Their eyes held. If he wanted her or any other Jewish woman, he must first submit to circumcision. He remembered Yusef telling him that a circumcised man was more sensitive and received enhanced pleasure from a woman. But first he would have to experience excruciating pain, the possibility of a fatal mistake, and be marked for life as a Jew.

Abulafia dropped the severed foreskin on the side table, poured wine on the infant's raw penis, and dressed it with clean linen. After the baby was unbound, its crying subsided.

"What is done with the foreskin?" Vicente asked Bento.

"It is buried without ceremony."

Menasseh recited a blessing over the child, which invoked God's special protection, and its father announced, "Welcome my first-born son, Joshua bar Daniel."

While Judah carried his godson around the room on its pillow, Menasseh led another communal recital. "Our God and God of our Fathers, sustain this child, whose name we give in Israel this day to be. May his father and mother rejoice in the offspring. And with love and wisdom may they be privileged to teach him the meaning of the covenant, which he has entered into today. To inspire him to practice righteousness in speech and in conduct, to seek the truth and the ways of peace. May this child grow into manhood as a blessing to his family, the Jewish people, and mankind. As he has entered the covenant, so may he attain the blessings of Torah, marriage, and good deeds, and let us say amen."

The prayer gave Vicente new respect for the Law of Moses. No pleas to idols and virgins. No need for intermediaries. No insolent demands for God or saint to gratify petty wishes. It was a prayer of love and hope for the boy to be wise and righteous.

Vicente congratulated the happy parents and drank toasts to their health and the baby's future. He watched the proud father show off his son to each man and woman before returning little Joshua to the arms of his anxious wife.

He was there and not there. Had the *Nasim* Natronai El-Makhiri carried Isaac-Guillherme the same way? Did Pepin and Charlemagne attend his *berit milah*?

He was alone and not alone. He sensed the presence of his ancestors. Their voices told him to come back to his people. Then they were gone.

Still not alone, Vicente caught both Abigail and Sara casting glances at him while they helped supervise the smallest children and kept them from the mother's bed so the baby could sleep. If he wanted to live among Jews, he would have to conform to their peculiar laws and rituals.

Premature. Why would he want to exchange his comfortable Catholicism for the Law of Moses, religion of outcasts, simply to belong to a community? In any case, he had more immediate and practical concerns. He intended to ask Bueno and Barossa how best to become a physician in Amsterdam, but Menasseh came over to him.

"Forgive me for ignoring you, Don Vicente. I have not asked what you thought of the *berit milah*."

"Despite the bloodletting and pain, your prayers were so stirring I may yet be inspired to follow the Law of Moses."

Menasseh called for silence and said, "Don Vicente has expressed his wish to join our congregation, and I shall sponsor him."

Vicente was appalled that the rabbi had construed his conditional language as absolute. Bento's eyes could not have opened wider. Abigail reacted with a smile for him. Sara whispered in earnest to her father.

Daniel embraced him. "Don Vicente, you have added to the joy of my son's *berit milah*."

Menasseh exulted, "Think what a prize he is to snatch from the bosoms of the Catholic Church and the Spanish Court. May his example encourage others to come back to us."

"Why did you not to come to Amsterdam sooner?" Bueno asked.

"Don Ephraim, I expected to accomplish great deeds in Spain."

After Vicente described his service to Olivares and the Crown and his failure to become Inquisitor General, Bueno shook his head. "He would not have been the first Inquisitor General of Jewish blood, and they were always our most ruthless persecutors."

"You will see worse now that Arce has control of the Holy Office."

Eliahu received a prod from his daughter. "Don Vicente, have you the means to survive here in Amsterdam, or must our community support you?"

"I have brought sufficient escudos, sovereigns as you call them."

"Then will you trade, sell, or invest?"

"No."

"Or grind and shape diamonds?"

"I know nothing of precious stones."

Eliahu's tone became more unctuous. "But of course you would be willing to learn, if you should marry a merchant's daughter. A Jew cannot be a complete man until he weds."

"I will be neither tradesman nor merchant." Vicente gestured towards Barossa and Bueno. "I will be a physician."

"Excellent, Don Vicente," Menasseh said. "For the Talmud teaches that to save one life is to save the entire world."

"First and foremost, he must learn to follow the Law of Moses," Bueno snapped.

All spoke at once:

"He will have to study Torah and Talmud."

"Observe the six-hundred-and-thirteen Laws."

"And answer all questions to our satisfaction."

Barossa commanded silence. "Don Vicente, we examine every stranger who comes to us, so please take no offense."

"I take none, if none is offered."

"Our greatest fear is that any newcomer from Iberia may be an informer or an assassin for the Inquisition."

"They would be my enemies."

"Indeed? We must also learn about those who seek refuge in Amsterdam if they have fled Iberia merely because of their varying degrees of Jewish blood."

"Why? Is not a Jew a Jew?"

"Not all individuals of Jewish blood come here to follow the Law of Moses and observe our rites." Bueno's harsh tone and words belied his benign, world-weary countenance and surname. "Such men carry into our community the plagues of heterodoxy, freethinking, and Christian idolatry. They can infect the entire community if we do not deal with them immediately. I always say cut off the infected part before it spreads and do not wait to dispose of the whole, as we did when we excommunicated the heretic, Uriel da Costa."

Vicente turned in surprise to Menasseh who described what had happened to the unfortunate heretic. He was disappointed to learn that the Jewish community excommunicated dissenters and those who questioned orthodox practices in a ceremony similar to that of the Catholic Church with curses of Sodom and Gomorrah identical to the Anathema of the Holy Office. He had not expected to discover in the middle of Dutch Calvinist Amsterdam an island of Iberia no less reactionary than Castile.

If not here, where else can I live?

The aroma of savory cooking wafted into the great room, and Daniel took Vicente's arm. "You will be my most honored guest at the feast, and in the near future, may we all witness your own *berit milah*."

Chapter 84
Don Isaac

After the men and older boys washed their hands, they went into a separate room to dine apart from the women. They sat at a long table decorated with silver candelabra and fine utensils, elegant porcelain plates, and delicate crystal goblets. Vicente ate heartily, drank liberally, and answered all questions put to him until Bueno whispered in Abulafia's ear. The *mohel* stared at Vicente horrified.

"You are a Dominican?"

"I suppose I still am in the eyes of the Church."

"I have never been to Sefarad. Is it true you Christians worship a woman there named Miriam and call her María?"

"In Spain," Vicente said, "Catholics believe that The Virgin intercedes on their behalf the way all mothers do when fathers are angry with their children. María has taken on additional importance because of Spain's obsession with *limpieza de sangre*. When a man enters another's house he says *Ave María* instead of Praised be God in order to avoid suspicion he might be a crypto-Jew or new-Christian."

Abulafia flavored his tone of voice with sarcasm. "The truth is they worship images, not our unseen Lord God, Who is One. How are they different from the Greeks and Romans, pagans all, who idolized Zeus and Jupiter as their supreme gods? But, what else can you expect from the credulous who believe bread and wine become the flesh and blood of their false messiah? Which is why they can also believe the lie we add the blood of our children to the unleavened bread we make for our Holy Days."

Abulafia's mockery offended Vicente. Ballebrera, Arce and Tomás too, would have been astounded to hear him defending the Catholic faith. "The purpose of the cross, statues, and other icons is not for Christians to pray *to*. They are symbols to pray *through*."

"No, Dominican, you have worshiped false idols, and all forms of idolatry are deceptions created by the Evil One. And that also includes your secular gentile teachings, all of which are helpless. Each must depend upon the others. One cannot become an astronomer without knowledge of geometry and algebra, logic and natural philosophy."

"Obvious and true, but what is your point?"

Abulafia spoke as if lecturing a schoolboy, "Listen to me, you, with your short-sighted brain. The study of our Holy Torah does not require the slightest knowledge of geometry, nor of any other secular study. For all is in it, and it is of itself. You still do not understand? Let me cite an example. The astronomical lore of our Talmud is a holy means towards the proper fixing of the Jewish calendar and its festivals. Whereas, your profane astronomy seeks to know the universe as an independent goal."

"And what is wrong with that?"

"One can never know God. Are you circumcised?"

"No."

"Have you kept our Sabbath and observed our Holy Days?"

"No."

"Then you have never Judaized."

"No."

Abulafia waved his hand as if to dismiss Vicente. "He is no Jew. Otherwise, he would have come here sooner to the New Jerusalem to follow the Law of Moses. He will spy on us, then return to Spain and continue to preach and worship the bastard false messiah and his whore of a mother, and serve the Order that condemns our people to the stake. Furthermore, what proof is there of his Jewish origins? As if it matters. I have no use for any partial-new-Christian Spaniard or Portuguese, whose last ancestor to follow the Law of Moses may have lived seven or more generations earlier. Such Jewish blood is diluted so thin as to seem like polluted water."

Vicente struggled to control his anger. "In Spain one suffers great penalties for having the slightest drop of Jewish blood, and, therefore, can never be Christian or Spanish enough. It seems among Jews like you, one can never be Jewish enough."

Menasseh raised his hands as a peacemaker. "Rabbi, Don Vicente, please . . ."

"Abulafia has the soul of an Inquisitor General, but one considerably less benign than Sotomayor. It seems your New Jerusalem would have a religion as intolerant as Spanish old-Christian Catholicism with an Index to stifle study and literature."

"His views are not shared by all of us in Amsterdam," Menasseh protested. "I welcome and accept you, as will so many others. I hope you will join our congregation in spite of what you have just heard."

Vicente hesitated. What were the alternatives? He could no longer survive as a Catholic. If he lived among Dutch Christian Protestants, he would carry the stigma of being an untrustworthy Dominican Catholic from their great enemy Spain. As a freethinker, he would

be more of an outcast than a Jew. To say no to Menasseh would isolate him from the Iberian Jewish community of Amsterdam. A qualified yes could buy him time to until he learned more about his options.

He evaluated Menasseh and the good will of the Touros against Bueno and Abulafia. The synagogue's lack of idolatry and the beauty of the prayers continued to impress him.

"Don Menasseh, I might if . . ."

Daniel slapped his hand on the table. "He means it."

I did not, but the perception is that I have.

"Even if he is sincere," Bueno said, "which I doubt, we have a serious problem. It would be different if we had proof of even one accusation that he ever Judaized in Spain. There is none. He is still a Christian, still a friar of our greatest enemy, the Dominican Order."

"If he has Jewish blood, he is still a Jew whether or not he has obeyed the commandments," Menasseh said.

Abulafia pointed at Vicente. "What proof? What proof can you offer us to show the purity of your Jewish blood?"

"Do I need a Jewish *limpieza de sangre* here in Amsterdam to satisfy Inquisitor Abulafia?"

The elderly rabbi screeched, "Those who come to the Law of Moses after worshiping your Christian form of paganism are a danger to our sons. Tell us. Why did you become a friar?"

Vicente related the story of his pledge of honor to Rafal. "I served my Infanta and the Count-Duke. I rescued Judaizers from the Inquisition. I hoped to become a reforming Inquisitor General and help Olivares abolish the *limpieza* statutes."

"And of course you were a sincere Catholic."

He ignored Bueno's irony. "Although I came to appreciate and admire much of the Church's teachings and functions, I did not believe all its dicta and dogma. I generally accepted the view of the Erasmian reformers who failed to alter the Church's direction in the previous century."

"Erasmians are no different than freethinkers and just as dangerous." Bueno said.

"A man who is devout in one religion, will be so in another," Abulafia preached, "and whomsoever is a hypocrite in one will be so in the other."

"And narrow minded dogmatists are as brothers in all religions," Vicente countered.

Bueno stood. "If I may continue, my objection to accepting this Dominican into our community is legal as well as theological. If any *mohel* circumcises him, the authorities will accuse us of proselytizing a Christian. We would be arrested and executed for breaking their law."

"Unfortunately Don Ephraim is correct," Menasseh said over murmurs of disappointment from the Touros. "Don Vicente, we must find a way for you to join our community without breaking the law."

"There is a simple solution." Vicente beckoned Bento to come closer and whispered in his ear. After the boy left the room, he pulled out his chair. "For the Prophet Elijah. As you all know, your first patriarch, Abraham, did not relegate his *berit milah* to another."

"What blasphemy is this?" Abulafia shouted.

"No blasphemy. I will circumcise myself. Here and now to prove my commitment."

What have I just said?

Vicente wished he could take back his words. Was it the amount of wine he had imbibed, a combativeness bred into his hot Valencian blood, the rational beauty of the *berit milah* prayers, or had he been possessed by the spirits of his *nasim* ancestors? He might never know.

Menasseh reached for a decanter and filled a silver goblet with wine. "I will recite the prayers for you."

"And be my *padriño*, my godfather?"

"I am honored to be your *sandak*, Don Vicente."

"And you honor my house." Daniel embraced Vicente then turned to the two physicians. "You will watch over him."

"Of course we will," Barossa said speaking for himself and Bueno, who was uncharacteristically speechless.

Vicente said to Abulafia, "Despite our differences, rabbi, will you guide me?"

"I want no part of this abomination, nor shall I permit any of my tools to be defiled."

Bueno helped Abulafia to his feet, and they left the room. Bento returned with a large tray containing a basin of hot water, soap, clean linen towels and pillow. Vicente hypothesized how self-circumcision might be done without a shield. Tighten a thread around the extended prepuce and cut? Pull and pinch the foreskin, then chop it off? Peel it back, then slice upwards and peel? Regardless, he would have to chance it with a steady hand and a good eye.

Menasseh offered him a cloth. "To bite on when you feel the pain."

"No need for it." Despite his bravado, Vicente was having second thoughts. He had announced his intention to circumcise himself here and now for all to hear. If he did not, what kind of impression would he forever leave in their memories, especially upon Bento and the young Touro males? If he did not, his word would be forever meaningless.

My word again. Honor might be the death of me yet, but without it, there is no life. Honor demands I go through with my self-circumcision, my personal Rubicon.

Vicente placed the pillow on the table. He intended to cut himself standing. He opened his doublet, dropped his breeches, and placed his uncircumcised penis on the linen pillow. He immersed in the goblet of wine the blade of the same dagger he had used to avenge his father's murder, let flames lick both edges, and spoke to the blade as if it were sentient: "Once the dispatcher of blood enemies, now the purified instrument of my *berit milah*."

Vicente had never heard so absolute a silence until Menasseh began to chant the same prayers he had recited earlier during Joshua bar Daniel's circumcision. Vicente wiped sweat from his brow and removed the blade from the flame. With thumb and forefinger, he stretched his foreskin to its limit.

He remembered Don Lope's final words: *Hear, oh Israel, the Lord our God, the Lord is One?*

Menasseh's eyes filled with tears, and he had difficulty speaking. "What patriarchal name will you take?"

"Isaac," Vicente said without hesitation.

"Isaac, our second patriarch," Menasseh announced with approval to the assemblage.

No, Don Menasseh, not that Isaac. I take the name of my great forebear, the Second Prince of Narbonne, son of Natronai, of the Royal House of David, and Alda, daughter of Charles Martel of the Royal House of Arnulf:

Isaac-Guillherme.

And Vicente brought down his dagger for the cut.

Historical Notes

From 1643 to 1645, Vicente, known as Don Isaac Israel de Rocamora, adapted to life in Holland. He began medical studies in 1645. No evidence exists that he followed the Law of Moses until 1647, the year he received his license to practice medicine and married Abigail in Amsterdam. Sons were born in 1648 and 1650.

Rocamora had difficulty accepting rabbinical tyranny over the most minute and intimate human functions, slavery to ritual, and spying within the Jewish community, so similar to Spanish Catholicism. The Sephardic Jewish community of Amsterdam was a piece of transplanted Catholic Spain, where ongoing tests of blood pedigree and orthodoxy dominated all existence. Even secular plays were prohibited, the same as in post-Olivares Spain.

Rocamora considered then rejected conversion to the Dutch Reformed Church in 1650. He settled for good in the Spanish-Portuguese Jewish community where his practice grew and prospered. He was respected as a learned man, philanthropist, and gifted poet in Spanish and Latin.

Seven more children were born to Rocamora and Abigail, the last in 1659 when he was fifty-eight years old. Rocamora served as *parnass*, warden, of the Jewish community, and provided medical and administrative services for the Jewish orphanage and the immigrant relief society.

In 1660, Rocamora received an exceptional honor; full privilege of Amsterdam citizenship, one of only three Jewish physicians so honored between 1641 and 1700.

After Abigail died in 1663, Rocamora married her cousin Sara Toura. They divorced two years later. He died in April 1684. His direct line continued through his second son, Solomon Isaac de Rocamora, and produced respected physicians over several generations.

Olivares died a lunatic in 1645.

Empress María died in 1646.

Philip IV's Queen Isabel died of fever in 1644, their son Baltazar Carlos in 1647. Their daughter María Teresa married Louis XIV. In 1649, Philip IV married his fifteen year old niece, Maria Anna, daughter of his sister, Empress María. He died in 1665; his retarded, deformed son, Carlos II, was the last Habsburg King of Spain.

In 1644, Jerónimo de Villanueva, Protonotario of Aragón, was denounced, arrested for heresy by Familiars of the Inquisition, and condemned. He was banished from Madrid. He died a broken man while his case was being reviewed by Rome.

During Arce Reynoso's tenure as Inquisitor General, 1643-1665, approximately twelve thousand new-Christian families fled Spain.

Charles I of England was beheaded in 1649 by Oliver Cromwell's Parliament.

Velázquez' canvas, *The Battle of Nördlingen*, was lost in a fire at Buen Retiro. No records or images of the masterpiece are extant.

Fernándo Cardoso left Spain in 1648 to practice Judaism in the Venetian ghetto; he changed his name to Isaac and became the greatest Jewish polemicist of the seventeenth century.

Manuel Cortizos de Villasante died in 1651; inquisitorial proceedings against his family revealed that he was a Judaizer, with a trust of six hundred thousand escudos in Amsterdam.

Rodrigo Méndez de Silva became known as the Spanish "Livy". Arrested in 1659 for Judaizing, he was tortured and abjured. Several years later, he appeared in the Venice ghetto, where he took the name Isaac and married an eighteen year old girl.

Manuel Fernández de Villareal became the Portuguese Consul in Paris and wrote a biography of Richelieu. He returned to Lisbon for reward of services in 1649. A careless letter from Menasseh ben Israel led to his arrest as a Judaizer. He died after an *auto-de fé* at the *quemadero* in 1652.

There is no evidence the Abbaye de St. Roch ever existed.

Documents confirming the existence of a Jewish Princedom in Septimania, ca. 760-900, survive to this day in various libraries.

Bodo, the Apostate, is a documented historical figure.

Rocamora's genealogy chart and other documents verifying his descent from King David and the House of Arnulf were lost or destroyed over the centuries.

Tomás de Rocamora became Bishop and Viceroy of Mallorca in 1644 and died 10 November 1653.

Francisco de Rocamora's direct line died out in the eighteenth-century; because of the *mayorazgo* between him and Jerónimo, the then Marqués de Rafal also became Conde de la Granja de Rocamora.

After Jerónimo de Rocamora died, Gaspar became the Second Marqués de Rafal and died without issue in 1666. Juan de Rocamora, *Maestro de Campo de Infanteria* as was his father, became the Third Marqués of Rafal.

In 1691, Juan's only surviving daughter, Jerónima de Rocamora y Cascante, Fourth Marquésa de Rafal, married Jaime Rosell Ruíz y Rocamora, grandson of his sister Isabel and Governor of Orihuela. They had no heirs, and various cousins inherited their titles. A Marqués de Rafal was elevated to grandee First Class in 1790.

Of interest concerning the de Rocamora purity of blood, a Jewish family donated two legal documents to the Bibilioteca Rosenthal in the Netherlands. One settled a dispute over which of two women should inherit the title Condessa de la Granja de Rocamora in 1660. The other was an inventory of property in a dispute over an inheritance in Murcia in the eighteenth century involving a Joseph (sic!) de Rocamora.

Also, in 1739, another Francisco de Rocamora, Deán of the Orihuela Cathedral, required a Royal Decree from the Spanish Borbón King Philip V confirming his *limpieza de sangre* against accusations.

And so, the direct titular line of Jerónimo de Rocamora died out in Spain while in the United Provinces, Vicente Isaac's seed multiplied fruitfully.

Characters
Where They First Appear

Those marked * are fictional.

In Valencia, 1617

Vicente de Rocamora, 1601-1684
*Alonso de Rocamora, Vicente's older brother
*Violante, Alonso's wife
*Don Lope (Diego de Fernández y Vega), physician, Vicente's mentor
*Fray Bernardo de Anglesola, Violante's cousin

Between Alicante and Orihuela, 1617

*Moraíma Royaya, a *morilla*
*Pablo Royaya, Moraíma's brother
*Yusef, Arab bandit leader
*Koitalel, runaway African slave from the Nandi tribe

In Orihuela, 1617

Jerónimo de Rocamora, Señor de Rafal and Benferri,
       Barón de la Puebla de Rocamora
Francisco de Rocamora, Señor de la Granja de Rocamora
Tomás de Rocamora, Dominican and Don Francisco's Brother
*Ramón de Rocamora, Señor de Ballebrera
*Fray António de Rocamora, uncle of the de Rocamora señores
*Jacinto de Rocamora, eldest son of Jerónimo
Gaspar de Rocamora, second son of Jerónimo
Juan de Rocamora, youngest son of Jerónimo

In Madrid, 1621-1632

Philip IV, King of Spain 1621-1665, b. 1605
Isabel (Elizabeth de Borbón), Philip's queen
Infanta Doña María, b. 18 August 1606, sister of Philip IV
Cardinal-Infante Don Fernándo, Philip IV's youngest brother
Infante Juan Carlos, dull witted younger brother of Philip IV
Gaspar de Guzmán, Count de Olivares, chief minister of the king,
    1621-1643
Countess-Duchess de Olivares
Fray António de Sotomayor, Philip IV's confessor,
    Inquisitor-General, 1632-1643
Count of Gondomar, Ambassador to England
*Sáncho de Fonseca, aka Marqués de Hombrecillo, midget court
    bufón (royal fool)
*Inéz, Hombrecillo's midget bride
*Xímena, Duchess of Astórquia, Ballebrera's, benefactress
Fray Rajosa, Infanta Doña María's elderly confessor
*Rodrigo de Lograño y Arce, master of the Spanish Circle
Margarita de Tavara, principal *menina* of the Infanta
Charles Stuart, Prince of Wales
George Villiers, Duke of Buckingham
Jerónimo de Villanueva, Marqués de Villalba, *Protonotario* of Aragón
Juan de Quiñones de Benevente, *Alcalde* of the Alcazar
*Padre Bartolomé Begoña, an *alumbrado*.
Félix Lope de Vega y Carpio, playwright, familiar of the Holy Office,
    Knight of Santiago
Francisco de Quevedo, satirist, Knight of Santiago
Cardinal António de Zapata, Inquisitor-General, 1627-1632
Fray Diego de Arce y Reynoso, Bishop of Palencia

In Valencia, 1629

*Brianda de Rocamora, daughter of Vicente and Violante

In Madrid, 1629-1632

Juan Adán de la Parra, inquisitor and poet
Fernándo Cardoso, court physician from Portugal

In the Battle of Nördlingen, 1634

*Karl Stauffacher, Swiss mercenary.
Ferdinand von Habsburg, King of Hungary, Doña María's husband
Gustav Horn, Protestant Swedish General
Bernard, Duke of Saxe-Weimar, Protestant General

In Brussels, 1634-35

*Jorge Álvarez, a physician
*Kaatje, a midwife

In Antwerp, 1635

Jaime Fernández y Vega, a Judaizer
Teresa, Fernández' daughter
*Martín Pinto, royal financier from Portugal

In Madrid, 1635-1643

Rodrigo Méndez de Silva, royal historiographer, royal council
      1640, author known as the "Spanish Livy"
Manuel Cortizos de Villasante, Portuguese financier, Knight of Calatrava
Manuel Fernández de Villareal, soldier, author, diplomat
*Padre Giovanni Malatesta, secretary to Papal Nuncio
*Sebastian de Silveyra, tobacconist
António Carnero, Olivares' personal secretary
*Catalina Bustamante de Faxardo, hostess of Madrid's most
      prestigious salon
*Pedro Zapata de Callosa, Catalina's cousin

In Roquemaure, 1643

*Pierre de Taurelle, Abbé de St. Roch

In Prague, 1643

Immanuel Bocarro Francês y Rosales, Empress María's physician
*Diego Muñoz de Castro, Spanish emissary

In Amsterdam, 1643

Menasseh ben Israel, rabbi, author, printer, Jewish link to the Christian
	community
Baruch (Bento) d'Espinoza, Menasseh's pupil
Abigail Toura, formerly Teresa Fernández of Antwerp
Judah Touro, Abigail's uncle
Eliahu Touro, Abigail's uncle
Sara Toura, Abigail's cousin, daughter of Eliahu
*Daniel Touro, Abigail's uncle
Jacob Barossa, once known as Diego de Barros in Castile;)
	parnass (warden of Amsterdam's Jewish community
Ephraim Bueno, physician, immortalized by Rembrandt
*Abraham Abulafia, rabbi and mohel
Rembrandt van Rijn, artist

Rocamora

Value of Spanish Money

In the 1600s, Castile's basic monetary unit of accounting was the maravedí. The ducado or ducat also was a unit of accounting and not a coin and for that purpose worth 357 maravedís

escudo (gold crown)	340 maravedís, 10 reales
pistole (gold coin)	escudo/doblon
doblon (gold coin)	2 escudos
doblon de la ocho (gold coin)	8 escudos
quartillo (vellón coin)	8 maravedís
quarto (vellón coin)	4 maravedís
real	34 maravedis
real de ocho (silver piece of 8 reales)	272 maravedís
Maravedi (copper vellón coin)	2 blancas
blanca (copper vellón coin)	½ maravedí
unskilled wage	4 reales/day
artisan	6 reales/day
physician	25 ducates/month
artillery lieutenant	40 ducates/month
grandee	60,000-100,000 ducates/year
priest	2-3 reales for saying mass
pound of bread	2-4 quartos
quart of wine	1 real
pound of mutton	8-20 maravedís
quart of oil	2 reales

Valencia, Aragón, and Catalonia count like the French:

12 diners	1 sou
1 Valencian lliura (livre)	20 sous
21 sous	1 Castilian ducat

Acknowledgements

Writing a book the scope of *Rocamora* required the research, support, and efforts of many. For those reasons, I thank the following for their contributions.

Pam Marin-Kingsley for her enthusiasm and commitment to *Rocamora*, her sense of humor, and brilliant cover design.

Genealogist Helga Becker-Leeser, of Arnhem, the Netherlands, whose extensive and invaluable research went far beyond my inquiries, all of which changed the original direction of *Rocamora* for the better.

Best-selling author Anita Shreve for her suggestions, encouragement, and attempt to find a publisher for *Rocamora*.

Famed author and matador Barnaby Conrad, whose Santa Barbara Writers Conference was a significant experience and who also offered encouragement and helpful suggestions.

Dr. Wilhelmina Chr. Pieterse, Director of the Amsterdam Municipal Archives, for sending information about Rocamora's life in Amsterdam.

Rabbi David Goldstein of Temple Beth David, Palm Beach Gardens, for his time, materials, and discussion regarding circumcision.

Dr. Joseph Kaplan, Professor of Medieval and Early Modern Jewish History, Hebrew University, for his correspondence, advice, and wisdom.

Mr. Romo, librarian at St. Vincent de Paul Seminary in Boynton Beach, Florida, who kindly allowed me to use the helpful resources in his library.

Jenny Yang Lambert for her research on my behalf at Oxford University's Bodleian Library.

Adelaide Andres of Salamanca who went out of her way to research for me in Spain.

The following for believing in *Rocamora* and trying to find a publisher for it: William and Amada Chohfi, Gary and Karen Brown, Larissa Henoch, Muriel Nellis, and Wendy Kowalski.

Seamon Glass for encouraging and promoting my writing.

Dr. Claudia and Sandy Samuels and Lt. Colonel Jeffery Kojac, USMC, for their positive comments after reading earlier drafts of the manuscript and their belief *ROCAMORA* should be published

The following for answering my inquiries and/or sending to me valuable information: H.M. Polak, Secretary of the Jewish Community of Amsterdam; Bob Drilsma, Antwerp; Fray Emilio Panella OP of Rome; Benjamin Gampel of the Jewish Theological seminary; Vicent Gomez Chornet of the Generalitat Valenciana; Dolores Alonso Roldán, Head of the Section on the Inquisition, of the Archivo Historico Nacional, Madrid; Sidney Cheyet, Professor of Jewish History, Hebrew Union College; and Rabbi Leila Gal Berner, Congregation Beth Israel, Media, Pennsylvania.

To the many historians living and dead whose writings contributed to what knowledge I have of seventeenth century Spain and Amsterdam.

And lastly but farthest from least, to my wife, Ellen S. Platt, for her unwavering belief, encouragement, superb editing, and suggestions.

About the Author

In Hollywood, Donald sold his writing to the TV series, *Mr. Novak*, and worked for and with diverse producers. After moving to Jupiter, Florida, Donald co-wrote *Vitamin Enriched*, 1999, for Carl DeSantis, founder of Rexall Sundown Vitamins; and *The Couple's Disease*, 2002, for Lawrence S. Hakim, MD, FACS, Head of Sexual Dysfunction Unit at the Cleveland Clinic.

Born and raised in San Francisco and a graduate of Lowell High school and U.C. Berkeley, Donald also has taught History, English, and Creative Writing and has been an Adjunct Professor of Writing at Polk Community College. He currently resides in Winter Haven, Florida with his wife, Ellen.

Photograph of Donald Michael Platt, courtesy of:
Richard V. Pezzimenti, Pezzimenti Photography
356 3rd St. NW
Winter Haven, FL 33881
Web site: http://pezzimenti.com/

www.ingramcontent.com/pod-product-compliance
Lightning Source LLC
Chambersburg PA
CBHW021137080526
44588CB00008B/102